KNOWLEDGE ASSETS

'In this book, Max Boisot presents a new, systematic analysis of information and intellectual property. If you accept that knowledge and the ability to use it is a key competitive resource, you must read this book. If you do not accept this, then also read it to discover where you are wrong before it is too late!'

John Child, Guinness Professor of Management Studies, University of Cambridge

'Max Boisot has written a book for any thinking manager, politician or lawyer interested in the role of information and intellectual property in the evolution of the information economy. He provides a challenging yet plausible framework for rethinking how today's advanced economies and the advanced firms within them operate. The framework is powerful and parsimonious. If you want to manage, legislate or design systems, you need the concepts in this book.'

Ian MacMillan, George W. Taylor Professor of
Entrepreneurial Studies, The Wharton School of Management

'Boisot's work is well-grounded theoretically, epistemologically and philosophically. Indeed we must see it as an exemplar of the kind of work necessary to make progress in our field.

J.-C. Spender, Dean of the School of Management, New York Institute of
Technology

'Max Boisot provides managers and academics with innovative and unique approaches to the linkage between information technology, organizational competencies, and knowledge management. Not only does this book make an important contribution for theory development by providing a model that is extended to various conditions, but practitioners facing complex situations will be rewarded with thought-provoking avenues to problem solving.'

Marjorie A. Lyles, Professor of International Strategy,
Kelley School of Business, Indiana University

'It is impossible to read even a few pages of Max Boisot's intelligent and persuasive book without encountering a powerful or provocative idea that challenges the way one used to think. Buy the book, absorb it slowly, and let the ideas influence you—the investment will be worth it.'

Rita Gunther McGrath, Assistant Professor,
Columbia University Graduate School of Business

Boisot's approach, which draws on material from a wide range of disciplines, calls for a fundamental change in our thinking and therefore requires and deserves a careful read. The ideas presented are exciting and challenging and even the reader who does not accept Boisot's analysis will find much thought provoking material in the book.'

Dr Keith Blois, Templeton College, University of Oxford

'In this book Max Boisot carefully considers the intricate relationship between physical assets and knowledge. The knowledge flow perspective offered by him is an important contribution to understanding organizations and what it means to manage in the 21st century. Read it, think about it, then dialogue about it.'

Johan Roos, Professor of General Management, International
Institute for Management Development (IMD), Lausanne

KNOWLEDGE ASSETS

Securing Competitive Advantage in the Information Economy

MAX H. BOISOT

OXFORD UNIVERSITY PRESS
1998

Oxford University Press, Great Clarendon Street, Oxford OX2 6DP

Oxford New York

Athens Auckland Bangkok Bogota Bombay
Buenos Aires Calcutta Cape Town Dar es Salaam
Delhi Florence Hong Kong Istanbul Karachi
Kuala Lumpur Madras Madrid Melbourne
Mexico City Nairobi Paris Singapore
Taipei Tokyo Toronto Warsaw
and associated companies in
Berlin Ibadan

Oxford is a registered trade mark of Oxford University Press

Published in the United States
by Oxford University Press Inc., New York

British Library Cataloguing in Publication Data
Data available

Library of Congress Cataloging in Publication Data
Boisot, Max.
Knowledge assets: securing competitive advantage in the
information economy / Max H. Boisot.
p.   cm.
Includes bibliographical references.
1. Knowledge management.   2. Organizational effectiveness.
3. Competition.   I. Title.
HD30.2.B64   1998   658.4'038—dc21   97–42642
ISBN 0–19–829086–1

1 3 5 7 9 10 8 6 4 2

Typeset by Hope Services (Abingdon) Ltd.
Printed in Great Britain
on acid-free paper by
Biddles Ltd, Guildford and King's Lynn

To the memory of my mother

FOREWORD

In the 1960s Marshall McLuhan declared new methods of communication would transform our society. Thirty years later we know work, skills, products, and the economy have been irreversibly changed by modern information technology and the knowledge it moves, stores and makes accessible. But one curious side effect of these changes is that our understanding of organizations and management is radically diminished. In this book Professor Boisot explores new ways of thinking about information, reminding us of the urgent need for a new system of managerial ideas and organizational practices appropriate to the Information Age.

Today's organization and management theories reflect ideas current at the turn of the last century, typically grounded in a Newtonian model which conceives the organization as a carefully designed and controlled mechanism for achieving explicitly stated goals and objectives. Individuals and resources are its specialized elements, working together much as the parts of a clock work together, conforming to the watchmaker's design. In the 1920s the human relations movement added an important dimension to the mechanical analysis, making us aware that formally designed organizational relationships were invariably accompanied by a system of interpersonal psychological and social relationships that became known as the informal organization. Even though this idea is widely accepted, the debate about how to manage the relationship between the organizational and the personal dimensions continues. In part this is because their contents seem to differ, one, formal, dealing with goal-related task issues, the other, informal, with psychological and group-maintenance issues. The different dimensions imply different types of knowledge and modes of communication but both seem necessary to the healthy organization.

Professor Boisot's theory deals directly with the knowledge articulated into organizational activity. In more technical parlance he provides the basis for a novel knowledge-based theory of the firm. This theory stands radically opposed to both the earlier machine and the later psycho-social models of the firm. Both of these now conventional models, of course, attempt to open up the 'black box' of the economists' theory of the firm and indicate the firm's important components and interactions. In this book Boisot's principal objective is to provide managers with insight into knowledge as the organization's key asset and to the practices which lead to the effective use and husbandry of that asset.

But knowledge is more slippery than the conventional concepts of cash, production equipment, or even product reputation and market share, seeming both too simple and too vague to bear the weight of a managerially relevant and decision guiding analysis. After all, the nature of human knowledge has puzzled philosophers for thousands of years without any single framework gaining general acceptance. So every attempt to use the concept of knowledge in organizational analysis must be preceded by an explanation of its nature. This is straight philosophy or, more precisely, the kind of straight epistemology that makes many of today's organizational and managerial theorists uncomfortable. But recent trends in the practitioner-oriented literature should remind us that managers have both an interest in and a solid grasp of these seemingly esoteric matters. The widespread popularity of the notions of corporate culture—one way of describing an organization's collective body of knowledge—and of tacit knowledge—an individual's difficult-to-communicate skill in generating and taking part in organizational activity—shows that many managers are epistemological sophisticates. Managerial discussion of core skills and competencies, the importance of intellectual capital, and the need to train knowledge-workers reinforces this conclusion.

It follows that knowledge-based theorists must be divided into categories according to the epistemology they adopt. There are those who take up a conventional position, such as that popularized by Karl Popper, believing that valid knowledge is the result of applying the scientific method. Disciplined experimentation produces explicit objective knowledge untainted by error, bias, or self-delusion. The growth of knowledge becomes a process of experiment-driven accretion. Thomas Kuhn famously suggested that this might not be entirely adequate, arguing that all types of scientific knowledge were embedded in wider non-scientific frameworks of social conceptions and practices. If, as history showed had occasionally happened, these frameworks changed, then much of what had seemed previously to be true and relevant would simply be wiped out. This kind of thinking is leading us away from conventional or monist epistemologies towards various kinds of epistemological pluralism, meaning that researchers and managers must recognize the possibility of several different kinds of human knowledge. The corresponding knowledge-based theory of the firm is necessarily more complex.

Economic theories of the firm focus on the process of maximizing profits. Organizational theories of the firm tend to focus on maximizing control, while human relations theories of the firm tend to emphasize maximizing individual satisfaction and possibly, thereby, individual productivity and creativity. A knowledge-based theory focuses on maximizing the results of the firm's knowledge generation, storage, and application processes, presuming the firm is also a mechanism for transforming that knowledge into profit. If the adopted epistemology is unidimensional, then maximizing knowledge growth or organizational learning is about setting up continuing experiments enabling the organization to learn about its environmental circumstances including, of course, how to satisfy its customers and deal with its competition. The focus is on the interaction of the organization and its environment. There is a methodological puzzle here for this interaction cannot be analyzed unless the environment has been described independently of the organization's knowledge. The theorist has to presuppose and take up an epistemo-logically privileged position denied to the managers being analyzed. Many theorists are troubled by this need to give themselves privileged knowledge preferring a more relative and interpretive position in which they focus on the managerial modes of knowing.

If the adopted epistemology is pluralist, the organization can still be seen as an instrument of knowledge growth, but now more types of knowledge are permitted. In addition to the quasi-scientific knowledge admitted by positivist convention, there is also the possibility of experiential and practical know-ledge of the type which Nelson and Winter have labeled 'organizational rou-tines'. Further, and most importantly given a pluralist epistemology, the firm can also be described as the locus of interaction between these types of know-ledge. For instance, if we allow, in Polanyi's terminology, for tacit 'personal' knowledge in addition to explicit 'impersonal' scientific knowledge, then the firm can be described as the process by which personal intuition and discov-ery can be articulated into objective rules and procedures which others can then follow as they re-articulate the ideas into organizational practices. In short, a creative or entrepreneurial individual's tacit knowledge can be lever-aged by forming a firm. This has to seem a more useful and practical way of theorizing about the firm than dealing merely with market behaviours.

Boisot's theory deals with these notions by definition alternative types of knowledge as positions or 'stations' in a three-dimensional epistemological space which he dubs the I-Space. His theory is bold on at least two grounds: (a) he adopts a pluralist epistemology, still unusual among organizational and managerial theorists, and (b) he theorizes about the interaction of these knowledge types as the firm follows the Social Learning Cycle and moves around the I-space. Thus he takes on much the same agenda as explored in Nonaka and Takeuchi's prize-winning *Knowledge Creating Company* (OUP, 1996) but his treatment and conclusions are widely different.

The principal difference is that while Nonaka and Takeuchi's epistemology is pluralist, it is only two-dimensional. Indeed they illustrate their theory as movement around a two-by-two matrix which is defined by the somewhat problematic distinction between the explicit and tacit types of knowledge. Boisot's pluralism is three-dimensional, defined by the more substantial dis-tinctions between abstraction, codification, and diffusion. This framing increases the degrees of freedom and makes the analysis potentially richer, but also more difficult to handle. His theory explores the interactions between these dimensions, as well as the consequences of moving the organization knowledge along them. It is trivial to observe that managers should realize that while ideas are plentiful an idea needs to be made explicit and communi-cated to others in ways that they can use if the firm is to be successful. Boisot takes this insight and with his pluralist analysis, lays out a system of manage-rial practices for maximizing the value the organization can extract from its ideas and knowledge.

There are obvious gaps and shortcomings. He wisely avoids too much discussion of the personal creativity that produces the knowledge in the first place. This means he does not need to address the complexities of the relationship between those who develop the ideas and those who have to put them into practice—an issue which caused Frederick W. Taylor, the author of the most widely appreciated knowledge-based theory of the firm, considerable difficulties. Boisot avoids discussion of the sociology of knowledge, notions explored by Kuhn and Merton but now being re-examined in the rapidly expanding field of science and technology studies. Like many of us exploring new idea systems, he also presumes they are able to explain too many of the social and economic phenomena that interest us. But these are minor deficiencies in what is a profoundly novel push into a new area of organizational and managerial theorizing and Boisot's work will unquestionably help shape this field.

And this is a field that presents management and organizational theorists with the most serious tasks it has faced in decades. Since World War II academic theorists have diverged further and further from managerial and organizational practice. While the academics' contributions to economic analysis, accounting, and financial practice increase, as exemplified in Porter's *Competitive Advantage* and Scholes and Merton's recent Nobel, the very opposite is true of managerial and organizational theory. Here the new ideas have emerged from firms themselves, such as downsizing, outsourcing, and globalization, and from the consultancies, such as in Peters and Waterman's *In Search of Excellence* and Wheatley's *Leadership and the New Science*.

But when it comes to making managerial sense of the concept of knowledge, the academics have a head start. The work of, for instance, Penrose, Polanyi, Winter and Nelson, and Nonaka and Takeuchi is grounded in the academic discipline necessary to deal with so problematic a topic. If there is to be a knowledge-based theory of the firm, it is highly likely that it will be based on the work of academics rather than only on the insights which practice provides. Boisot's work is well-grounded theoretically, epistemologically and philosophically. Indeed we must see it as an exemplar of the kind of work necessary to make progress in our field. It is a clear call to managerial and organizational academics to abandon the empirically intensive but philosophically impoverished research programs which currently dominate our literature and embrace the tough problems of an epistemologically grounded approach to management's tasks in the arising Information Age.

J.-C. Spender
New York Institute of Technology Ltd

ACKNOWLEDGEMENTS

The ideas that are developed in this book were pummelled into shape through many conversations, some of which took place face to face, some through the written medium, and some with self through the intermediation of whichever author I happened to be reading at the time. Although it is impossible to acknowledge individually all those whose writings, thinking, or utterances influenced the final product—the ideas that underpin it have been fermenting over nearly two decades—I can at least affirm that: first, conversations with Keith Blois, John Child, David Coates, Dorothy Griffiths, Bill McKelvey, Ian MacMillan, Ron Sanchez, and J.-C. Spender have helped me to make this work more rigorous than it otherwise would have been; second, conversations with Pat Henegan, Ken Ideus, Terry Lemmon and Manfred Mack have helped me to stay in the real world more than I am usually inclined to; and third, conversations with myself while reading Stuart Kauffman, Michael Polanyi, Ilya Prigogine, Herbert Simon, and Oliver Williamson have kept me both inspired and more humble than I am normally perceived to be.

Colleagues and friends acknowledged under the first two categories above were kind enough to read and comment on different drafts of this book, as were David Currie, Kent Greenes, Ira Herenstein, and Daniel Levinthal. Although, as author, I remain responsible for what is found in these pages, I would like to thank them all for their contribution. Margareta Bellander Puyoles, whose patience and fortitude never cease to baffle me, stoically churned out draft after draft. She is a prized collaborator. My institutional home in Spain, Esade, provided logistic support. David Musson, at Oxford University Press, gave me valuable help in giving the book a coherent shape. Finally, I would like to express my deep gratitude to my wife Dorota, who uncomplainingly granted me the sabbatical that I needed from domestic responsibilities to finish the work. Dorota, being Polish,won't accept a simple thank you like everybody else. So to her goes a big *dziekuje* instead.

PREFACE

This book is an exercise in theorizing about the impact of information on firms and economic processes. The work is conceptual but not particularly technical. Although I believe that the concepts discussed in its pages have deep implications for the way that we shall shortly be organizing firms and for the way these will be competing in the twenty-first century, the book offers no ersatz solution to what are a set of highly complex and interrelated issues. This is not a book of instant recipes for the policy-maker or the manager in a hurry. Its message needs chewing over and this requires time and concentration. Why on earth should the reader bother?

The decision to read a book, any book, is an exercise in cost-benefit analysis, usually conducted under conditions of uncertainty. The prospective reader must try and assess at the outset what kind of return on his or her efforts are likely to be on offer. What, then, is in it for the reader who decides to plough through the following pages? I offer below a few signposts to what the book is about.

In the closing years of the twentieth century, mankind faces both an unprecedented challenge and an unprecedented opportunity. The challenge arises from the fact that we are consuming natural resources at a rate that is likely to prove unsustainable over the long term. The opportunity comes in the shape of an information revolution that may allow us to substitute knowledge-based resources for energy-based ones in many areas of economic activity.

We live today in a post-industrial society in which knowledge has increasingly come to be recognized as a primary source of wealth. The evidence has become overwhelming that economies that are poor in natural resources but skilled in the production and exploitation of knowledge generally outperform economies that have abundant natural resources but are lacking in such skills. We are discovering, however, that knowledge is a very elusive thing. Wealth-generating assets, whose main component is knowledge, simply do not behave in the way that physical assets—with which we are more familiar—do. We do not as yet really know how to deal with knowledge-based wealth. One simple indicator of our predicament is that we are finding it ever more difficult to come up with robust GNP measures for the emerging knowledge-based economy.

Our predicament, it turns out, is not exactly a new one. Although we have by now come to take the phenomenon of energy for granted and thus find it unproblematic to measure the output of energy-based economic activity, the concept of energy itself took nearly two centuries to elaborate. It may be, therefore, that a couple of centuries hence the concept of knowledge will be equally taken for granted, and people will be wondering why we found it all so difficult. But why, it might be asked, do we find it so difficult?

Knowledge is a capacity that is built on information extracted from data. Knowledge assets yield a stream of useful services over time and hence have potential economic value. Unlike physical assets, however, knowledge assets can be shared with others and retained at the same time—a case of having your cake and eating it too. Yet while sharing knowledge does not reduce its utility for its original possessor—i.e., he or she can still go on receiving useful services from it after transmission—it does reduce its value. Shared knowledge loses scarcity. How do we deal with this issue? Typically, when trying to safeguard the value of our knowledge assets, we tend to treat them as if they were physical assets, putting barriers around them to stop them leaking out and having their scarcity value eroded.

For some types of knowledge—such as that contained in patents—this may work, but not always. With intellectual piracy becoming ever more rampant, we are learning that property rights in knowledge are a fragile institutional achievement. The founding proposition on which this book is built up is that knowledge diffuses naturally and rapidly in certain circumstances, whereas in others it does not—indeed, it then behaves more like physical objects. Understanding when it flows of its own accord and when it does not is crucial to mastering knowledge as a potential source of wealth.

When, then, is knowledge likely to flow readily and when is it likely to turn viscous? I argue that fluid knowledge is knowledge that is well codified and abstract: all extraneous data has been shed. Viscous knowledge, by contrast, is data rich, qualitative, ambiguous. It flows slowly, if at all. Think of the difference between transmitting a reference number and describing in detail a Rembrandt self-portrait, both on a long-distance telephone call.

Over time, some viscous knowledge can become fluid. As one gets to understand something, so it becomes easier to codify it and to abstract from it: one can then share it. Conversely, fluid knowledge, once it has become enriched by individual experience and idiosyncratic interpretations, becomes viscous once more: it then gets embedded in the heads of individuals who will again find it hard to share.

If knowledge is to be reliable and usable, then at some point it must lose some of its viscosity. Codification and abstraction make knowledge fluid and usable. By also making it more diffusible, however, they also make it more difficult to appropriate and extract value from. Knowledge assets thus have a paradoxical character. The more useful they become, the more difficult they are to hold on to. The successful exploitation of knowledge assets requires effective strategies for dealing with this paradox.

Knowledge assets are built up through a process of learning, an ability to exploit knowledge flows—both fluid and viscous—in adaptive ways. Much learning is a socially structured activity that feeds on what we might term an information environment. Some information environments encourage the pursuit of learning through the sharing of one's stock of knowledge assets, others through the hoarding of it.

The extent to which knowledge is structured and shared defines a culture. A bureaucratic culture, for example, likes to deal in knowledge that is well codified, abstract, and unambiguous. It is, however, not much given to sharing it, and acts to block its diffusion. A market culture, by contrast, while also showing a preference for well-codified and abstract knowledge—after all, what else is a price?—actually requires a high degree of sharing if it is to function effectively.

Not all cultures require the knowledge that they deal in to come in well-structured packages. Some actively thrive on ambiguity and vagueness. They like their knowledge to be viscous, like treacle. This makes it hard to share with anyone but insiders or clan members. It then becomes a source of personal power for those who have access to the knowledge relative to those who do not.

Does the information revolution that we are living through favour the creation of viscous or fluid knowledge? We argue that it favours both, but each under different circumstances. Understanding what those circumstances are is crucial both to a proper exploitation of knowledge assets and to the building up of corporate and national cultures appropriate to the emerging information age.

CONTENTS

LIST OF FIGURES

LIST OF TABLES

1

Introduction

CHARLES Babbage (1791–1871) is often referred to as the father of computing. His interest in the possibilities of mechanical calculation resulted from his exasperation at the extensive inaccuracies that plagued the mathematical tables then available to scientists, bankers, actuaries, navigators, engineers, and the like. 'I wish to God these calculations had been executed by steam', he exclaimed in 1821, after poring over two independently prepared sets of calculations for astronomical tables with the renowned British astronomer, John Herschel (1792–1871).

Babbage dreamt of a machine which, in addition to performing flawless calculations, would also eradicate transcription and typesetting errors by impressing the results of its calculations automatically on strips of papier mâché or on soft metal plates. He spent a decade designing, developing, and manufacturing components for a 'difference engine' (known as Difference Engine No. 1), a machine based on a mathematical principle known as the method of finite differences. The project collapsed in 1833 following a dispute with his chief engineer, Joseph Clement. The projected engine was of a staggering size and complexity for its day. Its design called for 25,000 parts to be assembled into a machine 8 feet high, 7 feet long, and 3 feet deep (2.44m × 2.13m × 0.91m). It would have weighed several tons and its cumulative cost at the time that the project collapsed was £17,450. By way of comparison, the steam locomotive built by John Bull in 1831 cost £740.

Difference Engine No. 1, however, could only perform one fixed task. Babbage's reputation rests on a second, more sophisticated device, conceived in 1834, which he labelled the analytical engine. This was a general purpose programmable device which in its basics bore a remarkable resemblance to modern electronic computers. Like Difference Engine No. 1, the analytical engine was never built, even though Babbage went on refining its design until his death. Yet work on the analytical engine inspired Babbage to design a simpler, more elegant difference engine, known as Difference Engine No. 2, which was finally built in 1991 to commemorate the bicentenary of his birth. Although Difference Engine No. 2 can calculate to a precision of 31 figures—10 digits more than had been envisaged for Difference Engine No. 1—it is made up of one-third as many parts as Babbage's original design. The machine, completed in May 1991, weighed 3 tons, and was built in public view at London's Science Museum at a cost of £300,000.[1]

Calculation has come a long way since Babbage's analytical engine. Every two years or so since the 1950s computers have become twice as fast, while their components have become twice as small. Modern electronic circuits now contain wires and transistors whose width is one hundredth of that of a human hair. Indeed, according to Seth Lloyd, a researcher at Los Alamos National Laboratories, the quantum computer is now within our reach.[2] The Pentium chip, released by Intel in May 1993, crowds 3.1 million flawless transistors on a square of silicon 16 millimetres by 17 millimetres. It can churn out calculations at up to 112 million instructions per second (mips).

There have been many varied attempts to explain such phenomenal gains in performance. The simplest and most widely accepted is that they reflect a continuous, systematic, and concentrated application of ever-expanding knowledge to an ever-increasing range of physical processes. In many areas, in fact, the knowledge has become more valuable than the physical substrate that carries it. For this reason, knowledge has to be viewed as an asset in its own right and not simply as an enhancement of other kinds of assets.

Conceiving of knowledge as an asset is not new. Sixteenth-century alchemists, for example, went to great length to protect the secrets of their craft. And as late as the nineteenth century, Britain imposed restrictions on the migration of its skilled craftsmen in order to deny continental firms the competitive advantage that their craft knowledge of industrial machinery could secure for them—it did not work. What is new in the late twentieth century is that knowledge assets are coming to constitute the very basis of post-industrial economies.

Prompted by the rapid spread of the information economy, we are only just beginning to think of knowledge assets as economic goods in their own right. Thinking of knowledge in this way is turning out to be more challenging than might be supposed, since there is a natural tendency to assimilate what is unknown to what is known. The early automobiles, for example, were known as 'horseless carriages'. In order to gain acceptance, they had to have, as far as possible, the 'look and feel' of a horse-drawn vehicle. So it is with information goods. In order to be accepted as such, an information good is expected to have the look and feel of a physical good. Unfortunately, the look and feel of knowledge assets are anything but physical.

A failure to properly conceptualize the nature of knowledge assets, however, condemns firms—and, indeed, whole economies—to fight tomorrow's competitive battles with yesterday's outdated weapons and tactics. Notwithstanding the information revolution that, with the approach of a new millennium, is gathering momentum both inside and outside their boundaries, the vast majority of firms remain firmly ensconced in the paradigm of

[1] D. D. Swade, 'Redeeming Charles Babbage's Mechanical Computer', *Scientific American*, February 1993.
[2] Seth Lloyd, 'Mechanical Computers', *Scientific American*, October 1995.

the energy economy. One reason for this inertia is that energy-based events are still much easier to observe and measure than information-based ones. Managers and policy-makers are vaguely aware that know-how and formal knowledge are a good thing, but they find it difficult to evolve a coherent orientation towards what remains for them a highly elusive phenomenon. Knowledge assets do not behave like physical assets—the carriage is now not only horseless, it has also become dematerialized—and attempts to reduce the former to the latter will give a firm a quite distorted view of the threats and opportunities that it will need to respond to in the years ahead.

What is an asset? An accountant would reply that an asset is a stock from which a number of services are expected to flow. In the case of current assets, services are expected to flow for less than a year; in the case of fixed assets, they are expected to flow for more than a year. Knowledge assets are stocks of knowledge from which services are expected to flow for a period of time that may be hard to specify in advance.

In contrast to physical assets, knowledge assets could in theory last for ever. Farming methods in certain parts of the world, for example, have remained unchanged for millennia, being handed down from one generation to another in the form of a tradition. By gliding from one physical substrate to another, a knowledge asset can prolong its existence indefinitely. The *economic* life of such an asset, however, is a function of how fast the knowledge base that sustains it is changing. Since old news is no news at all, for example, the economic life of a newspaper is typically less than twenty-four hours. The economic life of a physical asset is also a function of the economic life of its knowledge content. But because physical assets wear out in a reasonably predictable fashion—the average automobile lasts eight years, the average timber-framed house, forty years—it is much easier to put an upper limit on their value than in the case of knowledge assets. In spite of the inroads made by quantum indeterminism into our mechanical view of the world, Newton's three laws of motion continue to regulate our day-to-day interactions with phenomena in terms of mass, length, and time, imparting a useful—if not perfect—measure of stability to everyday physical objects. They have served us well for over three hundred years. How long will they continue to do so? No one can tell.

The open-ended value of knowledge assets means that there is no one-to-one correspondence between the effort required to create them and the value of the services that they yield. Knowledge assets, in contrast to pure physical assets such as raw materials, are—to use the jargon of chaos theorists—non-linear with respect to the effects they produce. When they are embedded in physical assets, therefore, as, say, in a manufacturing process, they can become a major source of discontinuity. Information organizes matter. The introduction of just-in-time (JIT) methods in manufacturing by Toyota and other Japanese firms, for example, significantly improved the coordination of complex operations, while reducing inventories. Yet JIT is built around little more than a simple signalling device.

In this chapter we briefly outline the working hypothesis that will be developed in the rest of the book, namely that a firm's distinctive competences, its capabilities, and its technologies can be viewed as emerging from the discontinuous impact of its knowledge assets on the spatio-temporal and energy systems that make up its physical assets. If accepted and acted upon, such a hypothesis profoundly transforms how we think of a firm's organizational and managerial processes, and challenges much established practice.

In particular, it invites us to rethink the conventional and mechanistic conceptualization of a firm as bundles of labour and capital brought together as productive factors under the control of an entrepreneur. Technologies, competences, and capabilities are holistic concepts that resist the incremental and 'linear' mixing of factors—neoclassical economists have tended to take such mixing as exhibiting constant returns to scale—by all-knowing entrepreneurs.

Technologies, competences, and capabilities, each in their own way, are manifestations of a firm's knowledge assets operating at different levels of organization. Since the use of these terms remains unsettled, however, whenever we use them in this book we shall adopt the following convention (see Figure 1.1):

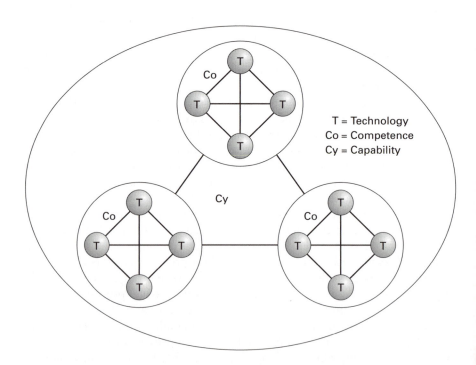

FIG. 1.1 Technologies, Competences, and Capabilities

1. We shall use the term *technology* to depict sociophysical systems configured so as to produce certain specific types of physical effects—the thrust of a jet engine, for example.
2. We shall use the term *competence* to depict the organizational and technical skills involved in achieving a certain level of performance in the production of such effects—i.e., an engine thrust with low fuel consumption and a high by-pass ratio.
3. Finally, we shall use the term *capability* to depict a strategic skill in the application and integration of competences—i.e., producing engines with price, performance, and delivery characteristics that respond to the needs of a wide variety of clients.[3]

The move from technologies to competences and on to capabilities takes us from the technical level usually found at the base of the firm, through the operational level traditionally associated with a firm's middle management, and then on to the strategic level, typically the province of a firm's top management. Each move up the organization involves a distinctive type of integration—knowledge assets residing at the base of the firm do not come together in the same way as do those at the top. At the base, integration brings together physical equipment and processes in response to technological and production imperatives. At the top, by contrast, integration is a more political business that requires a negotiated adjustment. Here, a variety of concepts, interpretations, and preferences—many of which may be quite divergent—have to be combined into a coherent whole.

Each move up the organization is also a move towards increasing *complexity*, taken here as the number of elements in interaction and the number of different states that those interactions can give rise to. The greater the number of elements one has to deal with, and the more varied their interactions, the more complex one's task. Clearly, the number and nature of technologies that have to be integrated into competences, and the number and variety of these that have to be mobilized to achieve a capability, will determine the level of complexity that a firm has to deal with.

By all accounts, that level is rising. Not so much because the number of elements to be integrated at any one level has risen—it may or may not have risen for the typical firm. Complexity is on the increase because in a regime of rapid technological change the rate at which new elements appear in a system and replace old ones has increased. New elements and their integration with existing elements of the system both have to be mastered, and this requires managerial attention and effort. Thus, whatever the level of objective complexity—i.e., the actual number of elements and relationships—that confront

---

[3] The relationship between a competence and a capability is still a subject of academic debate. Since the issue remains open and we do not wish to get drawn into a theological argument on the meaning of terms, we shall use our own definitions and hope that they strike the reader as plausible. For a further discussion of the issue, see G. Stalk, P. Evans, and L. Shulman, 'Competing on Capabilities', *Harvard Business Review*, March–April 1992; R. Sanchez and A. Heene, *Strategic Learning and Knowledge Management*, Chichester: John Wiley and Sons, 1997.

managers, the level of subjective complexity that they experience—i.e., the number of elements and relationships that they have *consciously* to attend to at any one time—has gone up. Just think, for example, of the manager getting to his desk every morning and finding two hundred e-mail messages posted on his screen as well as two dozen faxes sitting patiently in his in-tray. Filtering out what is noise from what is information in this pile of data, and responding to the latter in a timely fashion, will require far more presence of mind than was needed twenty years ago. Managers are being called upon to think on their feet as never before.

How do top managers cope with the increasing complexity that drifts up towards them from inside the firm, or that which floats in from outside? How do they avoid becoming overloaded and overwhelmed? The simple answer is by developing abstract models that help them to make sense of the complexity and reduce it to manageable proportions.

It turns out that if the challenge of complexity is a new one for us, the problem of abstraction is an old one in Western thought. At an intuitive level we perceive complexity and abstraction to be antithetical to each other: the more you have of the one, the less you will have of the other. Yet do abstractions have any basis in reality or are they just a handy way of describing the world, to be jettisoned and replaced as soon as more faithful descriptions become available? Although the question still gives sleepless nights to philosophers of a metaphysical bent, we ourselves do not need to lose much sleep over it. For our purposes, abstraction can be considered an act of cognitive simplification which spares us the need to deal with the complexities that surround us. Conversely, an ability to handle complexity at an intuitive level spares us the painful rigours imposed by abstract thought processes.

Whether we operate through formal abstract structures or through informal intuitions, our efforts are only productive to the extent that our representations connect with the real world in some way. The history of science teaches us that our representations often cluster into paradigms that are subject to inertia. According to the late Thomas Kuhn,[4] for example, it took 250 years for Copernicus's heliocentric model of planetary motion fully to displace Ptolemy's, barnacled as it was with epicycles. At least Copernicus was dealing with comparatively stable phenomena—on a human time-scale, that is. More problematic is what happens when the world changes, but our representations of it remain unaltered. As change accelerates, the gap between the world and our understanding of it, as mediated by ill-adapted paradigms, grows wider. A crisis then follows in which either the paradigms or those who hold them are junked.

---

[4] T. Kuhn, *The Copernican Revolution: Planetary Astronomy in the Development of Western Thought*, Cambridge, Mass: Harvard University Press, 1957; *The Structure of Scientific Revolutions*, Chicago: University of Chicago Press, 1962.

We face such a situation in the late 1990s. We are entering the information economy still firmly strapped to the paradigms of the energy economy.[5] These have acquired such a tremendous inertia that we find it easier to tinker with them as they drag us along, hoping that they might still turn up something useful, than to discard them. As we discuss in the next section, however, the challenges before us no longer allow us the luxury of such a Micawberish option: we are confronting an urgent need to develop paradigms appropriate to the age in which we live.

I.2 KNOWLEDGE ASSETS AND THE ENVIRONMENTAL CHALLENGE

The nineteenth century was a period of technological optimism. Many of the discoveries relating to the natural world that fuelled the scientific revolution of the sixteenth and seventeenth centuries were gradually adapted to the needs of industry. Building on the Enlightenment's belief in the power of reason and the inevitability of progress, men greatly extended their mastery over nature across a broad front. This was the age of the railway, the canal, and the large engineering project. As countries industrialized, standards of living rose. The high point of such optimism was London's Great Exhibition of 1851, an event through which Britain established its pre-eminent position as the workshop of the world in the nascent industrial order.

That there was a price to pay for industrialization in terms of human dislocation and suffering, of urban squalor and environmental decay, did not dim the optimism. Nor did Darwin's discovery that man's rightful place was in nature rather than above it, that he might turn out to be playing a quite contingent role in God's scheme of things instead of the central one that— *pace* Copernicus, Galileo, and those who argued for an infinite universe—he still arrogated to himself. The effects and implications of such developments took several decades to burrow through the thick layers of complacency that an uncritical faith in the omnipotence of science and technology was creating.

Two world wars and the loss of nuclear innocence gradually unveiled technology's dark side. Four centuries of well-intentioned effort and ingenuity had unwittingly prised open a Pandora's box that humankind was unable to master. Technological optimism has given way to technological pessimism, a mood that has been reinforced in the latter decades of the twentieth century by the realization that some of the by-products of uncontrolled industrialization, such as the greenhouse gases belching out from millions of factory chimneys and car exhausts, could materially alter the conditions—indeed, arguably, the very possibilities—for life on earth.

[5] P. Mirowski, *More Heat than Light: Economics as Social Physics, Physics as Nature's Economics*, Cambridge: Cambridge University Press, 1989.

Yet even as the crisis looms, policy-makers find it hard to disentangle cause from effect and hence to prescribe a credible course of action for dealing with it. Some experts, for example, will point to population growth as the cause of poverty and environmental degradation. Others will argue that poverty itself is the cause rather than the consequence of increasing numbers. In the absence of more compelling evidence and deeper understanding, such conflicting explanations will each continue to remain plausible and to attract their champions. The search for single causes, however, appealing as it may be to those who seek explanatory scapegoats, may well be futile. When it comes to the biosphere, we are dealing with a formidably interconnected and complex system in the face of which the old positivistic approach to diagnosis and explanation, namely, the breaking down of dynamic processes into isolated elements that could be separately classified as cause and effect, no longer convinces. Furthermore, explanatory strategies that rely on linear thinking—small causes have small effects and big causes have big effects—are likely to have only modest purchase in a world that is, as we now recognize, for the most part nonlinear.

Chaos theory has taught us that in systems whose evolution is highly sensitive to initial conditions, microscopic causes can sometimes have macroscopic effects. Where this is so, the fact that such microscopic causes are potentially numerous and hard to spot makes future states of the system hard to predict. It is not just a question of realizing that a butterfly flapping its wings over Wyoming can cause a hurricane over Florida. The challenge is to identify which *particular* butterfly is causing what *particular* hurricane. Applying the lessons of chaos theory to the biosphere, we discover that, contrary to our earlier assumptions, we are not just observers trying to predict its evolutionary trajectory in a detached fashion. We are also agents interacting with it and actively shaping its development—i.e., players as well as spectators. Perhaps the deflating influence of Darwinism has made us *too* humble. In the cosmic scheme of things we may well not rate much higher, causally speaking, than the gossamer wings of the proverbial butterfly. Yet, unwittingly, we may also be on the way to producing very big—indeed, possibly catastrophic—effects.

Optimism and pessimism are individual dispositions which, taken collectively, help to shape our responses to the environmental challenges that confront us. They may in part be accounted for by personality and cultural factors. They are also a product of cognitive processes, of the schemata that we deploy to make sense of things.[6]

For optimists, the environmental cup is half full. They draw comfort from the breathtaking progress that humanity has achieved in science and technology in the course of the twentieth century and persist in believing that our

---

[6] J. Piaget, *Play, Dreams and Imitations in Childhood*, New York: W. W. Norton and Company, 1962; J. Holland, K. Holyoak, R. Nisbett, and P. Thagard, *Induction: Processes of Inference, Learning and Discovery*, Cambridge, Mass: MIT Press, 1989.

capacity to solve the problems that we encounter will continue to outrun the rate at which these present themselves to us. For pessimists, the environmental cup is half empty. They point out that world population has more than doubled since 1950 and that it is set to more than double again by 2050. For pessimists, humankind's collective claims upon the natural resources of the biosphere have become unsustainable.

Unfortunately, the sheer complexity of the environmental challenges that we face makes it hard to decide whether optimism or pessimism is in order. Underpinning the optimistic view, for example, is a deep and perhaps unconscious faith in the healing power of self-regulating processes, whether these are driven by human action—as in the case of markets—or by nature's own activities: Lovelock's Gaia hypothesis.[7]

The pessimistic view, by contrast, owes much to our discovery that for all the progress that we have made in the realm of linear processes, the world remains stubbornly nonlinear, and that our essentially linear technologies have nonlinear consequences that we can neither understand nor master. With a few lines of code a determined hacker can bring a nationwide computer network to a halt. A few well-chosen TV pictures in a political campaign can change the course of an election. A 2 per cent technical edge in the performance of a critical component can secure for a firm the dominance of certain industries. The self-regulation on which optimists have pinned their hopes requires the timely operation of negative feedback to bring a system back into balance. Pessimists are concerned with the prevalence of positive feedback processes in many systems, processes that can drive them to new and unpredictable states, many of which could turn out to be life-threatening.[8]

In the late 1990s we are beginning to explore nonlinear phenomena across a broad range of disciplines both within the natural and the social sciences. These explorations are giving rise to a new discipline that is currently labelled the science of complexity.[9] Given the looming environmental challenges, however, it is unclear whether what we are learning about the behaviour of complex phenomena will give us ground for optimism or pessimism.

Yet, there are straws in the wind. If, past a certain threshold, complexity lapses into chaos, below that threshold it can also lead to order. More intriguing still, chaos itself can sometimes be a source of order. This can be seen, for example, in a phenomenon known as 'stochastic resonance'. One way of measuring the efficiency of information transmission is to compare a signal's

---

[7] See J. Lovelock, *The Ages of Gaia*, Oxford: Oxford University Press, 1990. It should be made clear that whatever optimism Lovelock expresses on the matter has been applied to the biosphere as a whole. He displays no particular optimism concerning man's own place in the biosphere.

[8] W. Brian Arthur, 'Positive Feedbacks in the Economy', *Scientific American*, February 1990; W. Brian Arthur, 'Competing Technologies, Increasing Returns, and Lock-In by Historical Events', *The Economic Journal*, 99 (394), 1989, pp. 116–31.

[9] For an introduction to complexity theory, see M. Mitchell Waldrop, *Complexity: The Emerging Science at the Edge of Chaos*, London: Penguin Books, 1992; J. Casti, *Complexification: Explaining a Paradoxical World through the Science of Surprise*, London: Abacus, 1994; G. Nicolis and I. Prigogine, *Exploring Complexity: An Introduction*, New York: W. H. Freeman and Co., 1989.

strength with that of the background noise that accompanies it. If one adds more noise to a fixed signal this will usually lower the signal-to-noise ratio. In the early 1990s, however, a French team of physicists built an electronic circuit around a nonlinear device known as a Schmitt trigger. To their great surprise, the French team discovered that the signal-to-noise ratio in their circuit rose to a peak as they increased the noise before tailing off as noise swamped everything else. This turned out to be stochastic resonance at work. It has since been picked up in a wide variety of settings.[10] An article published in *Nature* in July 1995 suggested that stochastic resonance might be at work in a variety of biological systems.[11]

The implication of the above example and of much recent experimental work is that complex processes may not allow much in the way of detailed prediction, but they may not be impossible to manage. We need to rethink our 'command and control' approach to such processes and in particular the level at which we need to gain knowledge of them if we are to cope successfully with their effects. Our ability to shift from an economy based primarily on physical resources to one built around information and knowledge depends on it. An example will make this clear.

I.3 KNOWLEDGE, INFORMATION, AND DATA

The earthquake that struck the city of Kobe in January 1995, claiming 5,000 lives, was a traumatic event that shook the confidence of many Japanese in their government's competence. Not only had the probability of an earthquake in the Kobe area been widely discounted by officials—it had not happened before, so why should it happen now?—but when it did occur, the systems, physical and organizational, that had been put in place to mitigate any damage were found to be sadly wanting. Invidious comparisons were drawn in Japan with the San Francisco earthquake of 1989, which had been of a similar magnitude but had caused much less damage and loss of life. Japanese seismic science was not what it had been trumped up to be, and the government officials responsible for coordinating the humanitarian response to the event proved to be inept and confused.

What was striking about the episode is that people had come to view cataclysmic events of this kind as manageable. Yes, of course, there would be damage, but it could be anticipated and minimized. It had not always been thus. East Asia lies across the so-called rim of fire and is particularly prone to giant earthquakes. The great Kanto earthquake of 1923, for example, had claimed over 100,000 lives, and in 1556 an earthquake followed by a landslide

---

[10] 'Come feel the noise', *The Economist*, 29 July 1995, pp. 71–2.

[11] See also H. von Foerster, 'On Self-Organizing Systems and Their Environments' in Youitz and Cameron (eds), *Self-Organizing Systems*, London: Pergamon Press, 1960; I. Prigogine and I. Stengers, *Order out of Chaos: Man's New Dialogue with Nature*, Toronto: Bantam Books, 1984.

in China had killed 830,000 people.[12] Clearly, earthquakes were not about to disappear. Nevertheless, a better understanding of seismology, improved civil engineering technology, and a responsive administrative infrastructure could work together to minimize their destructiveness and their disruptiveness.

We can usefully think of earthquakes as entropy-increasing phenomena—i.e., as disruptive events with a tendency to inject disorder into human affairs. We can then further think of scientific and technical knowledge relating to earthquakes as an entropy-minimizing resource. The more we understand the seismic behaviour of earthquakes the better we can design and organize our way around them, thus limiting the amount of disorder they are able to inject into human affairs.

Technically speaking, the entropy of a system relates its free energy available to do useful work to its bound energy that is not so available. It is a measure of the amount of disorder present in a system. The second law of thermodynamics teaches us that in a closed system increases in the level of entropy are irreversible. In an open system—one that exchanges energy and information with its environment—entropy levels can be reduced but only by increasing the production of entropy in the system's environment. Yet if the conversion of free into bound energy cannot actually be reversed, with some knowledge of the system's structure and behaviour, the *rate* of conversion can be minimized. More useful work can be squeezed out of a given stock of free energy, and a given quantity of work can itself be made more useful. In effect, minimizing a system's rate of entropy production enhances its efficiency. The term 'efficiency' as it is used here, in an open systems context, has much broader, ecological connotations than it has when applied in a closed systems context—i.e., to traditional engineering problems.

Knowledge and entropy production stand in some inverse relationship to each other. In the late 1940s the American engineer Claude Shannon demonstrated the existence of this inverse relationship in the case of information processes.[13] Yet it holds for physical processes as well. Whether it is held by a bat or a biologist, knowledge minimizes an organism's consumption of energy, space, and time for a given amount of effort. Since earliest times, human beings learnt how to use knowledge to get a good part of their work performed by artefacts, thus economizing on their own bodily consumption of energy. As they did so, however, their overall energy consumption went up, since using artefacts vastly increased their access to other energy sources—both animate and inanimate—while reducing the effort personally required of them in order to exploit these sources. Today, indeed, a country's standard of living is often defined in terms of the energy resources that it can place at an individual citizen's command.

---

[12] I. Simmons, *Changing the Face of the Earth*, Cambridge: Cambridge University Press, 1989.
[13] C. Shannon and W. Weaver, *The Mathematical Theory of Communication*, Urbana: University of Illinois Press, 1949.

Knowledge builds on information that is extracted from data. In practice, the three terms are often confused. Data is a discrimination between physical states—black, white, heavy, light, etc.—that may or may not convey information to an agent. Whether it does so or not depends on an agent's prior stock of knowledge. The states of nature indicated by red, amber, and green traffic lights may not be as informative to a Kung bushman of the Kalahari, for example, as certain patterns in the soil pointing to the presence of lions nearby. Thus, whereas data can be characterized as a property of *things*, knowledge is a property of *agents* predisposing them to act in particular circumstances. Information is that subset of the data residing in things that activates an agent—it is filtered from the data by the agent's perceptual or conceptual apparatus (see Figure 1.2). Information, in effect, establishes a relationship between things and agents. Knowledge can be conceptualized as a set of probability distributions held by an agent and orienting his or her actions. These either consolidate or undergo modification with the arrival of new information. In contrast to information, knowledge cannot be directly observed. Its existence can only be inferred from the action of agents. It follows from this that knowledge assets cannot be directly observed either; they therefore have to be apprehended indirectly.

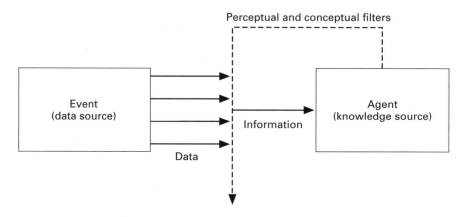

FIG. 1.2 Data, Information, and Knowledge

In human affairs, knowledge economizes on the use of physical resources (space, time, and energy) in three ways:

1. By in-forming them—i.e., by embedding itself in physical artefacts or processes, thus modifying their data structures and their information-bearing capacity. The regular size and shape of a building brick, for example, allows a wall to be erected faster, more reliably, and with less material than if it was built out of rubble or boulders.

2. By organizing them—i.e., by embedding itself as information in documents and symbolic support systems used to coordinate the creation or functioning of artefacts. The plans of a house or an office building depict in an abstract form a complex integration of physical products and processes within a confined space. Such plans usually have to be read in conjunction with detailed specifications and budgets.
3. By enhancing the understanding of intelligent agents that interact with physical resources—i.e., by embedding itself in the brains of individuals or organizations.[14] In drawing up plans for a house or an office building, an architect draws upon an accumulated stock of knowledge which reflects a collective understanding of human behaviour in space, the physical performance of structures and materials, the management of building projects, and so on.

In short, knowledge held by agents builds up the information structures latent in physical things, in documents, or in individual brains. Knowledge assets are those accumulations that yield a stream of useful services over time while economizing on the consumption of physical resources—i.e., minimizing the rate of entropy production.

I.4 DIFFERENT KINDS OF KNOWLEDGE ASSETS

We can classify knowledge assets along two dimensions:

Dimension 1: According to how far they can be given form. Knowledge that is to be embedded in mass-produced artefacts, for example, usually has to be more systematically formalized and codified than knowledge that is to be embedded more discursively in text. Many mass-produced artefacts are manufactured to fine tolerances that admit of little variation in dimension or performance. Their fabrication requires a precise description in the form of workshop drawings, specifications, or schedules. Knowledge that is expressed discursively, by contrast, usually allows for a greater degree of informality. Alternative ways of presenting it are possible, and these vary in the amount of redundancy that they require to be intelligible. Yet even discursive knowledge must be codifiable to some minimum degree if it is to be transmissible—much more so than most of the knowledge that individuals typically carry around in their heads. Many, and perhaps most, of the countless patterns that we hold in memory are never articulated. This is either because they are inarticulable—for example, the knowledge required to ride a bicycle or to evaluate a Rembrandt self-portrait—or because they are too idiosyncratic to justify the effort involved in articulating them—knowledge of a close relative's personal habits, of a childhood scene, etc.

---

[14] We take organizations such as firms to be intelligent agents in their own right. See J. B. Quinn, *Intelligent Enterprise: A New Paradigm for a New Era*, New York: The Free Press, 1992.

Dimension 2: As a function of their degree of abstraction. Knowledge that is embedded in artefacts, for example, of necessity has to be more concrete than knowledge that is set out in documents or in people's heads, even if it incorporates quite abstract principles. To illustrate: the type of knowledge deployed by Donald M. Eigler of IBM's Almoden Research Center in San José, California, when spelling out the company's logo by aligning individual carbon monoxide molecules, invoked both the abstract realm of quantum tunnelling effects as well as the very concrete realm of scanning tunnelling microscope technology.[15] A crucial difference between concrete and abstract knowledge is that the first type is confined to specific applications in space and time whereas the second type is more general and less restricted in its scope. Thus, the abstract knowledge embedded in the Schrödinger wave equation can find application in a far larger number of situations than can the more concrete knowledge embedded in the security code of my burglar alarm system.

Codification and abstraction constitute two founding concepts for our analysis of knowledge assets. They will be further discussed in Chapter 3. Here, we simply invite the reader to note that they represent two quite different though interrelated ways of economizing on information processing and transmission. The point is a key one. If knowledge assets allow us to economize on the consumption of physical resources per unit of effort, then codification and abstraction, in turn, allow us to economize on the data-processing and communication efforts required either to create or exploit knowledge. In short, *codification and abstraction lower the cost of converting potentially usable knowledge into knowledge assets.*

The point can perhaps best be understood by considering the relationship between science and technology. It is a commonplace that new technologies are often quite informal and *ad hoc* when they first make their appearance. As time passes, however, informal technical practices get standardized as certain abstract principles gradually come to light. Knowledge of the aerodynamics of flight, for example, followed rather than preceded the experiments of the early pioneers with different aircraft designs. And much contemporary medical practice is still a standardization of 'what works', with theoretical understanding only following later—indeed, sometimes, much later.

The thrust of any technological development, then, is towards a greater codification and abstraction of the technical principles involved, with progress towards the one facilitating progress towards the other. With each step comes some saving in the use of resources, often achieved in areas only indirectly related to the original work. The reason for this has already been mentioned: abstract principles enjoy greater scope and find more general application than concrete ones; as a developing field of knowledge becomes more abstract, therefore, so the areas in which it is applied grow more distant

---

[15] Philip Yam, 'In the Atomic Corral', *Scientific American*, July 1995, p. 13.

from each other. To illustrate: the miniaturizing skills developed by chip manufacturers as they seek exponentially to increase the number of transistors
they place on a microchip are now finding unexpected application in the
emerging field of nanotechnology. Drawing on processes and materials used
in microelectronics, researchers are today able to create microscopic beams,
pits, gears, membranes, and motors, whose size can be measured in microns—
a fraction of the width of a human hair. In this way, the technologies that gave
birth to microelectronics are increasingly being transposed into new fields of
endeavour.

1.5 TECHNOLOGY, COMPLEXITY, AND ENTROPY

We tend to think of economizing as a human activity. The science of economics is classified as a social science and in its current form it is just under a
century and a half old. Yet in the eighteenth century there was much talk of
the economy of nature—the tendency of all living things to exhibit economizing behaviour—and of Maupertuis's principle of least action, namely, the
idea that physical processes in general so organize themselves as to minimize
their consumption of a quantity known as the action. If we replace the term
action by energy, Maupertuis's principle still holds good: quantum mechanics, for example, causes atoms to arrange themselves in a minimum energy
configuration.

Could economics ever come to be considered a natural science as well as a
social one? At first sight the idea might seem surprising. Economics has experienced difficulty enough coming up with convincing accounts of human
behaviour—except in those elusive settings that economists label 'efficient
markets'—without taking on board the additional burden of explaining the
functioning of the natural world in terms of its concepts. Yet the idea may not
be as crazy as it sounds. What would have to be demonstrated is that physical and biological systems, no less than social ones, behave as if physical
resources were scarce. A first step might be to align a certain number of established physical and biological principles related to energy minimization with
the corresponding economic concepts.

Some lines of investigation are showing promise. Recent work in theoretical biology, for example, seems to confirm that biological systems tend to act
so as to minimize their rate of entropy production.[16] Such minimization
behaviour can be taken as expressing an economizing orientation. And within
inanimate physical systems themselves, one can observe both the principles of
least action and of least time at work.[17] Think of how a simple pile of sand

[16] D. Brooks and E. Wiley, *Evolution as Entropy: Towards a Unified Theory of Biology*, Chicago: University
of Chicago Press, 1986.
[17] The latter was put forward by the eighteenth-century mathematician, Pierre de Fermat.

tends to adopt a minimum energy configuration or how a beam of electromagnetic radiation follows the shortest trajectory between two points.

Furthermore, any process of self-organization can be plausibly interpreted as a quest for economy. A system exhibiting the property of self-organization aims to maintain itself in existence against the forces of disintegration on the one hand and of fossilization on the other. Life, for example, emerges from physical structures locatable in some intermediate state between the chaotic and the crystalline.[18] In such a state, it must hold entropy production at some minimum level consistent with its own continued maintenance. With too high a level of entropy production, life disintegrates in a chaotic cauldron; yet with too low a level, life is frozen out.

What applies to living systems applies by extension to the social systems that sustain them. Organizations and institutions must keep their rate of entropy production at a sustainable level if they are to survive. The challenge for firms in the twenty-first century will be to adjust to this simple idea. We are discovering that, being part of nature rather than above it, our species is constrained in its development by an entropy budget. But unlike the budgets with which we are all familiar, this one has an output side as well as an input side. On the input side our actions are limited by the amount of free energy available for their execution. Here, we can draw upon our energy 'income'—i.e., the renewable energy derivable directly or indirectly from the sun—or we can eat into our energy 'capital'—the non-renewable energy trapped in the earth's mineral resources. On the output side our entropy budget sets a limit to the amount of bound energy that we can safely generate per unit of time, since what cannot be exported into empty space has to be absorbed by the biosphere itself. If we exceed our allotted budget we will eventually choke on the effluents that we emit.

We are now aware that demographic and environmental considerations are steadily reducing the entropy budget available for each and every creature that inhabits the face of the earth, and that further reductions may be inconsistent with the long-term maintenance of human life on this planet. The limits-to-growth debate of the early 1970s framed the problem in terms of the earth's finite stock of resources—sooner or later, the raw materials on which modern industrial society has come to depend will run out.[19] This is a problem on the input side in our entropy budget. The problem, however, goes much deeper. At heart, it is about the inability of the biosphere as a system to go on absorbing the ever-increasing amount of entropy generated by our species. On the output side no less than on the input side of the entropy equation, then, we face an imminent crisis.

---

[18] A. Cairns-Smith, *Seven Clues to the Origin of Life*, Cambridge: Cambridge University Press, 1985; S. Kauffman, *The Origins of Order*, Oxford: Oxford University Press, 1993.
[19] D. H. Meadows, D. L. Meadows, J. Randers, and W. Behrens, *The Limits to Growth: A Report on the Club of Rome's Project on the Predicament of Mankind*, London: Earth Island Ltd., 1972.

Is there a way out? We are in no position to say. This book builds on the hypothesis that if there is, it will require a new theoretical understanding of how physical, biological, and information processes relate to each other. In particular, it will require an appreciation of the extent to which entropy production can be reduced by substituting information resources for physical ones in human activity. Yet this will only happen when the thinking about the environmental challenges that we face and about the information revolution we are currently going through are brought together into a single integrated set of concepts.

The synthesis will not be easy. At the broadest level we find two groups of individuals who are ostensibly addressing quite different issues. The first group is deeply concerned about the environment, the depletion of physical resources, and the pressures of demography. It has become intensely pessimistic about the ability of human institutions to keep human claims on the environment below the carrying capacity of the biosphere. The second group is concerned to make sense of the information revolution and the growing dematerialization of economic activity. Although it is trying to understand the nature of the discontinuity created by the emerging information society, this group remains optimistic concerning the potential offered by the new technologies to make inroads into the challenges that confront us as a species.

The two groups talk different languages and tend to attract different constituencies. For this reason there have been few attempts to link the issues that each group is concerned with. The exercise, however, seems worthwhile. Yet if it is to succeed, we need to rethink our approach to information phenomena and in particular to their economic characteristics. At present, they lie beyond the analytical reach of conventional economic analysis, steeped as it is in the paradigm of the energy economy.[20] By focusing on the nature of knowledge assets and on how they can be apprehended, this book aims to contribute to such a rethink.

I.6 THE PLAN OF THE BOOK

The book presents a framework for thinking about the relationship between physical and knowledge assets. Although it is addressed to people working in and around firms and thus refers to issues that operate primarily at the level of the firm, the bigger picture that we have just outlined should not be lost from sight. Good managers are rarely the unidimensional profit maximizers that they are portrayed to be. It therefore does no harm to assume—as I do— that they share the wider concerns of the communities in which they live.

The book is structured as follows:

---

[20] Mirowski, *More Heat than Light*.

– In Chapter 2 we present a way of thinking about information that brings out the extent to which knowledge assets and physical assets substitute for each other in economic processes. We argue that the act of learning imparts a long-term bias to the substitution process in favour of knowledge assets.

– In Chapter 3 we develop a conceptual framework for the analysis of knowledge flows within and between social groupings. We then informally derive a number of propositions concerning knowledge assets for further discussion.

– In Chapter 4 we use our conceptual framework to explore the paradoxical nature of knowledge assets with respect to economic value. We show that, in contrast to physical goods, information goods are indeterminate with respect to value and we explore some of the implications of this point.

– In Chapter 5 we look at how firms cope with these paradoxes and identify two generic strategies available for the management of knowledge assets. One pushes a firm to hoard its knowledge, the other encourages it to share it. We briefly look at the circumstances that will favour one strategy over the other.

– In Chapter 6 we explore how a firm's culture and organizational processes condition its choice of strategy and its overall approach to the management of knowledge assets. Our conceptual framework yields four distinct cultural types, each operating in its own information environment. The challenge for the firm is to match the information environment it finds itself in with an appropriate cultural response.

– In Chapter 7 we discuss the integration of a firm's knowledge assets at different levels of resolution—the product level, the technology level, and the organizational level. How far should these levels be integrated and how far should they be allowed to evolve autonomously?

– In Chapter 8 we examine a particular variant of the integration issue, namely, when it shows up as a distinctive competence or capability. We draw on our conceptual framework to show how such a competence can be identified and how it might evolve over time.

– In Chapter 9 we ask what is the impact of information technology on the pattern of knowledge flows and on the management of knowledge assets at the level of a firm and that of the industries in which a firm competes. Our conceptual framework indicates that current developments in IT are likely to bring about profound transformations in the culture of firms with implications that are quite counterintuitive.

– In Chapter 10 we apply some of the concepts presented in this book in two firm-level interventions, one in a chemical firm, the other in an oil major. We illustrate how the organization's knowledge assets can be mapped and show how such a mapping helps internal players to reinterpret the firm's technological posture.

– In Chapter 11 we recapitulate the main points presented in this book and assess their implications for the management of firms in the twenty-first century.

2

The Information Perspective

2.1 INTRODUCTION

ON 2 May 1991, on the centenary of *Rerum Novarum*, Pope Leo XIII's encyclical on unbridled industrialization, Pope John Paul II published his own encyclical: *Centesimus Annus*. In it, he embraced the new information age as being one which demonstrates that 'after the earth, the chief resource of man is man himself'.[1] As a resource, man can either be viewed, as Marx and his contemporaries did, as a source of labour power—i.e., as a *physical* phenomenon—or as a source of knowledge—i.e., as an *information* phenomenon. The energetic perspective on man has proved to be analytically more tractable than the information perspective although, of course, the two are thoroughly intermingled.

The intermingling itself presents us with further difficulties. It is particularly hard to understand the changing ways in which physical and information phenomena come together—whether in human beings themselves or in the artefacts that they create—to produce economic resources whose value often far exceeds the sum of their individual parts. Neoclassical economics wishes the problem away under the catch-all label of 'technological change' and then makes it 'exogenous' to neoclassical models of economic growth and development—it then ceases to be a problem that neoclassical economists feel driven to tackle. It shows up in their models sometimes as a 'residual', sometimes more politely dressed up as 'total factor productivity'. Either way, it robs their models of up to half of their explanatory power.

In this chapter we shall propose a way of integrating physical and information phenomena in a single unified representation, using—and modifying—a simple conceptual tool much loved by neoclassical economists: the production function. Before we start, however, and to avoid subsequent confusion, it will be necessary to reiterate once more the distinction, established in the preceding chapter, between data, information, and knowledge:

1. We take *data* to be simply a discernible difference between alternative states of a system. It is made up of low level energy that acts informationally rather than mechanically upon an observer. We know, for example, that single photons can fire retinal cells. Given their exiguous energy relative to the organism that they interact with, they cannot be said to act

---

[1] 'God's Invisible Hand', *The Economist*, 4 May 1991, p. 58.

mechanically on it. Their influence, if anything, is informational. By contrast, an Atlantic wave breaking over a swimmer acts on her mechanically as well as informationally—it can be felt as well as seen. In this second example, we would more readily describe the swimmer as a victim of the wave than as its observer.

2. *Information* is data that modifies the expectations or the conditional readiness of an observer. The more those expectations are modified, the more informative the data is said to be. To encounter a sequence of traffic lights in downtown Manhattan, for example, would surprise no one. To encounter the same sequence three kilometres from the South Pole, on the other hand, could prove quite disconcerting for those who have braved the elements getting there.

3. *Knowledge* is the set of expectations that an observer holds with respect to an event. It is a disposition to act in a particular way that has to be inferred from behaviour rather than observed directly. A knowledge of ash trays, for instance, can readily be built up by noticing that one tips one's cigarette ash into them, that one refrains from pouring tea into them, and so on.

Clearly, knowledge structures—i.e., expectations—are modified by the arrival of new information, and such information, in turn, has to be extracted from the data generated by phenomena.

What are knowledge assets in the above scheme? They can be thought of as that subset of dispositions to act that is embedded in individuals, groups, or artefacts and that has value-adding potential. In some cases the right to act on a given disposition is the exclusive property of an individual or group—i.e., it is an intellectual property right. Typically, it is not. We defer the discussion of the appropriability of knowledge assets to Chapter 4.

The structure of this chapter is as follows. In section 2.2 we discuss some of the salient features that distinguish an information economy from an energy economy. In section 2.3 we explore an idea first put forward by Kenneth Boulding: that information might be considered a factor of production.[2] We develop a production function that explicitly incorporates information as a productive factor, but in a way not envisaged by Boulding. In section 2.4 we discuss the difference between our production function and the more conventional neoclassical ones. In section 2.5 we apply our new production function to the environmental challenges facing firms, and in section 2.6 we extend our discussion to consider issues of entropy and complexity. The concluding section, 2.7, briefly develops the implications of our discussion for how we think of knowledge assets.

[2] K. Boulding, 'The Economics of Knowledge and the Knowledge of Economics', *American Economic Review*, 58 (May), pp. 1–13, 1966.

2.2 THE NEW ECONOMY

In the nineteenth century—and for a good part of the twentieth—wealth was associated with command over energy sources. The industrial revolution had substituted coal, a non-renewable source of energy, for wood, a renewable but fast depleting one. At the same time, it had greatly increased the efficiency with which this new source could be exploited. Some sources of energy, such as the wind and the sun, formed part of God's bounty—what, today, econo-mists would classify as 'free goods'. Other sources, although accessible and still bountiful in themselves, required some expenditure of energy in the form of animal or human labour power to make them available for use. How much energy had to be expended to get how much energy in return—work put in over work got out—was a function of the mechanical technologies available to carry out the conversion. In pre-industrial times these rarely extended beyond simple hand tools.

In the agricultural economies of the beginning of the nineteenth century, the critical factors of production were land and labour. Both were sources of energy. The first was provided by nature, the second by human or animal power. With the spread of industrialization, capital, typically in the form of machinery and plant, also came to be viewed as a factor of production. Yet some classical economists, most prominently Marx, considered capital to be little more than 'congealed labour'—i.e. the sum total of the labour power that went into its production.[3]

Thinking of capital in this way had interesting consequences. Factors of production had to be purchased and paid for. A key issue was the share of the total product that should be imputed to each factor. By reducing capital to labour, Marx was in effect denying that capital had any legitimate claim on the fruits of production at all. The capitalists were thus appropriating for themselves 'surplus value' created by labour, and rightfully belonging to labour. Marx went further. If capital had no legitimate role to play, then it followed that entrepreneurship, that delicate blend of knowledge and risk-taking that makes the intelligent commitment of capital possible in the first place, had none either. Even the intelligence, knowledge, and skill with which labour itself might be applied were all reduced to multiples of raw labour power by computing the total labour time required to acquire them. Clearly, Marx held a strictly energy-based view of economic processes.

Prevailing estimates of the extent of God's bounty were conditioned by reli-gious conceptions of the world and man's place in it. When, for example, Christ predicted that the meek would inherit the earth, it was implicitly assumed by those who heard him that there was plenty more where it came from. Economic interpretations of such divine munificence yielded a poten-tially limitless supply of productive factors at the prevailing market price.

---

[3] K. Marx, *Capital: A Critique of Political Economy*, London: Lawrence and Wishart, 1972.

Any limits on the supply side could then be attributed to venal behaviour such as hoarding, rather than to sudden fits of parsimony by the Creator. If any parsimony was called for, it would surely be in the use of human labour required to gain access to God's bounty. Ever since his fall, man had been condemned to earn his daily bread by the sweat of his brow. Yet God is merciful. By endowing his humble servant with a modicum of intelligence, he made it possible for him to maximize the bread while minimizing the sweat. *Pace* Marx, then, factor prices and factor productivity always reflected the effectiveness with which human knowledge and intelligence were applied to energy processes. Raw labour power has never been the whole story.

The knowledge and intelligence applied to productive processes found expression both in the technologies used in production as well as in the way that production was organized. The more effectively knowledge and intelligence were used, the greater the economies achieved in the consumption of productive factors. Yet, as we have seen, knowledge and intelligence are elusive; they are often idiosyncratic individual traits that do not interact in any direct mechanical way with the physical world. They are dispositional and therefore do not yield easily to either direct observation or analysis.

Nineteenth-century economists, and many of their twentieth-century successors, found a simple way of dealing with the analytical intractabilities posed by technology and organization: they pretty much ignored them. Technology was treated as a given. New technologies rained down from heaven following scientific or inventive breakthroughs and then mysteriously became immediately available to all economic agents. It turned out, then, that the earth was not the only thing that the meek inherited. As economists told it, they also inherited, ready-made, the technologies and organizational skills necessary to exploit it.

No less than Marx, classical and neoclassical economists decided to treat knowledge and information as parameters of their systems rather than as variables within them. Ignoring knowledge and information in this way allowed them to focus on the energetic dimension of economic processes.[4] Deprived of any interaction with knowledge and information, the energy systems that they studied exhibit the valuable property of linearity, wherein cause and effect operate continuously and proportionately. Knowledge and information, by contrast, can be highly nonlinear and hence disruptive. When injected into a physical system, they are capable of generating important discontinuities and of allowing small causes to exert disproportionately large effects. If we stop to think about it, has not the knowledge we have acquired of the humble electron effectively transformed the world we live in?

To repeat: in the agricultural economy, the productive factors were land and labour; in the industrial economy they were capital and labour. In each case, productive factors were brought together in what are called production

---

[4] See P. Mirowski, *More Heat than Light: Economics as Social Physics, Physics as Nature's Economics*, Cambridge: Cambridge University Press, 1989.

functions. A production function is a snapshot of the output levels that can be achieved with different input quantities of productive factors, with each input mix representing a different set of technological and organizational arrangements. These are assumed to be known by all producers of a given type of output.

A typical production function is shown in Figure 2.1. The curves AA' and BB' in the figure are known as isoquants. Each curve indicates the different mixes of capital and labour inputs—and by implication the technologies that bring them together—required to produce a given level of output. Moving along any given isoquant establishes the rate at which one factor can be substituted for the other at the margin using a particular technology. Productive factors exhibit constant returns to scale: double the inputs of capital and labour and you will get double the output.

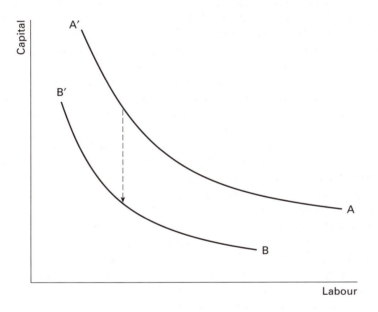

FIG. 2.1 A Production Function

Technical progress acts to reduce the quantity of inputs of capital and/or labour required to produce a given level of output. Technical progress shows up in the production function as a shift of the isoquant towards the origin—i.e., from curve AA' to curve BB'. It thus appears as a discontinuity that is exogenously given.[5] With conventional production functions, the growth of

---

[5] Here I shall use the term 'technical change' as it is used in daily discourse. Economists distinguish technical *change*—a move along a given isoquant—from technical *progress*—a move across isoquants towards the origin. I prefer to go for what is easy to read, even at the cost of a certain lack of terminological precision.

knowledge and information can form no part of the analysis. Yet given the role that knowledge and information play in the new economy, the use of such an ill-adapted tool condemns us in effect to play Hamlet without the Prince.

Typically, production functions single out in a highly simplified form those factors that society considers critical to the creation of wealth. In the agrarian economy of David Ricardo's day, the critical factors were taken to be land and labour. With the growth of the industrial economy in the course of the nineteenth century, capital came to replace land as a critical requirement for wealth generation. At the end of the twentieth century, across virtually all industries, knowledge has become a critical determinant of the wealth of nations. It might therefore be reasonable to conclude, as did the economist Paul Romer,[6] that one needs to add knowledge to labour and capital as a factor of production.

The idea has a certain appeal and Romer himself takes it further by embedding a measure of productive knowledge in human capital. He thus obtains four factors to play with: capital; unskilled labour; human capital—this might be measured by years of education; and ideas—possibly measured by patent counts. With these factors, constant returns to scale can no longer be assumed: Romer's production function shows increasing returns.

In spite of the problems this poses for neoclassical orthodoxy, Romer's analysis can be interpreted as an extension of it. I shall argue, as has Maurice Scott,[7] that Romer's attempt to incorporate knowledge into the existing neoclassical production function is untenable. But whereas Scott, given the difficulties involved, would have us abandon the use of production functions altogether, I will suggest the adoption of a radically different type of production function, one which at this stage of its development could only be used for a highly schematic type of analysis.

As Scott rightly perceived, Romer's addition of knowledge to a neoclassical production function made up of capital and labour involves us in double counting. By subdividing the labour factor into unskilled labour and human capital, Romer implicitly recognizes this. He fails, however, to deal with the knowledge that is already embedded in capital. Robots, for example, incorporate more up-to-date knowledge than mechanical lathes and may in certain cases cost less. Yet buying a robot registers as an expenditure on capital, not as one on knowledge or ideas. More problematic for Romer, much knowledge is embedded in organizational processes in ways that would quite escape his proposed measures. A firm's 'core competences', for example, constitute a form of organizational knowledge that would experience some difficulty showing up under any of Romer's proposed factors.[8]

---

[6] P. Romer, 'Endogenous Technical Change', *Journal of Political Economy*, 1990; 'Are Nonconvexities Important for Understanding Growth?', *American Economic Review*, 1990.

[7] M. Scott, *A New View of Economic Growth*, Oxford: Oxford University Press, 1989.

[8] For a discussion of core competence, see C. Prahalad and G. Hamel, 'The Core Competence of the Corporation', *Harvard Business Review*, May–June 1990; D. Leonard-Barton, 'Core Capabilities and Core

The reason that knowledge cannot stand as a factor of production in its own right alongside capital and labour is that the latter factors already incorporate knowledge in their fabric in ways that are hard to disentangle. Recall that the different mixes of capital and labour required to produce a given level of output are a function of the technology, skills, and organization available. Another way of saying the same thing is that they are a function both of the knowledge that is embedded in the factors themselves, and of that which is used to integrate them into productive configurations.

We conclude that if knowledge is to show up as a credible player on a production function, it cannot be as a bolt-on to existing ones. Such intellectual legerdemain would amount to little more than adding epicycles to a discredited Ptolemaic model in order to 'save the phenomena'. How the production function itself is constituted, then, must be rethought from the ground up. We turn to this next.

2.3 THE EVOLUTIONARY PRODUCTION FUNCTION

Let us take as our starting point the fact that the classical factors of production such as labour and capital are made up of entities that have both physical and information attributes. The physical attributes can be located along a continuum according to how much physical space and energy they consume over a given period of time. Information attributes, by contrast, are patterns extracted from data which, when properly applied, have the capacity to modify the behaviour of the physical attributes and hence to modify their rate of consumption of physical space and energy per unit of time. This capacity we call knowledge; it can be embedded in both animate and inanimate objects. Now, given that data has a physical basis, we can think of information that is extracted from data as an abstraction from productive factors, as, indeed, are the physical attributes of energy, space, and time. By separately abstracting both physical and information attributes from the capital and labour factors of a conventional production function, we can create a new one, better suited to our requirements.

To summarize the argument so far: if we are to give knowledge and information adequate representation as factors of production we will have to develop a production function that operates at a higher level of abstraction than the neoclassical one. Might we do this by simply having the physical attributes of energy, space, and time grouped together into a single physical factor that is represented by one dimension of our new production function, with knowledge and information grouped together into a second factor and represented by a second dimension?

Rigidities: A Paradox in Managing New Product Development', *Strategic Management Journal*, 13, 1992, pp. 111–25; J. Barney, 'Firm Resources and Sustained Competitive Advantage', *Journal of Management*, 17 (1), 1991.

It turns out on closer inspection, however, that this second factor cannot be made up of knowledge and information themselves. To see why, recall that information is something that is extracted from data in order to modify knowledge structures, taken as dispositions to act. Indeed, properly used, information *economizes on the consumption of data*. In a graph, for example, a single line can replace an infinite scatter of data points and—if we are lucky—a simple algebraic formula can replace an infinite number of lines. We therefore suggest that, as indicated in Figure 2.2, data, not information, should be considered the most suitable candidate for our second factor. Information, to be sure, retains an essential role as the product of extractive operations designed to economize on the consumption and processing of data—extractive operations that in effect trigger a move towards the origin along the vertical axis of Figure 2.2. Knowledge assets can then emerge as useful productive structures, located along an isoquant such as AA' in the figure, whose data-consumption characteristics are established by their information content.

Our new production function operates at a high level of abstraction, the physical resources of energy, space, and time making up one factor, and data making up the other. The countless ways in which these productive factors come together produce the world as we know it: the sun, the clouds, trees, animals, states of mind, movies, Mars bars, etc. We shall leave aside the question

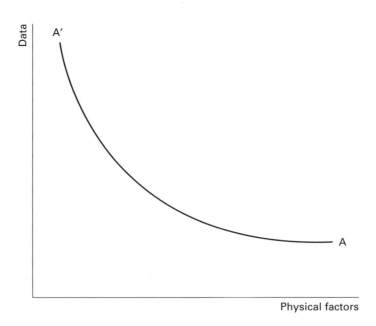

FIG. 2.2 An Evolutionary Production Function

of whether, in the absence of conscious human intervention, productive factors come together by design—which implies the action of a celestial entrepreneur—or whether the combinations evolved by accident. Either way, our production function indicates what we may expect by way of outputs for particular combinations of inputs. Of course, an act of abstraction such as the one we have just performed always exacts a price. What we gain in generality we lose in specificity. *Any* physical or data inputs could in principle find their way into our new production function. To apply it usefully in a particular context would require a far more detailed specification of physical and information inputs than we are offering here.

Our new production function, as depicted in Figure 2.2, nevertheless offers us two insights, one of which is implicit in the very idea of a production function, and one of which is not. The first insight on offer is that, within a given range, there is a trade-off in a system's consumption of data and its consumption of physical resources. By travelling up or down the transformation curve AA', a system can economize on the consumption of physical resources by increasing its consumption of data and vice versa. One promising example of this trade-off today is the gradual substitution of telecommunications in many areas of activity for physical transportation. Following the severe disruptions created by the Loma Prieta earthquake—measuring 7.1 on the Richter scale—that shook San Francisco on 18 October 1989, for example, many people switched on their PCs at home and started telecommuting to work, substituting an instantaneous flow of electrons for the energy-consuming movement of half a ton of metal on wheels along a crowded freeway. A second illustration of the point is offered by the nascent field of nanotechnology. Our ability to see and manipulate objects at the molecular or even at the atomic level, when further developed, promises a degree of precision and reliability in manufacturing that could deliver huge savings in the weight (energy) and size (space) of mechanical devices, as well as significant increases in their operating life (time).[9]

The second and less obvious insight on offer is that in any system capable of evolving over time, the trade-off between physical and information inputs is asymmetrical—i.e., it has a preferred direction. Between any two time periods, a system or its successors will exhibit a bias towards increasing its consumption and processing of data, and thus towards reducing its consumption of physical resources per unit of output. It does this through a process of differentiation, integration, and the creation of memory stores. In effect, our production function, in contrast to the more conventional ones used by economists, displays evolutionary tendencies.

To illustrate: living creatures are made up exclusively of cells. Cells are information-processing systems. Yet the information-processing capacities of prokaryotic cells such as bacteria—these appeared on earth some 3.5 billion

---

[9] K. Drexler, *Engines of Creation*, New York: Anchor Press/Doubleday, 1986.

years ago—are far exceeded by those of eukaryotic cells, which made their appearance some 1.8 billion years later. Prokaryotic cells, unlike eukaryotic ones, do not have a distinct nucleus within which genetic material can be carried. Although the latter are about 1,000 times bigger than an average bacterium—itself a prokaryote—their complexity allowed them to perform a trick that bacteria cannot hope to match: to come together in mutually dependent colonies such as animals, plants, and fungi. To do this, eukaryotic cells had to specialize and acquire communication skills—an achievement that required a lengthy and uncertain evolutionary process.

Shifting our focus from biological to human cultural evolution we witness further gains in data-processing capacities, but these now take place between rather than within organisms. They find expression in our new production function as institutions and society-wide data-processing and communication technologies.[10] Both are productive structures, and hence both count as knowledge assets. Working in combination, they brought about considerable savings in the consumption of physical resources per unit of output as hunter-gatherer cultures gradually gave way to settled agricultural ones, and these in turn metamorphosed into industrial ones (see Figure 2.3). Today, the information revolution promises further dramatic gains in our data-processing capacities. The hypothesis suggested by our evolutionary production function is that such a revolution should lead to a considerable saving in the consumption of physical resources per unit of output. Yet will such savings translate into tangible environmental benefits? Will they bring about any reduction in the pressures that, as a species, we exert on our environment in the form of entropy production? In short, will they allow us to make better use of our energy budget?[11]

We offer two answers to these questions: one is straightforward, the other less so. The obvious answer is that savings in physical resources consumed per unit of output will count for little if we go on increasing our total output indefinitely in response to uncontrolled population growth and rising expectations. In this sense the information revolution is no panacea. It merely points us in the direction of fruitful approaches to our environmental problems. These will not spare us hard choices, however, whether demographic or material, while our collective claims on the biosphere continue to exceed its carrying capacity.

The less obvious answer is that the substitution of data for physical resources cannot go on for ever either. We cannot eat data, nor can we keep ourselves warm by standing in front of a computer simulation of a log fire. Some irreducible level of physical resources is necessary to the maintenance of life. More importantly, perhaps, we cannot begin coherently to process all the data that the information revolution is immersing us in. Our brains are

---

[10] The institutional perspective we adopt is that of Douglass North. See D. North, *Institutions, Institutional Change and Economic Performance*, Cambridge: Cambridge University Press, 1990.

[11] The idea of an energy budget is discussed in Chapter 1.

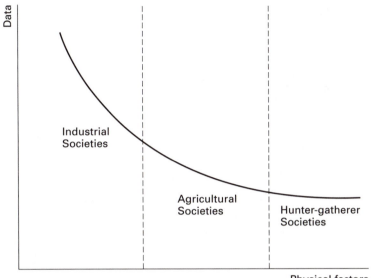

FIG. 2.3 Social Evolution in the Evolutionary Production Function

finite and our rationality is therefore bounded.[12] Where we confront data in volumes that exceed our capacity to process it, we either ignore it—i.e., sub-optimize—or suffer some kind of breakdown, overwhelmed by the complexity of it all.

Sooner or later, then, we confront the need to economize on the consumption of data as well as on that of physical resources. How do we do this? *By extracting information from data and then junking the latter*. This involves a discontinuous vertical jump down from curve AA' and on to curve BB', as shown in Figure 2.4. In other words, just like doctors, geologists, astronomers, and meteorologists, etc., we look for regularities in the data, for correlations that suggest an underlying pattern. When the pattern is found, it largely does away with the need to deal with the data directly. Our focus accordingly shifts from the data to the pattern.

Extracting information from data is a factor-economizing process that moves us towards the origin in Figure 2.4 through a series of discontinuous jumps. Thus, whereas economizing on physical resources through data sub-stitution involves an upward and leftward movement along a transformation curve such as AA', economizing on data involves jumping across curves and moving towards the origin. This is the reason why information cannot itself be a factor of production: it constitutes a factor saving. Just as with technical change in the neoclassical production function, the data-economizing process

---

[12] H. Simon, *The Sciences of the Artificial*, Cambridge, Mass: MIT Press, 1969.

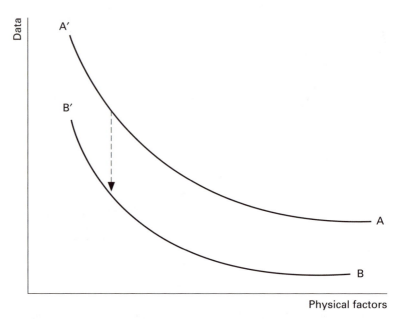

FIG. 2.4 Shifting Isoquant in the Evolutionary Production Function

is characterized by discontinuities, as is the knowledge to which it gives rise. Yet whereas neoclassical economics treats the discontinuity inherent in the creation of knowledge as exogenous to its explanatory scheme on account of its analytical intractability, we shall make it the focal point of our discussion. A potential for discontinuity is an inherent feature of all knowledge assets.

To recapitulate briefly: systems that evolve do so by economizing on their rate of consumption of physical resources. This involves, first, substituting the data factor for the physical factors in the production function of Figure 2.4 and, second, extracting information from the data factor. The process is represented by two distinct movements in the diagram: the first upward and to the left along the transformation curve AA', the second downward across transformation curves—i.e., from AA' to BB'—and towards the origin. The first movement is continuous and describes that slow accretion of data over time that we associate with learning from experience or with evolution. It is an inevitable by-product of the action of time on any evolutionary system— whether animate or inanimate—that can store data in the form of memory. Systems at different levels of complexity have different capacities for storing data and hence for learning from experience or evolving.

The second movement is discontinuous. We associate it with insight. The act of insight generates meaningful patterns that convey to the system useful information about the world it exists in and hence modifies its disposition to act—i.e., it creates knowledge. An insight reduces both the need for data processing and for data storage. In addition to relieving the pressure on the system's memory, it also reduces the load on data transmission, a point that will be developed in the next chapter. An insight, however, is an emergent outcome of the interaction that takes place between data and a system's data-processing apparatus. In other words, except in the most trivial of circumstances, its occurrence cannot be predicted from a prior knowledge of the data to be processed or of the characteristics of the data-processing agent. Extracting information from data, then, is a discontinuous, unpredictable process. As we shall see in the next chapter, there are essentially two ways in which a system can extract information from data—codification and abstraction—and they are quite distinct in their effects. The knowledge assets that are built up from these two activities inevitably reflect the discontinuities and unpredictabilities involved.

2.4 SOME ECONOMIC PROBLEMS WITH INFORMATION

What does our evolutionary production function have to offer that the neoclassical one does not? Both production functions take technical change to result from the exploitation of knowledge assets, and, as we have seen, in both cases this has the effect of moving productive processes towards the origin. With that move, both neoclassical production functions as well as our own have to cope with discontinuities. The two differ, however, in three important ways.

First, in the neoclassical case movement along a transformation curve could take place in either direction—that is, towards an increase in the use of labour or of capital. New knowledge, for example, in some circumstances, might well lead to an increased consumption of physical resources in order to save on data-processing ones. In the case of the evolutionary production function, by contrast, we hypothesize that there exists a direction to technical change: the trade-off between factors will usually favour the use of data resources over physical ones.[13] In other words, time matters in the evolutionary production function. In it, knowledge assets are generated by a sawtooth motion. Data, accumulating over time inside a system in the form of experience or memory, first moves productive activity upward and to the left, following a given isoquant, and then drops it vertically downward from one isoquant to another as data gets reduced through acts of insight that extract information from data. The dynamic is depicted in Figure 2.5.

Second, in the neoclassical case, the discontinuity associated with technical progress is only partly a reflection of the nature of that progress. It also owes something to the way in which productive factors were initially conceptualized. Students of management, in contrast to economists, have tended to

---

[13] In the short run, the price structure might well at times favour the use of physical resources over data resources. Evolution, however, is not a short-run phenomenon.

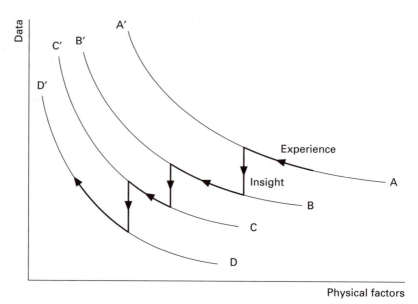

FIG. 2.5 Experience and Insight in the Evolutionary Production Function

portray technical progress as something continuous. Experience curves, for example, plot a steady reduction in the cost per unit of output as a function of both cumulative experience with that output and economies of scale. What is needed, however, is a way of giving both continuous and discontinuous forms of progress an appropriate representation. The evolutionary production function, by first distinguishing between experiential learning and learning by insight, and then attaching the discontinuity to the latter, achieves a tighter coupling between the discontinuity and the mechanism that actually creates it.

The most important difference between the neoclassical and our evolutionary production function, however, resides in their respective economic properties. Physical resources have an economically attractive property which, in the more esoteric context of the quantum theory, physicists define as 'locality'. Simply put, if they are here, then they are not there. Spatio-temporal locality imparts to physical resources an irreducible if minimal level of scarcity. It also helps to make them appropriable. Data resources have quite different economic properties: they are not naturally scarce. What is locked into a single individual's head at one moment in time can become common knowledge the next. In other words, in contrast to physical resources, data resources can proliferate uncontrollably. For this reason they are much more difficult to appropriate and subject to economic exchange than physical ones. Consequently, the more agents come to rely on knowledge assets as substitutes for physical resources, the more difficult they will find it to appropriate fully whatever value these create and to secure a maximum return on such assets.

This paradox of value will be discussed in more detail in Chapter 4. Suffice it here to point out that, to date, economics has no adequate theory for handling data—or information goods in general—as a factor of production. The nature of the problem is neatly highlighted by the following story reported in *The Economist*:

In 1978 a student at Oxford decided to improve his chances of academic success by borrowing a copy of his final examination questions. Not content with punishing him for cheating, the university prosecuted him for theft. The judge threw the charges out. The university, he pointed out, still had the questions. The student had not kept the piece of paper on which they were written. He had merely copied it. Because deprivation is the essence of theft, the student had not stolen anything.[14]

Is it any wonder that to the man in the street the term 'intellectual property' often seems almost a contradiction in terms? The need for adequate theorizing on information matters is well illustrated by this story.

2.5 INFORMATION AND THE ENVIRONMENTAL CHALLENGE

Our evolutionary production function has brought together information and environmental issues in a single representation as an interaction between data and physical resources. This allows us to reformulate anew some of the points made in the preceding chapter.

The greater the rate of consumption of physical resources per unit of output the greater the rate of entropy production. The major challenge that we face may not be limits on the supply of physical resources as such, but limits on the capacity of the biosphere to cope with increased rates of entropy production. Take plastics, for instance. On the input side they present nothing but advantages. They require less energy to produce than metal, and less energy subsequently to convert into products. These in turn are lighter, stronger, and more resistant to corrosion than the metal product they replace. On the output side, however, they present much more serious problems of disposal than metals do at the end of their useful life. The challenge, unfortunately, totally escapes detection in current formulations of national income accounts. Under current practice, for example, when a forest is cut down and sold, this registers as a wealth-increasing market transaction. The fact that the trees may not be replaced, and that their removal may result in soil erosion, flooding, and the loss of food, is conveniently overlooked. Or again, although pollution is likely to reduce welfare, it does not count as a reduction of GDP.

---

[14] 'The Eye of the Beholder', *The Economist*, 4 May 1991, p. 21.

It follows that cleaning it up should not count as growth. Perversely, however, cleaning up oil spills and buying catalytic converters count as GDP-increasing expenditures.[15]

The problem is that while the rate of entropy production per unit of output may well have started to go down significantly in industrial countries as information begins to replace matter on a broad front, uncontrolled demographic growth and rapid rates of industrialization elsewhere may be increasing the total units of output required to maintain a decent standard of living faster than can be compensated for by factor savings.

There is broad agreement on the need to bring down demographic growth rates to something close to replacement levels. There is much less agreement, however, on how to ensure that the least advantaged on our planet have access to the good life without inflicting irreversible damage on the biosphere in the process. Gains in efficiency will be essential, but if they are to be durable they will have to be complemented by an ethic of frugality. Yet who will vote for it? The Pareto welfare condition, so beloved of politically savvy economists, by favouring only policies that leave no one worse off, creates a theory-sanctioned impression that sacrifices can be avoided and that hard choices are unnecessary. A failure to achieve frugality, however, places virtually all the burden for meeting environmental challenges on to efficiency gains.

Our evolutionary production function does nothing more than suggest how such efficiency gains might be achieved. It offers no guarantee that it can be done. It indicates that one way to keep the rate at which entropy is produced by physical processes to a level consistent with the carrying capacity of the biosphere is to accelerate both the creation of knowledge and its application to physical resources in order to reduce our rate of consumption of the latter. In the evolutionary production function knowledge creation and application show up as two distinct phases:

1. *Creating knowledge*: The generation of insights through a process of extracting information from data. This appears as a series of downward movements across transformation curves and towards the origin, as shown in Figure 2.5.
2. *Applying knowledge*: Testing the insights created in a variety of situations that allow for the gradual accumulation of experiential data. This appears as a slow movement upward and towards the left along one of the transformation curves of Figure 2.5.

Knowledge assets emerge as the fruit of this two-step process. They are the product of two quite different types of learning working in tandem. The first is discontinuous and unpredictable. The insights that it generates may be quite trivial or they may revolutionize whole industries. The second is more incremental and manageable. It corresponds to what economists and corpo-

---

[15] 'Wealth of Nature', *The Economist*, 18 January 1992, p. 71, and R. Repetto, *Accounts Overdue: Natural Resource Depletion in Costa Rica*, Washington DC: World Resources Institute, 1991.

rate strategists call experience curves. Each type of learning prepares the ground for the other. Without a steady accumulation of experiential data, the act of insight has nothing to feed on. Without some fundamental insight, on the other hand, experiential learning has nothing to build on.

2.6 REDUCING ENTROPY AND REDUCING COMPLEXITY

The two types of learning operate within certain limits in the evolutionary production function. As we have already seen, the accumulation of experiential data cannot go on indefinitely. Increasing the quantity and diversity of data to be processed and transmitted merely increases the complexity of productive activity. Up to a point this is manageable: learning by doing has been shown to yield considerable savings in energy, space, and time. In many sports, such as skiing, tennis, or skating, the savings achieved produce elegant performances that are a source of pleasure for spectators. In commercial enterprises, the savings achieved by learning by doing and skilled performance, whether on the assembly line or in the boardroom, are a source of profit. Yet all systems, whether purely physical, biological, or social, have limits to their data-processing and storage capacities. If they are to maintain their ability to learn, at some point they have to metabolize the data they ingest.

They do this, first, by incorporating useful data within the information structures created by acts of insight, and then shedding surplus data through selective acts of forgetting. Metabolizing data in this way has the effect of reducing the load of complexity that a system has to deal with and frees up capacity for new learning. Complex systems are high producers of entropy. Where complexity resides solely in the way that the system handles the data, however—i.e., it is a product of a system's inability to process data on phenomena rather than a property of the phenomena themselves—then so does the entropy. Yet whatever the source of complexity, physical or informational, reducing it reduces entropy production.

We can illustrate this entropy reduction dynamic by examining the evolution of a new product. When a radically new type of product is launched, its design features remain quite fluid and its developers retain many degrees of freedom. The product is tried out in different markets with some market segments valuing certain performance attributes more than others. The process is initially quite *ad hoc* and high in entropy production. In this early phase no one yet knows which design features—or trade-offs between features—the different segments of the market will choose. Technologies used to manufacture the new product are often unreliable, crude and expensive. As Utterback points out, though, the product will still be able to function in some niche markets.[16] He cites the example of the Remington No. 1 typewriter, an

---

[16] J. Utterback, *Mastering the Dynamics of Innovation*, Cambridge, Mass: Harvard University Press, 1994.

inelegant and expensive contraption: yet in spite of Mark Twain's complaints about his infernal new machine, the author still needed to churn out text at a rapid pace. Utterback also gives incandescent lighting as an example. Although it was still highly experimental and costly, this did not deter the owners of SS *Columbia* from installing what was in effect Edison's first system. In closed spaces, where gas and oil lamps presented a fire hazard, the new lamps would clearly be superior.

As users gradually come to acquire experience of the product—an upward movement to the left along one of the isoquants of Figure 2.5—standardization and performance improvements tend to crystallize around those features that are valued by the greatest number of existing customers, and a stable configuration or pattern of product attributes emerges. At first, standardization can proceed in fairly large steps, since it is relatively unconstrained by other product attributes—these are still fluid enough to adjust to emerging product standards. We are now, in effect, in the early phases of a downward shift across isoquants in Figure 2.5. Standardization leads to performance improvements, and these in turn lead to further standardization. Both taken together lead to complexity reduction and subsequently to factor savings: the number of parts gets reduced, reliability increases, and a growing percentage of a product's manufacture can be automated. At least as important, product attributes coevolve to constrain each other mutually, thus further extending the scope for standardization while simultaneously limiting the scope for product variation. In this way a dominant design emerges and stabilizes.[17] Radical improvements or simplification become increasingly difficult to achieve once the first downward shifts across transformation curves have occurred.

So much for downward movements across isoquants. What about movements leftward and upward along isoquants? These have been taking place in parallel with the downward shifts. The improvements made possible by standardization will usually allow gradual savings in product weight, in product durability, in product size, and in manufacturing time. Such improvements will be introduced incrementally as users' and manufacturers' experience of the product builds up. Movements across and along isoquants thus operate in tandem. Note, however, that a leftward movement up an isoquant only reduces the complexity of a physical process by increasing data-processing complexity. Where the data of experience remains unmetabolized, information entropy goes up, not down. Nevertheless, this second type of movement tends to take place within a framework of structures and standards created by the first. And the closer this combination of movements gets us to the origin, the more constraining such structures and standards become. This is why, once they have become established, dominant designs are so difficult radically to alter—they gradually fossilize along a number of critical dimensions. The

---

[17] J. Utterback, *Mastering the Dynamics of Innovation*, Cambridge, Mass: Harvard University Press, 1994.

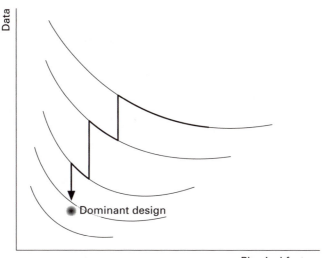

FIG. 2.6 The Trajectory of a Dominant Design in the Evolutionary Production Function

location of a dominant design in the evolutionary production function, together with the type of trajectory that produces it, are shown in Figure 2.6.

Focusing for a moment on the vertical axis of our evolutionary production function, it becomes apparent that, as data processors, we pay a price for complexity reduction. If, above a certain level of complexity, we face chaos—i.e., we cannot effectively process the amount of data we are confronted with at the speed it requires—reducing the complexity of experiential data, pushed beyond a certain level, fossilizes us and impairs our ability to cope with change and diversity. Effective learning requires us to blend complexity reduction—a downward movement in the evolutionary production function—with complexity absorption—an upward and leftward movement along a transformation curve. The sawtooth motion depicted in Figure 2.7, therefore, confines effective learning to a horizontal zone whose upper bound is chaotic—characterized by data overload—and whose lower bound is excessive order—characterized by an undersupply of data. Complexity theorists describe such a zone as 'the edge of chaos'; it is a region that complex systems are drawn to in their quest for dynamic stability.[18]

As with neoclassical production functions, movements along and across transformation curves are hard to distinguish in practice in the evolutionary production function. The key hypothesis that we are advancing, however, is that factor saving will be biased in favour of the consumption and processing

---

[18] For a discussion of this phenomenon, see S. Kauffman, *The Origins of Order*, Oxford: Oxford University Press, 1993; See also, C. Langton, *Artificial Life*, Reading, Mass: Addison-Wesley, 1992.

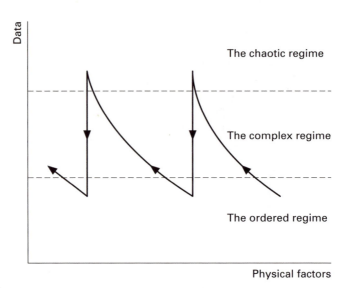

Fɪɢ. 2.7 Cognitive Chaos, Complexity, and Order in the Evolutionary Production Function

of data and against the consumption of physical resources. In other words, in contrast to the neoclassical production function, time's arrow is active in the evolutionary production function, and it points towards the left.

2.7 COMPLEXITY REDUCTION AND THE ARTICULATION OF KNOWLEDGE

In the preceeding section, we presented effective learning as a process of navigating at the 'edge of chaos' between excessive complexity and excessive order, steering productive activity now towards complexity reduction and now towards complexity absorption. Both strategies have the effect of saving on physical factors over time and hence of reducing the physical rate of entropy production.

Human productive organizations, however, have traditionally shown a strong preference for complexity reduction over complexity absorption—and this for practical reasons. As we shall see in greater detail in the next chapter, complexity absorption leads to a steady accumulation of tacit, experiential knowledge inside an organization. Although not necessarily ineffable, such knowledge can only be articulated and communicated with difficulty. It therefore tends to remain locked up in the heads of its possessors. Both its availability to the organization, therefore, and indeed its very existence, are precarious. Individuals come and go, they die off and their tacit knowledge dies with them. For this reason, productive organizations find it a better strategy to invest in the articulation of knowledge and complexity reduction than in the accumulation of tacit knowledge and hence in complexity absorption. Articulate knowledge can be shared and can thus be used to facilitate the coordination of productive activity. Tacit knowledge cannot be so easily shared.[19]

A preference for complexity reduction over complexity absorption translates into an organizational bias in favour of excessive order and a distaste for chaos in the evolutionary production function. Not all organizations, of course, are likely to experience this bias with equal intensity. Indeed, creative organizations may well at times exhibit a bias in the opposite direction and positively 'thrive on chaos' as Tom Peters puts it.[20]

Cultural considerations may also affect the direction of bias. Hofstede's researches into differences in national cultures, for example, show that some cultures are more comfortable with uncertainty than others.[21] One might reasonably infer that being at home with uncertainty will allow an organization to absorb complexity with greater ease than if it feels threatened by it. The case studies that we present in Chapter 10 explore the issue further. Organizations that seek excessive order—i.e., whose culture makes them, in Hofstede's terminology, high uncertainty avoiders—sooner or later hit the lower boundary of the learning zone shown in Figure 2.7. Unless they move back up the vertical scale, they and their knowledge assets are in danger of fossilizing.

Our analysis indicates that both organizational and technological innovation must be viewed as emergent phenomena in the evolutionary production function, the fruits of movements across as well as along transformation curves. They can also be thought of as outcomes of a process of structuration through which knowledge assets come into being.[22] Because this structuration process is discontinuous—i.e., nonlinear—it is hard to grasp using the traditional tools of economic analysis. The chapters that follow explore this structuration process at the level of social organizations called firms. Firms are instrumental in the development of knowledge assets. By implication, they have a key role to play in addressing the environmental challenges that threaten to overwhelm us. In this chapter, we have argued that knowledge assets do not yield to the tools of orthodox economic analysis. In our evolutionary production function physical and data resources each need to be

[19] M. Boisot, 'The Shaping of Technological Strategy: European Chemical Firms in South-East Asia', *Management International Review*, 2 (3), 1982; 'Convergence Revisited: The Codification and Diffusion of Knowledge in a British and a Japanese Firm', *Journal of Management Studies*, 20 (2), 1983, M. Boisot, *Information Space*, London: Routledge, 1995. See also I. Nonaka and H. Takeuchi, *The Knowledge Creating Company: How Japanese Companies Create the Dynamics of Innovation*, New York: Oxford University Press, 1995.

[20] T. Peters, *Thriving on Chaos*, New York: Alfred A. Knopf, 1987.

[21] G. Hofstede, *Culture's Consequences: International Differences in Work-Related Values*, Beverley Hills: Sage Publications, 1980.

[22] The concept of structuration is developed by Anthony Giddens. See A. Giddens, *The Constitution of Society: Outline of the Theory of Structuration*, Cambridge: Polity Press, 1984.

tackled with quite different conceptual orientations. Since the concepts needed to deal with physical resources are by now well established and uncontroversial, in the next chapter we shall concentrate on data resources, presenting a simple conceptual framework for their analysis. The framework will then be further developed and applied to firm-level issues in the chapters that follow.

3

The Information Space (I-Space)

3.1 INTRODUCTION

IN the preceding chapter, we presented knowledge assets as emerging from attempts at economizing on data processing. Data has become a factor of production in the new information economy; over time, it substitutes for physical resources through a learning process that blends the gradual accumulation of experience with discontinuous insights. The first part of the process increases the consumption and processing of data, the second economizes on data resources. In this chapter we take acts of codification and abstraction as holding the key to economizing on data. Further, we take the securing of such data economies as a crucial prerequisite of effective communication and, by implication, of effective organizational processes. These ideas are brought together in a single integrated conceptual framework, which we call the I-Space. I have described the I-Space in detail elsewhere.[1] In what follows we offer a brief outline of the framework.

In the next section (3.2) we show that codification can usefully be thought of as a process of giving *form* to phenomena or to experience. From our discussion it will emerge that, as well as being potentially valuable, the act of codification is fraught with problems and ambiguities.

In section 3.3 we turn to abstraction, the process of discerning the structures that underlie the forms. Codification and abstraction, often working in tandem, both reduce the data-processing load imposed on an agent, whether individual or organizational. They also facilitate communication processes and hence the diffusion of information whether inside or across boundaries— again, these could be individual or organizational. The diffusion of information is the subject of section 3.4.

Codification, abstraction, and diffusion are then brought together in section 3.5 in a single representation—the I-Space. This allows us to examine the flow properties of information within different agent groupings as a function of its degree of codification and abstraction. The dynamic behaviour of data flows in the I-Space is examined in section 3.6. Certain specific flow patterns give rise to the kind of learning from which knowledge assets emerge. These flows are broken down into their constituent components and each is discussed in turn.

In section 3.7 we indicate how a firm's knowledge assets might be represented in the I-Space, and discuss how such representations might be used by

[1] M. Boisot, *Information Space*, London: Routledge, 1995.

firms. Since a firm's knowledge assets are more broadly defined than its technologies, their identification poses delicate problems, exacerbated by the particular way they evolve over time. We discuss some of these problems as we
go along.

With section 3.8 we conclude the chapter, relating certain features of knowledge flows as they occur in the I-Space to properties of the evolutionary production function. We also briefly discuss the creation of knowledge assets,
drawing on concepts from complexity theory.

3.2 CODIFICATION

That firms are important generators of new knowledge has become a commonplace. It is also widely accepted that firms which consciously invest in the
creation of new knowledge through research and development activities or
through more informal learning processes generally tend to do better than
those which ride on the coat-tails of knowledge created by others. Yet it has
only recently become apparent that knowledge is far from being a homogeneous entity; over time it can undergo important transformations.
Knowledge which is hard to articulate or to share at one moment in time can
be reduced to a series of 0s and 1s inside a computer the next. Of late, this distinction between 'tacit' and 'codified' knowledge has attracted the attention
of practitioners and researchers.[2] The distinction, however, although it
appears to be rooted in neuroanatomy, remains ill-understood. As used, it
refers to little more than whether an item of knowledge can be set down on
paper or not. We will show that the distinction is much richer than has been
supposed and that it holds great theoretical promise.

In its most general formulation, the process of codification creates perceptual and conceptual categories that facilitate the classification of phenomena.
The act of assigning phenomena to categories once these have been created is
known as coding. The faster and the less problematically that coding can be
performed, the more effective the codification process and the more extensively it will be used. Effective codification is partly a matter of intellectual
and observational skill—an ability to discern contour and form in the data of
experience. Yet it also depends on the complexity of phenomena that require
partitioning into categories. The larger the number of distinctive attributes
associated with a phenomenon, for example, the more problematic the act of
codification. Not only will a large number of categories be required to capture

    [2] See, for example, I. Nonaka and H. Takeuchi, *The Knowledge Creating Company: How Japanese Companies Create the Dynamics of Innovation*, New York: Oxford University Press, 1995. I myself started stressing the distinction back in 1983, see M. Boisot 'Convergence Revisited: The Codification and Diffusion of Knowledge in a British and a Japanese Firm', *Journal of Management Studies*, 20 (2), 1983; Michael Polanyi predates us all. His book on personal knowledge was published in 1958. See M. Polanyi, *Personal Knowledge: Towards a Post-Critical Philosophy*, London: Routledge and Kegan Paul, 1958.

it—thus slowing down the coding process—but some of these may turn out to be spurious and thus undermine the validity of the exercise.

The following example will illustrate the point. Imagine having a number of boxes into which beads have to be placed according to their colour. The beads are picked up at random from a pile. If the beads turn out to be all of one colour, they can all be poured into one box. And if the colour of the beads can be ascertained beforehand, no assignment decision is needed. If the beads are one of two colours, however, then one can place them into two adjacent boxes, but now more time will be required to perform the assignment. As the number of colours grows, so will the time needed to match a particular bead to the box for the corresponding colour. Now suppose that in addition to variations in colour, the beads vary in their size. If one is required to classify by size as well as colour, the number of boxes in which the beads will have to be placed will increase once more, and the time required to decide into which box to place a particular bead will also go up. The number of boxes will go up as the product of the number of categories created to capture the colour attribute and the number of categories created to capture the size attribute. Thus, five colours and five possible bead sizes would require twenty-five boxes and twenty-five different types of assignment. If we then decided to classify by weight as well as by colour and size, and if we had five different weights of bead, we would end up with one hundred and twenty-five boxes and a matching number of assignments to make. Clearly, given how strongly our data-processing load is affected by the number of categories we have to deal with, it pays to choose one's categories with care. If, for example, we decided to classify our beads according to their texture as well as by size, colour, and weight, we could be creating a great deal of extra work for ourselves. The pay-off to classifying by texture would have to justify the extra effort involved.

The number of categories such as colour, size, or weight is one thing, the clarity of categories is another. If the beads vary continuously in size, colour, and weight, for example, it may take more time to decide to which specific box they belong. There will be borderline cases for which an intuitive approach to classification may no longer prove reliable. Formal measurement may then be required. Phenomena that vary discretely are easier to codify than those that vary continuously. However, the issue is rarely clear cut: what strikes one individual as a continuous variation may strike another as exhibiting the properties of discreteness. Humans, for example, are capable of recognizing approximately 10,000 different kinds of scent, from the pleasurable ones exuded by freshly cut flowers to the more distressful ones given off by an angry skunk. It is clear, however, that this capacity is exploited by individuals to very different degrees. Thus the olfactory discriminations performed by an expert wine-taster will be considerably more fine-grained than those of the non-expert.

The above example suggests that the degree of refinement of our classification schemes results partly from training and experience. An art historian will scan a work by Caravaggio with a far more developed set of cognitive filters than will an undergraduate taking an introductory course on mannerist painting. Yet, although these will affect how he perceives the Caravaggio—who was actually an anti-mannerist painter—the art historian's filters, in contrast to those of the wine-taster, will be conceptual as well as perceptual. He will thus be interested in the painter's relationship to the nobility and the higher clergy in *fin de siècle* Rome, the dynamics of the fashion he created among the *Caravaggisti*, the sources of his unbridled naturalism, and so on.

Codification constitutes a selection from competing perceptual and conceptual alternatives. The more of these there are to choose from, the more time such a selection will require and the more problematic it will become. Choice, in effect, links codification to the idea of complexity. Although there are many different definitions of complexity currently on offer,[3] we need only retain the fact that the more complex a task—such as, for example, a categorial assignment—the greater the amount of data processing required to complete it.[4] The same is true of codification: the less codified a task, the greater the time required to assign events to categories and hence the larger the number of bits of data that have to be processed in order to complete it.

The act of selection or codification is often conflict-laden. To select alternative A is to reject alternative not-A, a decision that can often be consequential for individuals or groups. To interpret the available evidence on human evolution, for example, paleoanthropologists must be capable of grouping hominids into species and genera. It is not always easy, however, to know exactly where one species ends and another begins. Since the fossil remains do not by themselves indicate which groups of individuals were interbreeding—species are often distinguished by their breeding patterns—classification remains partly subjective. Paleoanthropologists themselves can be divided into two groups according to their respective codification strategies: 'lumpers' will tend to group together as many creatures as possible, whereas 'splitters' will create new categories whenever they detect significant differences between samples. While some lumpers, for instance, recognize fewer than ten species, splitters can generate dozens of species from the known fossils.[5] One can surmise that a lumper's career prospects may not be as bright in a department staffed by splitters than in one staffed by fellow lumpers. In this way, the chances of obtaining research grants may well be affected by the codification strategy one chooses.

[3] See, for example, M. Gell-Mann, *The Quark and the Jaguar*, London: Abacus, 1994; I. Prigogine, G. Nicolis, and A. Babloyantz, 'Thermodynamics of Evolution', *Physics Today*, 25 (11), 1972, pp. 23–8; 25 (12), pp. 38–44; M. Mitchell Waldrop, *Complexity: The Emerging Science at the Edge of Chaos*, London: Penguin Books, 1992; R. Lewin, *Complexity: Life at the Edge of Chaos*, Middlesex: Penguin, 1993; J. Casti, *Complexification: Explaining a Paradoxical World through the Science of Surprise*, London: Abacus, 1994.

[4] This idea goes by the name of Algorithmic Information Theory. It is associated with the works of the Russian mathematician Kolgomorov and of Gregory Chaitin. See A. Kolgomorov, 'Three Approaches to the Quantitative Definition of Information', *Problems in Information Transmissions*, 1, 1965, pp. 3–11; and G. Chaitin, 'Information-Theoretic Computational Complexity', *IEEE Transactions, Information Theory*, 20 (10), 1974.

[5] C. Tudge, 'Human Origins: A Family Feud', *New Scientist*, 20 May 1995.

Battles for the establishment of technical or product standards—Betamax against VHS, Apple's Macintosh against IBM's PC—also provide instances of competing codifications. The fate of a product, or indeed a whole firm, sometimes hangs on whether it is capable of persuading the market to accept its way of structuring the world and of categorizing products rather than that of its rivals. Once codified, standards often create a lock-in effect that over time become irreversible.[6] In the battle for the VCR market, for example, the prizes would go to the system for which video outlets would stock the most prerecorded tapes, since this would enhance the value of owning that particular system. Increasing returns on early gains eventually tilted the competition in favour of the VHS standard, which then accumulated enough of an advantage to take virtually the entire VCR market. Ironically, increasing returns created a lock-in situation in which videotapes were now all prerecorded to the VHS standard, in spite of Betamax's technical superiority. Codification thus generates both cognitive and behavioural commitment. Skilfully applied, it constitutes a powerful strategic weapon.

Codification can be thought of as a procedure for shedding surplus data and hence for economizing on data processing. The not-As are discarded by the decision-making system once the As have been selected. They are no longer needed. This shedding of data makes commitment to a codification strategy an inherently risky business. If the strategy is faulty, the wrong data may be selected and valuable data discarded. In an organizational context, however, data discarded by the decision-making apparatus may actually be retained in an implicit form, embedded in the memory of individuals involved in the selection process. The British chemical firm Courtaulds, for example developed a revolutionary cellulosic fibre in the 1980s by drawing on employee knowledge of spinning technologies that had previously been rejected in other development projects.[7] Courtaulds' experience with this fibre is discussed further in Chapter 10.

By inviting selection from among a given set of alternative possible categories or states, the act of codification attempts to reduce uncertainty. If it is well performed, data processing will subsequently be facilitated and speeded up. Yet, uncertainty can only be effectively reduced if the suggested selection has some predictive value. A manufacturer of machine tools that segments its market on the basis of a prospective purchaser's taste in seafood, for example, is likely to make few sales. One that does so by focusing on the buyer's annual expenditure on capital goods, by contrast, is likely to fare a lot better.

In some cases the passage of time itself will reduce uncertainty, so that merely by waiting a little an appropriate codification strategy will suggest itself. Sooner or later, nature shows its hand. Yet, as we saw in the preceding chapter, organizations are often under pressure to reduce uncertainty, and

[6] W. Brian Arthur, 'Positive Feedbacks in the Economy', *Scientific American*, February 1990.

[7] M. Boisot, T. Lemmon, D. Griffiths, and V. Mole, 'Spinning a Good Yarn: The Identification of Core Competences at Courtaulds', *International Journal of Technology Management*, 2 (3/4), 1996, pp. 425–40.

consider waiting to be a luxury that they cannot afford. Codification, however, is akin to exercising an option, and can often be an irreversible act. Keeping an option open, on the other hand, buys time and can be far more valuable than exercising it. Absorbing uncertainty, therefore, like absorbing complexity, is a way of keeping one's cognitive options open. Premature codification is a false economy. Given that it can lead to positive as well as negative outcomes, uncertainty is not all bad and is not always to be avoided.[8]

Building on the link that we have established between codification and complexity, we can locate any task, physical or mental, as well as the knowledge assets required to execute it along a codification dimension scaled according to the amount of data processing it entails. At the uncodified end of the scale we will find tasks that require the processing of an infinite number of bits of data for their resolution. Such tasks cannot be articulated at all—indeed, it is not sure that they can even be described as tasks. They are ineffable, the province of the lone mystic. No amount of rational analysis can make them intelligible and hence communicable.

At the codified end of the scale, by contrast, we shall find simple tasks that only need one bit of data for their execution. A wall-mounted light switch, for example, will either be on or off and will be operated according to whether or not one requires light in a room. In between these extremes we find much of the everyday world. Riding a bicycle, for instance, might be thought of as involving uncodified rather than codified knowledge. Although the skill involved is not ineffable—it can at least be discussed—you cannot master the trick by simply reading about it and following instructions. Someone has to show you how to do it and you have to try it out for yourself. Learning to ride a bicycle, therefore, requires the interpersonal involvement of a learner and a demonstrator. Physical co-presence allows communication to take place across multiple sensory channels simultaneously, with instantaneous feedbacks and adjustments. Mastering a software package, by contrast, is a much more highly structured—and hence codified—business. A carefully sequenced set of instructions, each of which yields a particular outcome, has to be precisely followed. Here, instructions are found either in a manual or on a screen. Personal interaction with a teacher is not usually necessary.

Our codification dimension is scaled according to one particular definition of complexity: the number of bits of information required to carry out a given data-processing task. Computer scientists describe this as the 'algorithmic information complexity' of the task.[9] At the uncodified end of the codification scale we encounter a non-deterministic and almost chaotic regime which resists all attempts at task codification—here, task data is random. At the codified end we encounter a highly ordered regime, which reduces to a choice

    [8] This theme is developed further in A. Dixit and R. Pindyck, *Investment Under Uncertainty*, Princeton, New Jersey: Princeton University Press, 1994. See also R. Sanchez, 'Higher Order Organization and Commitment in Strategic Options Theory: A Reply to Christopher Bartlett', *Advances in Strategic Management*, 106, 1994, pp. 299–307.
    [9] Chaitin, 'Information-Theoretic Computational Complexity'.

between two states. As we shall see in the next section, other definitions of complexity are possible.

Clearly, economizing on data-processing resources entails moving away from the uncodified end and towards the codified end of the scale, from the inarticulate towards the articulate, from the complex towards the simple. As we saw in the last chapter, however, data-processing economies are by no means an unmixed blessing. A price is paid in terms of lost flexibility, of options forgone. The more completely one codifies a task, the more one effectively fossilizes it. For better or for worse it becomes an inert process. Complete codification, then, allows a task to be performed entirely by machine without human intervention.

Automation presents no problems for tasks whose actual variations fall within the range provided for by the codes. On the contrary, in such cases it offers both important economies as well as considerable gains in reliability. Yet recent trends have been towards increasing flexibility, with flexible automation systems coping with ever greater task variation. The ambition of many firms adopting a mass customization approach, for example, is to be able to segment markets down to the level of single individuals. Such a segment clearly needs more data to describe it than one that is more aggregated, and thus exhibits a higher level of algorithmic information complexity. The evolution of automation technology, therefore, if anything, has been moving away from the codified end of the scale and towards lower levels of codification. In sum, if efficiency considerations appear to be pushing for higher levels of codification in pursuit of data-processing economies, the need for effectiveness often pushes in the opposite direction, towards lower levels of codification and the pursuit of flexibility.

Operational effectiveness is not the only consideration that prompts moves back towards the less codified end of the scale. Recall that codification is a commitment akin to exercising an option. For many individuals, the loss of flexibility entailed by acts of codification also threatens a loss of personal power. Skilled craftsmen, for instance, will fiercely resist having their hard-won tacit skills reduced to a series of computer-generated machine instructions. Yet such skills are often more highly valued for the identity and status they confer than for the utility they yield. Whether it is labelled simple automation or deskilling, codification fossilizes hard-won skills and fossilization is disempowering and destructive of identity. As human beings, we retain our personal identity by operating, as do most living things, in a complex regime at the edge of chaos. We lose it by wandering too far along the codification scale, either towards the uncodifiable and the ineffable, or towards the codifiable and the excessively ordered.

3.3 ABSTRACTION

Mammography is widely seen as a key defence against breast cancer, which is a major killer. The technique, however, remains controversial. While some experts advocate annual mammograms for all women over the age of 40, others argue that the benefits are marginal, the harm caused substantial, and the costs involved enormous. One way to clarify the debate would be to refine the mammograms. Using normal techniques, radiologists can spot microcalcifications—little strong deposits in breast tissues that sometimes presage cancer—if they are more than a quarter of a millimetre across. Yet it is hard to extract these little signals out of a messy X-ray that is obscured by everything from ligaments to natural radioactivity.

Refining mammograms would correspond to an increase in the codification of data. It would improve the speed and reliability of the process wherein X-ray data can be classified as either microcalcification or not-microcalcification. Yet any gain in the sensitivity of mammograms would be double-edged. Microcalcification is highly suspect: not all of it leads to cancer. After testing, some sick people will be deemed healthy (false negatives) and some healthy ones will be deemed ill (false positives). Mammograms already have an extremely high false-positive rate, with more than 80 per cent of 'suspicious' mammograms turning out to be false alarms. Increasing the ease with which microcalcification is detected might well push up this false-positive rate.

Some doctors feel that the level of film resolution is already too great, since false positives cause patients a great deal of stress. Without a better conceptual understanding to facilitate interpretation of what is being seen, the sharper mammograms that are currently under development may end up doing more harm than good.[10] Clearly, then, as the example illustrates, looking at a photograph is more than a simple question of perception. It is well known, for instance, that animals cannot recognize objects depicted in photographs. Such recognition requires conceptual understanding.

Codification can be perceptual or it can be conceptual. In effect, when carried out by humans, to the extent that prior conceptual knowledge shapes the categories through which we apprehend the world, it is always a mixture of both. Where codification appears to be purely perceptual—as in the case of developing sharper mammograms—it still presupposes some conceptual understanding and interpretation of what is observed. On the other hand, where codification appears to be more conceptual, it is either directly or indirectly the result of an abstraction from perceptual data. Abstraction is the second of the three dimensions that make up the I-Space. We discuss it next.

Codification and abstraction often run closely together, so much so that they are frequently confused. They are, however, quite different. The first gives form to phenomena, the second gives them structure. If codification

---

[10] 'Sensitive Issue', *The Economist*, 12 August 1995, pp. 78–9.

allows us to save on data-processing resources by allowing us to group the data of experience into categories, abstraction allows us to realize further savings in data processing by minimizing the number of categories that we need to draw on for a given task. Abstraction then works by teasing out the underlying structure of phenomena relevant to our purpose. It requires an appreciation of cause-and-effect relationships to an extent that simple acts of codification do not.

To illustrate: imagine that we are grading tomatoes in order to price them for sale in the market. What are the attributes that we need to attend to? Clearly, those that are likely to exert a causal influence on consumers' decision-making processes. Some ability to understand how consumers think about tomatoes is thus presupposed. We might hypothesize that weight, size, colour, texture, shape, hardness, and taste constitute important attributes of a tomato for a consumer. If we were now to code each of these seven attributes along a three-point scale—good, average, and unacceptable—and classify our tomatoes accordingly, we would end up with 3^7 or 2,187 possible assignments for our tomatoes. This is an awful lot of data processing either for producers or for the consumers to deal with. How can we reduce it?

Well, for a start, we might note that certain attributes are strongly correlated so that some might serve as a proxy measure for others. Weight and size, for example, tend to run together, as do hardness, colour, and taste—tomatoes that are unripe are green and hard, those that are overripe are red and squishy. We might in this way reduce our task to dealing with four attributes. We would still, however, end up with 81 possible assignments, which might be considered excessive.

At this point our knowledge of consumers is likely to come into play. We may have learnt that in their preference for tomato shape and texture, consumers as a group exhibit no particular pattern, so that pricing according to grade may not be possible with respect to these attributes. Experience may also indicate that consumers value the opportunity to inspect goods and make their own selection. Our problem then becomes one of deciding how much of the data processing involved in the selection of tomatoes should be carried out by producers and how much directly by consumers themselves. Producers, for example, might decide that in order to safeguard their reputation, no unacceptable tomatoes should be put before the consumer. They thus face two possible decisions, acceptable or unacceptable, across four product attributes—i.e., 2^4 or 16 possible assignments—and the consumer also faces two possible decisions, acceptable or desirable, across four product attributes—i.e., 2^4 or 16 possible selections.

We have effectively reduced our data-processing requirements by a mixture of codification—reducing the number of points to choose from on a coding scale from three to two—and abstraction—reducing the number of attributes that need to be codified for the purposes of categorization from seven to four. Abstraction was achieved, first, by noticing and exploiting the way that different attributes were correlated with each other. Such correlations some-times point to higher-level patterns that reside in the data in latent form at dif-ferent levels of codification. Abstraction was also facilitated by discarding two product attributes that were deemed irrelevant for the purpose of grad-ing. If consumers do not vary predictably with respect to tomato texture and shape then it might be better to let them make their own selection and to leave the resulting choices outside the price equation. Note, finally, that without *some* amenability to grading, an attribute may not serve our purposes. If it is then dropped, we get abstraction by default. Where an attribute requires numerous fine discriminations to be performed for grading purposes, it will be much more time-consuming and costly to codify than where it can simply be judged acceptable or unacceptable on a two-point scale. The higher codi-fication costs incurred will then need to be weighed against the added value to customers in having a more discriminating grading scheme.

When properly carried out, abstraction allows one to focus on the struc-tures, causal or descriptive, that underlie the data. It generates concepts rather than percepts. Like percepts, concepts are devices that economize on data processing. Yet whereas percepts achieve their economies by maintain-ing a certain clarity and distinction between categories, concepts do so by revealing which categories are likely to be relevant to the data-processing task. Murray Gell-Mann has proposed a second definition of complexity which he contrasts with algorithmic information complexity and which pro-vides us with a useful metric for capturing the phenomenon of abstraction. If, as we have said, algorithmic information complexity is measured by the num-ber of bits of information required to carry out a given data-processing task, *effective complexity is measured by the number of bits of information required to specify whatever regularities characterize the task*. Effective complexity will clearly vary with the level of abstraction at which the task is specified.[11]

Abstraction, in effect, is a form of *reductionism*; it works by letting the few stand for the many. But are the products of abstraction real in the sense that percepts are real, or are they just convenient fictions? This is the age-old prob-lem of universals that so plagued medieval philosophy and which remains a teaser for much contemporary philosophy as well. Luckily, it need not detain us. Suffice it to say that abstractions become real to the extent that they shape the categories that we use to make sense of, and subsequently modify the world with which we interact.

To summarize so far: in addition to locating data-processing tasks and knowledge assets along a codification dimension, we can also locate them along an abstraction dimension scaled according to the number of categories that need to be drawn on. At one end of the scale one will be dealing with highly concrete experiences in which the knowledge produced will be pre-dominantly perceptual and local. Here, the categories employed will be rich

---

[11] Gell-Mann, *The Quark and the Jaguar*.

and dense and underlying causal structures may sometimes be hard to discern. At the other end of the scale, by contrast, one will be dealing with abstract thought and the knowledge produced will be predominantly conceptual and non-local. Each way of processing data offers advantages and drawbacks. Concrete perceptual knowledge offers vividness and intensity but does not reach out much beyond its immediate circumstances. Abstract conceptual knowledge, on the other hand, may find general application but may come across as rather pallid and bloodless—not exactly the stuff that dreams are made of. As Frank Zappa once put it, 'computers can give you the exact mathematical design, but what's missing is the eyebrows'.

Bloodless it may be, but abstraction is not free of controversy. Returning for a moment to our tomato example, the US judicial system has attempted a bit of biological classification on its own account. In the late 1800s the collector of customs for the Port of New York declared that the tomato was a vegetable—and hence taxable. Importers sued, arguing that the tomato is botanically a fruit. The case went to the Supreme Court in 1893, which found in favour of the defence.

Knowledge assets vary in their degree of abstraction. Some, located in scientific disciplines such as biochemistry, have a narrow range of applications in very specific circumstances. Others, located in more basic disciplines such as solid-state physics are much more generally applicable. Think of the difference, for example, between a wheat-starch paint-stripper called Envirostrip and a transistor. The first product, developed by Archer Daniel Midland, a Canadian agricultural conglomerate, is used to strip paint from B-2 stealth bombers. It manages to do this without dissolving the composite materials that the aircraft is built from, as other paint-strippers would. The second product is strongly science-based and emerged from the Bell Labs in 1947. The first responds to the very specific and limited need of a single large customer, the US airforce. The second has found its way into countless products the world over. Often, however, these blend bits of concrete and abstract knowledge together.

Abstraction, like codification, is a device for shedding data—i.e., for economizing on data-processing resources. Codification facilitates abstraction by giving categories an edge, and by making them more visible and manipulable. Abstraction, in turn, stimulates codification by reducing the number of categories whose boundaries need defining. Both, working together, have the effect of making knowledge more articulate and hence shareable. Both, however, retain an irreducible hypothetical flavour that imparts a provisional quality to whatever happens to have been articulated. For this reason, shared knowledge is always subject to revisions or improvements.[12] Abstract

---

[12] This point has been developed by the philosopher of science, Karl Popper. It forms the basis of his evolutionary epistemology. See K. Popper, *Objective Knowledge: An Evolutionary Approach*, Oxford: Clarendon Press, 1972.

codified knowledge is sometimes of great potential utility, but such utility has to be continuously demonstrated and reaffirmed in concrete applications.

3.4 DIFFUSION

The diffusion of information has been extensively studied. It covers processes that vary widely in complexity. Information diffusion, for example, is at its simplest when it takes place in purely physical systems and describes the random transfer of information between colliding particles under different thermodynamic conditions. Information diffusion in biological processes is more complex. Here, information transfer, say, between different organisms, is less the product of random encounters than of coordinated behaviour patterns— mating, migration, etc. Information diffusion in social processes, those with which we shall be dealing here, is the most complex of all, since behaviour patterns are more plastic—and hence wide-ranging—and, far from reflecting the blind operation of instinct or random physical motion, they are subject to the conscious exercise of free choice by data-processing agents.

For this reason we must distinguish between the physical *diffusibility* of data and information, and its deliberate uptake and use by a given population of data-processing agents. Diffusibility establishes the availability of data and information for those who want to use it. It does *not* measure adoption: information may be widely diffused and yet remain unused. There could be many reasons for this: its significance and potential utility might go unrecognized, its use might entail too much investment of time and effort, it may be subject to restrictions, and so on.

Diffusion is the third of the three dimensions that make up the I-Space. It can be scaled to refer to the proportion of a given population of data-processing agents that can be reached with information operating at different degrees of codification and abstraction. Such a population need not consist of individual human beings. It could be made up of firms, industries, or even countries. All that we require is that each member of a population exhibit a similar general capacity for receiving, processing, and transmitting data.

If the concept of population is to be analytically useful, however, it should amount to more than just a random assortment of data-processing agents. How are these to be selected? The answer is, with reference to the potential relevance to them of the data being processed and shared. In other words, a population located on the diffusion scale of the I-Space has to constitute a potential audience for a message or set of messages being transmitted. It does not follow, of course, that *any* given sender actually *wants* his or her message to reach every data-processing agent for which it has potential relevance. Data on IBM's production costs, for example, would surely find a large potential audience among clients and competitors. Yet IBM might quite reasonably be reluctant to share this data with outsiders. Nor does it follow that all members of a potential audience have an identical capacity to decipher all messages that might have relevance for them. Many of the chemical formulae that appear in the pages of the scientific journal *Nature*—generally available in many newsagents—may be highly relevant to me and may directly affect my future welfare. It is, however, beyond my ability to decipher them.

A particular act of diffusion might have many potential audiences: customers, professional colleagues, suppliers, etc. In practical applications of the I-Space, target audiences must be specified with great care before they are located along the diffusion dimension, since a faulty specification can seriously undermine the analysis. Once this is done, and using our diffusion scale, we can measure both the speed and the extent to which particular types of data and information spread within a target population. We can ask, for instance, what percentage of a given population can be reached with a message within a standard time period. Phrased in this way, it is clear that we are talking about the diffusibility of information and not about the rate at which it is actually taken up.

Whether the diffusion of information is the result of a conscious desire to communicate or the by-product of some other activity, it will be subject to three types of problem that Shannon and Weaver have associated with any communication process. These raise questions respectively at three levels:

1. Is the message received the same as the message sent?
2. Is the message received understood?
3. Is the message received acted upon as intended?[13]

The first type of question operates at a purely technical level. It deals with issues that are primarily of interest to communication engineers—i.e., issues of channel capacity, noise levels, information redundancy, etc. The second type of question operates at a semantic level—i.e., it is a question of meaning. It arises if, for example, sender and receiver do not share the same codes, or, if sharing the codes, they use them in different contexts or for different purposes. The third type of question identified by Shannon and Weaver works at a pragmatic level. A message may be meaningful, but it turns out to be ineffective in motivating action. For a message to lead to the desired effect, a sender and a receiver must share more than just coding schemes. They must share compatible orientations—i.e., values, attitudes, and motivations. Communication problems thus range from the technical to the existential. But technical problems can be a source of semantic ones and these, in turn, can create problems of a pragmatic nature. Lower levels thus exert their influence on higher levels, but not vice versa.

We see, therefore, that several considerations can affect the diffusion trajectory of a message within a given population:

[13] C. Shannon and W. Weaver, *The Mathematical Theory of Communication*, Urbana: University of Illinois Press, 1949.

1. The available means of communication will establish the nature and extent of the technical problems. Newspapers, television, the telephone, conferences, the internet, and face-to-face meetings all have quite different diffusion properties and will favour the transmission of particular types of message. Those to be found in newspapers, for example, compete for limited space which favour terse and often highly simplified description. Face-to-face meetings, by contrast, allow multiple channels and feedback to be used, thus allowing discourse to be replaced by expressive gestures.
2. The sharing of codes between sender and receiver will reduce the semantic problem but will require a joint investment in the communication nexus prior to any specific communicative act—i.e., if I want to sell in Japan, I will have to invest as much time mastering Japanese as my Japanese counterparts invest in understanding my pidgined use of their language.
3. The prior sharing of contexts between sender and receiver will ease the pragmatic problem between sender and receiver by ensuring a better alignment of mutual expectations. But it will, in turn, require a prior investment in shared experiences that may sometimes far exceed whatever investment is required by the sharing of codes. The sharing of expertise in a scientific community, for example, depends as much on prior socialization to collective norms and experiences as it does on the shared codes acquired in formal training.
4. The speed with which a message diffuses in a population will partly be a function of the rate and intensity with which agents interact with each other. In the case of face-to-face communication, this will depend on the spatial density and distribution of the relevant population. In the case of electronic communications, the frequency of interaction may have other determinants.
5. Traditionally, it could be assumed that information would diffuse faster within urban than within rural populations. Modern telecommunications may be changing this, although only in post-industrial economies. After all, recall that it required several weeks for accurate news of the 1989 Tiananmen Square massacre to reach most Chinese provinces.
6. Cultural dispositions will select which messages are likely to diffuse rapidly and which are likely to be ignored. Fads and fashions are built on people's innate tendency to watch and imitate each other. Who does the watching and who the imitating will vary from culture to culture.[14]
7. Legal considerations can affect the diffusion of information. Patent and copyright law, for example, although they do not prohibit the diffusion of technical or design information—indeed, in most cases they seek to promote it—severely restrict the uses to which it can be put without the approval of the sender. This has the effect of placing much of its diffusion under the sender's control. In other circumstances, there may be a legal

---

[14] S. Bikhchandani, D. Hirshleifer, and I. Welch, 'The Blind Leading the Blind: Social Influence, Fads and Informational Cascades', UCLA Working Paper, October 1993.

requirement to diffuse information—as in a takeover bid, for example, or a product recall.

To summarize: lower-level technical consideration will affect the diffusibility and hence the availability of information within a given population. Higher-level social and cultural considerations will influence the absorption of information within that population and hence the rate at which it is taken up and used.

3.5 THE INFORMATION SPACE, OR I-SPACE

We must now bring together the three dimensions of codification, abstraction, and diffusion into a single, integrated representation: the I-Space. The I-Space is a conceptual framework within which the behaviour of information flows can be explored and, through these, the creation and diffusion of knowledge within selected populations can be understood. The key hypothesis that we wish to advance is that codification and abstraction are mutually reinforcing and that both, acting together, greatly facilitate the diffusion of information. Stated thus simply, the idea may seem tediously obvious. As we have already noted, however, codification and abstraction do not necessarily facilitate the usage of the information thus made available. Abstract information may come in the form of easily digested words such as 'truth', 'beauty', or 'mankind' or in the form of indigestible symbols such as 'ß', '⊕', and 'h'. This insight has never been the focus of explicit theorizing or testing and, as we shall see in what follows, its implications are anything but obvious.

We can represent the proposed hypothesis by means of a simple curve traced out in our three dimensional I-Space, as shown in Figure 3.1. What the curve AA' indicates is that the more codified and abstract an item of information becomes, then, other things being equal, the larger the percentage of a given population it will be able to reach in a given period of time. As obvious as it may seem, it is worthwhile articulating the counterproposition: the less codified and abstract an item of information, then, other things being equal, the smaller the percentage of a given data-processing population it will reach in a given period of time.

To grasp the full meaning of the counterproposition, let us, briefly, follow neoclassical economic practice and make the perfect information assumption. Recall that in efficient markets, price and quantity information is made instantaneously available to all market players. Furthermore, price and quantity information is assumed to encode adequately all the data that players require to pursue their trades. They therefore operate in a world of zero information friction and inhabit the point A' of our diffusion curve. All other points in the I-Space imply the presence of information friction and hence a departure from the perfect information assumption.

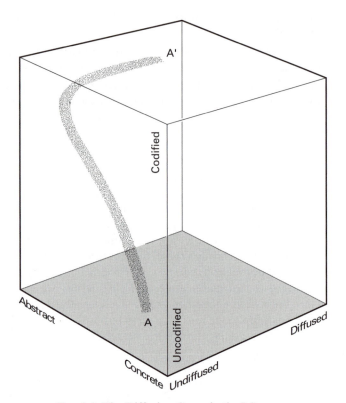

FIG. 3.1 The Diffusion Curve in the I-Space

Whence the friction? It is effectively symptomatic of Shannon and Weaver's technical, semantic, and pragmatic communication problems operating in various mixes at all other points in the I-Space. Their influence turns out to be at its most intense at point A on the diffusion curve. The communication problems identified by Shannon and Weaver relate, first, to the technologies used to communicate, second, to the context in which communication takes place, and finally, to the data-processing characteristics of senders and receivers. They are problems, in other words, that we find in the real world, which reduce the rarified one that neoclassical economists assume that we inhabit to a single point (A') in the I-Space.

An intuitive and somewhat loosely formulated version of our hypothesis by Nonaka and Takeuchi has attracted a great deal of attention recently. It is framed in terms of tacit knowledge.[15] What appears to have been underplayed in this formulation, however, is that tacit knowledge comes in three quite distinct variants.

---

[15] Nonaka and Takeuchi, *The Knowledge Creating Company*.

1. Things that are not said because *everybody* understands them and takes them for granted—i.e., knowledge of them has been consciously or unconsciously internalized over the years. Such knowledge *could* in principle (though not always) be articulated, but is not—it is what anthropologist Ed Hall refers to as 'high context'.[16]
2. Things that are not said because *nobody* fully understands them. They remain elusive and inarticulate. This is the kind of knowledge that the philosopher Michael Polanyi deals with in his book *Personal Knowledge*.[17]
3. Things that are not said because while some people can understand them, they cannot costlessly articulate them. This is the kind of knowledge that current students of tacit knowledge, such as Nonaka and Takeuchi, primarily have in mind when they use the term.[18]

The passage from tacit to codified and abstract knowledge incurs a cost. Recall that codification and abstraction are devices for shedding data. Consequently, structuring data for the purpose of sharing it creates a fundamental asymmetry between senders and receivers, between those who have to carry out the initial codifying and abstracting of information on the one hand, and those who receive it already structured, on the other. Many attempts to transfer knowledge assets within or between organizations come to grief because neither senders nor receivers appreciate this simple point. Whether they are aware of it or not, senders always know more than they can say. They will inevitably retain in their memories a great deal of tacit knowledge that will not be available to receivers. Whether this matters or not will depend on how effectively the chosen data-structuring strategies used by senders succeed in capturing the relevant dimensions of the knowledge to be transmitted. Unfortunately, data-structuring strategies designed to enhance communicative reach often unwittingly sacrifice communicative depth in the process.

To illustrate: in the early 1980s a large high-tech French firm undertook to transfer thirteen state-of-the-art electronic technologies to the Iraqi military. They were to be incorporated in a single large manufacturing plant located to the north of Baghdad. Being somewhat Cartesian in their approach, the managers of the French firm assumed that the knowledge embedded in their technologies had been fully captured in their drawings and manufacturing specifications. In fact, they vastly underestimated the amount of tacit knowledge required to operate them, the result being that their client encountered serious problems of implementation and became distrustful and quarrelsome. In order to maintain the goodwill of their client, the French firm was forced to send out to Iraq a team of French engineers to run the plant directly.

---

[16] E. Hall, *The Hidden Dimension*, New York: Doubleday, 1966; *Beyond Culture*, New York: Doubleday, 1976.
[17] Polanyi, *Personal Knowledge*.   [18] Nonaka and Takeuchi, *The Knowledge Creating Company*.

3.6 THE SOCIAL LEARNING CYCLE IN THE I-SPACE

The I-Space as represented in Figure 3.1 is static, depicting a functional relationship between codification, abstraction, and diffusion at a single instant in time. The framework, however, can also be used in a more dynamic mode.

It is possible, for example, to think of the relationship between codification, abstraction, and diffusion as setting up a data field, a configuration of forces that condition data flows over time through the I-Space and hence help to shape the evolution of knowledge assets. For data is indeed constantly on the move in the I-Space: much uncodified data sooner or later gets codified, much concrete data gradually increases in abstraction, and data that was the proprietary possession of a few individuals gradually becomes the common possession of all.

It should not be assumed, however, that all data movement in the I-Space is inevitably in the direction of greater codification, abstraction, and diffusion—i.e., from A to A' along the diffusion curve of Figure 3.1. As we shall see, movement in the reverse direction, from A' towards A, is equally likely: codified data over time gets internalized and becomes tacit, abstract data gets applied to concrete problems, and diffused data gives rise to unique insights which are appropriated by well-placed individuals.

The dynamic evolution of knowledge in the I-Space is illustrated in Figure 3.2. What starts off in region A of the space as highly personal idiosyncratic knowledge of particular events—these may be biographical or occupational—may, with successive efforts at structuring it, come to shed its tacit concrete particulars and gain in generality. It then becomes sharable and usable by others. If the diffusion of such knowledge is under the control of its creator—as, for instance, in the case of patents or copyright—it then becomes proprietary and can be traded for a position in region B of the space. Over time, proprietary knowledge falls into the public domain and becomes diffusible, moving into region C of the space as public or textbook knowledge. Such knowledge finds its way into journals, newspapers, textbooks, instruction manuals, consumer articles, and so on. To the extent that it gets used and applied in a variety of different circumstances, it gets internalized in region D, much of it becoming integrated in a tacit form into its possessor's common-sense view of the world. Common sense is widely shared—hence the term 'common'. It is not, however, a homogeneous entity. As individuals, we may share the same phenomenal data—relating to sunsets, traffic jams, inaugural speeches, etc.—but each of us passes this data through cognitive filters that have been tuned by our unique biographical circumstances. We thus convert a good part of what is taken to be a shared common-sense world back into what may be highly personal and idiosyncratic experiences.

The foregoing suggests that the creation and diffusion of *new* knowledge effectively activate all three dimensions of the I-Space, but that they tend to

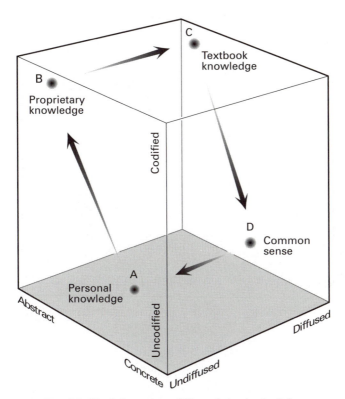

FIG. 3.2 The Movement of Knowledge in the I-Space

do so in a particular sequence. Where it occurs, such a sequence gives rise to what we shall call a 'social learning cycle' or SLC which, as illustrated in Figure 3.3, is decomposable into the following six phases:

1. *Scanning*: Identifying threats and opportunities in generally available but often fuzzy data—i.e., weak signals. Scanning patterns such data into unique or idiosyncratic insights that then become the possession of individuals or small groups. Scanning may be very rapid when the data is well codified and abstract, and very slow and random when the data is uncodified and context-specific. Consider how long it took for the scientific community even to accept as a plausible hypothesis that industrial emissions may be raising the mean temperatures of the biosphere.

2. *Problem-Solving*: The process of giving structure and coherence to such insights—i.e., codifying them. In this phase they are given a definite shape and much of the uncertainty initially associated with them is eliminated. Problem-solving initiated in the uncodified region of the I-Space is often both risky and conflict-laden. Witness the controversies that followed

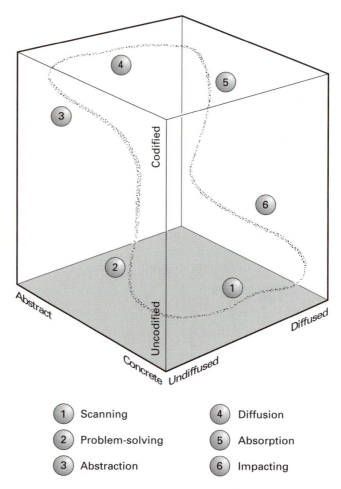

1	Scanning	**4**	Diffusion
2	Problem-solving	**5**	Absorption
3	Abstraction	**6**	Impacting

Fig. 3.3 The Social Learning Cycle (SLC)

Darwin's hypothesis that we are the product of random mutations and natural selection. Many of his detractors were deeply committed to a competing codification, namely, that we are the product of a divine intention.

3. *Abstraction*: Generalizing the application of newly codified insights to a wider range of situations. This involves reducing them to their most essential features—i.e., conceptualizing them. Problem-solving and abstraction often work in tandem. It is improvements in the technologies of detection and measurements—i.e., in codification—that allow scientists to probe the most basic and abstract structures of the material world.

4. *Diffusion*: Sharing the newly created insights with a target population. The diffusion of well-codified and abstract data to a large population will be

technically less problematic than that of data which is uncodified and con-text-specific. Only a prior sharing of context by sender and receiver can speed up the diffusion of uncodified and concrete data. The probability of achieving a shared context is inversely proportional to the size of the tar-get population. One's immediate family is the most plausible locus of shared context, followed by close work colleagues. Beyond the family and the workplace, the scope for shared context begins to diminish.

5. *Absorption*: Applying the newly codified insights to different situations in a 'learning-by-doing' or a 'learning-by-using' fashion. Over time, such codified insights come to acquire some context, that is, a penumbra of uncodified experience, which helps to guide their application in particular circumstances. In piano-playing, chess, or mathematics, mastery is achieved when one no longer has consciously to attend to the codes to offer a skilful performance.

6. *Impacting*: The embedding of abstract knowledge in concrete practices. Such embedding can take place in artefacts, technical or organizational rules, or in behavioural patterns. Absorption and impacting often work in tandem. It is by regularly practising emergency evacuation drills in specific situations that the crew of a ship or a submarine gradually comes to inter-nalize some fairly abstract and general principles concerning safety at sea.

The sequencing suggested by the SLC should be thought of as schematic. On a microscale many of these steps run concurrently so that what we are in effect dealing with are the broad resultants of data flows in the I-Space. Codification and absorption, for example, may well run almost together if those responsible for structuring new knowledge are also responsible for applying it in different areas. The same goes for abstraction and impacting. Furthermore, as indicated in Figures 3.4(a) to 3.4(c), many SLC shapes are possible, reflecting frictions or obstacles to data flows in the I-Space. For instance, cycle 1 (Figure 3.4(a)) would result from barriers to information dif-fusion which confine the operation of the SLC to a small percentage of those who could participate. The presence of barriers may reflect a conscious deci-sion to limit diffusion—as in the case of a patent—or it may be the unintended consequence of incompatible coding, of poor communication strategies, of a lack of shared context, etc. Small, specialized firms such as biotechnology start-ups are likely to display SLCs similar to cycle 1. Cycle 2 (Figure 3.4(b)), on the other hand, might suggest obstacles to effective scanning. Idiosyncratic perceptions are often deviant perceptions, and when they con-flict with a group's common-sense view of the world they may get discouraged or even penalized. Firms with strong developed norms concerning how things are done—certain professional or ideologically driven organizations—are well described by cycle 2. Finally, cycle 3 (Figure 3.4(c)) describes a popula-tion that is used to responding rapidly to well-codified and unambiguous sig-nals. This cycle, being located at the top of the I-Space is likely to be a fast

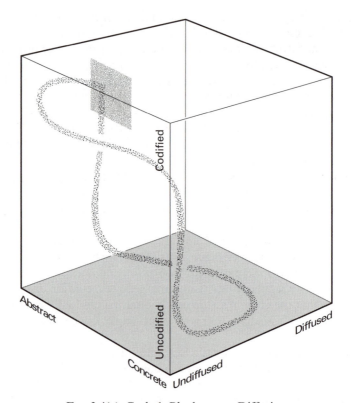

Fig. 3.4(a) Cycle 1: Blockages to Diffusion

one. Too fast, in fact, to allow the slow process of internalization through absorption to occur. In such a cycle, tacit learning is often not an option. Firms primarily engaged in trading rather than manufacturing and requiring rapid responses to well-codified price signals are candidates for cycle 3.

Although we have not explicitly indicated it in Figure 3.3, data can enter the I-Space from outside. Scanning, for example, might draw from a population external to that represented on the diffusion scale so that data might suddenly appear at any given point on that scale. Where this happens frequently or systematically it might argue for the construction of an I-Space which explicitly includes such a population. In certain circumstances several I-Spaces, each depicting populations at different levels of aggregation, might be used in combination.

To summarize, the SLC traces out the metabolic pathways used by a population of data-processing agents to process information. As we shall see in Chapter 6, that population's culture—organizational, industrial, national— is shaped by and in turn helps to shape these metabolic pathways.

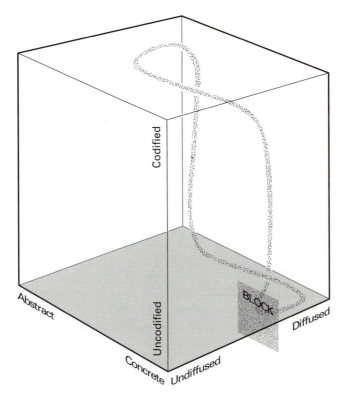

FIG. 3.4(b) Cycle 2: Blockages to Scanning

3.7 USING THE I-SPACE TO REPRESENT KNOWLEDGE ASSETS

If knowledge flows can be represented in the I-Space by means of SLCs, how do we represent knowledge assets in the space? Assets are stocks rather than flows and we have seen that knowledge assets can be stocked in people's heads, in documents, or in artefacts. A firm's knowledge assets therefore manifest themselves in its organization, its technologies, and its products. Recall that knowledge assets, like all assets, yield a stream of services.[19] In products, these services manifest themselves as a functionality (the product does something that the consumer values), reliability (it does it every time), and price (it does it at a price that the consumer is willing to pay). In a firm's technologies, the services of knowledge assets show up in the efficiency and speed with which a given set of inputs is transformed into useful outputs by people and machines working together. Finally, the organizational

---

[19] This is also true of products. See E. Penrose, *The Theory of the Growth of the Firm*, Oxford: Oxford University Press, 1959.

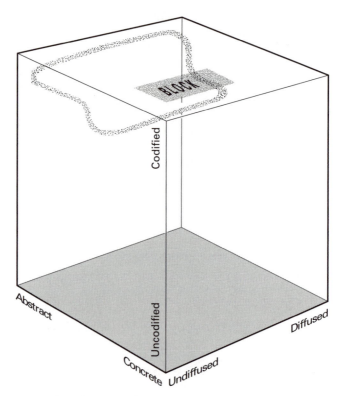

FIG. 3.4(c) Cycle 3: Blockages to Absorption

expression of the services yielded by knowledge assets appears in the way that technologies and organizational processes can be configured to respond to a range of contingencies such as shifts in demand, the emergence of a competitor, government regulations, and so on.

Knowledge assets are complex configurations of interrelated elements. In such configurations, what is an element and what is a link is often a matter of judgement and consensus. To the extent that knowledge assets can be made distinct and identifiable, however, they can in principle be located in the I-Space. Although the exercise can be carried out quite systematically, in my experience managers prefer to be intuitive and to offer 'eyeballing' estimates of their location. Using simple scales they are usually able to rate without too much difficulty the degree of codification, abstraction, and diffusion of their firm's products, technologies, and organizational elements. They first do this individually, reaching consensus iteratively through discussion.

The scales used can be applied at different levels of resolution, and at each level we find sets of interrelated elements. Different diffusion scales, for example, can be used to represent, respectively, employees within a department, units within a firm, firms within an industry, and industries within an economy. Other groupings are, of course, possible. In each case a specific level or type of knowledge might be mapped. It is important not to get the levels mixed up. To depict an automobile engine in fine detail in the I-Space, while representing the other elements of the vehicle as sub-assemblies in the same diagram, could well distort the analysis. Table 3.1 gives examples of simple three-point scales that have been used to assess a knowledge asset's degree of codification, abstraction, and diffusion.

TABLE 3.1 Scaling Guide

Position on Scale	Codification	Abstraction	Diffusion
	Is the knowledge:	Is the knowledge:	Is the knowledge:
High	Easily captured in figures and formulae? Does it lend itself to standardization and automation?	Generally applicable to all agents whatever the sector they operate in? Is it heavily science-based?	Readily available to all agents who wish to make use of it?
Medium	Describable in words and diagrams? Can it be readily understood by others from documents and written instructions alone?	Applicable to agents within a few sectors only? Does it need to be adapted to the context in which it is applied?	Available to only a few agents or to only a few sectors?
Low	Hard to articulate? Is it easier to show someone than to tell them about it?	Limited to a single sector and application within that sector? Does it need extensive adaptation to the context in which it is applied?	Available to only one or two agents within a single sector?

The scaling exercise is useful in that it helps to articulate, refine, and share perceptions of what exactly an organization's knowledge assets consist of and how they are distributed in the I-Space. What we obtain from such an exercise, in effect, when it is carried out by an organization's own members, is its view of itself. The result is often consciousness-raising even if, by its very nature, it cannot be fully objective since participants may hold quite distorted views of their organization's knowledge assets. The fact that their views often gradually converge through discussion can improve the degree of objectivity of the exercise, but it will also convert any distortion in perception that remains into a collective exercise.

A further gain in objectivity may be had, however, by comparing an organization's view of how its knowledge assets are distributed in the I-Space with an external and more systematically derived analysis. A judicious use of scientometric data on the organization's patenting and scientific publication activities, for example, could offer an independent check on how codified and abstract (i.e., science-based) its knowledge assets actually are, as well as how extensively they are available to competitors. Internal and external views on an organization's knowledge assets could then be compared and, where appropriate, adjustments made.

In the final analysis, however, an organization's view of itself is constructed out of the subjective perceptions of its members through a process of negotiation. Objective knowledge, to be sure, may be fed into the process to guide it, but this does not mean that the outcome can ever be fully objective. This limitation applies to all attempts to gauge an organization's strengths and weaknesses. In spite of the limitation, important insights into the nature of an organization's knowledge assets can be gained by bringing selected subsets of its products, its technologies, and related organizational processes together in the I-Space. Where, for example, its technologies are organizationally configured to deliver a distinctive performance that competitors find hard to match, we can speak of a competence or a capability. Where such competence or capability is central to the organization's operations, we can speak of a core competence or a core capability.[20]

Core competences and core capabilities have been the focus of a growing literature in the field of strategic management. They will be treated in greater detail in Chapter 8. All we need to note here is that since we can think of core competences or capabilities as organizationally integrated networks of technical processes, they can be represented in the I-Space in the same way as other knowledge assets. Indeed, given the difficulties that managers typically have in agreeing on exactly what their organization's core competences are, a proper use of the I-Space can greatly facilitate the identification and analysis of this class of knowledge assets.

3.8 SOME PROPOSITIONS DERIVABLE FROM THE I-SPACE

If data is taken to be a factor of production, and if the creation of information is a way of economizing on the consumption of this factor, then the I-Space offers a framework for analysing the production and distribution of

---

[20] C. Prahalad and G. Hamel, 'The Core Competence of the Corporation', *Harvard Business Review*, May–June 1990; G. Hamel and A. Heene (eds), *Competence-Based Competition*, Chichester: Wiley, 1994; G. Stalk, P. Evans, and L. Shulman, 'Competing on Capabilities', *Harvard Business Review*, March–April 1992.

information in a social system, whether at the level of a group, a firm, or some larger unit of aggregation. As we shall see in Chapter 6, we can use the framework to explore the way that different institutional structures condition exchange in different parts of the I-Space, and we can also analyse a variety of strategies adopted by economic agents in pursuit of such exchange.

When discussing problems of production and distribution we enter the realm of political economy. Unlike the industrial age, the information age does not yet have an articulate political economy of its own. The I-Space identifies codification, abstraction, and diffusion as foundational concepts for a political economy of information.

We conclude this chapter with a few propositions that will help to link it to some of the points discussed in Chapters 1 and 2.

1. Systems, whether social, biological, or purely physical, act to minimize their rate of entropy production per unit of activity. One way they do this is by substituting data for physical resources. Yet, as we saw, there is a limit to the quantity of data that a system can handle without breaking down. It therefore also acts to minimize the entropy generated by data-processing activities.
2. In the I-Space, the rate of entropy production is at a minimum in the region labelled E-min of Figure 3.5. Here, information is at its most codified and abstract and its diffusion is under central control. Region E-min is where the information environment is at its most ordered. By contrast, the rate at which entropy is produced by data processing reaches its highest level in the region labelled E-max. In this region, data can be given no structure and its diffusion in the social system is pervasive and quite random. If we were to use a thermodynamic analogy, we would say that in region E-min information achieves its maximum potential to perform useful value-adding work, whereas in region E-max it has exhausted this potential. The SLC links these two regions and transforms a given population of data-processing agents into an engine for putting knowledge to work.
3. In pursuit of some competitive advantage, organizations are constantly seeking to escape E-max, the region of maximum entropy production rates in the I-Space, and to move into E-min, the region of minimum entropy production rates. They do this in quest of order and economy, of predictability and security. The dynamics of the SLC, however, do not allow them to stay there. Sooner or later, and to varying degrees, firms are pulled back towards E-max.
4. Somewhere between the zones of maximum and minimum entropy production, firms encounter the phenomenon of complexity, a state of the world intermediate between chaos and excessive order. We encountered it as a horizontal band within which the sawtooth trajectories of the evolutionary production function were confined (see Figure 2.7). We encounter

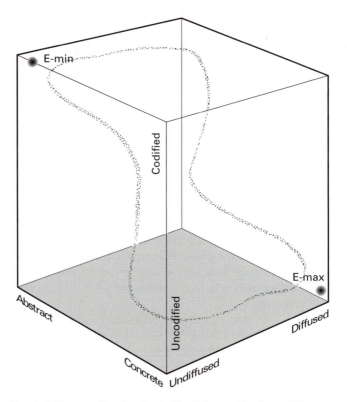

FIG. 3.5 Entropy Production in the I-Space: E-min and E-max

it here as a 'phase' in the I-Space. Once more, as depicted in Figure 3.6, it is an 'edge of chaos' phenomenon, activated by the SLC as it oscillates between region E-min and region E-max.

5. In the latter phase of its trajectory, as it moves towards region E-max, the SLC leads towards the data equivalent of thermodynamic equilibrium, a state from which it is impossible systematically to extract useful work. In this state, only data fluctuations can drive the SLC forward. These generate what are known as far-from-equilibrium states, stable and discernible patterns that emerge in region E-max of the I-Space but that have not yet been excessively ordered by successive acts of codification and diffusion. Thermodynamicists like Ilia Prigogine and Isabelle Stengers describe far-from-equilibrium structures as 'dissipative' because although they exhibit order, they remain comparatively high in entropy production.[21]

---

[21] I. Prigogine and I. Stengers, *Order out of Chaos: Man's New Dialogue with Nature*, Toronto: Bantam Books, 1984.

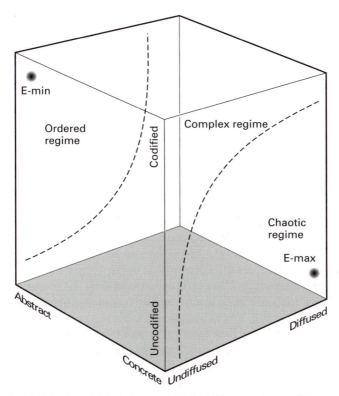

Fig. 3.6 Ordered, Complex, and Chaotic Regimes in the I-Space

The dissipative state is not a comfortable one for organizations to stay in. They seek a more stable and more static equilibrium further up the I-Space. Firms like Apple, for example, which start out as entrepreneurial and some-what 'chaotic', gradually acquire structure and become more 'bureaucratic' in their culture—sometimes excessively so. Yet, as we shall see in Chapter 5, firms will have to learn to be comfortable in *all* regions of the I-Space as well as with all phases of the SLC. This will call for a major shift in the way we think about organizations, since it will modify every aspect of their opera-tions. For one thing, it invites firms deliberately to allow for—indeed con-sciously to plan—the destruction of knowledge assets as well as their creation.

4

The Paradox of Value

4.1 INTRODUCTION

KNOWLEDGE assets are a source of competitive advantage for firms that possess them. They allow them to bring superior products or services to market faster and in greater volumes than their competitors can match. Yet the way that the possession of a knowledge asset translates into competitive advantage remains ill-understood. For example, while a firm like Glaxo was able to turn itself into one of the world's premier drug companies on the back of Zantac, a not particularly novel anti-ulcer drug, EMI in the late 1970s nearly bankrupted itself trying to commercialize its CT scanner, one of the biggest advances in radiography since the discovery of X-rays. It ended up ceding the market for scanners to General Electric and then quitting the business altogether. Clearly, competitive advantage does not flow automatically from the possession of knowledge assets. A firm has to know how to extract value from them.

Extracting value from knowledge assets requires an ability to manage them as they emerge, wax, and wane through the actions of the SLC. In moving its knowledge through an SLC, however, a firm incurs both data-processing and data-transmission costs. The costs of scanning, for example, are primarily those of extracting weak signals from numerous noisy sources both inside and outside the firm. Those of problem-solving—i.e., codification—result from searching problem spaces of varying sizes and from making risky selections under conditions of uncertainty. Abstraction costs arise when data-processing agents seek to amortize their investment in problem-solving over a wider and more varied class of problem by endowing their solutions with a generic quality. Courtaulds, for example, is seeking out a wide range of non-textile as well as textile applications for the revolutionary cellulosic fibre that it has developed and that we briefly mentioned in the last chapter. And the transistor only really came into its own when it was developed for applications that went beyond the mere replacement of valves. Diffusion costs are incurred when communicating with potentially large audiences in ways that can be understood and which lead to effective responses. The costs of absorption are those of getting potential recipients of new knowledge to internalize it and familiarize themselves with it. Finally, what we have called impacting describes the costly business of applying knowledge so internalized in a variety of concrete situations.

The costs just itemized are only worth incurring if, first, the potential value created by any given move along an SLC is large enough to compensate for the costs incurred in making it, and second, a sufficient proportion of the potential value created by such a move can be appropriated by the data-processing agent incurring the costs to cover them. To be considered innovative, a data-processing agent only has to satisfy the first of these two conditions. To be considered innovative *and* profitable, an agent has to satisfy both conditions. As we have already suggested, a data-processing agent might be an individual or a firm. It might even, under certain circumstances, be an industry. To keep things simple, in what follows we shall assume that the agent is a firm.

When it comes to the creation of value, knowledge assets differ from physical assets in important respects. A vivid way to summarize that difference is to observe that while one can photocopy the formula for benzene, one cannot photocopy an oilfield. In other words, the supply of physical goods is fully constrained by their spatio-temporal extension, while that of information goods is much less so. Information goods exhibit a natural scarcity only when they are deeply embedded in some physical substrate that is limited in space and time. Individual brains and certain physical products are good candidates for such a substrate. Electromagnetic waves are not.

In this chapter we use the I-Space to explore some of the issues posed by the behaviour of knowledge assets with respect to value. In the next section (4.2) we present a classical concept of value that remains influential to this day and is purely energy based—the labour theory of value. In section 4.3 we discuss some of the problems associated with applying an energy-based value concept to information goods. We conclude that it is misleading and sometimes positively harmful. In section 4.4 we examine the neoclassical theory of value as a possible alternative to the labour theory of value. We test its suitability for our purposes in section 4.5 by interpreting it in I-Space terms. In section 4.6, drawing further upon the I-Space, we posit the existence of a paradox of value that we associate uniquely with information goods, and in section 4.7 we look at the implications that such a paradox might hold for a firm's management of its knowledge assets.

The valuation of knowledge assets poses acute theoretical and practical problems that have to be addressed if the profound economic differences that distinguish an information economy from an energy economy are to be understood. As will become clear in the course of this chapter, these differences may be as marked as those that separate the world of classical physics from the world of quantum physics—and they might turn out to have a similar basis.

4.2 SOME ECONOMIC CONCEPTS OF VALUE

The term 'value' has always engendered controversy, both among economists and laypeople. Even as we approach the millennium there is no settled

definition of value that all those who use the term would wholeheartedly subscribe to. The working definition of the term that we shall apply to knowledge
assets will not please everyone and may even provoke some, but we shall
arrive at it after having considered some of the available options.

Until the so-called marginalist revolution that took place in economics in
the 1870s, economists took value to reside either in nature itself or in the
transformation that humans wrought upon nature. Those who looked to
nature itself as the source of value were either physiocrats or mercantilists, the
first focusing on agriculture, the second on mineral wealth. Physiocrats, reacting to the mercantilist policies of Colbert during the reign of Louis XIV,
held—but could not prove—that land is the main generator of value.
Contrary to what was claimed by Adam Smith a century later, they did not
regard industry as useless but simply as a sector producing no net additions
to income. The term 'laissez-faire, laissez-passer' was coined not by free
traders but by the physiocrats; it expressed the belief that neither industry nor
commerce added value as such, and therefore should not be subject to royal
taxes. Mercantilists believed that mineral wealth such as gold and silver—
specie—was the ultimate source of value and that countries grew rich accumulating these in the coffers of the state.[1]

Those who argued that value resided in the transformation that humans
wrought upon nature rather than in nature itself, by contrast, viewed human
or animal labour power as the source of all value. This way of thinking about
value was shared by the classical economists, notably by Adam Smith, David
Ricardo, and Karl Marx.

Whatever the differences that might have distinguished physiocrats, mercantilists, and classical economists in the way they thought about value, they
all took it to be energy based. For the physiocrats, the energy base was largely
renewable—mining was only a small part of human activity—and was considered to be the fruit of 'nature's bounty' mingled with the labour of men.
The classical economists, on the other hand, placed more emphasis on labour
alone and largely reduced value to some multiple of the subsistence cost of
labour—so many calories a day to keep an average labourer and his family
productive in a particular class of work.

What is striking about these pre-classical and classical theories of value is
that in no case does knowledge or information play any significant role. In
Marx's hands, for example, the value of labour incorporating different levels
of knowledge and skills could be derived from the quantity of labour time
necessary to acquire such knowledge and skills. The denominator was always
pure labour power, unadulterated with knowledge. Technical advances gave
rise to no particular claims: from the moment they appeared they took the
form of a public good—i.e., one whose availability is not diminished by its
consumption. Technical advances were thus taken to be a common posses-

[1] M. Blaug, *Economic Theory in Retrospect*, Cambridge: Cambridge University Press, 1978.

sion of humankind, and any attempts to render technical knowledge appropriable and to make it the property of particular individuals or groups was viewed by Marx as going against the nature of things.[2]

In sum, and as we have already established in section 2.1, land and labour, the factors of production treated by the early classical economists, were strictly physical in nature. Their notions of value, therefore, also had a purely physical basis.

4.3 THE VALUE OF AN INFORMATION GOOD

In the second half of the nineteenth century, and particularly after the marginalist revolution in economics got under way, value ceased to be regarded as an intrinsic property of the energy inputs required for productive activity. Value became relational and contingent, being established through the interplay of the supply and demand conditions for a good. The good in question, however, was still primarily conceived of as something physical, something that you could drop on your foot. Goods were thus bundles of frozen labour converted into potential energy, and services were bundles of living labour or kinetic energy. Value might be free to vary according to the laws of supply and demand, but it was still ultimately traceable to labour time.

The energetic foundations of value thus survived the marginalist revolution.[3] Knowledge and information, to be sure, had an important role to play in economic transactions, but it was always a supporting role—they were never treated as the central focus of a transaction and hence an object of exchange in their own right. There was, as yet, no such thing as an information good.

Recall that in Chapter 2 we developed an evolutionary production function by grouping together the physical inputs of space, time, and energy into a physical factor of production on the one hand, and by taking data—i.e. low-level energy that acted informationally rather than mechanically—as an independent factor of production on the other. To the extent that productive factors can be bought and sold in factor markets, we implicitly assumed that information goods could exist as economic objects and could be subjected to the laws of economic exchange.

We noted, however, that the economic behaviour of information goods was problematic since they could only properly enter into the process of economic exchange if they could be made appropriable. Only then could they partake of the scarcity that characterizes a good as being economic.[4] Yet it is

[2] K. Marx, *Capital: A Critique of Political Economy*, London: Lawrence and Wishart, 1972. See also M. Boisot, 'Institutionalizing the Labour Theory of Value: Some Obstacles to the Reform of State-owned Enterprises in China and Vietnam', *Organization Studies*, 17 (6), 1996, pp. 909–28.

[3] P. Mirowski, *More Heat than Light: Economics as Social Physics, Physics as Nature's Economics*, Cambridge: Cambridge University Press, 1989.

[4] Scarcity is an essential attribute of an economic good. See L. Robbins, *An Essay on the Nature and Significance of Economic Science*, London: Macmillan, 1935.

just those problems associated with the appropriability of an information good that continue to pose problems for economists and that make it so difficult to value. We can illustrate this by way of an example.

If I wish to buy a kilogram of oranges I can inspect them beforehand: I can infer their quality from their colour, their size, their weight, and their texture. I can have them weighed, I can smell them, and I can measure them. Furthermore, I can compare their quality/price relationship with reference to alternative offerings. And I can do all this *before* deciding to buy them. If my pre-purchase inspection does not satisfy me I can leave them with the vendor. Of course, such an inspection can never be complete. It cannot, for instance, replace the physical experience of actually eating an orange. Yet, being itself built on a prior sequence of such experiences and a general familiarity with oranges and other fruit, it does allow me to make some more or less valid inferences with respect to the particular kilo of oranges on offer. In other words, I can acquire information on a physical good prior to, and independently of acquiring the good itself, and that information will either confirm or disconfirm any *expectations* that I might have held with respect to the good.

An information good, by contrast, cannot be inspected prior to purchase: the very act of describing it partly transfers it, and the more complete the description, the more complete the transfer. More fundamentally, when I buy a kilo of oranges, I don't really want any surprises. Indeed, that is why I inspect them closely beforehand. When I buy an information good, on the other hand, surprise is precisely what I am paying for. If the good fails to surprise, it fails to inform. Recall that information, in contrast to data, modifies expectations. In short, it surprises. Once it has been transferred, however, it has lost both its capacity to surprise and its appropriability. Unlike a kilo of oranges, the possession of which resides either with the vendor or with the purchaser, an information good, once transferred, becomes the possession of both.

Following an exhaustive inspection of the information good by a prospective purchaser, then, wherein lies the surprise that constitutes the essence of what he is willing to pay for? It has vanished in the process of inspection itself. Why on earth, he or she might argue, should a pre-purchase inspection of an information good be paid for? After inspecting it he or she walks away, and, like the vendor, is now in full possession of the good. Yet no economic transaction has actually taken place.

Does this sharing of the information good lower its value? Many people would say that if two people possess an item of information where one did before, it has become twice as useful and hence twice as valuable. This cannot happen with oranges: either I consume them or you do. If we split them between us, we each gain half the utility. In sharing information, however, the operational usefulness of the information remains available in its entirety to whoever comes into possession of it, no matter how many people that might be. If, for example, I share with you my recipe for baking apple crumble, we can both enjoy the benefits of a remarkable dessert, whereas if I keep the recipe to myself, only I can benefit—unless, of course, I invite you to dinner. And it is precisely because I want to invite you to dinner and to impress you that I will keep the recipe to myself. Knowledge of the recipe will enhance my prestige in your eyes. This is less likely to happen if we both have the recipe. Such knowledge offers more than operational utility; it is a *positional* good that is more valuable to me if you do not have it.[5] Thus, utility is not the only determinant of value; scarcity is needed as well.

4.4 THE NEOCLASSICAL CONCEPT OF VALUE

Utility and scarcity were the prime ingredients in Leon Walras's definition of value. One of the founding fathers of neoclassical economics, Walras under-stood that things could be useful without being scarce—air, for example—and that, conversely, things could be scarce—water on Mars—without necessarily being useful.[6] In neither of these two cases would the good in ques-tion be considered *economically* valuable.

According to the neoclassical theory of value, utility is a personal matter and measures what an individual economic agent (it could be a person or it could be a firm) gets out of consuming a given quantity of an economic good. Utilities cannot be compared across agents. We may all pay the same price to see the movie *Gone with the Wind*, yet we shall each get something different out of it. Value, by contrast, is partly relational: it measures not only the util-ity of a good but also its scarcity relative to demand and to alternative offer-ings. Thus, even if the supply of a good is held constant, it could become scarce because of a sudden surge in demand. The watercolours that I occa-sionally produce on Sundays, for example, are in abundant supply relative to the demand for them, and I am assured by my less charitable friends that find-ing adequate substitutes for them presents little challenge. Yet if an eminent art critic were ever to fathom the subtle intricacies of my washes, and if, as a result, I were to be 'discovered' by one of the more up-market art galleries, then my watercolours could suddenly become scarce—and hence, potentially valuable—with no attempt at hoarding on my part.

Even though it has been primarily shaped by, and oriented towards the energy economy, the neoclassical perspective on value offers us a much bet-ter theoretical grasp of the difference between physical and information goods than its classical predecessor. Whereas physical goods are *inherently* scarce by dint of their spatio-temporal characteristics—in the hands of ordi-nary mortals loaves and fishes do not usually multiply—information goods

---

[5] The term 'positional good' was coined by Fred Hirsch. See F. Hirsch, *The Social Limits to Growth*, London: Routledge and Kegan Paul, 1977.

[6] See L. Walras, *Elements of Pure Economics or the Theory of Social Wealth*, Philadelphia: Orion Editions, 1984 (1926). Some people might argue that, given current environmental trends, this example may not serve us for much longer.

are not. They are scarce under some circumstances but not under others. Producing them in the first place might be very costly—creating a viable new chemical formulation might require several years of extensive screening, testing, and development prior to commercialization, and cost several million dollars—reproducing them, however, might be virtually costless and be carried out in seconds with the help of a good quality photocopying machine. For this reason, it follows that information goods cannot be subject to the same valuation procedures as physical goods. We shall draw upon the I-Space to examine the issue in more detail in the next section.

Before we do so, however, it is worth noting that neoclassical economics has addressed the problem of information goods somewhat schizophrenically. It has either treated information as a free good, not subject to trading and instantaneously available to all economic agents—here, its main function is to act as a support to economic exchange and to foster the perfect foresight so essential to efficient markets—or as a good that, through patenting, secrecy clauses, or other artificial means, can be made subject to all the scarcities that afflict physical goods and hence also to the normal rules of trading. In the first case, information has utility, but, lacking in scarcity, it has no value. In the second, it has both utility and scarcity and therefore has value. Which approach should we choose? The answer is: both. What we saw in the last chapter is that through an SLC, an information good evolves dynamically over time. The conventional economic approaches to its valuation thus capture in a static way two different moments in its trajectory. But the dynamic element is then lost to view.

As we shall presently see, the utility that can be extracted from an information good is a function of its location on the codification and abstraction dimension of the I-Space. Codification might predominate in the particular case, abstraction in the general case. A medical test illustrates the particular case. It will be more useful if the range of possible outcomes of the test can be fully specified and unambiguously distinguished from each other than if it admits of a significant percentage of false positives or false negatives; recall our discussion of mammograms in the last chapter. The general case is illustrated by the microprocessor. When it introduced the programmable integrated circuit in 1971, Intel did away with the need for dedicated chips and vastly extended the technology's range of applications. In effect, the firm had created a general purpose device.

Extracting value from an information good, by contrast, is a function of its residence time at a given point fixed by reference to all three dimensions of the I-Space.[7] In the case of value, therefore, the diffusion dimension is also acti-

---

[7] A patent allows a point located on the right in the I-Space to extract value as if it was located on the left. A patent increases the scarcity of knowledge by restricting access to its *utility*. The patent does not actually make knowledge scarce as such, it merely makes it useless to those not authorized to use it—but not always. Although the residence time of a patent is limited, for operational purposes we can treat it as a point as being on the left. For the ineffectiveness of licensing, see C. Taylor and Z. Silberston, *The Economic Impact of the Patent System: A Study of the British Experience*, Cambridge: Cambridge University Press, 1973; and

vated. It is this dimension that allows us to establish the scarcity of information goods—i.e., how few agents actually possess them—and that highlights their distinctive character with respect to scarcity.

The value of a knowledge asset is derived partly from the utility of the services that it yields over time, and partly from its positional status—it confers a competitive advantage because others do not possess it. A proper exploitation of knowledge assets calls for maximizing their residence time in value-generating regions of the I-Space. The information goods out of which knowledge assets are built, however, are continually prey to the actions of an SLC. The SLC tends to move information goods both into the value-generating region of the I-Space as well as out of it. In the next section, we shall see that the dynamic behaviour of information goods in the I-Space imparts a precariousness to knowledge assets that is not shared by purely physical assets.

4.5 THE CONCEPT OF VALUE IN THE I-SPACE

The three dimensions that make up the I-Space—codification, abstraction, and diffusion—allow us to establish how far a particular group of knowledge assets are structured and shared within a given population. They also allow us to draw up a value map for the analysis of knowledge assets. We begin the construction of our value map by noticing that the scarcity of an information good is a function of its location along the diffusion dimension of the I-Space. The further to the left in the I-Space we locate it, the less it is shared by other members of a target population and hence the scarcer it is. Conversely, the further to the right we place it, the more it has the character of a public good devoid of scarcity.

To the extent that the diffusion of an information good depends on its degree of codification or abstraction, we can see that its scarcity is a natural product of these two variables. Knowledge that is hard to articulate and to structure does not travel far. On the other hand, knowledge that can be compressed into a few well-chosen symbols can, with the right communication infrastructure available, travel globally in a matter of minutes or even seconds. The first type of knowledge places us in a world of Zen Buddhists who transmit their wisdom by example to a small and intimate community of disciples. The second type of knowledge places us in a world of bond traders, each sitting in front of a screen and transmitting well-codified price and quantity information instantaneously and on a global scale to agents they have never met.

What about the utility of an information good? Utility, in effect, has two dimensions: first, how useful the good turns out to be in a *particular*

R. W. Wilson, 'The Sale of Technology Through Licensing', Ph.D. thesis, Yale University, New Haven, Conn., 1975. See E. von Hippel, *The Sources of Innovation*, Oxford: Oxford University Press, 1988.

application, and second, how many different potentially useful applications can be found for it. Assuming that an information good is relevant in at least *some* application—and the decision to locate it in the I-Space at all is built on the assumption that it has some a priori relevance for a given population—then its utility is a function of how well articulated, how well standardized, and how reliable it can be made. In the first instance, therefore, the utility of an information good is partly a function of its degree of codification. But an information good also gains in utility if it is generalizable across a wide range of potential applications. Typically, the attributes of a good that are generalizable across applications in this way are fewer in number than those required within applications. The information good thus increases in utility as it moves towards a higher level of abstraction, acquiring a generic quality that increases the size of the population for which it has potential utility. Note, however, that if by increasing its degree of abstraction one also increases the size of the population for which it has relevance, then, at the very moment that one increases its utility, one also effectively increases an information good's relative scarcity.

Through the three variables of codification, abstraction, and diffusion, then, both the scarcity and the utility of an information good can be expressed in the I-Space. It should be clear from the foregoing that the maximum value of an information good in the space is achieved when its diffusion is at a minimum but its degree of codification and abstraction are at a maximum. Conversely, the minimum value of such a good is reached when diffusion is at a maximum and codification and abstraction are at a minimum. In Figure 4.1 we present the I-Space as a value map in which the points of maximum value (maximum scarcity and utility) and a minimum value (minimum scarcity and utility) are indicated. The different curves notionally link together points of equal value in the I-Space, with value increasing as the curves approach region V-max and decreasing as they approach region V-min. Note that the point of maximum value, V-max, is reached in the region of the I-Space in which the rate of entropy production is at a minimum. Conversely, minimum value, V-min, is reached in the region in which the rate of entropy production is at a maximum. The value of information goods and the knowledge assets they give rise to is thus intimately related to their capacity to produce order in a world where order is a scarce commodity. Note also that both the points V-max and V-min can be made to lie along a single SLC—as indicated in Figure 4.2—something which implies that *both* the regions in which the points are located will need to be activated by any effective learning process.

How is one to interpret this? Can learning, for example, ever be a value *decreasing* activity? Can it become a source of disorder rather than order? The answer is, as indicated by the SLC itself, that effective learning takes one through different phases in the I-Space, not all of which are necessarily directly value-adding. Take absorption and impacting, the two phases of the SLC that lead one into the minimum value region of the I-Space. Taken

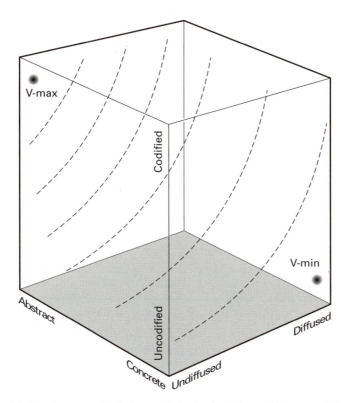

FIG. 4.1 Maximum and Minimum Value in the I-Space: V-max and V-min

together, they correspond to a process of learning by doing or learning by using that involves repetition in the use of newly acquired codes and a willingness to try them out in new situations. To be effective, this phase often has to be exploratory and quite playful. It involves numerous false starts and much trial and error—possibly mostly errors. In these two phases, learners often feel that they are going backwards and decreasing rather than increasing in mastery. The range of possible applications for the codes seems to outgrow the learners' capacity to apply them, and it is only by spending a great deal of time internalizing them that any competence at all is acquired.

Of course, it is all a question of *reculer pour mieux sauter*. With the attainment of competence, one gradually begins to move to the left in the I-Space relative to those who, having encountered the codes, fail to internalize and apply them—i.e., they have abandoned the learning race and hopped off the SLC. The leftward move leads one away from the minimum value region around the point V-min, and once more towards the maximum value region around V-max. When described as part of a learning activity, this move presents no particular problem. It is the outcome of a scanning process, the

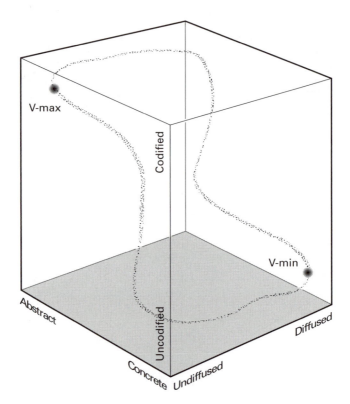

Fɪɢ. 4.2 V-max and V-min on the SLC

spotting of promising new patterns in generally available data. Not everyone who has the data, however, is able to see new patterns. Hence the move to the left, from the many who have the data, to the few who see the patterns. Such a move cannot be explained in conventional economic terms. The reason is that neoclassical economics draws much of its inspiration from classical physics[8] and classical physics claims that when a system attains thermodynamic equilibrium it tends to stay there unless it receives additional inputs of energy from outside. Unaided, the system cannot by itself move away from equilibrium and towards a high level of order—and hence gain in value.

Yet, as thermodynamicists like Prigogine, Nicolis, and Babloyantz have pointed out, thermodynamic equilibrium in physical systems is characterized by fluctuations of varying size.[9] For the most part, these are inconsequential and short-lived so that the system returns to its original state of equilibrium. Occasionally, however, a particular fluctuation can drive the system to a new,

    [8] Mirowski, *More Heat than Light*.
    [9] I. Prigogine, G. Nicolis, and A. Babloyantz, 'Thermodynamics of Evolution', *Physics Today*, 25 (11), 1972, pp. 23–8; 25 (12), 1972, pp. 38–44.

more ordered far-from-equilibrium state. Prigogine labels such a state 'dissipative'. In this new state, the system may well increase its overall rate of entropy production. But it may also demonstrate a greater capacity to do *work*, so that its rate of entropy production per unit of work can still be lower than what it was under conditions of thermodynamic equilibrium.

As with energy-driven systems, so with data-driven systems. Neoclassical economists perceive departures from market equilibrium as being the result of externally administered 'shocks' rather than the product of fluctuations originating within the system itself. In effect, they fail to distinguish between market *data*, which can be quite stable and homogeneous in appearance, and the variety of patterns that the data give rise to. Data can accommodate multiple overlapping patterns that reflect different attempts to structure and extract useful information from it. Patterns can thus be quite heterogeneous and hence, on occasions, a source of endogenous fluctuations. Most of these do not threaten long-term market equilibrium. Some of them, however, following a process of absorption and impacting, will sometimes lead to destabilizing insights—i.e., novel patterns—that will drive the economic system into a new and ordered far-from-equilibrium state on the left of the I-Space. In this way, order emerges out of chaos, both states being necessary for a proper functioning of the SLC.

There is more. As we argued in the preceding chapter, order is a scarce commodity located on the left of the I-Space. Yet order can also propagate towards the right in the I-Space through a diffusion process. As it does so, it loses its scarcity value. Value in the I-Space is thus inherently unstable. It behaves paradoxically.

4.6 THE PARADOX OF VALUE

We now briefly explore the paradox of value that afflicts information goods in the I-Space. It poses an unusual challenge for the effective management of knowledge assets, and for this reason needs to be well understood. In the next chapter we shall explore two quite different ways that firms can deal with the paradox.

Order can propagate within or across systems in several ways. A system can, for example, replicate itself, as in crystal growth and crystal break-up. Or it can reproduce itself, as in the growth and spread of organic species. All kinds of variants are possible between these two possibilities. With replication, the transfer of information is direct, with the structure of one entity mapping directly on to the structure of another. With reproduction, by contrast, information transfer is indirect. It takes place through the transmission of a genetic programme which subsequently drives and guides a development process within the organism to be reproduced. In both examples, information, the ordering agent, is borne on a physical substrate which determines the

conditions and physical reach of the ordering process. Durable spatial contiguity, for instance, is required in the case of crystal growth.[10] And physical
encounters—episodic spatial contiguity—are usually required for biological
reproduction.

In social systems, information transfer does not usually require physical
contiguity. The cultural patterns that constitute the ordering principles on
which social systems are built can today be borne on electromagnetic waves.
In earlier times, although spatial contiguity was not required, spatial proximity certainly was. In fifth-century Athens, for example, although up to 50,000
adult males were entitled to participate in the Assembly (ecclesia), the quo-
rum was 6,000. From the time of Cleisthenes, the usual meeting place for the
Assembly was the hill of Pnyx, a short distance west of the Acropolis.
Meetings took place under an open sky. It is doubtful, given the physical setting, that active participation was an option for more than a few hundred of
those who attended.[11] In the twentieth century, however, modern telecommunication technology has considerably loosened the constraints on physical
proximity and thus greatly extended the spatial reach of information's ordering potential.

Recall, though, that in order properly to exploit the spatial reach offered
by telecommunication technologies, information flows have to be made more
codified and more abstract. Yet, because there is a cost to codifying and
abstracting, only that information whose potential utility and value is
thought to justify the time and effort involved in its structure will be selected
for transmission. More importantly, the exercise will only be worthwhile if
the transmission of information takes place under controlled conditions, that
is, those that allow agents required to make the investment—usually
senders—to extract value from the process.

Here we encounter an interesting problem: if I want to communicate with
a limited yet spatially dispersed audience, I may have to structure my message
to the same extent as if I wanted to reach a much larger one. The actual diffusion of my message may be limited by my choice of codes—I may use jargon known only to the audience I wish to reach—but its diffusibility is not
thereby affected. Where information has a transient value—as, for example,
in many transactions on the Internet—the returns to code-breaking may be
virtually nil. Where, however, one is dealing with durable knowledge assets—
e.g., the legendary formula for Coca-Cola, the manufacturing specification
for a nuclear weapon, etc.—the returns to code-breaking may suddenly turn
positive. At that point, the diffusibility of information may become a better
guide to its future value than its actual diffusion at a given moment in time.

To summarize, order has value, but within a social system the speed with
which order-generating information can propagate, by reducing its scarcity,
may reduce its value. This becomes clear from an examination of the diffu-

[10] A. Cairns-Smith, *Seven Clues to the Origin of Life*, Cambridge: Cambridge University Press, 1985.
[11] J. A. Fine, *The Ancient Greeks: A Critical History*, Cambridge, Mass: Harvard University Press, 1983.

sion curve in the I-Space: the closer we move towards the theoretical maxima along the codification and abstraction dimensions, the more diffusible becomes the information created, and hence the more precarious whatever scarcity is achieved.

We thus reach a paradoxical situation: the greater the utility we achieve with an information good as we increase its degree of codification and abstraction, the more difficult it becomes to secure its scarcity. The problem has both a production and an exchange dimension. The production one has just been discussed: the very act of producing useful information through codification and abstraction by enhancing its diffusibility reduces its value. The exchange dimension was touched upon in section 4.3. There, we noted that the value of physical goods is established by comparing them with each other. In order to be able to do this, some information about such goods must be widely diffused—this is required by the efficient market hypothesis. Information about information goods, however, cannot be so diffused without compromising their scarcity. Thus, when information ceases to play merely a supporting role in economic transactions, when it becomes instead their central focus, the logic that regulates the production and exchange of physical goods ceases to apply.

The message of the paradox of value is a disconcerting one for those who believe that economics is or should be an exact science: it is that information goods are indeterminate with respect to value. And just as the discovery of indeterminacy in physical processes entailed a shift in paradigm from classical physics to quantum physics,[12] so the indeterminacy of information goods calls for a distinct political economy of information. Our understanding of knowledge assets will thus require a different set of concepts to those through which we apprehended purely physical assets. Furthermore, to the extent that knowledge assets get embedded in physical assets—to varying degrees, the case with all artefacts—the new concepts that we shall have to draw on to deal with the former will also change the way we think of the latter.

We have identified a fundamental difference in the behaviour of physical and information goods. We then concluded that firms which trade primarily on the basis of knowledge assets need a different theoretical perspective to those that trade primarily on the basis of physical assets. The new perspective is likely to affect the ways that knowledge-based firms conceive their strategies, their technologies, their human resources processes, and their environment.

We discuss strategy issues in Chapters 5 and 8, technology issues in Chapter 7, human resources in Chapter 6. We end the book with a discussion of the firm's environment in Chapter 11. In the next and concluding section of this chapter we briefly explore some of the implications of the paradox of value.

---

[12] A. Pais, *Inward Bound: Of Matters and Forces in the Physical World*, New York: Oxford University Press, 1986.

4.7 SOME IMPLICATIONS OF THE PARADOX OF VALUE

How might the paradox of value shape the way that firms manage their knowledge assets? Consider, for example, the way that a firm might classify its technologies: one popular classification is shown in Table 4.1. Technologies so classified would be located in the I-Space as shown in Figure 4.3. *Base technologies*, being mature, are well structured—i.e., codified and abstract—and largely diffused within the relevant industries. The technologies to be found in a typical bottling plant would qualify as base technologies. Everybody has them and nobody gains a competitive advantage thereby. *Emergent technologies*, on the other hand, are comparatively unstructured and as yet undiffused. Work on superconductivity, for example, remains for the most part confined to the research laboratory. Superconductors are materials that lose electrical resistance at a particular temperature known as the critical temperature, or Tc. Developing materials with a high Tc—superconducting metals typically exhibit a Tc below 20 K and are therefore not commercially viable—has become a major research objective in the late 1990s. Yet since the mechanism for superconductivity in new materials like ceramics remains poorly understood, the theoretical challenge remains formidable and few players fully master the demanding technologies involved.[13]

Table 4.1 Classifying a Firm's Technologies

Base Technologies	*Key Technologies*	*Emergent Technologies*
1. Well codified	1. Usually well codified and mastered	1. Not yet codified
2. Often generic	2. When properly leveraged they are generic	2. Only a few concrete applications
3. Well diffused within or across industries	3. These are not, as yet, diffused. They are specific to a handful of firms	3. Specific to a handful of firms. Not yet diffused
4. Without them a firm is not even a player	4. They are a source of competitive advantage for firms that have them	4. They could become a source of competitive advantage for firms that develop them

Finally, we can think of *key technologies* as emerging technologies on their way to becoming base technologies—i.e., by following the diffusion curve—that have been hijacked by a firm and held captive in the maximum value region of the I-Space. For late twentieth-century high-speed trains, for exam-

---

[13] G. Vidali, *Superconductivity: The Next Revolution?*, Cambridge: Cambridge University Press, 1993.

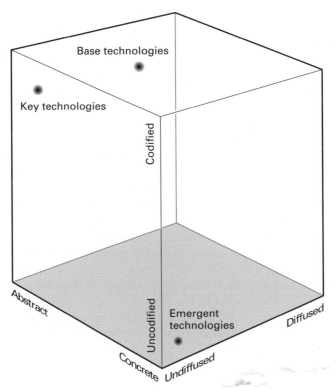

Fig. 4.3 Different Types of Technology in the I-Space

ple, railway bogies have become a key technology, providing dynamic stability and comfort under very demanding conditions. For supersonic aircraft, composite materials providing a high strength to weight ratio as well as a high resistance to heat also constitute a key technology. The value that can be extracted from a key technology is a function of how long it can be held in residence in that region. Security of tenure is not guaranteed, since there are usually plenty of potential claimants for the space it occupies. Residence time in the maximum value region may be a function of how well intellectual property rights are protected in that region, but these offer at best partial protection. A second issue is how well a key technology can be integrated with a firm's other knowledge assets. The higher the degree of integration achieved, the greater the technology's inertia in the I-Space with respect to diffusion, and the longer its prospective residence time in the maximum value region. Finally, residence time will be cut short by a rapidly changing knowledge base. Unlike weak property rights which erode the relative scarcity of knowledge assets, a dynamically evolving knowledge base erodes their utility as more attractive alternatives loom into view.

Investing in emerging technologies is an uncertain and sometimes risky business. Yet firms competing on the basis of knowledge assets often have little choice. The opportunity costs incurred by not investing are often punishing. Such investments can usefully be thought of as the equivalent of purchasing options to operate these technologies at some date in the future.[14] Options are devices for absorbing rather than reducing uncertainty. At some definable cost they allow one to buy time and to exercise value-enchancing choices. Uncertainty frequently offers positive as well as negative pay-offs, and investing in options effectively allows one to filter out the latter while retaining the former where they are potentially on offer. In developing its key technologies, a firm places, and at the same time hedges, its bets. It must, first, assess the expected value of investing in a given technology by estimating the probability that out of all emerging technologies available it will become a key technology—in the case of high-speed trains, for example, a key issue is whether magnetic levitation technology, possibly based on superconducting solenoids, will one day replace wheel-on-rail technology; in the case of computing, the challenge is deciding whether gallium arsenide could overtake silicon as a substrate for chips. It must then estimate the possible residence time of the technology in question in the maximum value region of the I-Space. Finally, it must gauge its own ability to transform an emerging technology into a key technology. After all, moving an emerging technology into the maximum value region may call for hefty up-front investments. Is the firm well placed to carry these out, or could it be overtaken by a competitor? Clearly, developing and exercising options will carry different costs for different players.

The paradox of value holds that the further into the maximum value region the firm manages to move its knowledge assets, the more precarious becomes their residence time in the region on account of the competitive forces at work there and of the resulting diffusion of know-how that they set in motion. As we shall see in the next chapter, the strength of these forces varies by industry and sometimes as a function of organization structure. Knowledge assets, for example, may be easier to hold on to in, say, the pharmaceutical than in the automobile industry.[15] On the other hand, in industries characterized by high degrees of job mobility and informal 'knowledge trading' between professionals working for different firms,[16] firm-specific knowledge may begin to leak out and diffuse fairly early in the process of codification and abstraction and hence well before it reaches the maximum value region of the I-Space.

From its earliest days, for example, the semiconductor industry has been characterized by frequent job-hopping and brains walking out of doors. Robert Noyce and seven of his colleagues left William Shockley's labora-

---

[14] R. Sanchez, 'Higher Order Organization and Commitment in Strategic Options Theory: A Reply to Christopher Bartlett', *Advances in Strategic Management*, 106, 1994, pp. 299–307; A. Dixit and R. Pyndyck, *Investment under Uncertainty*, Princeton, New Jersey: Princeton University Press, 1994.
[15] Von Hippel, *The Sources of Innovation*.   [16] Ibid, p. 6.

tory—actually a barn—in Mountain View, California, in 1957 to set up the Fairchild Semiconductor Corporation in Palo Alto. The secession was the first of many that were to affect Fairchild itself. In 1968 alone, the new firm begat thirteen spin-offs.[17]

Ironically, being aware that such informal and uncontrolled diffusion of its knowledge assets can take place is actually likely to intensify a firm's efforts to move into the maximum value region, as it attempts to extract tacit experiential knowledge out of the heads of its employees and embed it in proprietary firm-specific processes. Why should this be?

There is an old legal dictum that 'possession is nine-tenths of the law'. The dictum is particularly applicable to knowledge assets. Firms may legally *own* the tacit knowledge assets accumulated by employees in the course of their employment, but they do not actually *possess* them. To make good their ownership claims, firms must be able to take possession of such knowledge in a meaningful way. The only course available to them for doing this is to get such knowledge articulated. It can then be codified and either embedded in organizational procedures or in the firm's physical assets—i.e., stored in the organization's memory.

Yet even where skilled knowledge workers helpfully articulate their tacit knowledge assets, as we saw in section 3.1, the process is never complete. A large residue of tacit knowledge—perhaps the largest and the most important part of it—will remain with them. The possessors of such knowledge will therefore always 'know more than they can say'. For this reason tacit knowledge can never fully be in the possession of the firm. Much of it remains inalienably the possession of individuals, working singly or in teams.[18] It is individuals or small groups who experience the countless hitches and glitches that usually pock-mark the development of a new product or process. They are the ones who are then called upon to explore formal or informal ways of overcoming them.

This has implications for the way that a firm manages the SLC and also for what we mean by a learning organization. Where uncertainty and complexity cannot be reduced and, as a consequence, knowledge cannot effectively be transferred, it may remain beyond the reach of organizational action. It can then only be managed by individuals in possibly idiosyncratic ways. Knowledge assets carried primarily around in people's heads rather than embedded in organizational processes or in physical plant characterize craft-based firms. Such knowledge assets rarely move very far up the I-Space and hence cannot ever be made fully proprietary. They are scarce, but too fuzzy to be subject to trading independently of the physical skills in which they find themselves embedded. They occupy the region A in the I-Space of Figure 4.4.

[17] H. Queisser, *The Conquest of the Microchip: Science and Business in the Silicon Age*, Cambridge, Mass: Harvard University Press, 1988.

[18] For team production, see A. Alchian and H. Demetz, 'Production, Information, Costs, and Economic Organization', *American Economic Review*, 62, 1972.

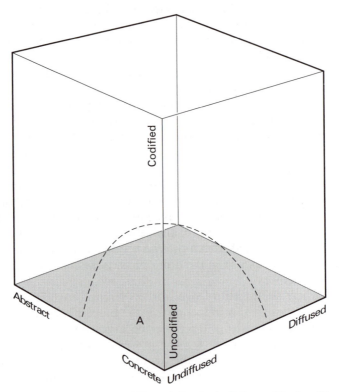

FIG. 4.4 Tacit Personal Knowledge in the I-Space (Region A)

The only codification and abstraction that they might be subject to is that of branding, the creation of an easy-to-remember word or symbol that refers to a complex knowledge domain not itself accessible to outsiders.

It is often not much accessible to insiders either. Craft-based knowledge is jealously guarded by its possessors. Being uncodified, it does not easily diffuse. Its utility, however, is also limited by its lack of codifiability and abstraction. Craft-based knowledge is for the most part personal and concrete. It cannot easily be standardized or made highly reliable, and its productivity is circumscribed. The only strategy that can properly exploit craft-based knowledge makes a virtue of its scarcity characteristics by stressing its exclusivity. The point is sometimes lost on the creators of powerful brands who try to extend their reach beyond what the underlying craft base will allow. A plethora of hastily licensed products, for example, virtually ruined Pierre Cardin in the 1980s,[19] and by the mid 1980s Gucci had slapped its logo on more than 14,000 different products, from T-shirts and key-chains to sun-

---

[19] 'The Luxury Goods Trade', *The Economist*, 26 December 1992, pp. 91–4.

glasses and coffee mugs. Branded positional goods such as these rapidly lose their exclusivity when mass-marketed.

The challenge posed for firms by the issue of tacit knowledge has a cultural dimension. Where the firm has the character of a total institution, as was the case of large Japanese firms until the early 1990s, the mobility of skilled employees is much reduced and so is the danger that the brains will walk out of the door. There is therefore much less pressure to get employees to articulate their tacit knowledge. The lack of opportunities outside the firm, together with the firm's own socialization processes, predisposes employees to place whatever tacit knowledge they possess at the service of the firm.[20] Thus, although Japanese firms are no less subject to the paradox of value than their Western counterparts whenever they move up the I-Space, they arguably hold a larger part of their knowledge assets in its lower regions, in the uncodified practices of individuals and teams.[21] Being less codified, these practices are also more rooted in concrete applications rather than in abstract principles. They do not diffuse so easily—a competitive advantage when it comes to preventing imitation by competitors, yet a disadvantage when it comes to establishing such practices abroad. The internationalization of the Japanese economy and the spread of Japanese manufacturing production outside its own borders are forcing Japanese firms to articulate and to structure their organizational practices in order to transfer these to foreign workers. The latter, in contrast to their Japanese counterparts, have not been socialized since leaving school to the Japanese way of doing things. And, as experience with Japanese automobile plants in the USA and in the UK indicates, Japanese practices turn out to be eminently codifiable when they have to be—and therefore imitable too. The paradox of value is thus currently eroding what was once believed to be an unassailable and almost mystical cultural advantage, a unique possession of the large Japanese firm.

---

[20] I. Nonaka and H. Takeuchi, *The Knowledge Creating Company: How Japanese Companies Create the Dynamics of Innovation*, New York: Oxford University Press, 1995; R. Dore, *British Factory—Japanese Factory: The Origins of National Diversity in Industrial Relations*, Berkeley: University of California Press, 1973; J. Abbeglen, *The Japanese Factory*, Glencoe: The Free Press, 1958.

[21] In *The Knowledge Creating Company*,Nonaka and Takeuchi, for example, point out that in developing new products, Japanese engineers are encouraged to employ metaphoric forms of thought.

5

Neoclassical versus Schumpeterian Orientation to Learning

5.1 INTRODUCTION

IN the last chapter we argued that knowledge assets were indeterminate with respect to value. Maximizing the utility of such assets compromises their scarcity, and maximizing their scarcity, in turn, makes it difficult fully to develop and exploit their utility. This paradox of value adds an extra dimension to the risks that are usually associated with investments in knowledge assets. When investing in such assets, one is typically concerned with whether one will actually be able to create valid and useful knowledge—i.e., one's focus is on the risks associated with codification and abstraction. Issues of scarcity, to be sure, are also taken into account, but they are often addressed in limited ways and primarily in terms of intellectual property rights. If these can be unambiguously established, it is assumed, then scarcity can also be secured.

Misunderstanding the paradox of value has cost some firms dearly. Believing itself to be secure behind its all-too-fragile patent barriers, for example, EMI lost control of its scanner technology to General Electric. Through an ill-judged outsourcing strategy, IBM lost control of the market for personal computers, one which it had been instrumental in bringing into existence. The dynamics of the paradox, then, need to be better understood.

The value of many buildings, for example, is expected to decline over time on account of physical wear and tear, independently of gradual shifts in demand, changes in land-use patterns, etc. The depreciation schedule for a building is an estimate of the time over which it will yield useful services. Here, however, one usually distinguishes between its economic and its physical life. In socialist economies, by contrast, depreciation schedules relate primarily to the physical life of a good. It is not usually replaced until it is incapable of yielding any useful services, and this even if superior alternatives are available. Such depreciation schedules constitute one of the main causes of low productivity in state-owned enterprises—i.e., they are made to work with clapped-out plant and equipment. In market economies, certain types of building receive a similar treatment; sometimes they may be kept in existence because the services that they yield are cultural and emotional and not purely technical. In certain circumstances, for example, the physical wear and tear undergone by an old building may actually enhance its aesthetic appeal and hence its market value.

The pace of innovation in the construction industry is not such as to curtail systematically the economic life of old buildings. In industries characterized by high levels of innovation, however, the economic life of a good tends to be much shorter than its physical life. Although capable of yielding further services, it is often made obsolete by competing alternatives. A new generation of microprocessors, for example, is often technologically out of date by the time it is launched on the market, together with the equipment used to manufacture it.[1] The difference between the physical and the economic life of a good in part measures the stochastic impact of either newly created knowledge or the rapid diffusion of existing knowledge on the knowledge assets currently associated with the good. Computer-integrated manufacturing systems, for example, typically have a much shorter economic life than residential buildings, because even though their physical life may be quite similar, each new system generation typically embodies a greater quantity of new and useful knowledge assets than its predecessor.

One may well ask why anyone would bother to invest in anything as precarious as knowledge assets given the risks involved and the uncertainty of the returns. Much, in effect, depends on devising effective strategies for dealing with the paradox of value. In this chapter we identify and discuss two distinct strategic orientations to the paradox. Each builds on quite a different set of assumptions about how learning emerges from information flows and organizational processes. Each yields an identifiable approach to the management of knowledge assets. The two orientations are not mutually exclusive and can often coexist within a single firm, either in different parts of the organization at the same time, or in the same part of the organization at different times. Typically, however, one orientation will tend to predominate, predisposing the firm either to hoarding or to sharing its knowledge assets.

In the next section (5.2) we briefly describe and discuss the different assumptions concerning the nature of knowledge that respectively underpin each of the two orientations to the paradox of value. In sections 5.3 and 5.4 we present the two orientations to the paradox. We show that they correspond respectively to a static and a dynamic view of the evolution of knowledge assets and that they operate at different levels of complexity. The first encourages us to view the firm as an equilibrium phenomenon, and is thus in line with orthodox economic thinking. The second invites us to see the firm as a phenomenon that can operate within both an equilibrium and a far-from-equilibrium framework.

In section 5.5 we show how a firm's choice of a learning orientation may be affected by how it conceives of its knowledge assets. While some firms think of these in portfolio terms, others think of them as systems. Each perspective, being influenced by both industry and technology characteristics, will be appropriate for a different set of contingencies. In section 5.6, therefore, we

---

[1] E. Braun and S. Macdonald, *Revolution in Miniature*, Cambridge: Cambridge University Press, 1982.

look at how a firm's industrial environment and its competitive position within an industry can influence its orientation towards learning. How far is such an orientation imposed upon it from outside by the circumstances that it finds itself in, and how far is it the product of autonomous internal factors such as managerial perception or an idiosyncratic corporate culture? In section 5.7 we conclude the chapter with a brief discussion of recent trends in industry evolution that could affect the firm's choice of an appropriate learning orientation.

5.2 EXPLOITING TECHNOLOGICAL ASSETS: TO HOARD OR TO SHARE?

IBM spends more on creating new knowledge than any other company on earth—between 1988 and 1992 its research and development expenditures exceeded $US25 billion—yet by the mid 1990s the firm had lost two-thirds of its 1987 market value. Clearly, creating knowledge assets and profiting from them are two different things. IBM's strength has traditionally been in the mainframe business. These large and expensive machines, fiendishly complex and built to proprietary standards, had the effect of locking corporate customers into a lifetime of IBM systems. Yet the low volumes that characterized the mainframe business robbed manufacturers like IBM and Digital of the huge benefits generated by learning curve effects available in the semiconductor business. Learning curve benefits—lower costs, faster cycle times, improved reliability, etc.—are the fruit of cumulative volume and, by implication, of large market shares in mass markets. These were, in principle, available to IBM when it made its belated entry into the personal computer business in 1981. Yet because the firm was in a hurry and anxious to make up lost ground, it had been forced hastily to assemble its machines from off-the-shelf components, thus making it possible for competitors to build machines to the same standard. Most crucially, IBM incorporated the Intel microprocessor and Microsoft's DOS operating system into its PC without restricting those firms' sales to competitors. The result was that IBM created a standard within the industry from which it was unable to profit. Intel was able to reap all the learning curve benefits that could have gone to IBM, and Microsoft became the world's largest software company.

IBM's entry into the personal computer industry called for radically new patterns of behaviour and thought, patterns that the firm proved slow to master. It had been accustomed to phase out old technologies as slowly as possible and only gradually to bring in new ones. In this way it would avoid disrupting the sales of its oldest machines. IBM, then, was something of a technology hoarder. By contrast, the two firms that have pretty much controlled PC technology since its birth have grown rich by selling their technologies to all comers. They are primarily technology sharers. IBM's crucial problem is that it had internalized the hoarding habit to such an extent that when, as a result of rapid improvements in performance, the technological environment called for sharing, the firm found itself wrong-footed. To be sure, it dabbled in sharing, but failed to learn how to profit from it—in the process it handed leadership of the industry to Intel and Microsoft.

Hoarding and sharing, like selfishness and altruism, are emotionally laden terms that one associates with individual character. They also characterize the behaviour of firms. Just as with individuals, the labels should be applied with understanding and discrimination. Whether a firm opts for hoarding or sharing its knowledge assets turns in part on how it thinks of knowledge and its evolution over time. Two polar cases can be identified.

In the first, knowledge is seen as cumulative. Learning consists of gradually eliminating errors so that better-quality knowledge gradually accumulates in the memory of social systems and organizations. It does so through well-formed codifications and abstractions that over time weave a fine tissue of well-tested and integrated facts and propositions. The knowledge base is hierarchically organized with abstract covering laws regulating the deployment of facts and lower-level theories within the tissue. Scientific textbooks often project an image of knowledge as cumulative, as a carefully yet unproblematically assembled collection of facts and theories, hierarchically organized into a vertical network. Although this image of how knowledge builds up has been criticized as being too simple and sometimes downright misleading, there are many fields for which it offers a plausible and certainly useful account.

In the second, knowledge is seen as cumulative but only within the confines of a paradigm. Over time, paradigms displace each other and much old knowledge is destroyed. In this second case, codifications and abstractions build up alternative networks of facts and theories that can either collaborate or compete.[2] These networks are, in effect, patterns that we ourselves impose on the data, and in most cases the data turns out to be consistent with a potentially infinite number of patterns.[3] Networks or paradigms, then, are not inherent in the data and just waiting to be discovered. They are free constructions of the human mind. And just as one can change one's mind, one can modify the constructions that one overlays on the data of experience. One classic study of such a 'paradigm shift' was carried out by Kuhn when he examined the switch from a geocentric Ptolemaic cosmology to a Copernican heliocentric one in the sixteenth and seventeenth centuries.[4]

Technologies can be thought of as embodiments—physical or otherwise—of paradigmatic knowledge. The IBM example that we presented above describes a shift of technological paradigm from mainframes to personal computers. Note, however, that the shift involved no sudden change in the

---

[2] T. Kuhn, *The Structure of Scientific Revolutions*, Chicago: University of Chicago Press, 1962.

[3] We say that theory is undetermined by the data.

[4] T. Kuhn, *The Copernican Revolution: Planetary Astronomy in the Development of Western Thought*, Cambridge, Mass: Harvard University Press, 1957.

paradigms that made up the technology's scientific base. It was not any radical discontinuity in our knowledge of electronics that brought about the transformation of the industry. It was a discontinuity in the industry's knowledge of customers and their needs. The introduction of the 8-bit microprocessor by Intel in 1971 had vastly expanded the potential market for computing. For the first time it could reach out beyond the data-processing departments of large firms and service bureaux and connect directly with small firms and even individuals. IBM's problem was that a certain technological narcissism had blinded it to these developments, leading the firm largely to ignore these new customers and their distinctive needs. Commitment to a concept of large corporate customers buying large expensive machines had led it to overlook—or at least vastly to underestimate—the market potential of small customers buying small machines.

Although Kuhn himself had initially presented paradigms as incommensurate knowledge systems providing no independent benchmark for ascertaining whether one was superior to the other, there is still room to argue that a move from one paradigm to another can be progressive.[5] Yet, this does not change the fact that paradigm shifts often involve the destruction of existing knowledge assets and the building up of new ones on different foundations. To be progressive is not necessarily to be cumulative.

It is possible to hold a position midway between the two polar cases presented. A shift of paradigm, for example, may involve a destruction of codified and abstract knowledge embedded in organizational processes, but leave intact the tacit knowledge base from which such knowledge is derived. It will then live on in the heads of employees, in folk memories, and in the oral traditions that often lend spice to an organization's culture. Such archaeological knowledge will gradually erode or deform over time if transmission mechanisms remain informal or unreliable. While it survives, however, its effects can either be destructive or constructive: destructive in that it may constitute an atavistic threat to the newly articulated and competing paradigm; constructive where it is prized as an extension of an organization's cognitive repertoire and hence of its knowledge assets, to be drawn upon should circumstances warrant it. Many technologies that were once destined for the scrapheap have been rescued from oblivion because changes in prices or demand suddenly made them viable once more—recall Courtaulds' resurrection of discarded spinning technologies in developing its revolutionary cellulosic fibre. When that happens, those who carry prior experience of that technology in their heads become much sought-after. The preservation of this fund of tacit experiential knowledge is one of the main challenges that face technology-based organizations when projects come to an end and highly skilled teams disband. Indeed, in the late 1960s it was one of the main justifications put forward for keeping the Concorde supersonic airline project

[5] Kuhn himself came to acknowledge as much. See I. Lakatos and A. Musgrave (eds), *Criticism and the Growth of Knowledge*, Cambridge: Cambridge University Press, 1970.

in existence long after it had become clear that it would never recover its costs.

Our two polar conceptions of knowledge operate at different levels of complexity. The cumulative view of the evolution of knowledge makes it a relatively stable hierarchical process. Where discontinuities occur, they can be for the most part contained within a small region of the hierarchical structure. The paradigmatic view of knowledge evolution, on the other hand, is much more disruptive. Discontinuities can propagate throughout the structure and trigger *gestalt switches*, that is, major changes in the patterns wrought by the data. There is no way that such propagation can be hierarchically confined, since it is the structural foundation of the knowledge base itself that is undergoing transformation. In the second case, therefore, the evolution of the knowledge base is characterized by a degree of complexity and unpredictability that is absent from the first. It is, in effect, an 'edge of chaos' phenomenon out of which new knowledge structures suddenly emerge.

The hypothesis that will be developed in this chapter is that conceptualizing knowledge as cumulative leads to the adoption of hoarding strategies, whereas conceptualizing it in paradigmatic terms favours sharing strategies. The grounds for this thesis will be presented in sections 5.3 and 5.4, and the implications of the thesis will be explored in sections 5.5 to 5.6.

Firms typically do not apply hoarding or sharing strategies in a stark doctrinaire fashion. Much judicious sharing of information with customers and suppliers, for example, can go on within the broad context of a hoarding strategy in order to enhance the value of the knowledge that is being retained within the firm. Pharmaceutical firms, for example, are often important sources of up-to-date medical knowledge for doctors, pharmacists, and hospitals, even if they keep their formulations to themselves. Conversely, information sharers will often hold back key items of knowledge in order to give themselves a competitive advantage over their recipients. Microsoft, for example, has often outraged competitors by allegedly hiding sets of instruction or 'code' in its popular Windows operating-system software. A book published in 1992 called *Undocumented Windows* claimed that Microsoft's own spreadsheets and other applications took advantage of features of Windows that were not reported in the documentation available to external software developers.[6]

As indicated by our earlier discussion, then, hoarding and sharing strategies can coexist, as can the different conceptualizations of knowledge that underpin them. Yet while the latter are not necessarily incompatible with each other, when one predominates within a firm it leads to a distinctive approach to investment in knowledge assets. Arguably, the two strategies should be viewed as being complementary rather than competitive, but, if so, the circumstances under which either will apply need to be clearly specified. In what

[6] 'Mad at Microsoft', *The Economist*, 19 September 1992, p. 76.

follows we first present the theories of learning that respectively underpin hoarding and sharing strategies; we then explore the different conditions under which each theory might hold.

5.3 NEOCLASSICAL OR N-LEARNING

Knowledge can be considered cumulative if over time knowledge assets yield ever more faithful representations of the world, as falsehoods are weeded out, gaps are filled, and fuzzy areas are brought into sharper focus. Learning thus becomes a stabilizing process through which individuals and organizations—firms, professional associations, universities, government laboratories, etc.—through repeated error detections and corrections, gradually gain access to an objective world and adapt to it. In this way valid knowledge gradually spreads and replaces faulty knowledge in a given population. As it does so, however, it acquires a certain inertia.

The inertia that accompanies stability is double-edged. On the one hand it imparts a certain robustness to the knowledge base. People can then rely on it to support technical applications or further learning without having it collapse on them. A solid and trustworthy knowledge base is itself a great asset that spares its users the need to reinvent the wheel every time they want to move forward. On the other hand, as the knowledge base stabilizes, whatever foundational errors happen to be locked into it become ever more difficult to deal with. Error detection and correction activities thus gradually get confined to minor adjustments and improvements.

In the economic realm, cumulative knowledge creates a world of rational expectations and efficient markets.[7] As with pricing, successive acts of codification and abstraction gradually capture all relevant information on given phenomena, and newly structured knowledge eventually diffuses to all. The system is self-adjusting and ensures that people will not continue to make systematic errors. Knowledge is shared at a pace and in a way that ensures that only random errors will remain in the system to act as background noise.

Over time, the economic value of knowledge assets leaks away. Their potential utility having been fully coded, their rapid diffusion eliminates both scarcity and, with it, any rents that might be earned through the possession of such assets. As happens in the right-hand region of the I-Space, when everyone either possesses or has equal access to a tradeable item of knowledge, market equilibrium is reached and no trades are possible at a price above the cost of providing such knowledge. Entrepreneurs, by exploiting any transient differential possession of knowledge by market players—whether the differences concern prices or product attributes—actively contribute to the process of knowledge diffusion and hence to the attainment of market equi-

---

[7] D. Begg, *The Rational Expectations Revolution in Macroeconomics: Theories and Evidence*, Oxford: Philip Allen, 1982.

librium.[8] Notice that where learning is cumulative, tacit knowledge has little part to play in the economic process save as a raw material for successive acts of codification. What is shared are hard, codified, and abstract facts, instantaneously diffusible and shorn of any ambiguity. If the facts of the matter are well captured by the codes and everyone is in possession of the codified facts then there is nothing left to learn beyond the facts themselves.

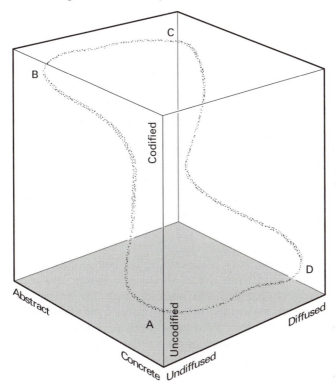

Fɪɢ. 5.1 The Four Regions Activated by an SLC

In such a world there is no incentive for economic agents to invest in the SLC beyond region C of the I-Space, as indicated in Figure 5.1. Its rent-generating potential now exhausted, the SLC effectively comes to a halt in that region. In this respect, market equilibrium marks the termination of social learning. One can thus only go on extracting value from knowledge assets by slowing down their progress towards region C, that is, by maximizing their residence time in region B and erecting barriers to their diffusion. In effect, learning is treated as a unidirectional rather than a cyclical phenomenon in the I-Space, better described by Figure 3.1 than by Figure 3.3. It is

---

[8] I. Kirzner, *Competition and Entrepreneurship*, Chicago: University of Chicago Press, 1973; *Perception, Opportunity, and Profit: Studies in the theory of entrepreneurship*, Chicago: University of Chicago Press, 1979.

initiated in region A of the I-Space, where it draws upon undiffused *local* knowledge that is highly concrete and uncodified. Through successive efforts at structuring the data it encounters, learning terminates in region C having produced a diffused and generic type of knowledge that is abstract and highly codified. There this knowledge remains, until disturbed or displaced by new knowledge that has followed a similar trajectory.

The concept of learning as an equilibrating process that comes to a halt in region C of Figure 5.1 is one associated with the neoclassical perspective in economics. For this reason we shall label it *N-learning*. It offers a Newtonian perspective on the production and distribution of knowledge in social systems: inertia keeps such systems on track so that change, when it occurs, registers as a disturbance originating outside the system. What has to be explained, therefore, is not stability, the system's natural condition, but change, the exogenously administered shock. In the early years of the twentieth century, Newtonian mechanics was subsumed under a more encompassing set of theories; one, the general theory of relativity operating at the macroscale, the other, quantum mechanics, operating at the microscale. Newtonian mechanics was not thereby refuted, but its relevance and utility became confined to phenomena that operate at a scale that we can apprehend intuitively—that of everyday objects such as cars, aeroplanes, and falling apples.

N-learning exhibits all the advantages and drawbacks of its Newtonian muse. If offers a handy way of describing the coarse-grained behaviour of knowledge flows—and these are at their most visible and coarse-grained where knowledge is codified and abstract. For that reason it intuitively appeals to managers concerned to extract value from their current stock of knowledge assets—i.e., long-lived capital-intensive plants, a key patent, a powerful brand.[9] Common sense tells them that if they are properly to exploit such assets they had better keep them to themselves—i.e., hoard them. And in many cases, perhaps even the majority, common sense serves these managers well. Patents, secrecy clauses, scale-induced barriers to entry are so many institutionally created ramparts behind which visible and diffusible knowledge assets can accumulate. Yet while ramparts work fine if one is fighting a war of position in which all players husband their cognitive resources behind protective fortifications, if some of the players are fighting a war of movement, a war for which the primary requirements are speed and nimbleness over a large territory, then ramparts can become impediments to mobility at a time when it is most required. Where speed and adaptability are called for, N-learning sometimes creates a 'Maginot Line' mentality that deprives a firm of the flexibility it needs. A different model of the learning process is then called for.

---

[9] The phenomenon of brand recognition tells us that brands are a form of knowledge shared with customers but not available for exploitation by competitors.

N-learning builds on an essentially linear view of the world: small causes have small effects and big causes have big effects. It is linearity that gives the world its stability and its predictability—i.e., that makes it analytically tractable and computable. N-learning, by moving us up the I-Space into an information environment that is codified, abstract, and intersubjectively stable (i.e., objective), affords us considerable data-processing economies. That is what makes it so attractive to firms with scarce data-processing resources. For most practical purposes, an N-learning strategy works well enough. In some circumstances, however, the data economies secured by N-learning turn out to be false ones.

5.4 SCHUMPETERIAN OR S-LEARNING

Today we have come to realize that the world is for the most part nonlinear, that microscopic causes can have macroscopic effects, and that change not stability is the natural order of things. It follows that moves up the I-Space and towards greater abstraction can never fully eradicate or stabilize the energy and data fluctuations to which we are subject. By their very nature, therefore, acts of codification and abstraction are, perforce, incomplete; they are at best hypotheses about the structure of the world that will always remain provisional and subject to revision. From this perspective, knowledge may be progressive in the sense that successive approximations may give us a better grasp of the underlying structures of reality, but, as pointed out in section 5.2, it is not necessarily cumulative. Subsequent hypotheses cannot always reliably build on preceding ones to create a single monolithic edifice. In a way that is reminiscent of Schumpeter's 'gales of creative destruction', new hypotheses are often destructive of old ones.[10] For this reason, and in honour of Schumpeter, we label our second perspective on learning Schumpeterian learning, or *S-learning*. In contrast to N-learning, it sees the SLC as continuing its course beyond region C in the I-Space, and moving down once more into those uncodified and highly local concrete regions—i.e., D and A of Figure 5.1—in which disequilibrating discontinuities originate.

It is only recently that the influence of nonlinear dynamics has spread beyond the world of physics and chemistry. The discovery that the world is overwhelmingly nonlinear and that linearity is very much the exception rather than the rule has led to a profound rethink concerning the nature of the physical world. One implication of this rethink is that effective learning strategies often require coming to terms with nonlinearities rather than trying to eliminate them. S-learning, therefore, in contrast to N-learning, actively explores the creative potential of the lower regions of the I-Space and the nonlinear phenomena therein.

---

[10] J. Schumpeter, *The Theory of Economic Development: An Inquiry into Profits, Capital, Credit, Interest and the Business Cycle*, London: Oxford University Press, 1961 (1934).

Nonlinear phenomena are inherently hard to codify, and for that reason occupy the lower regions of the I-Space. If, as we have suggested, the world is for the most part nonlinear, then we must conclude that it, too, for the most part occupies the lower regions of the I-Space. The upper regions of the space, the realm of codifications and abstractions, then becomes little more than the repository of our episodic and tentative attempts at structuring, at extracting information from a recalcitrant world. Seen in this way, we have no reason to suppose that our codified and abstract constructions can ever free themselves sufficiently of systematic error to act as anything more than a fragile scaffolding for our daily lives.

An agent who acts as if the SLC moves beyond region C and then down and across the I-Space towards region D is making assumptions about the nature of learning and knowledge that differ significantly from those that prevail in orthodox economic thinking. Structured knowledge that has been diffused gets absorbed and impacted in a wide and possibly unpredictable variety of new situations. It may then be tentatively applied to the identification of dimly apprehended opportunities or threats, and this in areas where outcomes cannot simply be extrapolated in a linear fashion from past experiences. In other words, codified and abstract knowledge, having diffused, is applied in new contexts and circumstances that themselves resist systematic articulation. It is thus subject to a wide variety of subjective interpretations, and the larger the population within which absorption and impacting takes place, the greater the cognitive variety that is thereby generated. Consider, for example, the fact that a McDonald's hamburger is variously perceived as a fast food in the USA, a highly desirable luxury item in many ex-socialist countries, a symbol of American cultural dominance in France, and a symptom of the globilization of markets by many business school academics,

As it moves into the lower region of the I-Space, therefore, the SLC encounters a range of interpretative schemes which either confirm or challenge the codes and abstract structures employed. Where these are confirmed, the process is equilibrating and after a while learning will come to a halt. We thus remain in the world of N-learning, a world in which codes and structures are internalized unproblematically. Where, however, the interpretative schemes used do not align with the chosen codes and structures, the process becomes disequilibrating and a source of discomfort and puzzlement for data-processing agents. They will then reject either the codes, the structures, or the interpretative schemes that they have been using. Alternatively, they may engage in scanning and problem-solving activities in an attempt to reconcile them, thus initiating a new round in the SLC. Existing schemes and patterns may be retained, but they will be juggled around until a better fit between codes, structures, and data is achieved.

By way of illustration, consider the USA's response to the Japanese challenge in the automobile sector. Throughout the 1960s, Japanese industry was perceived as a source of cheap, low-quality imitations competing on price.

Figures on the competitive performance of Japanese automobile manufacturers in the 1970s, however, led to a major revision of schemes used to assess their strength as potential competitors. Some schemes were abandoned altogether, others profoundly modified. Either way, the change process initiated by the figures was long and painful.[11] The outcome was a shift in the paradigms that had hitherto been used by US and European automobile manufacturers to organize production: from a mass-production orientation that aimed at 'good enough' levels of defects, inventories, and product variety, to a lean production orientation that aimed at perfection—i.e., zero defects, zero inventories, endless product variety, all within a framework of continually declining costs. Out of this process of revision and modification, important new knowledge was created, and existing knowledge, both structured and tacit, was modified or discarded. We label the process 'creative destruction' because it operates at a high level of uncertainty in the sense that probability distributions cannot be specified a priori for the range of outcomes that it might produce.

Given the above remarks on the absorption and impacting phases of the SLC, how are we to think of knowledge sharing? Is the diffusion of codified knowledge equilibrating—as assumed by neoclassical economists—or is it in fact disequilibrating? The answer to the question turns on one's conception of what is knowledge and what is information. To a neoclassical economist, for example, the sharing of information such as is contained in prices is, in principle, equilibrating, and the larger the number of market players that are in possession of the market price at a given moment in time, the more easily equilibrating mechanisms can do their work. What is disequilibrating in this view is the asymmetric possession of price information—i.e., some players knowing the price and others not. Yet, even here, the forces of equilibration will eventually come into play, providing a sufficient number of players are in possession of the relevant market information.

For shared knowledge to be equilibrating, economists are required to make two crucial assumptions, one of which they are aware of, the other usually not. The first is that economic agents all exhibit rationality in the way they handle the information they receive. This assumption has been much criticized on the basis of recent research. The computational powers available to agents for dealing with complex data-processing tasks turn out to be quite limited[12] and this frequently leads them to make decisions which are irrational. Bluntly stated, over a wide range of activities few real world agents can actually chew gum and walk at the same time. Individual responses to new information, therefore, are not fully predictable. Yet this is not fatal to the

[11] J. Womack, D. Jones, and D. Roos, *The Machine that Changed the World: The Story of Lean Production*, New York, Harper Collins, 1991.

[12] H. Simon, 'The Logic of Heuristic Decision Making', in Rescher (ed.) *The Logic of Decision and Action*, Pittsburgh: University of Pittsburgh Press, 1967, pp. 1–20, reprinted in H. Simon, *Models of Discovery*, Dordrecht, Holland: D. Reidel Publishing Co., 1977; D. Kahneman, P. Slovic, and A. Tversky (eds), *Judgement under Uncertainty: Heuristics and Biases*, Cambridge: Cambridge University Press, 1982.

assumption of rationality providing that the computational errors that agents are prone to are not biased in one direction rather than another—i.e., they are not systematic—when averaged over all players. Recall that it is systematic errors that compromise efficient market outcomes.

Enter the second assumption that economists make concerning the diffu-sion of information. In Chapter 3 we described knowledge as dispositional, that is, as a set of probability distributions that we apply to events. New information modifies these probability distributions and hence modifies our knowledge base. The nature of the modification is largely dependent on the schemata by means of which information will be interpreted, that is, on the shape of the probability distributions held by data-processing agents prior to the reception of new information. The crucial assumption made by orthodox economists is that *new information biases interpretative schemata of different agents in the same direction.* How reasonable is this assumption?

In many cases, interpretative schemata will themselves be quite codified and abstract and will thus lend themselves to quite manageable computational processes. Such is the case, for example, with many problems in Bayesian statistics. Here, over time, we might well expect some convergence of different interpretative schemata, as computational outcomes are shared, compared, and adjusted. Yet the further down the I-Space we travel and the more concrete and richly textured our computational task, the more implicit, complex, and varied the knowledge that we draw upon in carrying out interpretations. Not only is such 'contextual' knowledge more diverse, but it is also harder to share and hence to subject to mutual adjustment.

In this second case it is much harder to believe that Bayesian processes can work their magic, and to the extent that the interpretation by agents of new information diverges, we are entitled to view such information as disequilibrating. Systematic differences in the interpretation of new information, each traceable to different implicit models of how the world works, now become possible. Differences in interpretation might be the product of differences in cognitive style, computational capacity, or individual circumstances. They often constitute a source of new insights and patterns and hence act to prolong the SLC beyond region C in the I-Space of Figure 5.1. What consequences flow from this?

One is that knowledge is more likely to be cumulative within a single interpretative scheme than across a number of such schemes. Where schemes structure and organize large tracts of knowledge we talk of paradigms and refer to moves from one scheme to another as paradigm shifts. The economic life of a given item of knowledge is likely to be limited by the life of the paradigms or interpretative schemes that it inhabits. When automobiles began to replace horses as a means of locomotion in the early twentieth century, for example, the craft of saddle-making retreated into niche markets and much technical knowledge that had been judged essential until then virtually disappeared. A single item of knowledge, however, may well find a place in several paradigms, although in each it will enjoy a different degree of utility. It may therefore be able to survive the demise of any one of its host paradigms providing that others are still available to accommodate it. Yet in such a case it can hardly be argued that the common possession of an item of knowledge or information has equilibrating effects or is determinate with respect to value.

A second consequence of prolonging the SLC beyond region C is that the economic life of a piece of knowledge is more likely to depend on the durability of the interpretative schemata with which it is associated than on that of the codes or structures through which it is articulated. By implication, where interpretative schemata are changing rapidly, the time available for extracting value is typically short. The limited life of existing knowledge assets in a regime of creative destruction, therefore, makes their continued retention and hoarding a highly dubious strategy. Such a strategy only really makes sense if one enjoys some measure of control over the speed of the industry level SLC that one faces.

Sometimes, of course, one does. When the existing knowledge assets used by an industry are highly integrated and complementary, new knowledge, even if superior and more productive, may yet fail to dislodge them. Existing assets then become 'locked-in'.[13] Think, for example, of the QWERTY keyboards on today's PCs and word processors. A problem encountered with early mechanical typewriters was the jamming together of typebars as an operator's speed increased. Christopher Scholes, the developer of what later became the first commercial typewriter, the Remington No. 1, experimented with various keyboard layouts in order to address the jamming problem. He discovered that the problem could be minimized by locating keys likely to be struck in quick succession on opposite sides of the keyboard. The resulting QWERTY layout is known to be suboptimal from an ergonomic point of view, and the shifts from mechanical to electronic typewriting has long made the jamming problem irrelevant. Yet it constitutes the foundation of all existing typing skills. The costs of giving up QWERTY for something more efficient have become human and institutional as well as technological: habits would have to be unlearned and retraining undertaken on a massive scale in moving to a new keyboard layout. Furthermore, whereas the bulk of benefits on offer from switching to some improved keyboard layout would benefit future generations, the bulk of the costs involved in doing so would be internalized by the current generation of QWERTY users. Here, the SLC is slowed down by the inertia of existing practice.[14]

Another example of industry-level lock-in blocking the progress of an SLC concerns high-speed trains. Magnetic levitation technology offers the prospects of ground speeds well in excess of what is achievable through wheel-on-rail technology. The railway infrastructure in place, however, is built around the wheel-on-rail system so magnetic levitation technology would

[13] W. Brian Arthur, 'Positive Feedbacks in the Economy', *Scientific American*, February, 1990.

[14] P. David, 'Clio and the Economics of "Qwerty"', *American Economic Review*, 75, May 1985, pp. 332–7.

have to offer quite disproportionate benefits to compensate for the extra costs involved in installing a brand new infrastructure. In this way, the prior diffusion of an inferior technology can sometimes block the emergence of a superior one.

In a regime of creative destruction, however, control by one or two firms of the industry-level SLC—one in which the agents populating the diffusion dimension of the I-Space are firms—is unlikely. Here, the best available strategy is to be among those who drive the industry level SLCs forward. Such cycles, although they involve the sharing of knowledge assets, may do so in ways that allow an innovating firm to retain its competitive advantage.

Consider, for example, Figure 5.2, which represents an industry-level I-Space with an SLC covering just a handful of players (i.e., firms) located towards the left on the diffusion dimension. How should we interpret such an SLC? At first glance it would appear that we are dealing with hoarding: new knowledge does not diffuse much beyond a handful of firms. Note, however, that absorbing and impacting still takes place and that knowledge assets, therefore, are still being renewed. Learning, although confined to a few, has not actually come to a halt. The knowledge sharing described in the diagram might cover a firm's key subcontractors and perhaps a number of 'lead users' among a firm's customers.[15]

A key issue for S-learners is exactly who to involve in the sharing of their knowledge assets, and how extensively to involve them. Compare Figures 5.2 and 5.3. In the latter figure we see a new SLC, indicated by a dotted line, operating to the right of the first. This second SLC is built on a selective diffusion of knowledge that is generated in the first. The knowledge so selected is diffused much more extensively in the second SLC than in the first. A firm or group of firms may well have good reasons to initiate such a controlled diffusion of its knowledge assets. For example:

1. To create industry standards that lock customers into their product range.
2. To build up interest and understanding among potential users, thus increasing demand. This sometimes requires extending the diffusion scale to the right in the I-Space by pushing existing knowledge out to new populations.
3. To collaborate with users in the absorption and impacting phases of their own SLCs and thus subsequently to participate in a more broadly based scanning activity. Deep cycles confined to the left of the I-Space sometimes suffer from 'parochialism' and a 'not-invented-here' (NIH) mentality.

Note that in Figure 5.3 the firm operates not with one but with two SLCs, one restricted to 'insiders'—i.e., firms such as suppliers and customers with whom the firm actively collaborates—and the other admitting 'outsiders'. Operating two SLCs is only worth doing if the restricted SLC can run more rapidly than the unrestricted one. If they are to derive any competitive advantage from

---

[15] E. von Hippel, *The Sources of Innovation*, Oxford: Oxford University Press, 1988.

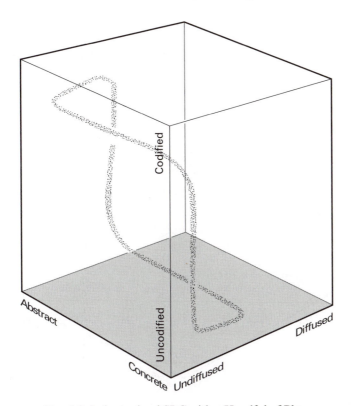

FIG. 5.2 Industry-level SLC with a Handful of Players

defining themselves as such, insiders must be capable of learning faster than outsiders.

5.5 TECHNOLOGY SYSTEMS

But will such 'fast learning' actually allow a firm to extract adequate value from its knowledge assets? Residence time in the maximum value region of the I-Space is likely to be much shorter in a fast-learning regime than in a slow-learning one, and cautionary tales abound of firms that have raced down their learning or experience curves into a state of profitless competition in which their every innovation or improvement is immediately matched by rivals. Japanese semiconductor manufacturers, for example, unwittingly became the victims of their own fast-learning strategies in the late 1980s. Many of them were only saved from going bust by the US government's insistence on putting a floor price underneath the two countries' trade in semiconductors.

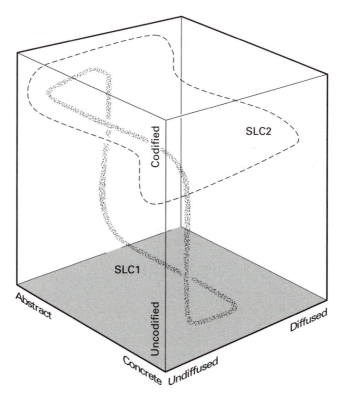

FIG. 5.3 Internal and External SLCs Operated by a Firm

Where the rate of imitation and the speed of diffusion of new knowledge in an industry are both faster than the rate at which an innovating firm can internalize the knowledge that it has helped to create in new applications—i.e., where the diffusion component of the SLC undermines the advantages to be had from investing in the absorption and impacting components—then control of the SLC is likely to shift to other players. Once more, the choice seems to reduce either to fast learning or to hoarding knowledge assets.

Under S-learning, however, calculations of the costs and benefits of different SLC strategies can no longer be based on the residence time of isolated knowledge components in the maximum value region of the I-Space. It must be based instead on the residence time of knowledge components that have been integrated into a technology system. This requires us to move from a portfolio to a systems view of knowledge assets.

To illustrate: where knowledge assets can be configured as a technology system, the latter's constituent technologies are interlinked, with the interfaces between them being either organizational or technological. In a job-shop production system, for example, the sequence of operations is mediated by individuals working to a schedule which is constantly being adjusted in response to organizational priorities. At one moment a particular order has to be rushed through, at another, inventories have to be reduced, and so on. Here, the linkage between the different technical operations is organizational. In an automated assembly line, by contrast, the sequence of operations is pretty much predetermined and mediated technologically by transfer machines. We shall discuss such systems in more detail in Chapter 8. What we must note here is that whenever technologies can be linked in this way, then as long as *some* of them can be located in the maximum value region of the I-Space, others can be allowed to migrate out of the region and diffuse to outsiders without compromising a firm's proprietary grip on its knowledge assets. Indeed, as we have just seen, if the technologies that are allowed to migrate towards the right in the I-Space are sufficiently useful to potential adopters located there *and* well attached to technologies that remain firmly located on the left in the space, then the overall value of the technology system might well increase since the diffused technologies can stimulate demand for those that remain as yet undiffused. This was, in part, the reasoning behind ATT's decision to license transistor technology freely to all-comers following the development of the transistor by Shockley, Bardeen, and Brattain at the Bell Labs in 1947.

The critical skill required to manage the systemic deployment of knowledge assets is systems integration. Sometimes it is achieved through modularization,[16] where what is codified and abstracted is the relationship or interface between technologies which themselves remain 'black boxes'. These may or may not be codified or abstract. Well-structured interfaces allow a rapid diffusion of technologies without necessarily giving potential adopters access to them. Automobile assemblers, for example, use modularization to maintain their control of the system integration component of the manufacturing process while decentralizing much technological development to first-line subcontractors. These can develop proprietary technologies for their respective subsystems—electrical, cooling, braking, etc.—and have these treated as black boxes within the larger system. As long as all work to standardized—i.e., well-codified and generic—interfaces so that the different subsystems fit well together in the final assembly, no one need be threatened by technology leakages.

At other times, integration calls for tacit skills that are hard for outsiders to imitate even if the system components being integrated are themselves quite accessible. The integrated know-how that goes into creating an outstanding yet complex building—for example Utzon's Sydney Opera House or Pei's Bank of China building in Hong Kong—has this tacit quality.

In sum, what is selectively shared in an S-learning regime is either knowledge at the component level or knowledge at the level of linkages between

---

[16] R. Sanchez, 'Strategic Flexibility, Firm Organization and Managerial Work in Dynamic Markets: A Strategic Options Perspective', *Advances in Strategic Management*, 9, 1993, pp. 251–91.

components—i.e., their architecture (see Figures 5.4(a) and 5.4(b)). If both are shared, then either one has to be an exceptionally fast learner to retain a competitive advantage with respect to the knowledge assets that one has created, or one loses control of them. In the latter case, the centre of gravity of the knowledge system as a whole begins to drift away from the maximum value region as it begins to diffuse—unless, of course, other players pull it back into that region.

The judicious management of a knowledge system, therefore, requires a strategic sense of when to invest in selected knowledge assets in order to steer them towards the maximum value region and when to let go of those that are already there. For what is actually being maximized in a knowledge system, is the *throughput* in the maximum value region, not the residence time of any single knowledge asset taken in isolation. Effectively managed, however, such a system should be able to maintain its centre of gravity in close proximity to the maximum value region of the I-Space, no matter how rapidly its constituent elements pass through it. S-learning strategies thus require a systemic approach to the management of knowledge assets. In contrast to N-learning strategies that seek to block the effects of the passage of time, S-learning strategies positively thrive on them. The former pursue monopoly rents based on a portfolio approach to their knowledge assets. They treat such assets atomistically, trying to maximize the residential time of individual technologies in the maximum value region. The latter, by focusing on the average residential time in that region of knowledge assets configured into an integrated system, are quite happy to see individual assets moving out of that region providing that this has the effect of accelerating the SLC to the benefit of the system as a whole.

5.6 THE LINK TO INDUSTRY EVOLUTION

In the preceding section we suggested that whereas in some cases a firm could exert some control over the speed and shape of an industry-level SLC, in others it would have to adapt itself to the realities of the industry's characteristic learning processes. Which case applies will depend on the structure of the industry in question and where the firm finds itself within that structure. Some industries—oil, power, generation, air transport, etc.—are highly concentrated, with economies of scale and high barriers to entry conferring on a few privileged players the power effectively to control the industry SLC. Others, by contrast, are highly fragmented and competitive, and few players have the possibility of controlling the shape of the industry SLC. It is often assumed that industry concentration is a consequence of industry maturity. This is not necessarily the case. Many mature industries, such as the building industry, are highly fragmented, whereas some emerging industries—e.g., aerospace— are characterized by above average degrees of concentration.

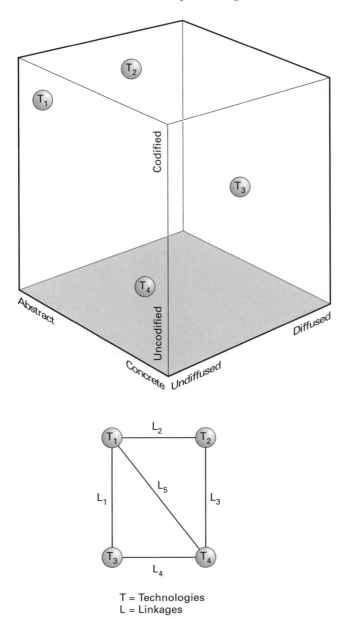

T = Technologies
L = Linkages

FIG. 5.4(a) Locating Technologies in the I-Space

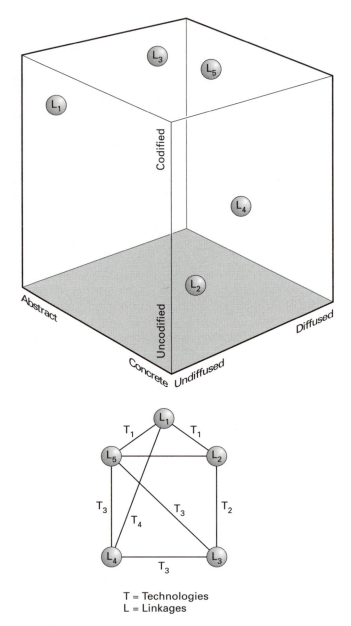

T = Technologies
L = Linkages

FIG. 5.4(b) Locating Linkages between Technologies in the I-Space

The scope for profitably investing in the creation of knowledge assets and one's choice of strategy for doing so—whether oriented towards N- or S-learning—are both strongly dependent on the nature of the learning environment associated with different types of industry structures, as well as on the specific configuration of their respective knowledge bases in the I-Space.

Not all types of knowledge assets can be tightly integrated into systems. The knowledge assets held by, say, a major university in the form of faculty and research facilities, for example, or those held by a large hospital, do not easily lend themselves to system-like configurations. In these cases, therefore, it may make more sense to treat them as discrete elements in a portfolio. Nor are all SLCs necessarily harbingers of creative destruction. The choice to be made between an N-learning and an S-learning approach to the strategic management of knowledge assets, then, depends on the specific characteristics of an industry's knowledge base as well as on the shape and dynamic properties of its SLCs.

Technology-based knowledge assets, for instance, can often be located on an SLC as a function of where they are in their life cycle. Emerging technologies retain many degrees of freedom, reflecting the fact that many choices concerning standards and performance requirements remain as yet provisional. This is why these technologies are initially located in the lower region of the I-Space. Where they cluster around a single new product, they may, after a while, become codified and integrated into a single dominant design,[17] which, while possibly suboptimal, reflects a complex interplay of competing stakeholders' interests and historical circumstances. The stabilization of automobile design in the early decades of the twentieth century, for example, triggered a massive investment in co-specialized assets such as freeways, petrol stations, car parks, garages, etc. Each of those assets is supported by one or more lobbies with a strong stake in limiting design variations to minor improvements. As already seen, then, a dominant design enjoys a certain inertia that will make it hard to modify radically once it comes into existence.

Clearly, a firm's ability to influence the evolution of a technology will depend, first, on the latter's location on the SLC at the time the firm encounters it—this will partly reflect the technology's progress through its own life cycle—and second, on the firm's technical capacity for exerting leadership within the industry—as expressed by its own overall location on the industry-level diffusion scale in the I-Space. A firm located far to the right on the scale, for example, is less well placed to leverage its knowledge assets than one located well to the left.

A firm's influence will also depend on the shape and speed of industry-level SLCs in which it participates. As already mentioned, these will vary from industry to industry. Choosing between an N-learning and an S-learning orientation, therefore, requires a two-step analysis:

---

[17] J. Utterback, *Mastering the Dynamics of Innovation*, Cambridge, Mass: Harvard University Press, 1994.

1. Locate the knowledge assets critical to the industry as well as the linkages
   between them in the I-Space. It is important that knowledge assets and the
   links that facilitate their integration be recorded separately in the I-Space.
   Knowing how to link individual knowledge assets together, and thus to
   integrate them, also counts as a knowledge asset and needs to be represented as an independent point in the space as indicated in Figures 5.4(a)
   and 5.4(b).
2. Assess the shape and speed of the industry-level SLC as it applies to each
   of the critical knowledge assets and to the linkages between them.

These two steps may require a fair bit of analysis and deliberation. Chapter
10 illustrates the process in the case of two firms, albeit schematically for the
second step.

It might be anticipated that where the industry-level SLC is slow and its trajectory confined to the left of the I-Space, and where the industry is characterized by a high degree of fragmentation, the residence time of knowledge
assets in the maximum value region of the space may well be sufficiently long
to justify a hoarding strategy. With a slow-acting SLC, the rate of throughput in the maximum value region may not deliver a sufficient volume of
knowledge assets for value extraction, so that even if these are tightly integrated into systems, the firm could find itself giving away too much too fast
and at too little profit to itself. Some technology transfer operations carried
out by large firms in emerging markets turn out to be profitless for this reason. In such circumstances, the returns to the incremental accumulation and
internal deployment of knowledge assets are likely to exceed those to be had
from sharing them. An N-learning strategy would then be appropriate.

Industrial fragmentation makes the building of common industry standards costly and hazardous, and in the absence of such standards market
shares are likely to remain modest. Pursuing a fast S-learning strategy in a
slowly evolving and fragmented industrial environment runs the danger of
squandering knowledge assets. Neither the residential time nor the throughput in the maximum value region allow for a full recovery of the investment
in learning.

Where, by contrast, an industry-level SLC is fast-moving and spreads right
across the diffusion scale, a hoarding strategy runs the danger of starving a
firm's internal SLC—the one that places its own employees along the diffusion scale—of essential nutrients. Information and knowledge may still flow
rapidly and extensively inside the firm, but it will be increasingly stale stuff,
robbing the firm of the cognitive vitality required to stay competitive. Stale
knowledge assets may remain undiffused under a hoarding strategy, but they
will rapidly come to lose their utility relative to competing alternatives, and
hence their value to the firm. After a while they atrophy and get dislodged
from the I-Space altogether.

5.7 SOME CURRENT INDUSTRY TRENDS

Industries evolve and so do the characteristics of industry-level SLCs. We can illustrate this by returning to one of our earlier examples. In the early 1980s, IBM, believing itself to be in an environment that favoured N-learning, carefully hoarded its knowledge assets. The arrival of low-cost, user-friendly personal computers greatly extended the size of the population that clamoured for computer knowledge as well as access to machines. The relevant industry-level SLC underwent a change of shape. From a tall one located on the left of the I-Space which allowed players to pursue their learning in a controlled fashion and at a leisurely pace behind barriers to diffusion, it changed into a flat one spread across the diffusion scale in the upper region of the I-Space. IBM failed to adapt to the kind of learning implied by the new SLC. The two different types of SLC are shown in Figure 5.5.

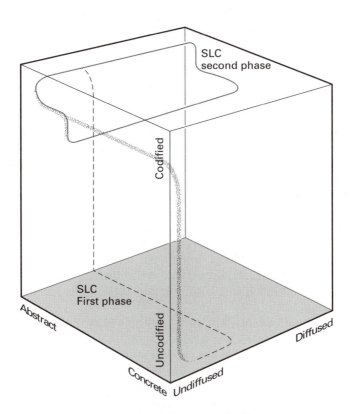

FIG. 5.5 The SLC Changes its Shape

Because the second type of SLC is located in the upper reaches of the I-Space, diffusion and scanning processes are highly structured and very rapid—too rapid, perhaps, to allow the kind of reflective activities associated with S-learning to take root. Recall that S-learning is the fruit of an absorption and impacting process which allows for alternative interpretations of structured data. Competing patterns emerge from this 'reflective' activity, some of which, if further developed, might lead to radically new and potentially valuable technological, scientific, or managerial insights.

A rapid SLC operating in the upper regions of the I-Space, however, does not allow enough time for this much slower interpretative activity to take place. Such an SLC typifies the kind of learning that develops in an industry following the emergence of a dominant design. By then, many degrees of freedom have been eliminated through the establishment of industry-wide technical standards so that the highest returns available to investments in learning favour a quick succession of incremental, well-structured, and rapidly diffusible improvements. Post-dominant design, moving down the I-Space to explore alternative patterns and paradigms, threatens a destruction of the industry incumbents' existing knowledge base. There will thus be few takers within the industry itself for a major investment in the absorption and impacting phases of the SLC. If and when such investment does occur, it is usually the work of new entrants coming in from outside the industry with a quite different approach to its problems. The threat posed to Swiss manufacturers of mechanical watches by Japanese electronic firms in the late 1970s readily springs to mind as an example. The Swiss had their strength in watch segments based on older mechanical technologies. Their market shares for watches incorporating the new electronic technologies were much lower. When electronic watches gained rapid and widespread acceptance, Swiss manufacturers found themselves at a disadvantage against the Japanese, who had invested heavily in the new technologies and therefore had the edge.

We conclude that flat cycles spread across the top of the I-Space may reflect N-learning strategies no less than deep ones occurring on the left of the space. Both pass through the maximum value of the I-Space, but whereas the first maximizes its residence time in the zone by slowing down the SLC and blocking the diffusion of knowledge assets, the second mimics the S-learning approach and maximizes its throughput in the zone by carrying out a rapid succession of small, incremental, and rapidly diffusible improvements to the knowledge base.

Both N-learning variants, however—and this is the point—take an equilibrium condition to mark the termination of the learning process. There comes a time when knowledge has become totally structured and diffused so that no further learning is possible. The returns to codification and abstraction then disappear, as does the time available for absorption and impacting. Yet, whereas the first type of N-learning responds to the threat of equilibrium and the consequent loss of rents by trying to slow down the SLC and prevent it spreading towards the right in the I-Space, the second exploits opportunities for generating incremental rents on the approach to equilibrium. In contrast to S-learning, however, the second type of N-learning shuns all investments in absorption and impacting. Both N-learning variants are responding to a rightward shift in the centre of gravity of the industry's knowledge base along the diffusion curve as the industry evolves.

Where does a throughput-maximizing N-learning strategy—the second variant—leave S-learning? We have already suggested that S-learning is both a generator and a beneficiary of cognitive diversity, of alternative and often competing conceptions of how the world works. S-learning builds upon the absorption and impacting phases of the SLC, phases in which codified abstract knowledge is first internalized and then applied in a variety of concrete situations. The trajectory followed by S-learning strategies has the effect of periodically and deliberately moving knowledge assets *away* from the maximum value zone in the I-Space and thus of temporarily reducing their attractiveness as an investment proposition. This has to be counted as a cost of S-learning strategies. The increase in uncertainty entailed by moving down the I-Space, taken together with the lack of appropriability of the resulting insights when they arise from the interactions of many industry players, inevitably reduces the short-term pay-off to investing in this phase of the SLC.

Investment, when it occurs, then, takes two different forms: first, the form of government subsidies to industry research consortia such as SEMATEC or JESSI; second, the form of industry outsiders who are not yet located in the industry-level I-Space and who therefore remain unconstrained by the prevailing valuations of existing knowledge assets. The first approach rarely takes one very far down the I-Space, since it usually involves players committed to preserving and reinforcing existing technology paradigms. It seeks to create without destroying. The second, by contrast, can be quite unpredictable, since outsiders often have no commitment to an industry's existing investment in knowledge assets. One of the reasons, for example, that new entrants ended up dominating the semiconductor industry following the development of the transistor was that incumbents were too committed to their existing valve technologies—for which they viewed the transistor as a replacement—to respond adequately to the new opportunities that presented themselves.

In practice, no firm can afford the single-minded pursuit of either an N-learning or an S-learning strategy. The first strategy would lead it into an excessively ordered regime in the north-west corner of the I-Space and sooner or later to a fossilization of its knowledge assets. These would go on being hoarded and squeezed for all they were worth long after they had passed their 'sell-by' date. The second strategy would lead the firm aimlessly to explore the chaotic regime of the south-east corner of the I-Space until it disintegrated as an identifiable entity. Life at the edge of chaos is always being pulled in opposite directions simultaneously, towards the mortifying security of excessive order and fossilization on the one hand, and towards the exciting uncertainties of excessive disorder and disintegration on the other. As learning entities, firms are subject to the same tensions.

James March makes a useful distinction between exploratory and exploitative learning.[18] Exploratory learning generates variety and, with it, uncertainty. It creates options that allow the acts of selection and commitment associated with codification and abstraction to be postponed. Such learning tends to be naturally playful and unconcerned with efficiency considerations. Exploitative learning, by contrast, pursues efficient outcomes. It exercises options, and, in so doing, eliminates variety and choice.[19] It reduces uncertainty through successive acts of codification and abstraction.

Clearly, the first type of learning will gradually move us towards the lower region of the I-Space, and the second towards the upper region. Yet, whereas the second corresponds directly to what we have labelled N-learning—it will gradually flatten the SLC, as in Figure 5.5(b)—S-learning requires a blend of exploratory *and* exploitative learning, as well as an ability to balance out the claims of each. S-learning thus incorporates a measure of N-learning as a subsidiary process. It is, for this reason, inherently more complex than N-learning and requires a distinctive culture for its operation, one that is capable of profiting simultaneously from the certainties that it manages to attain as well as from the uncertainties that it still confronts. In effect, S-learning requires the fostering of what we might label an 'edge of chaos' culture. We discuss the role played by culture—corporate, industrial, and national—in shaping the operations of SLCs and the evolution of knowledge assets in the next chapter.

---

[18] March draws his inspiration from Holland 1975. See J. March 'Exploration and Exploitation in Organizational Learning', *Organization Studies*, 2 (1), February, 1991; J. Holland, *Adaptation in Natural and Artificial Systems*, Cambridge, Mass: MIT Press, 1975.

[19] R. Sanchez, 'Strategic Flexibility'.

6

Culture as a Knowledge Asset

6.1 INTRODUCTION

TECHNOLOGY has been treated by many anthropologists as an extension of culture. Each in its own way, in so far that it has an enabling function and yields useful services can be considered an asset. And since each also embodies socially validated and useful knowledge, it can be classed as a knowledge asset. The proposition has perhaps been more visible, and hence more readily convincing, in the case of technology than in that of culture. Much of what we call technology is knowledge physically embodied in objects that you can touch or physically manipulate. You flick a switch and a lamp bulb lights up. You are dimly aware that a great deal of knowledge concerning electron flows has gone into establishing that effect. Or again, you gently push down on the accelerator and your vehicle moves forward, an outcome that would be unthinkable without a deep knowledge of the Carnot cycle.

The case of culture, by contrast, is more problematic. Only a small part of what we call cultural knowledge gets itself embedded in technologies and artefacts. A large part is embodied in social processes, institutional practices, and traditions, many of which are carried around in people's heads. For this reason most cultural knowledge has tended to be taken for granted rather than treated as an asset to be prized and exploited. At best, it is perceived to be behaviourally useful knowledge. When, for example, do we order a white wine with our meal and when a red one? What is the appropriate dress code for a wedding? At what point in a developing business relationship is a Frenchman likely to switch from the *vous* form of address to the less formal *tu*? In what circumstances should an agreement be committed to paper? When would it be offensive to do so? Knowing how to answer such questions, to be sure, provides an essential lubricant for what are often quite unconscious cultural processes. Such knowledge, however, is viewed as having but a limited reach.

In recent years our appreciation of culture as a knowledge asset has undergone a transformation. The rise of Japan as a world-class competitor over the last three decades has brought home to Western managers that much of the managerial and technical knowledge that they have taken to be universal in its application is often in fact specific to a culture and draws on deeply rooted and value-laden assumptions of how organizations and institutions function. It can be adopted—and, indeed, sometimes improved upon—but only with a considerable prior investment in cross-cultural understanding and adaptation.

Culture operates at many levels of aggregation. We can talk of the culture of a group, of a firm, of an industry or a profession, of a region, of a country, or even of a group of countries. Yet at whatever level we choose to define it—national, regional, industrial, or corporate—culture remains the means by which non-genetic information is transmitted either within a given generation of agents or from one generation to the next. Technological practice forms an integral part of such cultural transmission. But technological practice usually combines theoretical knowledge that may itself be pretty well universal in scope with more practical knowledge that is often much more local and culture-specific in its application.

Take, for example, the case of just-in-time production (JIT) systems. Their basic principles as inventory-minimizing devices and their signalling function are not hard to grasp and have been described in any number of operations-management texts. Yet their effective implementation rests on a number of specific cultural and institutional practices as well as submerged assumptions about how organizations function. These are much more elusive to grasp and difficult to manipulate or change. One such assumption concerns relationships with suppliers. The arm's length contractual relationship between purchaser and supplier promoted by competitive market cultures often does not allow the growth of exclusive and collaborative trusting relationships that are essential to a proper application of the JIT concept.

In JIT, loosely coupled relationships are converted into tightly coupled ones as inventories and cycle times are reduced. This has the effect of intensifying the coordination that is required across organizational boundaries well beyond what can be handled by arm's length market relationships. The interorganizational relationships associated with JIT reflect the institutional and organizational practices specific to a culture. They are partly the product of a life-long socialization process, and do not travel nearly as well as the concept themselves. Many US firms which in the 1980s turned to JIT as a universally applicable technique, for example, only discovered the hidden layers of cultural knowledge required to make it work after they themselves had failed to do so. In some cases relationships with suppliers were too adversarial for trust and collaboration to flourish. In other cases it was the firm's own workforce that turned out to be distrustful of management—sometimes with good reason—and uncooperative.[1] Blinded by the highly visible knowledge assets associated with JIT, they had failed to spot the less visible but no less essential ones that lurked in the penumbra. These were not only harder to detect; they were also much harder to adopt.

The Western bias towards classifying as knowledge only that which can be given a codified and abstract formulation has led knowledge assets—whether embodied in physical objects such as plant and machinery, or in organizational practices such as planning and budgeting systems—to be treated as if

---

[1] J. Womack and D. Jones, *Lean Thinking*, New York: Simon and Schuster, 1996.

they were essentially technological in nature. They are not. *They are first and foremost cultural and only then technological.* The potential value of a knowledge asset is largely a function of how it is used and in what context. A proper understanding of context, social or otherwise, is thus essential to the proper application of technique.[2]

To illustrate: the Chinese have a long-established craft tradition in fine porcelain. In the early 1980s, as the country opened up to commercial relations with Western economies, a number of Chinese collective enterprises manufacturing porcelain sought to act as subcontractors to Western firms. Responding to a solicitation from a Jiangsu-based collective enterprise, one British firm from the Potteries in Staffordshire shipped a sample plate design to China to be reproduced three hundred times. Unfortunately, unnoticed by the British firm, the sample had a fine hairline crack that had spread from one edge of the plate to its centre. Back came three hundred plates with the design beautifully reproduced—along with the hairline crack, which had unwittingly been taken as forming part of the design.

As the example suggests, knowledge assets not only vary in the discretion they allow when applied, but also in how that discretion is interpreted. The discretion available is a function of the degrees of freedom that characterize a knowledge asset. The degrees of freedom allowed by the simple on/off operation of a light switch, for example, are fewer than those allowed by the use of a hammer—one of the reasons why hammers are more likely to end up as the focus of creative brainstorming exercises than light switches.

The higher the degrees of freedom associated with a knowledge asset, then, the greater is the scope for its evolution and application to be shaped by cultural preferences. In the case of knowledge assets embodied in physical products, the degrees of freedom available for the expression of cultural preferences will be greater prior to the emergence of a dominant design—where this occurs—than subsequently. If cultural preferences do change following its emergence—by the early years of the twenty-first century, a large-scale switch by consumers away from PCs and towards so-called network computers that process data within the network itself rather than at terminals could provide an interesting example of such a preference change—the knowledge assets involved may be too committed to the earlier preferences to survive the transition. They may in effect be too culture-specific. They then have to be discarded rather than adapted.

This chapter builds on the premiss that it does not make much sense to talk of knowledge assets independently of the cultures in which they are embedded. It takes culture as operating through institutional structures that must themselves be considered knowledge assets. Over time, culture shapes these institutional structures and is in turn shaped by them. Cultures and institutions, then, exert a reciprocal influence on each other through the actions of SLCs.

---

[2] W. Bijker, T. Hughes, and T. Pinch, *The Social Construction of Technological Systems: New Directions in the Sociology and History of Technology*, Cambridge, Mass: MIT Press, 1987.

In the next section (6.2) we look at how different types of cultural action and cultural orientations to action can shape the evolution and exploitation of knowledge assets. In section 6.3 we interpret cultural actions and orientations in I-Space terms; this allows the discourses on technology and those on culture to be reconciled within a single conceptual framework. In section 6.4 we show how information flows in the I-Space give rise to different types of institutional structures, and in sections 6.5 and 6.6 we examine the impact of cultural and institutional action first on the scope and then on the boundaries of firms. We discuss the implications of our investigation for the management of knowledge assets in the concluding section (6.7). We show how SLCs, by constantly redeploying knowledge assets within and between different types of institutions, effectively help to shape the evolution of the cultural order.

6.2 THE SOCIAL DIMENSION OF KNOWLEDGE ASSETS

The scope of a knowledge asset turns on how it is structured and shared among its potential users and producers. Structuring, by facilitating the diffusion of a knowledge asset, helps to expand the size of the information field within which it could be shared. The field itself is made up of data-processing agents susceptible to being 'oriented' by the reception of a relevant item of information.

As was seen in section 1.2, however, how far such information is structured through acts of codification and abstraction establishes the scope for embedding it in objects, in documents, or in the minds of data-processing agents. The nature of the embedding that occurs conditions the possibilities for the transmission and hence for the sharing of knowledge assets within a target population. The relationship between codification and abstraction, on the one hand, and diffusion, on the other, is thus mediated by the physical properties of the information storage and transmission media available.

All physical substrates are subject to physical decay and to the entropy law. Objects wear out, documents fade, agents—both human and organizational—go senile and die. Thus the storage of information and of knowledge assets is prey to the ravages of time. A second and related problem concerns the ability of knowledge assets to propagate across space. After all, cultural transmission has to be *spatio*-temporal if it is to have any discernible effect. An item of knowledge has to be internalized by contemporaries as well as by descendants before it can properly be considered cultural. Furthermore, the chances of it being internalized by descendants partly turns on how effectively it has been incorporated in the culture of contemporaries and then given some minimum level of stability. We can thus think of culture as a kind of collective memory whose spatio-temporal reach is determined by that of its biological and purely physical substrates.

Physical substrates for information vary in their storage and transmission properties. Properly maintained, a metallic object may last longer than a piece of paper, but beyond very small distances it is usually easier to mail a document than to move a piece of equipment made out of metal. It is also easier than dispatching an agent unless the type of knowledge being transmitted is hard to embody in equipment or to set down on paper—i.e., like artistic or craft-based know-how, it is highly concrete and uncodifiable.

Finally, some types of knowledge assets can transmit well over time but not at all in space. Their information content is deeply embedded in, and hence confined to a specific location and cannot travel at all. Some works of architecture have this quality. No photographs of the west portal of Chartres Cathedral or of the nave of Amiens Cathedral, for example, can ever fully replace the direct spatial experience of them. Verbal and written descriptions of these two works can, of course, refer to the experience, but they cannot replace it. Medieval cathedral builders located outside the Ile-de-France, the wellspring of the gothic style, were thus at a disadvantage when trying to capture and replicate the spirit of such works. They had to rely on the rough sketches and notes of travellers like Villard de Honnecourt, a master-architect from Cambrai, whose 'Album' became a codification of architectural idioms and motifs.[3] Yet what Villard and others like him could capture in their codification was thin gruel indeed compared to what is on offer *in situ*. Indeed, the further one travels away from the Ile-de-France and the more borders one crosses, the more the churches encountered appear as misinterpretations of the qualities to be found in those of the likes of Beauvais, Sens, Reims, and Notre-Dame.

The irreducibly local nature of some knowledge notwithstanding, the spatio-temporal reach of data flows has been greatly extended by the information revolution. In the last decades of the twentieth century, the physical capacity to store data has been expanded by several orders of magnitude through the development of silicon substrates. Likewise, the capacity to transmit data has been similarly extended by the ever more efficient exploitation of electromagnetic waves. And although in the architectural examples given above, the substrates used respectively for storage (i.e., stone) and transmission (i.e., paper or parchment) are not the same, the converging technologies of computation and telecommunication are today exerting a strong reciprocal influence on each other's development as well as on the possibilities of social information processing.

Cultural evolution is deeply affected by the technical means available for the social articulation and transmission of knowledge. Studies of early Babylonian society indicate that the development of writing led to a larger, more complex, and stratified social structure than what had hitherto prevailed. Control of the technology of writing, however, remained in the hands

---

[3] G. Henderson, *Gothic*, Middlesex: Penguin Books, 1967; E. Panofsky, *Gothic Architecture and Scholasticism*, Cleveland: The World Publishing Company, 1951.

of a priestly caste that could use it to consolidate its power base within the system. It was only with the advent of printing in the fifteenth century, based on the technology of movable type, that literacy and political power could spread to new social strata and that, partly as a consequence, the spatio-temporal reach of Western culture could extend beyond Western Europe.[4]

It is worth noting that movable type, in the absence of an alphabet that could exploit its flexibility, did not lead to the spread of printing technology. The Chinese, for example, had developed a simple movable type technology long before the West, but could not exploit it on account of the complexity and number of Chinese ideograms.[5] Ideograms differ from alphabets in their capacity for abstract reference. They tend to attach themselves to a large number of specific referents at the concrete end of our abstraction scale. In our own day, it is doubtful that information technology could have developed with the speed that it did had it not been possible to map the alphabet on to a binary code. Here again, the difficulties that confront the Japanese with their Chinese-derived characters in developing a competitive software industry are instructive.

6.3 TECHNOLOGY AS AN EXPRESSION OF CULTURE

There have been many definitions of culture of widely varying types. No matter how a definition is formulated, however, most would take the structuring and sharing of information within a population distributed across space and time as a central ingredient.[6] For this reason, the I-Space lends itself well to the study of cultural transmission. Here, the structuring of information is captured by the codification and abstraction dimensions of the I-Space, and the sharing of information is captured by the diffusion dimension. Central to the idea of using the I-Space in this way is the observation that cultures vary in their ability or propensity to structure knowledge and hence in their spatio-temporal reach. Something that will be ineffable within one culture, and thus remain the closely guarded property of a small esoteric group, might well be a codified commonplace readily available to all within another. The cultural codes available to data-processing agents, then, will help to demarcate regions of knowledge that will be asymmetrically distributed within a population from those that will be more evenly distributed. Where information asymmetries are strong, the resulting discontinuities will sometimes spawn

    [4] J. Goody, *The Interface between the Written and the Oral*, Cambridge: Cambridge University Press, 1987.
    [5] Ibid.; C. Ronan and J. Needham, *The Shorter Science and Civilisation in China*, Cambridge: Cambridge University Press, 1978.
    [6] A. Kroeber and C. Kluckhohn, *Culture: A Critical Review of Concepts and Definitions*, Papers of the Peabody Museum of American Archeology and Ethnology, Vol. 47, Cambridge, Mass: Harvard University Press, 1952, p. 181; M. Douglas, *Natural Symbols: Explorations in Cosmology*, Middlesex: Penguin Books, 1973; E. Hall, *Beyond Culture*, New York: Doubleday, 1976; M. Boisot, *Information and Organization: The Manager as Anthropologist*, London: Harper and Collins, 1994.

distinctive subcultures, each of which might usefully give rise to its own independent I-Space representation. Why so?

Recall that the population of data-processing agents to be located along the diffusion dimension must be specified prior to any analysis. This is not as straightforward as it might seem. A population of employees within a firm, for example, would focus the analysis on corporate culture, whereas a population of firms within an industry would orient it towards industrial culture. In each case, a separate I-Space would need to be constructed. Yet individual agents typically have multiple affiliations—to family, work colleagues, clubs, charitable organizations, etc.—and are therefore subject to multiple cultural influences that interact and overlie each other. In effect, they operate in a number of overlapping information fields.

Selecting a population of agents that exhibits a coherent pattern of cultural behaviour is therefore not always as easy as it might appear. It is easier where clear boundaries can be drawn around a population than where they cannot. Such boundaries should ideally mark critical discontinuities in the information flows that shape the actions of agents, whether these be individuals, firms, or other data-processing entities. Discontinuities arise where the density of information flows tails off in such a way that distinct groupings begin to form within a population. Communications within groups of agents then become both more frequent and more intense than across groups.[7]

Nation-states, for example, often deliberately create such discontinuities at their borders in order to foster a sense of cultural identity among their citizens. Language, laws, currencies, traditions, and institutional practices will thus differ on either side of a national border. Firms do likewise. Here, language, laws, and currency may or may not vary as one crosses different boundaries within the firm—they will do so in the case of an international firm but not in the case of a domestic one—but, technologies, institutional practices, traditions, and internal regulations will differ from one firm to the next, giving rise to distinctive corporate cultures.

Differences in corporate culture will not always be as strong as differences in national cultures,[8] but they may nonetheless be important enough to offer a firm a differential advantage in the accumulation of knowledge assets. Drawing a boundary around a firm for the purposes of cultural analysis, however, remains problematic. Do we, for example, take the *organizational* boundary to be coextensive with the *corporate* boundary as defined by the population of employees? What about the subcontractors, suppliers, and customers, with whom the firm may be collaborating? Studies of Japanese subcontracting practices strongly suggest that the organizational reach of a corporate culture may extend well beyond the firm's legal boundaries,

---

[7] K. Deutch, *The Nerves of Government: Models of Political Communication and Control*, New York: Free Press, 1966; T. Allen, *Managing the Flow of Technology: Technology Transfer and the Dissemination of Technological Information within the R and D Organization*, Cambridge, Mass: MIT Press, 1977.

[8] G. Hofstede, *Culture's Consequences: International Differences in Work-Related Values*, Beverley Hills: Sage Publications, 1980.

allowing it to impose its procedures and ways of doing things to external agents as if they were insiders. Indeed, much of the current interest in outsourcing and downsizing implicitly builds upon the possibility of leveraging an organization's culture so as to allow it to exert influence beyond its boundaries. Where this happens, the critical discontinuities that shape the distribution of knowledge assets will not necessarily occur at the firm's own boundaries, but rather at those of an organized grouping of firms or other entities.

At whatever level of social aggregation they take place, where discontinuities in knowledge flows exhibit stability and robustness they become candidates for institutionalization. The way that knowledge assets distribute themselves in the I-Space, and the trajectories of the SLCs that bring them into being, are both profoundly affected by cultural considerations and by how these are expressed in stable institutional structures. We examine these structures next.

6.4 CULTURES AND INSTITUTIONS IN THE I-SPACE

Information flows, in their disembodied form, are not particularly well suited to the analysis of cultural action. They are hard to capture and too complex to make sense of. We need a framework that helps us to classify and interpret them, even if crudely. It turns out that one is ready to hand. It will need some adaptation, though, and will have to be used with care.

Following the lead given by the new institutional economics, we shall take the *transaction* as our unit of analysis.[9] For our purposes, a transaction can be thought of as any act of social exchange that depends on information flows for its accomplishment. Transactions can be as simple and brief as the purchase of a packet of cigarettes, or as complex and extended as those which bind a Zen master to his disciples. Like institutional economists, we are interested in the relationship that can be established between different transactional characteristics and the phenomenon of institutionalization. Our use of the term transaction, however, will extend beyond that of institutional economics where the focus has tended to be primarily on transaction costs and efficiency considerations. These, to be sure, are relevant. But, as we shall see, they are not the whole story.[10]

Transactions vary in their information requirements as well as in the cultural circumstances in which they occur. The purchase of a packet of cigarettes, for example, may require little more than a knowledge of the brand and the price, whereas the effectiveness of a transaction between a Zen

---

[9] O. Williamson, *Markets and Hierarchies: Analysis and Antitrust Implications*, Glencoe: The Free Press, 1975; *The Economic Institutions of Capitalism: Firms, Markets, Relational Contracting*, New York: The Free Press, 1985.

[10] M. Granovetter, 'Economic Action and Social Structure: The Problem of Embeddedness', *American Journal of Sociology*, 91, 1985.

master and his disciples may require that the parties be intimately acquainted and possess extensive idiosyncratic knowledge of each other's personal foibles and character traits.

Economic and social organizations are indeed concerned to reduce the cost of transacting, as transaction cost economists have argued.[11] One way of doing this is to economize on the data-processing and transmission costs associated with a given transaction. This in turn can be achieved through two distinct strategies. The first, we have already identified. It consists of moving the transaction away from the origin in the I-Space and along the codification and abstraction scales in order to reduce the volume of data that one has to deal with. Lower volumes of data to be processed will reduce both data-processing and data-transmission time. Yet moving along the scales is only feasible if there exists enough understanding of transactional issues to shed data surplus to requirements without losing essential information. If codification and abstraction are carried out prematurely, that is, in the absence of such understanding, the effectiveness of the transaction will be undermined. Transactional efficiency and economy are then purchased at too high a price.

The second strategy economizes on transaction costs without necessarily relocating the transaction in the I-Space. Instead of trying to modify the information characteristics of the transaction, it creates a transactional infrastructure that takes such characteristics as a given and secures economies in exchange by exploiting scale effects. When transactions of a particular type reach a certain volume, an effort is then made to give them a stable structure and to institutionalize them. The existence of such structures will lower the marginal cost of transacting in a particular region of the I-Space and make the returns on transactions in that region attractive relative to alternative locations.

Figure 6.1 identifies four different types of transaction in the I-Space, each of which, if it becomes central to a culture, is capable of giving rise to a distinctive institutional order. In Table 6.1 we list some of the cultural characteristics associated with each type of transaction. Each will now be discussed in terms of the information environment required to make it function.

Let us initiate our discussion by returning to the purchase of a packet of cigarettes. What can we say about the information environment or about the social relationships involved in purchasing a packet of cigarettes?[12] The first point to make is that the transaction draws heavily on public knowledge that is both well codified, abstract, and diffused. A packet of Marlboros is understood to contain twenty cigarettes of a certain quality and length. Many purchasers will not even talk about the price, as it is already well known through advertising or prior purchases. The tobacconist will possibly hand over the

[11] D. North, *Institutions, Institutional Change and Economic Performance*, Cambridge: Cambridge University Press, 1990; D. North and R. Thomas, *The Rise of the Western World*, Cambridge: Cambridge University Press, 1973.
[12] This section draws heavily on Boisot, *Information and Organizations*.

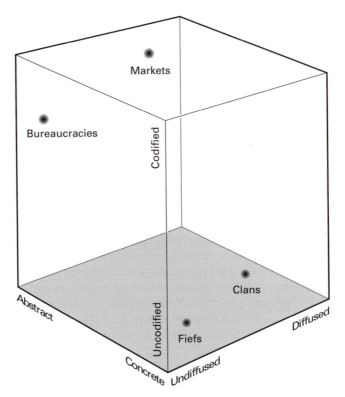

FIG. 6.1 Transactions in the I-Space

packet without a word, take the money, and give the right change without commenting. A perfunctory thank you may follow, but if it does not the purchaser may not even notice.

Thus, the second point is that the transaction is usually quite impersonal. As suggested in Chapter 3 the degree of personalization may vary, but it is not essential to the transaction. The purchaser may be a hardened criminal on the run or a Nobel prizewinner for physics—but he or she will still get the packet of Marlboros. The tobacconist may be a Trotskyist or regularly beat her or his four-year-old daughter—it is all the same to the buyer. Clearly, the transaction is *more* likely to take place in certain cases where such personal biographical information is *not* diffused and available to the other party. Transacting parties, then, do not have to share common interests, values, or beliefs in order to do business.

The third point builds upon the second: it is that each party is free to pursue its own interests and goals in the transaction. The vendor earns a living by selling as many cigarettes as possible; the purchasers find salvation in purchasing as many cigarettes as they think they need. The tobacconist may

TABLE 6.1 Transactions in the I*-Space

Bureaucracies	Markets
• Information is codified and abstract	• Information is codified and abstract
• Information diffusion is limited and under central control	• Information is widely diffused, no control
• Relationships are impersonal and hierarchical	• Relationships are impersonal and competitive
• Submission to superordinate goals	• No superordinate goals—each to themselves
• Hierarchical coordination	• Horizontal coordination through self-regulation
• No necessity to share values and beliefs	• No necessity to share values and beliefs
Fiefs	**Clans**
• Information is uncodified and concrete	• Information is uncodified and concrete
• Information diffusion limited by lack of codification and abstraction to face-to-face relationship	• Information is diffused but still limited by lack of codification and abstraction to face-to-face relationships
• Relationships are personal and hierarchical (feudal/charismatic)	• Relationships are personal but non-hierarchical
• Submission to superordinate goals	• Goals are shared through process of negotiation
• Hierarchical coordination	• Horizontal coordination through negotiation
• Necessity to share values and beliefs	• Necessity to share values and beliefs

disapprove of people who smoke. But who cares? The parties have enough information available to decide for themselves what they each want out of the transaction. The area in which the respective objectives of buyer and seller converge is the one in which they can do business. The rest is irrelevant.

The final point to be made is that the availability of well-codified and abstract price information to all makes the system largely self-regulating. Should the tobacconist wish to raise the price, he or she must reckon with the strong possibility that some customers will go elsewhere. Should the latter try to haggle over terms, they know that the vendor can find other customers who will trade at the going price. The self-regulating character of the system is due to the large number of tobacconists and cigarette buyers who can readily provide substitutes and who thus impose behavioural adjustments on the parties.

What we have just described is, of course, a classic *market* transaction under conditions of perfect information. As economists have long been telling us, market transactions, to be efficient, require that information on price, quantity, and quality be widely distributed to both buyers and sellers. Other conditions, such as ease of entry into the market and the divisibility of goods on offer, also influence market efficiency, but this need not detain us. We simply note that the information environment of a pure market transaction requires the codification, abstraction, and diffusion of relevant transactional data.

The next type of transaction we shall discuss will follow a cigarette purchaser from the tobacconist, and assume that he returns to his office, having just finished his lunch break. During his absence, a number of documents have piled up on his desk and await his signature. One of them is marked 'Confidential' and turns out to be a spending request by one of his subordinates working in a branch office of the organization in a neighbouring town. The request is set out in a standard format as required by the company's investment department and has a number of supporting documents attached. These turn out to be insufficient, so a number of files and additional documents must be consulted before a decision can be made. Perhaps the proposed expenditure must be compared with competing alternatives; or perhaps it must be evaluated in the light of the organization's development policy, and so on. So what can we say concerning this transaction?

First, much of the information on which the decision will finally be made, although set out on paper and kept in files and therefore well codified and abstract, is not generally available either within or outside the firm and so is not widely diffused. We are therefore dealing with a form of proprietary knowledge. The subordinate will not know on what grounds the decision is made because much of the information is not available at his level of the hierarchy.

Second, it is perfectly conceivable that this particular decision-maker has never met the subordinate making the request, so the relationship is, in effect, an impersonal one. The decision will rest on the merit of the case and will be taken on rational grounds that will (or should) ignore the identity of the petitioner. Certain formal procedures will have to be followed in order to arrive at a defensible conclusion, calling for a certain number of skills and prior training—say in financial analysis or in marketing—that the current incumbent is deemed to possess. Thus, in contrast to a market transaction, neither party is free to pursue its own personal objectives but is constrained to serve a well-defined 'higher' organizational purpose with rationality and impartiality. Yet, as with a market transaction, the parties are not required to share common values, beliefs, and attitudes beyond those just mentioned, to wit, rationality and impartiality. They may both enjoy golfing and turn out to be fanatical chess players, or one may be a Sunday sky-diver and the other an amateur snake-charmer. No matter. The decision will be made in total disregard of such personal niceties. After all, it may one day have to be submitted to the cold scrutiny of a higher authority.

The fact that superior and subordinate pursue a common and well-defined organizational purpose allows the first to delegate a certain decision-making authority to the second in the knowledge that, providing he is given the requisite information and possesses the relevant skill, he can be trusted to take the same decision that his superior would have taken in his place. Thus, a controlled and highly selective diffusion of information, usually performed on a strictly 'need to know' basis, is the key to effective delegation of hierarchical authority. To illustrate: below a certain sum of money, the subordinate may be free to make the spending decision himself, but he should then be prepared to defend it on substantially the same information grounds that were used when referring the decision upwards.

With increasing delegation comes the need for a hierarchical coordination of the work of subordinates. Where they encounter problems in their work that do not fall within the provision of the organizational rules prescribed, they pass the problems up the hierarchy to the level at which the rules can be modified or, if needs be, set aside. But this means that, as one moves up a hierarchy, the rules readily available to decision-makers actually reduce in number, and the information environment in which decisions are made becomes less and less structured. A firm, for example, may require a 15 per cent return on its new investments, but how exactly do you establish where you stand in relation to that hurdle when launching a technically new product in a new market? Does the analysis asked for really signify anything more than a ritual tendency to quantify wishful thinking?

In spite of the lack of codification and abstraction that characterizes the information environment as one approaches the top of the organizational pyramid, the transaction that we have just described is typical of *bureaucracies*. Information is well codified and abstract, but its diffusion is strictly regulated by the operation of a hierarchy. The pyramidal structure of an organizational hierarchy shows information flowing up—this could be regarded as something of a scanning motion—and also flowing down. It is clear that, while the base may hold on to much concrete and uncodified information, and that not everything gets systematically reported to the boss, the top of the hierarchy, by piecing together the information elements transmitted from the base, can build up a composite picture of an organization's activity which is not available at the base. This offers hierarchical superiors a strategic information advantage which can often be converted into power over subordinates.

Let us now leave our executive to his decision and shift our attention to another part of his organization. We might assume, for example, that he works for a large industrial firm with a sizeable research and development effort. As we enter one of the laboratories carrying out basic research, we meet a small group of scientists sitting around in a corner of the space and engaged in an intensive discussion. The team leader, a world-class specialist in crystallography, is listening to the results of an experiment recently carried out by her laboratory colleagues. Transactionally speaking, what do we have?

The scientific knowledge use by the team leader in evaluating what her colleagues are telling her is in large part codified, and there may be daunting quantities of it. But those critical knowledge elements that put her in a class of her own, and perhaps to which she owes her reputation, are personal. They are uncodified and reflect the slow accumulation, absorption, and impacting of high-quality idiosyncratic experience within a single brain. They are the fruit of a lifetime's investment in a particular branch of learning. Such knowledge, or 'know-how', cannot readily be described. It can be transmitted in a limited way to close colleagues by force of example, as when, for instance, they participate with the team leader in setting up and conducting an experiment, and, by observing and sharing directly in the experience, they pick up the little 'tricks of the trade'—the calibration of an instrument, the interpretation of a reading, and so on—that gradually contribute to their own stock of personal knowledge. Note, however, that it then becomes *their* personal knowledge and no longer that of their leader. Certain elements may be shared, but for the most part such knowledge remains a singular possession.

For this kind of group to transact effectively it must be very cohesive. Its various members must 'get along'. Relationships are of necessity much more personalized than in the case of the bureaucratic transaction. The research group has been built up into a highly productive team by their leader over a number of years. She is concerned to develop to the full the potentialities of individual researchers. To do this well she must get to know each one of them individually: their backgrounds, their aspirations, their strengths and weaknesses, and possibly their personal circumstances. The outcome is the kind of research team that the Nobel laureate Enrico Fermi managed to develop in his Rome laboratory: a group of scientists who, as Gerald Holton observes, 'had practically grown up together'.[13]

The personalized relationship between team members is essential to the building up of a sense of shared values and trust between them, and essential to the very personal authority of the team leader. The power she wields over her team is of a very intangible kind. It does not essentially reside in her official position on the organization chart, nor on her ability to offer promotions or salary increases, but rather on professional ability and personal qualities. This is charismatic authority. It creates disciples rather than subordinates, and its power to command obedience depends on the existence of personal loyalty based on trust and shared values rather than—as with bureaucratic authority—on the ability to coerce. The team and its leader may share the same scientific objectives, but these may well be personal to the leader herself and express her own long-term professional aspirations. Although some corporations might dispute this, in industrial research and development, when it comes to choosing research projects, what is good for the individual researcher often turns out to be good for the corporation as well.

As in the case of a bureaucratic transaction, coordination will also be hierarchical, although less so, and certainly less formally so. Team members will

---

[13] G. Holton, *The Scientific Imagination: Case Studies*, Cambridge: Cambridge University Press, 1978.

be 'on the same wavelength' and will coordinate their work according to a set of implicit norms that reduce the felt weight and the visibility of hierarchy.

The transactional style just outlined works best with small, highly dedicated groups. Charisma's writ does not usually run very far: its power is inversely proportional to distance, and it is only in the twentieth century, when the media have been able to diffuse selected features of the 'face to face' and the personal touch to a large population—think, for example, of President Roosevelt's 'fireside chat', or the Elvis fan club—that it has been able to extend its dominion. Yet, with distance, its effects are hard to sustain over the long term, so it is most effectively exercised with a small band of followers with whom intimate personal contact can be maintained on a regular basis.

The word I have chosen to describe this type of transaction is the *fief*, a term that expresses the absolute yet circumscribed reach of personal power. If the word has accumulated more negative than positive connotations, it is because we tend to associate it with abuses of personal power. Personal power is redolent of a feudal order that in an industrialized society is considered the hallmark of corruption and underdevelopment. Yet a moment's reflection will show us that, where personal knowledge is of a quality that can translate into personal power, something like a fief will often emerge. Fiefs abound all around us: in firms, on the university campus, inside the home, and so on. Only in exceptional cases, however, do they enjoy any institutional legitimacy. Where they do, we can observe what Max Weber called the 'routinization of charisma', a move over time from a fief to a bureaucracy, an attempt to inject some institutional stability in what is an inherently transient and unstable transactional form. In our analysis, we shall accept the 'feudal' transactions characteristic of fiefs as constituent elements of a cultural order.

The last type of transaction that we wish to study still concerns our crystallographer. When her research team's work is completed, she will write up its findings in the form of a research report that she will present at the next meeting of her professional scientific network. This will be a pre-publication presentation through which she will solicit comments and criticism from her professional colleagues. Her research findings will probably be put forward in an abbreviated form and couched in a professional jargon that implicitly assumes much prior shared and taken-for-granted knowledge among network participants. Yet what might therefore appear as common sense to an assembly of crystallographers may be somewhat inaccessible to the person in the street, untutored in the arcane concepts and terminology of the discipline. Such jargon, however, allows an extensive use of 'restrictive codes' in which much uncodified knowledge is shared with professional colleagues.[14]

---

[14] For a discussion of restricted codes, see Douglas, *Natural Symbols*; B. Bernstein, *Class, Codes, and Control Vol. I. Theoretical Studies Towards a Sociology of Language*, London: Routledge and Kegan Paul, 1971.

In any professional association, relationships are built up through a network of personal contacts with one's peers, so it is likely that our crystallographer will know a good number of those present at the meeting. Scientific meetings like this one are supportive events in which colleagues, through their presence and their behaviour, affirm their joint commitment to a common set of goals—e.g., the disinterested pursuit of scientific truth—as a shared set of values. Our crystallographer's findings may be criticized, but it will be done constructively and in the service of a joint cause. In some professions, shared values are articulated in a code of behaviour that practitioners undertake to observe. The code, however, is usually a loosely formulated set of general principles or moral maxims that are often difficult to enforce, so that transactions still depend a good deal on the existence of trust between practitioners and their colleagues or clients. As might be predicted from our earlier discussion, the more codified the skills required in a given profession, the lower the degree of trust required in a given transaction and the easier it becomes to write a contract for it. It is easier to sue an auditor for negligence than a neurosurgeon, and a neurosurgeon than a psychoanalyst.

The professional norms and values that regulate the behaviour of our crystallographer in relation to her professional association are not hierarchically imposed as in a bureaucracy or a fief. They evolve through a process of face-to-face negotiations between peers, in which politics and personal power may sometimes weigh more than rational deliberation. Where such interpersonal power is evenly distributed among participants, we may speak of a collegial process. But where it ends up concentrated in one or two hands, we are, in effect, back in a fief. The resulting transactions themselves are also the outcome of negotiations, often conducted implicitly—a horizontal process akin to a market rather than a vertical bureaucratic one. Yet as a market it is very inefficient. The need for common values and the uncodified nature of the information shared by participants tend to limit the number of players to what can be handled in face-to-face relationships—oligopoly rather than pure competition; smoke-filled rooms rather than the trading floor. Entry is restricted and individual players are expected to observe the 'club rules' which serve both to mitigate the extent to which they can pursue their own individual interests, and also to impose upon them some minimum concern with the common weal. Such transactions are characteristic of *clans*.

Where entry is not restricted and the number of players increases, clans tend to break down. The uncodified norms and values that act as a social cement lose their power to bind. A good example of a clan structure breaking down in the 1990s is offered by the City of London, where a rapid increase in the number of international financial institutions competing for business in what is rapidly becoming a global industry has led to an erosion of the uncodified City norms and values that traditionally drove informal interpersonal networks in the 'Square Mile'. Aggressive competition by newcomers, some marching to the beat of a quite different drum, is slowly moving the City away from a clan and towards a market culture. The 'Big Bang' of 27 October 1986, designed to do away with restrictive practices in Britain's financial markets, has turned out to be merely an inevitable—albeit big—step on the slow road from clans to markets. Typically and almost inevitably, cultures— corporate, industrial, and national—mix these different transactional forms so that the resultant institutional order must be described as a configuration that blends together markets, bureaucracies, clans, and fiefs. What then makes a culture distinctive is how it distributes transactions in the I-Space.

The particular shape of knowledge flows and, hence, of SLCs in the I-Space is sensitive to the availability of transactional infrastructure in a given region of the space. By lowering the marginal cost of transacting in its immediate neighbourhood, a transactional infrastructure acts as an attractor for uncommitted transactions and can often counterbalance the pressure that exists to move information exchanges towards the maximum value region of the I-Space in quest of higher returns on information processing. The prior existence of strong clan norms within a group, for example, eliminates the need for formal contracting and for policing contracts. Conversely, the ready availability of workable contract-enforcement mechanisms reduces the need for time-consuming investments in personal trust relationships. Nevertheless, the dynamic that propels transactions towards the maximum value region remains a strong one, and, if institutional infrastructures are also available there, they will often lower the costs of transacting below what they are elsewhere.

For this reason, economic organizations, as they grow and develop, gradually develop a bias towards the upper region of the I-Space when assigning transactions. This shapes the evolution of firms and their internal culture as they grow. Over time, as shown in Figure 6.2, fief-like family businesses or start-ups, built on the personal and sometimes charismatic authority of their founder, gradually give way to more bureaucratically structured functional firms. As these continue to increase in size, they are gradually led to decentralize and divisionalize their operations, allowing more competitive 'internal market' processes to regulate the allocation of human and financial resources between organizational or strategic business units (SBUs).[15] As already discussed, however, firms pay a price in moving their operations up the I-Space. Data economies are often achieved at the expense of data richness. With the increased standardization and routinization of transactions, organizational processes and the employees who operate them, by degrees, come to lose their capacity to deal with fuzzy and uncertain data. Managers are taught to expect clear answers to clear questions and to penalize vague or hesitant replies. Will the new technical process that we have developed work or not? Will we hit this year's budget figure or will we not? Is the market there or should we pull out? etc.

[15] A. Chandler, *Strategy and Structure: Chapters in the History of the American Industrial Enterprise*, Cambridge, Mass: MIT Press, 1962; *The Visible Hand: The Managerial Revolution in American Business*, Cambridge, Mass: The Belknap Press at Harvard University Press, 1977.

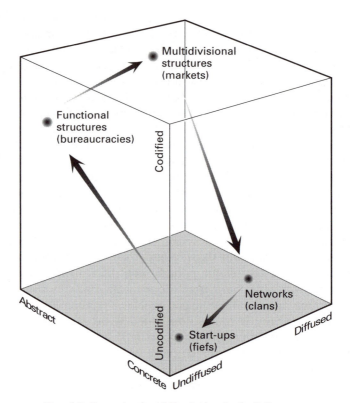

Fig. 6.2 Organizational Evolution in the I-Space

Yet where the world itself is vague or uncertain, the clarity sought by managers can often be positively dysfunctional. It discourages the less codified
and abstract forms of scanning—a casual remark by a customer, the atmos-
phere in a meeting, a holiday encounter, etc.—that might pick up hard-to-
detect signals of threat or opportunity. For this reason, a number of firms are
today seeking to move once more down the I-Space by adding to their cultural repertoire more personalized and less codified and abstract organizational processes. Some, like Hewlett-Packard and ABB, break themselves up
into numerous and smaller clan-like units with which individual employees
can identify. Others—and here 3M provides a ready example—encourage
their more entrepreneurial employees to build up small businesses (fiefs)
around new product concepts that they might dream up. Note that these
moves down the I-Space *add* to the firm's institutional repertoire and do not
involve liquidating the bureaucratic and market structures already created in
the upper parts of the space. They therefore enrich a firm's culture and
enhance its capacity to act and interact.

Clearly, the range and diversity of transactional structures that a firm constructs for itself to manage information flows will influence its approach to the creation of knowledge assets. Firms that have strong cultures in the bureaucratic region of the I-Space, for example, are more likely to exhibit N-learning values and behaviours than firms which transact primarily out of the clan region. Arguably, the latter will feel more comfortable with an S-learning orientation.

The first type of firm will treat knowledge assets as if they were a physical good to be preserved and confined to the left in the I-Space, whereas the second type of firm will treat them as lubricants for its learning process, a vital fluid that allows it to move rapidly around different SLCs. As we shall see in section 6.6, however, much will depend on the attractive strength of different institutional forms in the I-Space. Cultures that are built exclusively around a single institutional order often deprive themselves of the diversity required for effective learning. As indicated in Figure 6.3, a broadly based SLC will activate *all* the institutional structures that we have been discussing. Yet

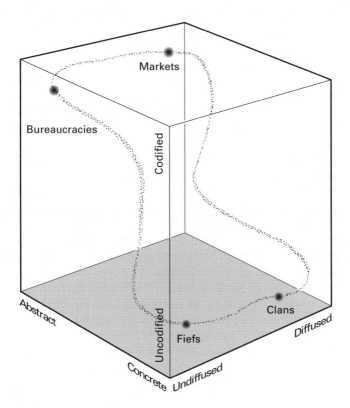

F<small>IG</small>. 6.3 Institutions in the SLC

whenever one of these structures is promoted to the systematic exclusion of others, a culture becomes ideologically driven. And as history abundantly demonstrates, ideology, whether it operates at the corporate, the industrial, or the national level, has the effect of blocking effective learning.

6.5 CULTURE AND THE SCOPE OF THE FIRM

We have stressed on several occasions the importance of properly specifying the characteristics of the population of data-processing agents that will be located along the diffusion dimension of the I-Space. In many cases one population will act as an external environment for another. The population of employees that make up a firm, for example, has a further population of firms as customers, suppliers, and competitors which constitutes its immediate industrial environment. Thus, the cultural influences that bear down on a given data-processing agent—whether the agent be an individual human being, a small group, or a firm—are often superimposed on each other in overlapping layers.

Whatever the cultural complexities that data-processing agents have to face, the larger the population of agents that make up an information field— and hence susceptible to being represented in an I-Space—the more abstract the level at which the interests that bind agents together will appear. Universalistic cultural values will usually command more legitimacy when confronted with a multitude of competing individual interests than the particularistic cultural orientation that gives priority to some of these interests— brothers, classmates, neighbours, etc.—over others. Particularisms are inherently divisive.

The institutional structures that we described in the last section can facilitate transacting both within and across organizational or industry boundaries. In Figure 6.4, for example, we adapt our transactional typology to indicate the kinds of transacting that might link a firm to its external environment. In this figure, the diffusion population would be made up of agents that the firm typically interacts with—i.e., customers, suppliers, competitors, etc. The informational and cultural characteristics of each type of transaction depicted in the figure are set out in Table 6.2. External transactions link firm-level learning activities to those of a larger population that the firm interacts with. For reasons just given, we would expect that the knowledge which flows between a firm and a larger, external population to have a more generic and universalistic quality than that which flows only within the firm. Through transactions such as licensing, joint ventures, service contracts, and the like, and the information exchanges that they entail, a firm, consciously or otherwise, trades in knowledge assets, judiciously increasing its overall stock of them where there is a goodness of fit between the type of information exchanged and the transactional structure selected to channel it, and decreas-

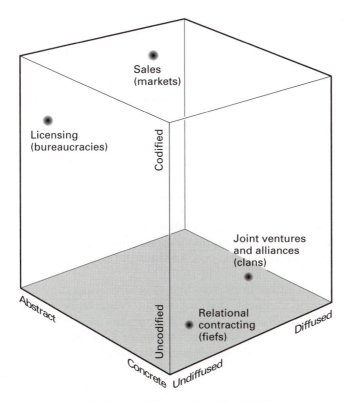

FIG. 6.4 External Transactions in the I-Space

TABLE 6.2 External Transactions in the I-Space

Transactional Features	Sales	Licensing	Joint Ventures and Alliances	Relational Contracting
Location in I-Space	Markets	Bureaucracies	Clans	Fiefs
Relations	Impersonal	Impersonal	Personal	Personal
Typical Information Characteristics				
• Codification	High	High	Medium	Low
• Abstraction	High	High	Medium	Low
• Diffusion	High	Low	Medium	Low
Importance of Shared Values	Low	Low	Medium to high	High
Coordination	Self-regulating	Hierarchical	By negotiation	Loyalty

ing it where such a fit is absent. In making this statement, we assume that a firm can selectively let go of discrete knowledge assets—as for example through a licensing agreement or a joint venture—without necessarily eroding its overall asset base.

Our analysis gives us a different perspective on transactions from what is usually offered by transaction cost economics (TCE). Transaction cost economists typically take bureaucratic transactions to be *internal* to a firm and market transactions to be *external*. This leads them to confuse the cultural *style* of a transaction—i.e., whether it is configured as a market, bureaucratic, clan, or fief transaction—with its *governance*—i.e., whether it is conducted inside the firm boundaries or partly outside them.[16] Clearly, many transactions that might be characterized as market-oriented take place inside firms. The allocation of investment resources between SBUs, for example, might well be carried out on a competitive basis using external market-determined 'hurdle rates' as a basis for selection. Again, a firm might operate an internal labour market in order to assign scarce human resources to their most productive uses.[17]

In a similar manner, firms may find themselves operating in an external transactional environment that we would characterize as bureaucratic. Anyone who has operated in command economies such as that in China will be aware that, prior to the economic reforms of the 1980s, state-owned firms confronted an institutional environment that was strongly bureaucratic, with both the acquisition of inputs and the disposal of outputs being determined by a central plan. As we shall now show, this conflation of a bureaucratic order with internal transactions on the one hand, and of a market order with external transactions on the other, seriously distorts the way we think of knowledge assets.

The confusion arises because in the TCE scheme of things transacting is located on a single continuum between centralized and decentralized forms of governance, with internalization standing as a proxy measure for centralization and externalization acting as a proxy for decentralized transactions. Somewhere in the middle of the continuum we find hybrid forms like joint ventures and strategic alliances. TCE recognizes that transactions involving tacit knowledge are harder to decentralize and hence to externalize, but it lacks a conceptual scheme for explicitly relating the structuring of a transaction to the possibility of decentralizing it. Our three-dimensional framework does just that. Yet, to the extent that the same transactional options are available both inside and outside the firm, the choices on offer are both more extensive and more complex than what is indicated by the TCE perspective.

---

[16] See M. Boisot, 'Markets and Hierarchies in Cultural Perspective', *Organization Studies*, 7 (2), 1986, pp. 135–58. The issue is further discussed in M. Boisot, *Information Space: A Framework for Learning in Organizations, Institutions and Culture*, London: Routledge, 1995.

[17] P. Doeringer and M. Piore, *Internal Labor Markets and Manpower Analysis*, Lexington, MA: Heath, 1971.

Let us elaborate. The marginal cost and revenue of a particular type of transaction will be a function of a firm's prior investment in supporting infrastructure in the appropriate region of the I-Space—i.e., it will depend on its cultural orientation. ITT under Harold Geneen, for example, with its competitive culture of 'rule by numbers', was heavily invested in the market region of the I-Space. Apple Computers under Steve Jobs and his Macintosh 'clique', by contrast, was better characterized as a fief culture. Changing the style of an internal transaction entails liquidating part of an existing transactional infrastructure and investing in the creation of a new one, a costly and time-consuming process of cultural transformation. Changing the governance of a transaction is even more complicated. In effect, it involves a three-step process:

1. Identifying the costs and benefits of transacting internally under all four transactional options—i.e., markets, bureaucracies, clans, and fiefs. These will be a function of how the firm's internal infrastructure is distributed in the I-Space and of how effectively the firm's culture supports such a distribution.
2. Comparing these costs and benefits with those of transacting externally, again under all four transactional options. The latter costs will be a function of how the external infrastructure available to the firm is distributed in the I-Space, and of how effectively the wider culture—industrial or national—supports such a distribution.
3. Where the costs and benefits of transacting externally compare favourably with those of transacting internally, establishing the costs to the firm of aligning its internal transactional structure with the requirements of the external infrastructure available. A strongly bureaucratic firm seeking a joint venture in the clan region of the I-Space, for example, will need to develop some capacity for handling less certain and more informal 'trusting' forms of exchange if it is to succeed.

Following this three-step process, a firm will only modify the governance of a transaction—i.e., move it in or out across its organization boundaries—if the benefits of doing so exceed overall costs *after* those of organizational realignment have been taken into consideration. Very often, the sheer costs of changing an organization's culture impart a certain inertia to existing arrangements in spite of the ready availability of apparently superior transactional alternatives—a case of institutional 'lock-in'.

When discussing internalization and externalization issues, one problem that arises concerns the boundaries of the firm. How, exactly, are these to be drawn? In the upper regions of the I-Space, this may not pose much of a problem. Tasks and roles are clearly articulated and easy to demarcate from each other. What goes on inside the firm can readily be separated from what does not. In the lower region of the I-Space, by contrast, tasks and roles are fuzzy, ambiguous, and hard to define. What properly belongs inside the firm's boundaries is not always easy to distinguish from what should remain outside. Consequently, not only are contracts hard to write, but exactly who the contracting agents are may not be readily identifiable. Here, therefore, transactions will be largely conducted on the basis of trust.

Yet trust does not just pop up whenever it happens to be required. It is itself the fruit of an extensive prior investment in interpersonal relationships. Where they reliably bind agents to each other, such relationships may compensate for the absence of clear organizational boundaries and ambiguous agency. But they will only do so if the long-term interests of transacting agents are properly aligned. The time required to socialize them into such an alignment must be counted as a cost of doing business in the lower region of the I-Space.[18] Outside the immediacy of spot-market contracting, then, the temporal horizon of a transaction emerges as a critical cultural variable, and trust-building as a significant transaction cost.

The response of many firms to the problems of trust and opportunism that plague the lower regions of the I-Space has been to try and avoid the issue altogether by giving transactions a more codified and abstract character. Bureaucratic and market transactions are both more visible and more impersonal than those arising in fiefs or clans. They are also less time-consuming and easier to manage. Where this response reflects the intrinsic logic of the transactions that confront a firm, it will be successful. Difficulties arise, however, when the response merely reflects a firm's cultural orientation. Transactions are then shifted into the bureaucratic region not because they display the required informational characteristics, but because the firm's own bureaucratic culture makes it more comfortable to transact in that region. Where this happens, the firm's ability to trade in less structured knowledge assets, whether internally or externally, will suffer.

The reason for this is that transactions involving exchanges of tacit knowledge operate with a different cultural logic to that in which explicit knowledge is traded. In the upper regions of the I-Space such exchanges might be labelled contract-oriented. The terms of an exchange and the respective obligations of the parties to a given transaction can be explicitly specified, as can the remedies for a breach of contract. In the lower regions of the space, by contrast, exchange is driven by what we might call the logic of the gift.[19] As the French anthropologist Marcel Mauss has shown, gift-based transactions have a much broader focus than short-term and utilitarian contract-oriented exchanges. Their primary function is often nothing to do with achieving gains from trade, but rather to affirm a relationship. Indeed, as anthropological field studies have shown, in certain gift-based transactions, utilitarian concerns count for so little compared with relationship building that sometimes

---

[18] On agency costs, see M. Jensen and W. Meckling, 'Theory of the Firm: Managerial Behaviour, Agency Costs, and Capital Structure', *Journal of Financial Economics*, 3 (4), 1976.
[19] W. Hagstrom, *The Scientific Community*, New York: Basic Books, 1965.

identical articles are exchanged.[20] The gift relationship is far more open-ended and uncertain than the contract. Neither the terms nor the time-horizon of the exchange are specified a priori. It thus operates at a much lower level of codification and abstraction than contract-oriented exchange. Gift-based transactions not only require trust for their consummation, they create it as well.[21]

Firms that master the logic of the gift will feel comfortable transacting within or across the organizational boundary in the lower region of the I-Space. In so doing, they will extend their organizational reach beyond what can be achieved through contractual means alone, building up durable if intangible links with subcontractors, suppliers, customers, and alliance partners. They will then be able to access external sources of tacit knowledge and thus build up their knowledge assets in ways that are unavailable to more contract-oriented firms, those whose culture confines them to the upper reaches of the I-Space. Firms that have developed a transactional capacity throughout the I-Space do not view the world exclusively in terms codified by abstract corporate boundaries. For them, no clear dividing line systematically demarcates insiders from outsiders. Such firms effectively leverage their transactional and cultural skills to expand their organizational capacities well beyond their legally determined boundaries.

There is strong evidence that national culture and institutions play a part in predisposing firms to transact from a given region of the I-Space. National values and beliefs influence socialization practices, legal frameworks, and economic behaviour patterns in ways that strongly skew the distribution of transaction costs in the I-Space. US culture, for example, with its strong preference for competitively determined contractual relations, is a plausible candidate for assignment to the market region of the space. French culture, on the other hand, although equally committed to the rule of law, accords a greater role to the state in the contractual relations that citizens establish with each other than does Anglo-Saxon culture. This more centralized, state-centred view of contracting would place the country in the bureaucratic rather than the market region. Both China and Japan, by contrast, exhibit a strong cultural preference for more informal and tacit forms of exchange, albeit that in China these will tend to be more centralized than in Japan.[22] A tentative assignment of these national cultures in the I-Space is offered in Figure 6.5. The word 'tentative' is worth emphasizing. As our earlier discussion of overlapping cultural patterns indicates, we have no reason to think of national cultures as homogeneous. They exert their influence on individuals

---

[20] M. Mauss, *The Gift: Forms and Functions of Exchange in Archaic Societies*, London: Routledge and Kegan Paul, 1954.

[21] Ibid.

[22] Hall, *Beyond Culture*; M. Boisot and J. Child, 'The Iron Law of Fiefs: Bureaucratic Failure and the Problem of Governance in the Chinese Economic Reforms', *Administrative Science Quarterly*, 33, 1988, pp. 507–27; M. Boisot and J. Child, 'From Fiefs to Clans and Network Capitalism: Explaining China's Emergent Economic Order', *Administrative Science Quarterly*, 41, 1996, pp. 600–28.

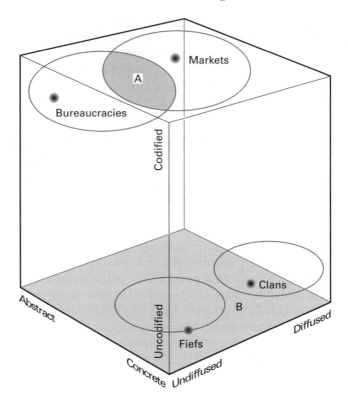

FIG. 6.5 National Cultures in the I-Space

in competition with regional, corporate, and professional cultures. It is when these become aligned and thus mutually reinforce each other's influence that data-processing agents may come to feel that transacting in a given region of the I-Space forms part of the natural order of things.

For an illustration of how corporate and regional culture can work together, consider the case of the Italian firm Benetton, a firm that, in the 1980s and 1990s, built up a powerful and highly effective network of subcontractors by skilfully exploiting a regional culture centred on clans in the I-Space—as one Italian journalist noted, there was no manager at Benetton who was not at the same time owner, president, or director of a leading subcontracting or supplying company in the Lombardy-Venetia area.[23] The firm successfully fostered a climate of collaboration with suppliers and subcontractors based on a culture of trust and long-standing personal relationships. However, it faced a major challenge when it expanded into the USA, where the prevailing cultural orientation was towards markets and impersonal arm's-length contracting, rather than towards clans.

[23] J. C. Jarillo and J. Martinez, Benetton Spa (A) Harvard Business School Case 9—389-074, 1988.

6.6 CULTURAL ATTRACTORS

A transaction can be represented as a dot located in the I-Space according to the characteristics of the critical information flows required to support it. To the extent that a transactional infrastructure is available in the neighbourhood of a transaction's chosen location in the I-Space, it will have the effect of lowering the cost of that transaction. The availability of infrastructure will also attract transactions as yet uncommitted to a particular location in the I-Space. We can then think of institutions as transactional infrastructures that create *basins of attraction* for transactions in the I-Space. We can further view a cultural order as that configuration in the space which results from a given scatter of transactions, a configuration that emerges from the interplay of competing institutional attractors.

In those regions of the I-Space where basins of attraction overlap and hence compete, a transactional assignment is likely to be unstable, and transactions will migrate in a discontinuous fashion to more stable regions. Where there is no overlap between basins of attraction, a transaction's location in the I-Space is more likely to be dictated by the dynamics of information flows alone and of the SLCs that result. These alternative possibilities are depicted in Figure 6.6. In the diagram we see transaction A located precariously between two competing and overlapping basins of attraction, covering, respectively, bureaucracies and markets. Transaction B, by contrast, sits more placidly between the non-overlapping basins of fiefs and clans. The latter's trajectory over the short term is more likely to be dictated by the action of the SLC acting upon it than by the pull of competing infrastructures. Transactions may be assigned pragmatically on the basis of cost and benefit, or more 'ideologically' on the basis of principle. Assignments are guided by prevailing social norms. In most cultures, for example, it would be difficult to sell one's grandmother on the open market, no matter how attractive the offers one might receive.

Institutional structures that act as strong attractors in the I-Space create quite distinctive cultures, that is, cultures which manage to confine the larger part of their transacting to a particular region of the space. If the institutions of Marxism-Leninism, for example, tried to restrict the economic and social transactions of the planned economy to the bureaucratic region of the I-Space, those of Thatcherism, by contrast, attempted to channel what many would consider to be non-economic transactions towards the market region of the space. In each case, a distinctive culture was aimed for, one in which ideology was in the driving seat. Ideology, by legitimating transactional assignments on other grounds than their own merit, can render a given region of the I-Space—at least temporarily—almost impervious to transactional competition from other regions.

For this reason, when an ideology gets institutionalized, it can profoundly

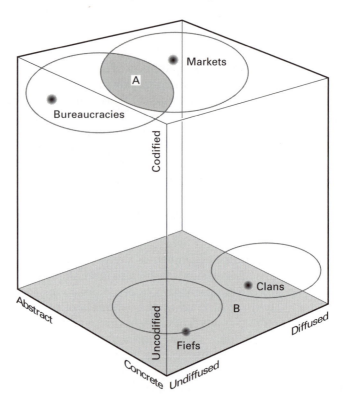

Fɪɢ. 6.6 Overlapping and Non-Overlapping Basins of Attractions in the I-Space

transform the cultural landscape. Whether they are driven by ideological or more utilitarian considerations, we shall label strong cultures characterized by strong institutional attractors *centripetal*, to distinguish them from *centrifugal* cultures, those in which the attractive power of competing institutional structures in the I-Space is either weak or more evenly balanced. In the latter case, the resulting transactional scatter is more broadly spread out—see Figures 6.7(a) and (b).

Our analysis leads us to a view of corporate culture that differs from much of what passes for conventional wisdom in the popular management literature. Strong cultures are typically held to be a mark of corporate distinctiveness and a source of competitive advantage. They are the product of a powerful founding vision and corporate single-mindedness. Yet in the sense that we are using the term, strong centripetal cultures also lead to tunnel vision. Whether they operate at the national, the industrial, or at the corporate level, *centripetal cultures block learning whereas centrifugal ones promote it*. Let us explore this idea further.

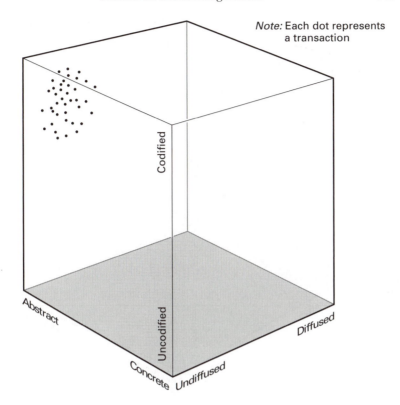

Note: Each dot represents a transaction

FIG. 6.7(a) Centripetal Transactions in the I-Space

Recall that institutional structures, by modifying the transactional costs and benefits associated with particular patterns of information flow, help to shape the trajectories of SLCs. A strong or centripetal culture will have the effect of confining an SLC to a small region of the I-Space and hence of limiting the scope for learning of the data-processing population as a whole. To take one example, many large firms would like to foster internal venturing activities in order to rejuvenate their businesses.[24] Where such firms have strongly bureaucratic cultures, however, they tend to set up internal control and monitoring procedures that kill the very intrapreneurial impulses that they are trying to foster. Entrepreneurs, whether internal or external, tend to operate in the uncertain and fuzzy worlds of fiefs and clans. They are no great respecters of organizational boundaries and procedures. Yet, unless they are given some leeway to operate outside an organization's established ways of doing things, they either leave or come to grief.

[24] G. Pinchot, *Intrapreneuring*, New York: Harper and Row, 1985; Z. Block and I. MacMillan, *Corporate Venturing: Creating New Businesses within the Firm*, Boston: Harvard Business School Press, 1993.

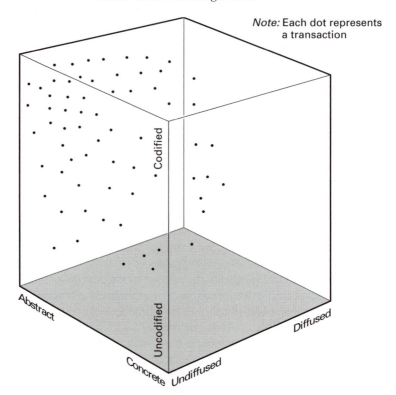

FIG. 6.7(b) Centrifugal Transactions in the I-Space

On the other hand, many small owner-managed businesses become accustomed to doing things in an informal way that suits the fief-like orientation of their founders. Owner-managers often maintain their managerial discretion—and hence their personal power—by committing as little as possible in writing and by dealing with issues personally rather than delegating. They therefore often fail to develop enough structure in the bureaucratic region of the I-Space to create a stable platform for further learning and growth. When this happens, the firm's development remains stunted, until the founder either leaves or retires—Steve Jobs's departure from Apple after the arrival of John Sculley once more comes to mind.

Finally, the competition and conflict that sometimes characterize the relationship between the different organizational units of large firms may have divergent cultural orientations at their origin. To the extent that these units operate in different information environments and according to the distinctive values and beliefs that correspond to these, they will have difficulty understanding each other and coordinating their efforts. Figure 6.8 offers an illustration of this point by locating the different functions of a firm in the I-

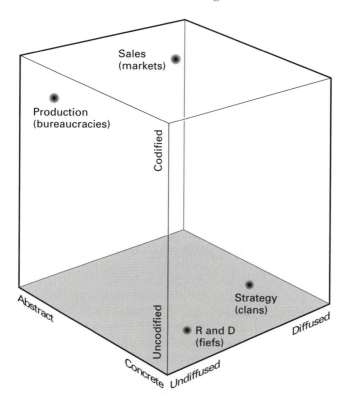

Fig. 6.8 Organizational Functions in the I-Space

Space. Table 6.3 gives the basis for the assignment. Where one of these functions predominates and acts centripetally, the cultural claims of the other functions will go unrepresented in the organization's strategic processes. Conflict may be avoided, but at the expense of the learning that would result from addressing it. Consider the following example provided by Hill and Jones of a firm in which the marketing function was under-represented:

When demographic data indicated that houses and families were shrinking, planners at General Electric's appliance group concluded that smaller appliances were the wave of the future. Because the planners had little contact with home builders and retailers, they did not realize that kitchens and bathrooms were the two rooms that were not shrinking. Not did they realize that working women wanted big refrigerators to cut down on trips to the supermarket. The result was that General Electric wasted a lot of time designing small appliances for which there was only limited demand.[25]

---

[25] C. Hill and G. Jones, *Strategic Management: An Integrated Approach*, Boston: Houghton-Mifflin, 1995.

TABLE 6.3 Internal Transactions in the I-Space

Transactional Features	Sales	Production	Strategy	R and D
Location in I-Space	Markets	Bureaucracies	Clans	Fiefs
Relations	Impersonal	Impersonal	Personal	Personal
Typical Information Characteristics				
• Codification	High	High	Medium	Low
• Abstraction	High	High	Medium	Low
• Diffusion	High	Low	Medium	Low
Importance of Shared Values	Low	Low	Medium to high	High
Coordination	Self-regulating	Hierarchical	By negotiation	Professional loyalty

Mahoney and Sanchez suggest that the formulation of a strategy by General Electric that was unrelated to market trends may have resulted from the strategic decision-makers ignoring the signals from marketing staff.[26]

Only cultures which display some minimum amount of centrifugalism will be able to create SLCs that effectively activate the data-scanning and processing capacities of the agent population as a whole. Effective social learning thus requires cultural variety no less than cultural single-mindedness, and firms that operate with a restricted institutional repertoire unwittingly limit that variety.

Sometimes the attempt to limit variety is deliberate. Variety is a source of complexity, and, as we have seen, complexity can either be reduced or absorbed. Centripetalism can then plausibly be interpreted as an uncertainty reduction strategy, whereas centrifugalism is a strategy for absorbing complexity. Of course, each of the transactional structures that we have discussed in this chapter varies with respect to the complexity that it is capable of absorbing or reducing. But such structures deal with complexity in the small, at the level of the individual transactions. Centripetalism and centrifugalism, by contrast, pose the problem of complexity at the more strategic level, that of the system as a whole.

6.7 TECHNOLOGY, CULTURE, AND ORGANIZATION LEARNING

What are the implications of our discussion of cultures and institutions for the management of knowledge assets? Recall that technology—an important

[26] J. Mahoney and R. Sanchez, 'Competence Theory as Integrating Product and Process of Thought: Beyond Dissociative Theories of Strategy', unpublished paper, 1995.

class of knowledge assets—and its associated know-how can be thought of as extensions of culture. The concept of a technological system, presented in the preceding chapter, makes it clear why this is so. A technological system is a network of interlinked technologies. Both the technologies and the links between them are permeated to varying degrees by organizational processes activated by transactions between agents. These need to coordinate their actions in order to keep the technological system operational: machines have to be switched on in a certain sequence and at certain times; equipment has to be cleaned and maintained; meters have to be read and reported on; and so on.

Technological and transactional structures reciprocally influence each other. By implication, technology and culture do so as well. We can illustrate this by first locating a variety of technological systems each within the orbit of one of the transactional structures that we have presented, and by then examining their respective information characteristics. Figure 6.9 and Table 6.4 present the results of this exercise. Technological systems, then, are

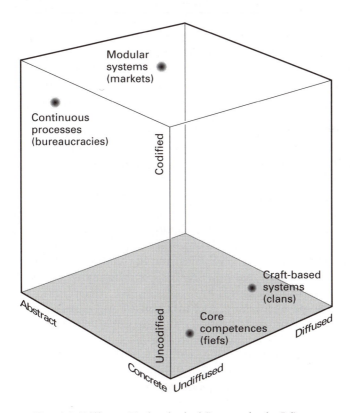

FIG. 6.9 Different Technological Systems in the I-Space

TABLE 6.4 Transactional Attributes of Technical Systems

Attributes	Modular	Continuous Processes	Craft-Based	Core Competence
Transactional Orientation	Markets	Bureaucracies	Clans	Fiefs
Information Characteristics				
• Codification	High	High	Low to medium	Low
• Abstraction	High	High	Low to medium	Varies
• Diffusion	High	Low	Medium	Low
Coordination	Self-regulating	Hierarchical	By negotiation	Loyalty
Facilitates	Decentralization	Centralization	Adaptation	Uniqueness

culture-laden. The manner in which they are operated reflects their location in the I-Space and the institutional options available there. We hypothesize, therefore, that there has to be some goodness of fit between the specific cultural requirements imposed by a given technological system and the cultural options made available to the system by a firm's prior investment in institutional infrastructure. It is no more feasible, for example, efficiently to run a tightly integrated continuous production process using solely the informal and consensual management-style characteristic of clans than it is to operate a complex craft-based system that draws heavily on the shared tacit knowledge of highly skilled individuals as if it were an impersonal and quasi-automatic bureaucratic machine.

The fit between technology and culture, however, should not be too tight if learning is to take place—i.e., if there is to be any knowledge-generating movement around an SLC. On the one hand, too great a gap between technological requirements and technological culture leads to breakdown. On the other, too good a fit leads to stasis. Progress through an SLC, whether technological or organizational, will only take place when there is an optimal gap between the two. The point we are making amounts to a new interpretation of the distinction first drawn by Marx—in a quite different context—between the forces of production (technologies) and the relations of production (organizational and institutional practices).[27] For Marx, any gap between these two forces could only be closed by revolution. We argue, contra Marx, that it can also be closed by learning. As Marx himself well understood, if a perfect fit between these two sets of relations is not desirable—after all, it would eliminate the opportunities and justification for revolution—it is also not sustainable. SLCs may sometimes be slow-acting, but they are never static. They are always opening new gaps between technological opportunities and needs on the one hand and organizational and cultural provisions on the other.

---

[27] K. Marx, *Capital: A Critique of Political Economy*, London: Lawrence and Wishart, 1972.

At the level of firms, therefore, only those whose cultural repertoire gives them transactional capacity throughout the I-Space can summon an adequate *learning* response to any emerging gaps between technology and culture. Those operating from too narrow a cultural base in the space, however, must of necessity lose control of the SLC unless they can complement their limited cultural repertoire through carefully selected interfirm and intercultural collaborations—i.e., through an externalization of transactions that link them with agents located elsewhere in the space. However, they will then confront the same problems of integration that more culturally diverse firms encounter *inside* their organization when trying to coordinate the activities of different functions or businesses. There is no cheap grace.

7

Products, Technologies, and Organization in the Social Learning Cycle

7.1 INTRODUCTION

WE have discussed the need to establish a goodness of fit between the institutional and cultural requirements imposed on a firm by its technologies on the one hand, and what is to be provided by way of an institutional and cultural order on the other. In this chapter we explore the issue further. But in addition to a firm's organization and its technologies, we shall also discuss its product offerings in terms of the I-Space. Why do we do this?

Much of the strategy literature until the end of the 1980s could be framed in terms of products and their performance in markets. Product-market matrices, for example, would allow a firm to diagnose its competitive potential as a function of the market share commanded by its products in markets exhibiting varying degrees of growth. Firms would readjust their strategies by reallocating their investment resources across existing products or product groups as a function of their market potential, modifying the composition of their product-market portfolios as required.[1] In the early 1980s, the strategic focus shifted from products to the industrial environment within which firms competed. A firm's performance within a given product-market became a function of industry characteristics and of the firm's position within the industry.[2] The new perspective gave the firm more scope in deciding its fate: competitive advantage could be secured as much by mastering the dynamics of industry competition as by a somewhat mechanical manipulation of a product-market matrix. Yet although competitive strategy became more complex and sophisticated, the emphasis remained primarily on securing advantage through 'positioning' the firm in an appropriate environment— i.e., the approach remained mechanical.

In both the portfolio and the industry approaches to strategy, the flavour could be described as behaviourist. The environment, whether framed in terms of product-markets or of industry players, exerted predictable, and sometimes controllable influences on firms and shaped their behaviour in determinate ways. The science of strategy largely consisted of analysing these

---

[1] D. Abell and S. Hammond, *Strategic Market Planning: Problems and Analytical Approaches*, New Jersey: Prentice-Hall, 1979.

[2] M. Porter, *Competitive Strategy: Techniques for Analyzing Industries and Competitors*, New York: The Free Press, 1980; *Competitive Advantage: Creating and Sustaining Superior Performance*, New York: The Free Press, 1985.

external influences and of specifying appropriate firm responses. What might be called the environmental imperative severely circumscribed a firm's room for manoeuvre. The 'logic of the situation' that it found itself in precluded idiosyncratic and creative approaches.

In the next chapter we shall present a perspective on strategy that gained popularity in the 1990s, one that gives greater scope to autonomous and creative processes within the firm. By fostering a learning orientation, it makes the firm less a creature of the circumstances that it finds itself in than earlier perspectives.

Firm-specific learning and creativity will sooner or later find its way into a firm's product portfolio. No less than the technologies used to produce them, products are an extension and an expression of a firm's culture. Products not only tell us something about themselves, they also often reveal much about the firm that made them and about the technologies that it used in doing so—a detailed comparison of, say, a Rolls Royce luxury car and a Zil (the Russian equivalent) would suffice to make the point. And just like a firm's cultural and technological processes, its products act as a substrate for a part of its knowledge assets. For this reason, an understanding of knowledge-based competition must cover a firm's products as well as its technologies and organization. In saying this, however, it must be recognized that products are often the most transient carriers of a firm's knowledge assets. The products themselves may be highly perishable, while the knowledge they impart may last for decades. The know-how that goes into baking bread, flying an aircraft, or singing a melody is pretty durable, even if the services yielded by this know-how typically last but a few hours.

This chapter's main message is that as a firm becomes more information-intensive, the boundaries drawn between its products, technologies, and organization are often hard to establish. A firm's knowledge assets transfer with increasing speed and ease from organizational processes to technological ones and from thence into products. Take, for example, office-cleaning services. They used to be rendered by organized human labour alone, working, at most, with buckets and mops. Since about the 1970s, they have gradually given way to services carried out by labour assisted by machines and equipment, such as automatic polishers and heavy-duty vacuum cleaners. In some cases—the intelligent office—cleaning services have been dispensed with altogether and replaced by products that clean themselves at the flick of a switch. A reverse migration of knowledge from products to the technologies that create them is also possible, and then on to the organizational processes that accommodate these technologies. Personal computers, for example, have transformed the technical and administrative routines of organizations while at the same time profoundly modifying our traditional notions of hierarchy, authority, and control. And e-mail has given everyone in the firm much easier access to senior management—so much so that even the latter are today beginning to find it a bit unmanly not to be able to type.

The fluidity of the boundaries that demarcate an organization from its technologies and its products calls into question the viability of strategic frameworks whose analytical power depends on stable boundaries. Thus, many tools of product-market, technological, and organizational analysis, while providing useful snapshots, will all need complementing by a more unitary and dynamic view of a firm's strategic processes. Although a unitary view is not yet on offer, I believe that the I-Space provides a conceptual framework within which one could be developed. We take the first few steps in this chapter.

We shall proceed as follows. In the next section (7.2) we examine the viscosity of information flows and the 'stickiness' of knowledge assets as a function of their substrate. We then look, in section 7.3, at how flow viscosity modifies the evolution of SLCs respectively for products, technologies, and organizations. This prepares the ground for a discussion in section 7.4 of 'goodness of fit', taken as an appropriate degree of integration across the three different types of SLC. In section 7.5 we relate our discussion of fit to the paradox of value and to our earlier discussion of N- versus S-learning. In section 7.6 we show how an analysis of SLCs at the product, technological, and organizational levels can be used to diagnose a firm's learning strategies and its deployment of knowledge assets. A conclusion follows in section 7.7.

7.2 THE PHYSICAL SUBSTRATES FOR KNOWLEDGE ASSETS

Recall from our discussion in Chapter 1 that information is something immaterial that is extracted from data and that modifies an agent's disposition to act. Such a disposition constitutes an agent's knowledge base so that knowledge is a possession of individual agents. Information connects the agent to the data of the world, data itself being a discrimination between the different energy states of some physical process. Agents themselves are physically constituted to receive, store, and process data. Where the data received is informative, it helps to align the agent's internal states with those of some relevant region of the external world. Information, then, is a particular property of data structures; it acts as a bridge between physical states that are external to the agent and those that are internal.

So far, we have taken data-processing agents in the I-Space to be individuals, firms, or even entities larger than firms—i.e., industries. Should these different types of agents, operating at different levels of aggregation, be taken to possess knowledge or knowledge assets in the same way? The answer to this question turns on how far we are willing to accord genuine powers of agency to organized entities larger than individual human beings. If we do not—the position of many orthodox economists who take individual *human* agent behaviour as the bedrock of economic analysis—then we are committed to denying any reality to emergent phenomena such as group minds or learning organizations.[3] These expressions then become little more than a convenient shorthand for describing structured groupings of individual human agents. Firms, for example, in spite of possessing a legal personality which allows them to sue and be sued are viewed as nothing more than a nexus of contracts that binds together individual human agents.[4] We may choose to treat firms as data-processing agents for I-Space purposes, but this is a convenient fiction that should not blind us to the fact that human agents are where the action is. In such a case, knowledge and knowledge assets must be viewed as residing at least in part outside such human agents, and in the organizational props and artefacts that they use to support their data-processing activities. If, on the other hand, we do—the position we have adopted in this book—then we also hold that in so far as organizations as a whole display a disposition to act, they also 'have' knowledge, albeit not consciously held. In this second case, knowledge assets, whether embedded as data in documents, physical objects, or in the heads of employees, may indeed form part of the agent's internal systems, where the agent is now an organization rather than an individual employee.

Some readers may feel that we have been indulging in mere philosophical quibbling. Does it really matter, they may ask, whether a knowledge asset is deemed to be located outside or inside an agent? Most assuredly it does. In Chapter 1 we defined a knowledge asset as knowledge that yields an appropriable stream of benefits over time. The appropriability of such benefits, however, is likely to vary according to whether the assets that give rise to them are located in physical substrates external to the agent or in physical substrates that make up the very system that we call the agent. After all, knowledge embedded in these two types of substrate is likely to exhibit quite different diffusion properties. A firm's orientation to its knowledge assets will then be a function of where it believes its critical knowledge resides—i.e., in the heads of the individual agents that it employs, or within other components of its organization. Its willingness to embed useful information in physical artefacts, in documents, or in the heads of employees will reflect these beliefs and will determine what it will choose to treat as a black box and for whom.

An example will illustrate the point. All artefacts carry information that is pressed into them: they are *in*-formed. By their shape, they communicate to their prospective users what they are and how they are to be used and manipulated. Few people today, for instance, except possibly a New Guinean highland tribesman, risk mistaking a telephone receiver for a shower head and attempting to wash their hair with it. People have encountered telephones in most societies, and have either used them or at least watched them being used. Nevertheless, by themselves, objects can only convey a limited amount of

---

[3] See K. Weick, *The Social Psychology of Organizing*, Reading, Mass: Addison-Wesley, 1979. K. E. Weick and K. H. Roberts, 'Collective Mind in Organizations: Heedful Interrelating on Flight Decks', *Administrative Science Quarterly*, 38, 1993, pp. 357–81.

[4] S. Cheung, 'The Contractual Nature of the Firm', *Journal of Law and Economics*, 3 (1), April 1983.

information, even to those who are familiar with them. If my television set plays up, I may fiddle around with the controls for a while in order to try and retrieve the picture, but should I need to get inside the casing, which to me is pure black box, I will ultimately have to call the local repair-person. A repair-person who is new to the job will bring a checklist (a procedure that is sometimes now computerized) to guide his or her efforts at diagnosis. By far the greatest number of repairs to TV sets are, of course, carried out on the spot. Occasionally, however, the repair-person encounters another black box nested inside the first: neither the TV set as an object nor the diagnostic checklist of themselves yield sufficient information to cover all repairing contingencies. In certain cases, a black-boxed component, or sometimes the set itself, has to be shipped back to the manufacturer and the knowledge stored in the head of certain specialized employees has to be mobilized and added to that of the other two sources in order to complete the repair.

If we now locate on a diffusion scale the kind of knowledge of TV sets held by myself as a customer, by a repair-person, and by the manufacturer's technical personnel, relating its position on the scale to the nature of the substrate in which this knowledge is embedded—i.e., in objects, documents, or heads (see Figure 7.1)—it becomes clear that the kind of knowledge that is most widely diffused, and hence available to customers is embedded in the object itself. The information imparted in documentary form to repair-persons is much less diffused, and that carried around in the heads of specialist technicians does not extend much beyond the manufacturing organizations that they work for. What the diagram indicates is that as information gains in

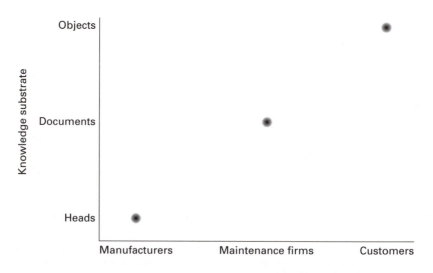

FIG. 7.1 Diffusion by Substrate

complexity so its diffusion becomes more limited.[5] It is only as complexity is mastered and reduced—and this often calls for abstraction skills—that knowledge carried in one's head can be structured and either set down on paper or embedded in objects—i.e., it can be codified. Once information has been transposed from individual brains into documents or physical objects, it acquires a life of its own and can diffuse rapidly and extensively, more so perhaps in the case of physical objects—especially if these are portable—than of documents. The latter typically presuppose some prior knowledge of the codes and conventions used. Everyday consumer objects such as a telephone, for example, may of course require some prior familiarity by users, but in much smaller doses and in a less codified form than what is required, say, to interpret the instrument printouts relating to a chemical experiment.

Prior familiarity with context is often as important as a prior knowledge of codes. Codification and abstraction always involve a data sacrifice. A residual of concrete, uncodified data stays behind in the minds of those who create or activate the codes, generating a natural information asymmetry that is often valuable to them. Whether consciously or otherwise, they have experienced the full range of coding options from which a selection was made—i.e., in addition to the codified and abstract knowledge which they may share with others they have *contextual* knowledge which is much less accessible and articulable. Sometimes this knowledge is valuable, sometimes not, depending on how comprehensively codification and abstraction strategies capture relevant knowledge. Comprehensiveness, of course, is not always the aim. In many cases, technology strategy becomes a game between those who seek to maintain and renew information asymmetries, and those who seek to eliminate them. For creators of new knowledge, the issue becomes one of choosing which items to keep tacit and which ones to structure. The game is not only played between firms, but often also between a firm and its own employees—as, for example, when a senior researcher keeps to himself a discovery with commercial potential that is unrelated to the project that he is paid to work on. Yet whatever the short-term outcome of the game, publicly useful knowledge, whether it be the possession of firms or of individual employees, over time tends to move in the direction of greater codification and abstraction.

Where exactly the firm decides to place the boundaries between the knowledge to be held by its customers, external collaborators such as maintenance technicians, and its own company employees will materially affect what it defines respectively as a product, a production technology, and an internal organizational process. The firm, of course, is not free to set these boundaries as it pleases, since the action of competitors, as well as consumer attitudes and expectations, must also be taken into account. Consumers, for example, do

---

[5] M. Polanyi, *Personal Knowledge: Towards a Post-Critical Philosophy*, London: Routledge and Kegan Paul, 1958; A. Reber, *Implicit Learning and Tacit Knowledge: An Essay on the Cognitive Unconscious*, New York: Oxford University Press, 1993.

not want to be overloaded with product data or instructions that vary from one brand to another and that are soon forgotten when not regularly used. Personal computer sales only really took off in the mid-1980s when this simple truth was taken on board in the development of standardized user-friendly products. Or again, much technically skilled maintenance activity will disappear as a product increases in reliability and is replaced rather than maintained. As we have already seen, with increased reliability, the replacement decision is dictated by a product's economic life rather than its physical life, and its economic life, in turn, will be a function of the pace of product innovation. This is often decided by the actions of competitors.

A firm that is treated as a fictional agent and hence perceives its knowledge assets to lie outside itself—i.e., it takes them to be the possession of individual human agents—will feel more vulnerable to their loss than one that is treated as an agent in its own right. The latter will view its knowledge assets as deeply embedded in its internal systems whether or not they are carried around in the heads of individual employees. In the first case, all knowledge that flows outward across the organization's formal boundaries constitutes a potential asset transfer that reduces the future benefit streams flowing into the firm. And the way to limit such transfers is to place as much of this knowledge as possible into black boxes that block or slow down its diffusion.

The second case is more nuanced. Some knowledge flows will constitute an asset transfer, but only in so far as they reduce the dependence of the recipient on the firm. This will only happen where the knowledge flowing is self-contained and detachable, as, say, when a licensee, through reverse engineering, acquires the know-how necessary to manufacture for itself the critical components that the licensor used to supply it with. Where the knowledge in question is tightly integrated with the rest of the firm's knowledge assets, however, its flow will, if anything, *increase* rather than decrease the dependence of the recipient on the firm's knowledge base, and hence increase the future benefits that accrue to the firm. When making use of the firm's knowledge, the recipient, in effect, becomes locked in to its knowledge base through its particular norms or practices. In selectively transferring TGV (*train à grande vitesse*) technology to its South Korean customers, for example, GEC-Alsthom has increased the risk that one day they might be tempted to go it alone. Yet at the same time the transfer ensures that until they succeed in doing so—and this may not be easy—they will be committed to a railway infrastructure of tracks, power generation, signalling systems, and safety equipment that strongly favours GEC-Alsthom as a supplier.

The firm has thus leveraged the flow of knowledge taking place across its corporate boundaries to increase its organizational reach and, in so doing, has actually expanded its asset base. Goodwill is one of the labels that we can give to such leveraging. It is classified as an intangible asset on a firm's balance sheet and expresses a consumer's predisposition to buy from the firm. This predisposition may well reflect the consumer's knowledge of and familiarity with the firm's products. If so, the knowledge diffused to consumers must be taken as forming part of a firm's knowledge assets. Even if it is held by external data-processing agents, it is still knowledge capable of generating future benefit streams for the firm.

But can knowledge which is available to a firm's customers always be considered to form part of a firm's knowledge assets? After all, much of this knowledge usually leaks out in an uncontrollable fashion through the product itself. And in some cases much more leaks out than the firm ever intended, thus allowing its products to be reverse engineered, and then either imitated or even improved upon—recall from our earlier discussion the fate that befell the British firm EMI in the late 1970s. Here the knowledge gained does not simply help purchasers to *use* the product, but also to replicate it for themselves if they so wish, thus turning them into competitors. In other cases, by contrast, a firm may not even be giving out enough information to allow a prospective purchaser to use its products as intended. Where the product is novel and somewhat complex, inadequate information may put off purchasers unwilling to invest in the necessary learning and experimentation. They will therefore often settle for a more familiar, even if possibly inferior, alternative. Many consumers of innovative electronic gadgetry, for example, are today suffering from 'function fatigue': so many switches, bells, and whistles to manipulate; so little indication in the instructions of what these are for.

Clearly, directing part of a firm's knowledge flows to customers is a matter of balancing out at the margin those who might, as a result, be created and those who might be lost, as well as the net benefit streams accruing respectively to knowledge-hoarding and knowledge-sharing strategies. These calculations cannot be carried out in the abstract, since they depend in part on the firm's own future intentions as well as those of its competitors.

In sum, there is an optimal amount of value that a firm can extract from information-sharing activities. Above a given level of information flows, the firm is underexploiting its knowledge assets, giving away the shop, and possibly making itself dispensable. Yet at some point below that level, customers will buy less from the firm than they otherwise might. Note that in both cases the firm is loosening its bonds with either existing or prospective customers. Knowledge located in the heads of customers can only plausibly form part of a firm's knowledge assets, therefore, to the extent that it keeps them profitably oriented towards the firm—i.e., it keeps them inside its information field.

Finally, how a firm embeds its knowledge assets in things, documents, or individual heads can significantly affect the shape of the SLCs that it then has to manage, as well as their speed. Knowledge that flowed slowly and in a largely uncodified form when it was primarily organizational in nature may well become highly codified and modularized when it gets embedded in physical objects.[6] It will then flow much more rapidly to outsiders, thus possibly

[6] R. Sanchez, 'Strategic Flexibility, Firm Organization and Managerial Work in Dynamic Markets: A Strategic Options Perspective', *Advances in Strategic Management*, 9, 1993.

expanding the diffusion population that a firm has to deal with—for better or worse. When that happens, it may make sense to track the resulting changes in knowledge flows through a number of different I-Spaces, some representing populations of agents internal to the firm, such as individual employees, small groups, or even whole businesses, others representing populations of external agents such as suppliers, customers, and competitors. These different populations will not always fit comfortably on a single I-Space. A firm has to decide for itself which agent populations are critical to particular knowledge-management processes and construct its I-Spaces accordingly.

7.3 THE STRUCTURING OF TECHNOLOGICAL KNOWLEDGE ASSETS

The knowledge embedded in things, documents, and people's heads evolves over time in response to life-cycle effects. If, for example, we look at the evolution of computers over time, what do we see? In their early years, little of the knowledge required to operate them was standardized, so only a limited amount of it could actually be embedded in the product itself. Much of it resided in complex or voluminous documents and even more in the heads of operators.

The first machine to be labelled an electronic computer, for example, the ENIAC (Electronic Numerical Integrator and Computer), weighed 30 tons, sported 18,000 thermionic valves, and several kilometres of cables and wires. Any change in its program required a modification in the physical configuration of valve connections. This had to be performed manually. Not surprisingly, operators were considered to be specialists, requiring extensive training and experience. Such training did not always transfer easily from one set of machines to another. Given the scarcity of specialists and the cost and size of the machines that they operated, therefore, the early data-processing operations of firms tended to be centralized.

With the growth of the industry came standardization, and with standardization a focus on space and time as the critical performance parameters that would shape the evolution of the industry's technologies and product characteristics. Computers were to become ever smaller and ever faster. Performance gains allowed more and more knowledge to be embedded in the physical hardware of a computer as well as in its operating system. The valves of the ENIAC consumed 174 kilowatts of electricity per second, enough to run a small house for a week. The valves were later replaced by transistors and these were subsequently miniaturized so that thousands of them could be placed on a silicon chip the size of a thumbnail. Less expertise was necessary to operate the machines and less documentation was required. The advent of the PC in the late 1970s further reduced the amount of tacit knowledge that needed to be carried in the heads of users or in documents, since most of it was now designed into the machine itself in the form of pull-down menus and graphic user interfaces (GUIs). By structuring computer knowledge and by embedding it in standardized hardware and software—the development of high-level languages such as Fortran or Cobol constituted a move towards both codification and abstraction—four things were achieved:

1. A significant reduction in the volume data processing and the mastery of codes required of users. The machine took over many tasks that users had hitherto been required to perform for themselves.
2. A rapid diffusion of computers and of computer-related know-how to potentially new users. People who had never been near a mainframe computer were now playing computer games on small home machines.
3. A considerable reduction in the absorption of codified and abstract knowledge required of users. Three days of computer training could get you going instead of the three months to three years required previously.
4. A decentralization of knowledge-based power within organizations from providers of data-processing services to consumers of these services. With PCs on almost every desk, the IT function now had to become more 'customer-driven'.

In the I-Space, the evolution of computing from mainframes to PCs can be viewed as a change in the shape of the relevant SLCs from ones that were deep and concrete and located on the left-hand side of the I-Space—i.e., they were application-specific and in the hands of few highly experienced specialists who kept their know-how to themselves—to ones that were flat and abstract and located in the upper region of the I-Space—i.e., the technologies they covered were generic, readily available, and could be used with a minimum amount of skill and experience (see Figures 7.2(a) and (b)). With the change in the shape of SLCs came a change of industrial culture, from one that was dominated by large technology-driven, corporate bureaucracies protected from new entrants by economies of scale and heavy research budgets, to one that was more fragmented, more market-oriented, and more entrepreneurial. As a consequence of intensifying price competition, product life cycles in many segments of the industry became shorter and the returns to learning in depth—i.e., to absorption and impacting in the SLC—perhaps more elusive.

Many industries experience the transition from a deep, technology-driven cycle in the early to middle phases of their evolution, to a flatter, more market-driven one as they mature. The transition from the one to the other is often marked by the emergence of a dominant design,[7] a product configuration that, as we have already seen, while not necessarily optimal,[8] remains stable enough for industry-wide standardization to take root. In industries characterized by significant economies of scale, standardization may facilitate

[7] J. Utterback, *Mastering the Dynamics of Innovation*, Cambridge, Mass: Harvard University Press, 1994.
[8] W. Brian Arthur, 'Positive Feedbacks in the Economy', *Scientific American*, February 1990.

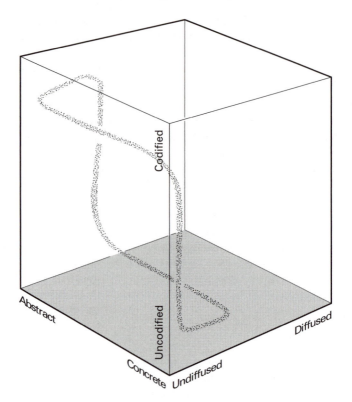

Fɪɢ. 7.2(a) SLC for Mainframe Computers

concentration. In contrary cases, standardization may actually help to fragment and open up the industry. This is exactly what happened with PCs.

Following the emergence of a dominant design, innovation often becomes incremental. Through high levels of complementary investments by industry players, a new product's basic configuration comes to acquire a strong inertia and then resists all attempts at radical restructuring. The cost of disruptions to existing structures by anything other than incremental and compatible innovations often far exceeds their perceived value either to users or to providers. We then have a form of lock-in, a situation in which radical change will only be accepted by existing industry players when it is competence-enhancing.[9] Such was the case with jet travel, for example, which, when it was introduced in the late 1950s, greatly expanded the market for air travel without directly threatening the position of existing players. Where innovation is competence-destroying, on the other hand, it will be resisted. For this reason, radical change, when it appears, is often the work of outsiders. Outsiders took

[9] M. Tushman and P. Anderson, 'Technological Discontinuities and Organizational Environment', *Administrative Science Quarterly*, 31, 1986.

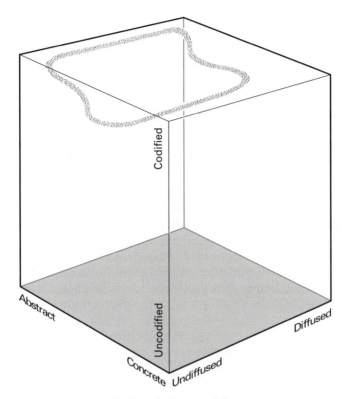

FIG. 7.2(b) SLC for Personal Computers

over the emerging market for transistors from valve manufacturers in the 1950s because the latter were reluctant to cannibalize their existing products. It was a collection of small entrepreneurial firms, such as Apple, that led the charge against mainframe computing in the late 1970s and that forced IBM to enter the market for personal computers. It was Japanese electronic manufacturers that introduced cheap quartz watches at about the same time and that nearly annihilated a Swiss watch industry determined to stick to mechanical timepieces.

The emergence of a dominant design eliminates uncontrollable product variety and much of the tacit knowledge required to cope with it. Idiosyncratic craft-based skills gradually give way to mechanical routines, and informal eye-balling is replaced with cold calculations. Standardization codifies and abstracts some of the key elements of product design in such a way as to maximize the appeal of a good or service to as large a number of prospective purchasers as possible. Today, mass customization and modularization are both restoring a measure of controlled variation in product characteristics, but they do so in ways that preserve the benefits of standardization.

Dominant designs, by channelling the evolution of a product's performance characteristics along certain dimensions, commit it to following a given technological or product paradigm—e.g., petrol engines rather than steam engines, rubber wheels rather than air cushions, etc. Incremental change within the paradigm then yields greater net benefits to existing industry players than a switch from one paradigm to another. It is only when the total costs of cleaving to a given paradigm rise and become apparent—something that may be slowly happening with the automobile—that alternative paradigms will be explored.

To summarize, both the emergence and the demise of dominant designs are foundational events that change the shape of SLCs operated by firms and industries as well as the location of key players on them. At one moment in an industry's evolution, codification, abstraction, and diffusion will be the critical learning skills to focus on. At another, absorption, impacting, and scanning skills will turn out to be all important. With a change in the kind of learning required to be an effective industry player, comes a change in the kind of culture that can foster such learning. Firms that operate centripetally, from a narrow cultural base in the I-Space, may then find it hard to manage the transition.

7.4 SHOULD KNOWLEDGE FLOWS BE INTEGRATED?

As discussed in the last chapter, Marx saw social evolution—and revolution—as driven by the gaps that inevitably open up between a society's technical processes on the one hand, and its institutional and organizational systems on the other. We can reformulate Marx's insight as a tension that exists between the different kinds of learning imposed on individuals, organizations, and industries, and caused by changes in technological and product regimes. If too little tension is experienced, the learning that results becomes mechanical and uncreative: it runs in grooves. Yet, where the tension is too great, blockages to learning will emerge. The trick is to find the optimal amount of tension that will balance out the need to explore and the need to exploit.

Knowledge assets are embedded in things, documents, and in people's heads, and these in turn are configured to produce organizations, technologies, and products. In Figure 7.3 we can see knowledge assets shifting from one type of physical substrate to another and thereby modifying their diffusion properties as well as the scope and shape of the SLCs that they participate in. In the computer industry in the late 1990s, for example, consumers participate in SLCs that fifteen years earlier were still only accessible to producers. Since then, the cycle has pushed out along the diffusion scale of the I-Space to incorporate—indeed to create—a much larger population of data-processing agents. Many of the tensions referred to above are the result

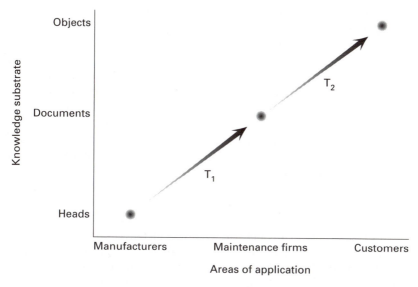

Fig. 7.3 The Migration of Knowledge Assets

of the stretching and pulling of SLCs as they move across different substrates.

The mercurial nature of I-Spaces does not make them any easier to construct. In sections 6.7 and 7.2 we suggested that a firm's organizational and its technological knowledge might sometimes usefully be represented either by different I-Spaces, or by different SLCs within the same I-Space. We can equally apply this suggestion to the firm's products, given that much product-related knowledge has to be shared with customers. Where a firm's customers are known this might not pose too many problems. But what happens when the customer is an anonymous consumer, an occasional purchaser of the firm's—and its competitor's—products? To what extent should we take the episodic consumer as forming part of a firm's information field, given that at some point episodic consumption shades off into non-consumption—or worse, the consumption of a competitor's product offering? The challenge of accurately specifying the population that should be placed along the diffusion dimension of the I-Space remains a delicate one.

It is also a crucial one to address for an effective deployment of knowledge assets. As indicated by Figure 7.3, the diffusion properties of knowledge assets will be affected by the choice of substrates for carrying them. A chisel, for example, of itself, imparts very little of the knowledge required for its proper use. The same goes for a paint brush. The information communicated by the chisel or a brush has to be complemented by a great deal of tacit prior knowledge if the tool is to be skilfully exploited. The documentary support usually provided with a software package, by contrast, may be sufficiently self-explanatory to allow the average PC-owner to operate the software by carefully following instructions. In the case of the chisel and the brush, easily diffusible knowledge embedded in the design of the product must be complemented by not-so-diffusible knowledge residing in the head of an experienced user. In the case of the software, however, both the knowledge embedded in the product and that contained in the supporting documents may diffuse quite rapidly, largely untethered to experiential knowledge.

Arguably, and with some notable exceptions, knowledge becomes more diffusible as one moves up the diagonal of Figure 7.3. Such knowledge may vary in utility. It may only allow a recipient to *use* a given object. Or it may, in addition, allow the user to maintain it. In the case of simple objects, it may even allow the recipient to reproduce the object. The exceptions, of course, are where the transmitter deliberately limits access to the knowledge embedded in diffusible objects through the creation of black boxes. Black boxes notwithstanding, the trend has been for a firm's knowledge assets to migrate up the diagonal of Figure 7.3 over time. Knowledge that once resided in the heads of employees gradually finds its way into documents or objects as it gains in stability and predictability—i.e., in codification and abstraction.

The migration of knowledge across physical substrates partly accounts for the emergence of gaps between the location of a firm's organization, its technology, and its products in the I-Space. Firms whose culture was initially built up around highly personalized craft-based processes located in fiefs, after a period of growth, can find themselves having to deal with impersonal standard operating procedures located in bureaucracies. Others, geared to the manufacture of highly complex and customized products are confronted with the challenge of volume production, experience curves, and price competition—a shift from bureaucracies to markets in the I-Space that many firms shifting from, say, defence-contracting to civilian markets have had to manage. Not all of them made it: changes in the product's attributes drive changes in the technologies used for making it; these in turn drive changes in the firm's culture; they occur after a delay. Rare is the firm that transforms its culture ahead of product and technological changes. The result is often a mismatch between the product and technological challenges that confront a firm in a given region of the I-Space and its cultural capacity to respond to it.

7.5 BENEFITING FROM ONE'S CHOICE OF LEARNING STRATEGY

The foregoing adds a new twist to our earlier discussion of a firm's learning strategies. Recall that slow-moving SLCs will foster N-learners who tend to hoard their knowledge assets, whereas fast-moving SLCs will foster S-learners who tend to share them. Any choice between these two learning strategies cannot be sensibly made without careful thought being given to its impact on the firm's culture (see Chapter 5). A strategy that appears to make sense in the abstract may prove to be a disaster when implemented within an ill-matched corporate culture.

Whatever the choice of strategy, however, we hypothesize that S-learners will be more willing to embed their knowledge assets in substrates with rapid diffusion properties—such as, say, consumer products—than N-learners. The latter will prefer to immerse their knowledge assets deeper within their own organization, or, if they do embed them inside products, they will enclose them as far as they can in black boxes and thus limit an outsider's access to them.

Each strategy has its dangers. S-learners may fail fully to exploit the absorption, impacting, and scanning phases of the SLC that allows them to benefit properly from sharing their knowledge assets. Moving down into the lower right-hand region of the I-Space, and then on into concrete applications, takes time and is full of uncertainty and risk. As the knowledge that results from learning by doing becomes more tacit and ambiguous, the scope for misinterpretation and misunderstanding increases. The move thus requires being in touch with customers and suppliers at a deeper, more intimate level than impersonal spot-market transactions allow. It assumes an ability to go beyond the abstract, codified articulations of market demand in order to explore the much less codified but more concrete phenomenon of individual need.

A firm's existing customer and supplier base will not always be representative of the range of needs that a firm could address—in that sense, a firm can get *too* close to its customers.[10] IBM's long-standing fixation on its mainframe customers, for example, blinded it to the emergence of a latent and unmet need for inexpensive computing. And Intel's commitment to its D-Ram customers kept it shackled to its Japanese competitors well after D-Rams had become a low-margin commodity—thus slowing down its shift to the emerging microprocessor business.[11] Effective S-learning requires a firm to scan beyond its immediate constituencies, so that, even before working its way down the I-Space, it has to move further to the right, reaching out to latent constituencies.

The only commercial justification for freely sharing knowledge assets with customers, suppliers, or more remote constituencies, is where doing so either facilitates and accelerates a firm's own learning with respect to the environment it confronts, or skews the learning of its constituencies in the firm's favour. Where the firm fails to exploit the learning opportunities opened up by knowledge sharing—either because it is not following through on the

---

[10] C. Christensen and J. Bower, 'Customer Power, Strategic Investment, and the Failure of Leading Firms', *Strategic Management Journal*, 7 (3), March 1996, pp. 197–218.

[11] R. Burgelman, 'Fading Memories: A Process Theory of Strategic Business Exit in Dynamic Environments', *Administrative Science Quarterly*, 39, 1994, pp. 24–56.

trajectories of the SLCs that it has created, or because it is sharing knowledge with the wrong agents, or, finally, because it is sharing the wrong kind of knowledge—it will not extract full value from an S-learning strategy.

N-learners face the opposite problem. Being reluctant to share their knowledge in the first place, they may fail to participate properly in their customer's learning at all, and may then hold on to increasingly stale knowledge assets well past their sell-by date. In other words, their hard-won knowledge becomes obsolete. N-learners may operate deep learning cycles inside the firm, but, being turned inward, these become unresponsive to either tangible or intangible market signals. They successfully maintain the *scarcity* of their knowledge assets, but only by allowing their *utility* to erode as better adapted alternatives emerge. In effect, the market has been learning faster than they have and eroding the value of their knowledge assets.

Large firms switching from defence to civilian markets often encounter this problem. Being accustomed to deal with a single large client in a symbiotic fashion over long periods of time, these firms often lack the responsiveness and skills needed to cope with rapidly moving consumer markets that emit fuzzy and ambiguous signals. Their instinct is to ignore such signals and to keep doing what they are good at. Hypnotized by the potential value of their accumulated knowledge assets, they fall into a competence trap.[12] In 1973, for example, one of the principal contractors on the Apollo programme, Rockwell, decided to enter the field of consumer electronics. Through its acquisition, Admiral, it introduced what was then considered to be the 'Cadillac of TV sets', a product that incorporated all the latest improvements in video technology. Unfortunately, it was a 'cost-plus' product of the kind Rockwell had always produced for the government. It was too expensive and did not sell. Or again, in the early 1980s, McDonnell Douglas diversified into information technologies and systems, creating a time-sharing computer system and automated manufacturing units. By 1985, the firm was facing a $109 million loss for a turnover of $1.1 billion.[13]

An organization with a centripetal culture, one which confines it to transacting in a narrow region of the I-Space, may be less well placed to pursue an S-learning strategy than one with a broader, more centrifugal culture. The latter's more varied institutional repertoire facilitates the operation of a wide-ranging SLC, since it enjoys some transactional capacity to pursue learning activities over larger regions of the I-Space.

Where a firm with a centripetal culture needs to operate an S-learning strategy, it will often be led to collaborate closely with outsiders offering complementary cultural orientations. Yet the obstacles to such collaboration are sometimes as great as those to developing the required cultural capacity

[12] Tushman and Anderson, *Technological Discontinuities*; Utterback, *Mastering the Dynamics of Innovation*; D. Leonard-Barton, 'Core Capabilities and Core Rigidities: A Paradox in Managing New Product Development', *Strategic Management Journal*, 13, 1992, pp. 111–25.

[13] J. C. Derian, *America's Struggle for Leadership in Technology*, Cambridge, Mass: MIT Press, 1988.

in-house. Many alliances, mergers, and acquisitions have come to grief by failing to address the elusive issue of cultural compatibility. Just consider how difficult it is to get nimble-footed, highly paid investment bankers to work effectively with more methodical commercial bankers following a merger or a takeover. The examples of Swiss Bank Corporation and S. G. Warburg, of Deutsche Bank and Morgan Grenfell, and of American Express and Shearson Lehman all readily spring to mind.

7.6 UNDERSTANDING SLCS

What emerges from our discussion is the idea that the shapes of the SLCs in which a firm participates, at whatever level of aggregation,[14] are somehow expressive of what Mintzberg labels its 'realized' strategy. As he points out, a firm's intended strategy rarely gets fully realized and what does get realized was not always wholly intended.[15] The real world inconveniently interposes itself between intentions and outcomes and continuously feeds the strategy process with unanticipated events—some positive, some negative for the firm. An intended strategy, therefore, has the character of a hypothesis about how the firm and the world interact together. It leaves plenty of scope for the unexpected and the emergent. A firm's realized strategy, then reflects its ability to cope with whatever unexpected threats or opportunities the world has chosen to throw at it and to adapt to them—in other words, its ability to learn.

It is not easy to map out in the I-Space the SLCs in which a firm participates in any rigorously objective way. Depending on how these are constructed, some will straddle a firm's boundaries, while others will operate with a limited population deep inside the firm. SLCs are best handled as social constructs, interpretative tools for the visualization of a firm's critical learning processes. Constructing an SLC starts with some specification of the kind of knowledge that will be tracked, of what it is being tracked for, and of the populations that are likely to make up an information field for that knowledge. Switching from one set of knowledge assets to another changes the populations relevant to the analysis and hence the field within which the assets flow. Given the multiplicity of knowledge assets that a firm deals with and the number and complexity of information fields that these give rise to, it is unrealistic to hope for a single, unified representation of a firm's learning processes. No Grand Universal Theory beckons.[16] In the messy realm of human affairs, the most that can be hoped for is a sense of the *kinds* of SLCs that a firm's culture tends to generate, and, with luck, the emergence of suggestive patterns to guide its knowledge-management processes.

---

[14] As we have already seen, these may need representing on different I-Spaces.

[15] H. Mintzberg, 'Crafting Strategy', *Harvard Business Review*, July–August 1987; H. Mintzberg and J. Walters, 'Of Strategies, Deliberate and Emergent', *Strategic Management Journal*, July–September 1985.

[16] Grand Universal Theories (GUTs) are the holy grail of a certain class of physicist, single overarching theories to which all other theories are subordinated.

We can gain a sense of what the approach involves by developing a checklist of questions that should be addressed in developing an SLC. For each phase of the SLC, we have constructed tables of questions (Tables 7.1–7.6) that help to describe or specify the behaviour of a firm's products, technologies, and organization in the three dimensions of the I-Space. Each table produces nine cells which can gradually be filled in by answering the questions they contain. The cells can be filled in intuitively in a first iteration and more systematically later. The pay-off resides in the pattern that emerges when the answers given for different cells are compared and evaluated. If the exercise is carefully done, a firm will gain a deep understanding of its learning processes. Different answers to the questions posed can yield very different shapes for an SLC. Yet, whatever its shape, for an SLC to have any strategic value for the management of knowledge assets, at one moment or another it must either approach or come to terms with the maximum value region of the I-Space. Among the many cycles that are possible and that do this we find the two that were discussed in section 7.3: those, respectively, of the technology-driven and the market-driven firm.

Recall that the technology-driven firm tends to operate deep industry-level cycles on the left of the I-Space. It may or may not be science-based and it may or may not deploy generic technologies. The technology-driven firm invests considerable time and resources moving newly created knowledge assets up the I-Space towards greater codification, and extending their range of applications—a move towards abstraction. Pharmaceutical firms, for example, can spend more than a sixth of their revenue in research and development and on the regulatory processes that their products must submit to before they can be allowed on to the market.

Firms that invest heavily in deep SLCs typically opt for knowledge-hoarding strategies that protect their knowledge assets from the rent-dissipating effects of competitive markets, so that they have time to profit from their investments. Knowledge-hoarding strategies work best where industry-level SLCs are discontinuous and slow. They will also be easier to implement where a firm's critical know-how is embedded in its organizational and technological processes than where it is embedded in products. In the latter case, the know-how has to be encased in carefully designed black boxes if it is not to leak out.

The market-driven firm, by contrast, tends to operate flat industry-level cycles at the top of the I-Space. Here, time-to-market and competitive response time is all. To keep it focused, the firm thinks in terms of product-market competition and strategic business units (SBUs). In the market-driven firm, technological evolution, although rapid, is typically incremental. The firm does not necessarily share all its knowledge assets, but, in order to shape industry standards and the rules of the competitive game to its advantage, it is led to diffuse more of its technology and know-how than knowledge hoarders. Such a firm will have more transparent production processes and fewer

TABLE 7.1 SLC Phase—Scanning

	Product	Technologies	Organization
General Identifying signals of threats and opportunities to which the firm must respond	Scanning should identify new products or services that could impact the firm's product-market posture	Scanning should identify emergent or developing technologies that could either complement or threaten the firm's existing technology base	The firm should monitor its organizational processes and its interfaces with other organizations for trends and developments.
Codification Scale How much should the firm invest in scanning for 'weak', i.e., uncodified signals?	How should the firm scan for products that are still under-going development—i.e., codification?	How should the firm scan for technologies that have not yet been codified through a patent? What about hard-to-diffuse process technologies?	How should the firm manage its informal organization processes? How far should it tolerate 'deviant' insights and behaviours among organizational members?
Abstraction Scale How extensively should the firm scan for general trends as opposed to focusing on its own product-markets and industries?	Should the firm scan *classes* of products or particular products?	To what extent should the firm scan the science base as well as the technology base? How generic should be the technologies that it scans for?	How much should the firm's scanning focus on the more abstract issues of norms, beliefs, and values, rather than concrete problems and opportunities?
Diffusion Scale From how broad an internal or external population of agents should the firm scan?	In relation to which group of agents should the firm be undertaking product scanning?	How extensively should the firm scan for technologies? How big should its reference population be?	What agents should count as forming part of the organization's processes for scanning purposes?

Table 7.2 SLC Phase—Problem-Solving

	Product	Technologies	Organization
General Articulating an adapted response to what has been scanned	Developing and testing a product until it meets its performance requirements	Developing and testing a technology until it meets its performance requirements	Structuring and standardizing organizational processes in order to achieve predictability and reliability
Codification Scale To what level of detail and resolution should problem-solving take place?	How far should a product be standardized and its design stabilized before it is launched on the market?	How far should one rely on the tacit craft skills of employees and how far on automation in operating given technologies? Is there an optimum trade-off for the firm?	To what extent should the firm's procedures be rule-governed? How much should be left to the discretion and judgement of employees?
Abstraction Scale How specific or general should the problem focus be?	Should the firm develop generic products or products that are highly targeted to particular customers with specific applications?	Should the firm be developing and using general purpose technologies or processes that are specific to particular applications?	Should organizational processes be framed in terms of general principles or particular outcomes?
Diffusion Scale How many agents should be involved in the problem-solving process?	To what extent should the development of new products be a matter of consensus among stakeholders and to what extent should it be a matter of personal initiative by individual entrepreneurs and product champions within the firm?	To what extent should the development of new technologies be a matter of consensus among stakeholders and to what extent should it be a matter of personal initiative by individual technical employees within the firm?	How many stakeholders should be involved in the framing of an organization's internal processes?

TABLE 7.3 SLC Phase—Abstraction

	Product	Technologies	Organization
General Generalizing the response to new classes of problems and opportunities	Adapting a given product to the needs of new markets	Extending the use of a firm's technology into new areas of application	Extending particular organization practices to all parts of the firm
Codification Scale What level of formalization is required to ensure a general application?	Should product standards adopted be universal or should they vary according to the circumstances of their application?	How far should the technology standards developed be science-based? How far should they be empirically derived and specific to the firm?	Should the firm's standard operating procedures focus on general cases or on particular ones? If the first, how should exceptions be dealt with? If the latter, how to ensure comparability and consistency across cases?
Abstraction Scale What are the limits to the generalization of an application?	Should the differentiating features of a product be kept to a minimum in order to broaden its appeal to as many consumers as possible?	How general should a general-purpose technology be?	If the focus is on general cases, how general should they be? If it is on particular ones, how narrow should the focus be? This is the problem of establishing the coverage of a rule.
Diffusion Scale To what extent does generalizing the response make it accessible to a wider group of agents?	Should the product aim to become a commodity that is universally consumed?	To what classes of agent should a firm's technology be accessible? This does not establish the number of agents within the class that should gain access to the technology	How many stakeholders should be involved in establishing the coverage of an organization's procedures?

TABLE 7.4 SLC Phase—Diffusion

	Product	Technologies	Organization
General Making the response accessible to a wider number of agents	Making the products accessible to a wider number of agents	Making the technology accessible to a wider number of agents	Making the firm's knowledge available to a larger number of organizational stakeholders
Codification Scale At what level of codification should diffusion occur?	How extensively should product attributes be standardized? To what extent does this facilitate diffusion?	How far should a technology be codified given the way that codification affects diffusibility?	How far should a firm's organizational processes be codified for the purposes of affecting their diffusion?
Abstraction Scale At what level of abstraction should diffusion occur?	How universal or generic should product attributes be in order to achieve a given level of diffusion?	How far might the fact that an organization's technology is science-based facilitate its diffusion?	How far should the firm's organizational processes be framed in a general way in order to facilitate their diffusion?
Diffusion Scale How extensive should the diffusion be?	How rapidly and extensively should a product be allowed to diffuse within a target population?	How rapidly and extensively should a firm's technologies be allowed to diffuse within a target population?	How extensively should knowledge of a firm's organizational processes be diffused inside the firm? Should it be anything more than 'on a need to know' basis?

TABLE 7.5 SLC Phase—Absorption

	Product	Technologies	Organization
General Internalizing knowledge acquired by using it in different circumstances	Gaining intuitive familiarity with a product through a process of 'learning by using'	Gaining intuitive familiarity with a technology through a process of 'learning by doing'	Gaining intuitive familiarity with an organizational process by frequently experiencing or applying it.
Codification Scale How far down the codification scale should absorption be taken?	How much intuitive familiarity is required to use the product as intended?	How much intuitive familiarity is required to operate the technology with competence?	How much intuitive familiarity of an organization process is required in order to implement it competently?
Abstraction Scale In how wide a variety of circumstances should absorption be undertaken?	In how wide a variety of circumstances does a product have to be used in order for an agent to gain intuitive familiarity with it?	In how wide a variety of circumstances does a technology have to be used in order for an agent to gain intuitive familiarity with it?	In how wide a variety of circumstances and settings does an organizational process have to be experienced by an agent in order for him or her to gain intuitive familiarity with it?
Diffusion Scale How large a population of agents should participate in the absorption process?	Do all users of a product need to gain intuitive familiarity with it?	Do all users of a technology need to gain intuitive familiarity with it?	Do all participants in a given organizational process need to gain intuitive familiarity with it?

TABLE 7.6 SLC Phase—Impacting

	Product	Technologies	Organization
General Applying the knowledge absorbed in concrete circumstances	Skilfully using or consuming the product in new circumstances	Skilfully applying the technology absorbed in new circumstances	Skilfully adapting the organizational process that has been mastered in new circumstances
Codification Scale How structured should the application be?	How explicitly should circumstances be defined for the consumption or use of the product?	How explicitly should circumstances be defined for the application of the technology absorbed?	How explicitly should the circumstances be defined for the application of the organizational processes that have been absorbed?
Abstraction Scale How specific should the application be?	How specific should be the circumstances in which the product is used or consumed?	How specific should be the circumstances in which the absorbed technology is applied?	How specific should be the circumstances in which the organizational processes are applied?
Diffusion Scale How many agents should be participating in the application of absorbed knowledge?	How many agents should be able to use or consume the product in given circumstances?	How many agents should be able to apply the technology in given circumstances?	How many agents should be able to apply the organizational processes mastered in given circumstances?

and smaller black boxes distributed across its products. In the late twentieth century, PC manufacturers provide an example of market-driven firms.

In spite of differences in the respective learning cycles of these two kinds of firm, and in spite of the greater willingness of the market-driven firm to share its knowledge, they both reflect an N-learning rather than an S-learning orientation. Why?

In order to answer this question, consider Figures 7.2(a) and (b) once more, where the two types of SLC have been superimposed. They share in common two features. The first is that both cycles pass through the maximum value region of the I-Space, albeit that the deeper cycles will visit the region less frequently and will stay there longer when they do so than the flatter ones. The second feature is the most interesting: *both cycles shun the minimum value region of the I-Space*. This can only mean that in spite of significant differences in the way that each type of firm handles its knowledge assets, each behaves as if it believed that little useful learning is to be had in operating a deep cycle of the kind depicted in Figure 7.4, one that is both broad and deep in the I-Space. This is the S-learner's cycle; it describes the behaviour of what we have called the Schumpeterian firm.

The Schumpeterian firm combines characteristics from the two types of SLC just discussed to operate a wide and deep cycle in the I-Space. Such a firm, for example, might help to set industry standards by rapidly sharing its knowledge. But it is also willing to invest time and resources in follow-through activities—i.e., in exploiting the industry's collective learning. In contrast to N-learners, the Schumpeterian firm is capable of contemplating the creative destruction of its own knowledge assets if what it learns from the market and the industry suggests that this will enhance its survival prospects—i.e., in its quest for transformation and renewal it is willing to enter the region of maximum entropy in the I-Space. Put in biblical terms, it is ready to lose its life in order to save it. Put in managerial terms, it is ready to bet the company.

Predictably, pure S-learners are not too thick on the ground. Firms typically aim to hold on to what they have built up, and to exploit it in a world that they understand. S-learning often involves a switch of technology paradigm and a willingness by a firm to reconstruct its identity—in part or in whole—in order to be able to operate within the logic of the new paradigm. It is sobering to realize, for example, that the Swiss were actually the first to introduce an electronic wristwatch in 1967—at the Concours de Chronometrie of the Neuchâtel Observatory—with which they smashed all accuracy records. Yet they dismissed the new technology as a fad and continued to rely on their mechanical timepieces where most of their research efforts were concentrated. Not so the Japanese, who began to expand their share of the market with inexpensive quartz watches. By 1980, Switzerland's share of the world market had fallen to 20 per cent—down from 56 per cent in 1952. It was only with the introduction of the Swatch in 1983, a product that

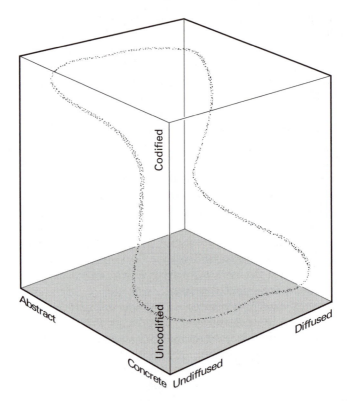

FIG. 7.4 The S-Learner's Cycles

redefined the watch as a high fashion accessory, that the Swiss position began to recover. The Swatch, in effect, constituted a paradigm shift for watch manufactures, calling for a radically different approach to pricing, product positioning, distribution, and branding. Under the leadership of Dr Ernst Thomke, ETA, the prime supplier of watch movements to Swiss watch manufacturers, undertook the painful reconstruction of its identity and culture in order to accommodate the new product paradigm. Many watch manufacturers, however, decided to stay with mechanical timepieces and became niche players.[17]

In contemplating the S-learner's SLC in Figure 7.4 we can discern the terms of the cost-benefit calculation that is undertaken. The costs of creative destruction will only be bearable to those who have not built up too many knowledge assets in the maximum value region. S-learners, then, travel light. They have less to lose than N-learners. They are often youngsters or outsiders who have not yet built up a base of knowledge assets that can be destroyed.

[17] Arieh Ullman, 'The Swatch', in Bob de Wit and Ron Meyer (eds), *Strategy: Process Content, Context*, Minneapolis, St Paul: West Publishing Company, 1994.

Yet, at times, even seasoned industry players can become S-learners when the dynamics of industry competition demand it. As we saw in Chapter 5, some industries will foster an N-learning culture, others an S-learning culture. When the 'dominant logic'[18] that shapes industry behaviour shifts, some firms are able to adjust their cultural repertoire accordingly. It all suggests that S-learning should be thought of as a cultural capacity to deal with a crisis of limited duration rather than as a permanent willingness to engage in the creative destruction of knowledge assets.

7.7 CONCLUSION

SLCs are varied and variable. They are also highly schematic representations of what are, in effect, complex learning processes. They can only be tracked by observing the behaviour of the information-bearing substrates through which learning manifests itself. In this chapter we have discussed three such substrates: first, the products that a firm offers to customers, second, the technologies through which a firm generates its products, and third, the organizational processes that provide the firm with a framework for managing its technologies. To the extent that all three substrates are capable of sustaining SLCs, all three can foster the development of knowledge assets. A firm, then, has to manage a multiplicity of SLCs and has to do so in a coordinated fashion. When these get out of sync, tension results. This is no bad thing where tension elicits a creative or a learning response. Often, however, the inertia of a firm's existing knowledge assets itself blocks the required process of adaptation. The firm then finds itself increasingly lagging behind, reacting to events rather than shaping them. And what it already knows so well blinds it to the reason why.

[18] C. Prahalad and R. Bettis, 'The Dominant Logic: A New Linkage Between Diversity and Performance', *Strategic Management Journal*, 7, 1986, pp. 485–501.

8

Competence and Intent

8.1 INTRODUCTION

THE term 'core competence' has been much in vogue among management academics and practitioners since Prahalad and Hamel's *Harvard Business Review* article on the subject in 1990.[1] Core competences, however, are more discussed than understood and are easily confused with other popular concepts such as core businesses and core capabilities.[2] Drawing upon Molière's *Monsieur Jourdain* for inspiration, many CEOs have managed to persuade themselves that all these years their firms have been demonstrating core competences without realizing it. Most of them, alas, are deluding themselves, believing that a firm's competence is the product of managerial fiat.

Japanese managers are no more exempt than Western managers from such delusions. NEC's chairman in the 1990s, Tadahiro Sekimoto, for example, is a great believer in the powers of synergy, and has been proclaiming the natural fit between computing and telecommunications since 1980. It is a fit, however, that has yet to translate into a demonstrable core competence at NEC, a firm operating as ten vertically integrated product divisions, each acting as a rigid fief in isolation from the others.[3] In a similar manner, the synergy that was supposed to justify Sony's and Matsushita's excursions into Hollywood between 1988 and 1990—one that, by bringing together the hardware and software sides of the media and entertainment business, would bestow on each firm some unique competitive advantage—proved to be nonexistent.

If a firm has a core competence, then as well as forming part of the rhetoric of its top managers, it will show up as forming part of a firm's knowledge assets. Sometimes—more rarely—the line of causation runs from managerial rhetoric to the competence: by talking about competences in inspirational ways, managers actually succeed in fostering their growth within a firm. More typically, however, it works the other way round: it is the possession of a competence that justifies the rhetoric. As a knowledge asset, a competence affects a firm's disposition to act. It should therefore find a place in the I-Space.

In this chapter we discuss core competences as I-Space phenomena. The idea is to see what light our conceptual framework can shed on a popular if

    [1] C. Prahalad and G. Hamel, 'The Core Competence of the Corporation', *Harvard Business Review*, 68 (3), 1990.

    [2] G. Stalk, P. Evans, and L. Shulman, 'Competing on Capabilities', *Harvard Business Review*, March–April, 1992; D. Leonard-Barton, 'Core Capabilities and Core Rigidities: A Paradox in Managing New Product Development', *Strategic Management Journal*, 13, 1992, pp. 111–25.

    [3] 'What's Japanese for Synergy?', *The Economist*, 4 November 1995, p. 84.

still elusive strategic concept. The next section, 8.2, explores the meaning of the term 'core competence' and traces its evolution from the work of management theorists in the late 1950s to the end of the century. Section 8.3 examines the possible sources of a firm's core competence and the contribution these can make to its strategic posture. In section 8.4 we use the I-Space to extend our conceptual understanding of the term, and in section 8.5, still within an I-Space framework, we look at the evolution of core competences over time. In section 8.6 we discuss the way that a competence maintains or renews itself when confronted with the paradox of value. Finally, in the concluding section, 8.7, we place our discussion within the emerging intellectual perspective offered by complexity theory by suggesting that a core competence may best be viewed as a complex adaptive system.

As a complex adaptive system, a core competence is likely to prove quite refractory to treatment by conventional management tools. As the late Friedrich Hayek might have put it, it is the fruit of human action rather than human design and as such cannot simply be wished into existence by managerial fiat or plans.[4] The implications of this point for the management of knowledge assets further indicate the need for a new intellectual paradigm to cope with the strategic and managerial challenges of the information-based economy.

8.2 WHAT IS A CORE COMPETENCE?

As far back as the late 1950s, scholars such as the late Edith Penrose and Philip Selznick were stressing the need for firms to compete on the basis of distinctive competences and resources.[5] This 'resource-based view'—as it came to be called—was gradually replaced in the 1960s and 1970s by the 'positioning view' discussed in the introduction of the preceding chapter, which rooted a firm's competitive advantage in its ability to respond to identifiable configurations of external forces. As we saw, there is something faintly behaviouristic about the positioning view. A proper analysis of environmental stimuli, resolvable as industry structure and competitor behaviour, is translated somewhat mechanically into robust firm-level prescriptions. The element of strategic choice, however, the creative and unpredictable exercise of managerial judgement, almost drops out of sight.[6] If economists treated the firm as a black box whose inner workings were beyond the reach of analysis, corporate strategists chose to treat it as a 'Skinner box', whose inner workings were almost irrelevant to analysis.[7] Between the bell of profitable market opportunities and the salivation of shareholders lay a piece of organizational

---

[4] F. Hayek, 'The Use of Knowledge in Society', *American Economic Review*, September 1945.
[5] P. Selznick, *Leadership in Administration*, New York: Harper and Row, 1957.
[6] J. Child, 'Organizational Structure, Environment, and Performance: The Role of Strategic Choice', *Sociology*, 6, 1972, pp. 1–22.
[7] The Skinner Box was a box named after the behaviourist B. P. Skinner and used to condition pigeons.

machinery that could be operated unproblematically and in a behaviourist fashion by the all-seeing strategist. It was only with the publication of Prahalad and Hamel's article 'The Core Competence of the Corporation' (1990) that the resource-based view was placed firmly back on the agenda of practising managers, and that complex internal organizational processes were once more given the attention they deserved.[8]

A firm's competences are elusive phenomena. Their existence can only really be inferred from a firm's performance. Yet whereas, from a positioning perspective, performance is a predictable and almost mechanical response to identifiable environmental influences, from a resource-based perspective, it is the outcome of an interaction between such influences and far more intangible firm-specific factors.

For Prahalad and Hamel, a core competence displays the following attributes:

1. It delivers a clear and valued customer benefit such as a lighter, smaller, cheaper, or more versatile product. Sometimes a competence manifests itself through superior performance along a number of dimensions simultaneously. Each new generation of microprocessor, for example, represents a saving in weight, time, space, energy—and ultimately in cost—over its predecessors.

2. It is largely tacit and hence hard to imitate by competitors. The speed with which a firm can bring innovative products to market, for example, may depend upon the intangible ability of its product development team to coordinate the actions of its members.

3. It is organization-wide and can thus be applied across an organization's product offering. Miniaturization is a skill that Sony applies across its whole product range in consumer electronics. A competence developed in one area of firm activity can thus be leveraged and applied elsewhere.

4. Unlike physical assets, it appreciates with use. A core competence is the fruit of an organizational learning process. As it gets used repeatedly in a variety of circumstances, so does it deepen. Thus, properly managed, a core competence can become more valuable over time. JVC, for example, successfully exploited OEM relationships in the 1970s with leading national consumer electronic companies like Thomson, Thorn, and Telefunken to extend and deepen its videotape competence, thus outpacing Sony and Philips.

5. It cannot be traded. Only the organization incorporating the competence can be traded. It follows that competences have to be grown in-house, they cannot be bought in the market. As intangible assets, this distinguishes competences from brands. Whereas brands gain their value from the tacit

    [8] See also J. Barney, 'Strategic Factor Markets: Expectations, Luck, and Business Strategy', *Management Science*, 32, 1986; M. Peteraf, 'The Cornerstones of Competitive Advantage: A Resource-based View', *Strategic Management Journal*, 14, 1993; B. Wernerfelt, 'A Resource-based View of the Firm', *Strategic Management Journal*, 5, 1984.

knowledge—i.e., behavioural dispositions—of *consumers*, competences gain theirs from the tacit knowledge of *producers*.

Since none of these attributes is free of ambiguity, many firms have felt able to claim the possession of core competences where a closer and more rigorous examination might suggest that there are, in fact, none to be had. The IBM consulting group and the London Business School, for example, conducted an audit of 203 British factories at the beginning of 1994. Although 73 per cent of companies believed that they matched the best in the world, the auditors reckoned that only 2 per cent of them could be considered 'world class'.[9] Heeding the Delphic Oracle's exhortation to 'know thyself' is not, apparently, something that managers are much inclined to do!

Establishing whether or not one's firm possesses the attributes of a core competence is plagued by problems of definition. For example:

1. The benefit to the customer of the firm having a competence may be overestimated. Motorola's commitment to quality is legendary. Yet it has sometimes led the firm to bring its products late to the market—e.g., its 68040 chip.[10] Is the trade-off that is made by the firm, between product availability and product quality, actually valued by the customer?
2. If competence attributes are tacit, how can they be identified? Company players may be no better at accessing the tacit attributes of a competence than outsiders. It took Corning seventeen years to get the performance of optical fibres to the point where it could compete with copper. In doing so, it built up a great deal of tacit knowledge. But can the firm specify what it is, exactly, in its tacit knowledge base that will keep it competitive?
3. What is the unit organization that possesses the competence? If it is tacit, does the competence reside in the heads of a few individuals working as a team? Or is it widely distributed within the firm? How effectively a competence can be leveraged will largely depend upon the answer to this question.
4. Over time, a core competence can become a core rigidity.[11] Motorola's commitment to quality, for example, could easily blind it to the fact that, in future, the competitive game will revolve around swift product development times, turnover of work in progress, and low selling prices. Overcommitment to one dimension of performance can deprive a firm of the flexibility needed to switch to another when circumstances require it.

The examples given by Prahalad and Hamel in their article indicate that they view core competences as an organization-specific integration of technologies that yields a set of core products, that is, a physical or intangible configuration of value-adding attributes that forms the basis of a product range (see Figure 8.1). The functionality achieved in core products—i.e., the specific

[9] 'A Contender Again', *The Economist*, 28 May 1994, p. 104.
[10] 'Future perfect', *The Economist*, 4 January 1992.
[11] Leonard-Barton, ' Core Capabilities'.

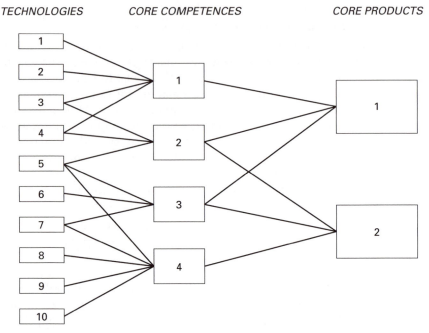

FIG. 8.1 Technologies, Skills, Core Competences, and Core Products

benefits on offer to prospective customers—then becomes an emergent property of the firm's configuring and integrating skills.

Core competences are a source of differentiation and individuation for a firm, bestowing on it a distinct identity and capacities. A question that might be asked is how distinctive does a firm's performance have to be in order to be considered symptomatic of a core competence at work? Given the multi-dimensionality of a competence, the answer is likely to be pretty subjective. As human beings, for example, what distinguishes us from other species rests in part on a unique combination of genes. Yet we share 98 per cent of our genes with chimpanzees, our humanity residing in the remaining 2 per cent. As with genes, so with competence. Minute differences in the way that knowledge assets are deployed and exploited might account for huge differences in performance between firms. The relationship between competence and performance is likely to be nonlinear.

A second question concerns the nature of the technologies being integrated by the organization. Prahalad and Hamel often draw their illustrations from large firms using state-of-the-art technologies. But are these a necessary ingredient of a core competence? Consider, for example, the story of Unipart. When John Neill led an employee buy-out of Unipart in January 1987, he was urged by his financial advisers to quit manufacturing as soon as possible. The Oxford manufacturing plant that Neill was inheriting was sixty years old, and stocked with drab workshops and elderly machine tools. Under Honda's tutorship, the firm decided to switch over to lean production, a coordinated deployment of teamwork and communication capabilities to secure continuous improvements and a more efficient use of resources. Its most crucial investment, however, was not in new plant and machinery, but in its workforce. New working methods gave the older machines a new lease of life and they were therefore retained. Working in teams, the factory's labour force discovered new, faster ways to set up stamping presses—some of these were fifty years old—allowing smaller batches of goods to be produced for just-in-time delivery. Inventory turnover went up from 3–4 times a year to 27 times a year, thus shrinking the space required by operations. Organizational coordination and integration, not technological performance, brought about the gains in performance.[12] To be sure, having the right technology is bound to help. But in many cases it may not be essential to what one understands by a core competence.

Finally, given competences as a source of distinction and individuation, how restricted must their distribution be? Each individual human being, for example, possesses a configuration of personality traits that makes him or her unique. Does each firm, then, simply by dint of being unique, possess a core competence?

Prahalad and Hamel see a large firm as typically possessing between seven and fifteen core competences. Given their supposedly tacit nature, this may be hard to demonstrate. Furthermore, it can easily foster the belief that a firm *ought* to have them and thus lead managers to claim competences for their firms where none is, in fact, evident. Firms, like people, can be unique without necessarily being distinctive, and vice versa. The key point about the possession of a competence is not that it should be unique but that it should be scarce, that is, a source of competitive advantage that other firms would like to have. A number of firms, for instance, may possess similar competences, so that none is, in fact, unique. Yet as long as these firms are few in number relative to the demand for the performance secured by the competence, then scarcity and competitive advantage can be maintained.

8.3 THE SOURCE OF CORE COMPETENCES

If a core competence is an emergent property of a firm's configuring and integration skills, what is it that allows such skills to deliver extraordinary performance in some cases and not in others?[13] Prahalad and Hamel, in an earlier article in the *Harvard Business Review*, give us one possible clue: strategic intent.[14] Drawing mostly on Japanese examples, the two authors discuss

---

[12] 'Unipartners', *The Economist*, 11 April 1992, p. 89.

[13] Our respective uses of the terms 'competence' and 'capability' was given in section 1.1. For an alternative set of definitions, see G. Hamel and A. Heene (eds), *Competence-Based Competition*, Chichester: John Wiley and Sons, 1994.

[14] G. Hamel and C. Prahalad, 'Strategic Intent', *Harvard Business Review*, May–June 1989.

the importance of developing a rigorously derived vision around which a firm's organizing and strategic efforts can crystallize. Thus, for example, Toyota's exhortation to its managers and workers to 'beat Benz' or Komatsu's to 'surround Caterpillar' provide a simple—some would say very simple—focusing device that provides guidance and motivation under conditions of competitive uncertainty. But is it enough to allow the firm to build up its core competences?

The illustrations provided by Hamel and Prahalad tend to be adversarial and zero-sum in nature. The world that they depict is populated by malevolent fast learners who enter into collaborative relationships with the worst of intentions. The visions on offer are all of market conquest and dominance. This is unfortunate, since it deflects attention away from a vision's or intent's potentially powerful contribution to the process of self-organization.

Of course, not all visions work. Edward Reuter's attempt in the 1980s to turn Daimler-Benz into a high-tech conglomerate, for example, overstretched the company, and, if anything, deprived it of any viable focus. The strategic intent was flawed and the grandiose 'synergies' that Reuter pursued proved illusory. The same might be said of ATT's attempt to exploit an assumed convergence of the computer and telecommunications industries—its purchase of NCR in 1991, a computer company, proved disastrous. As we subsequently learned, computer-making remains essentially a manufacturing business, and telecommunications a service business.

In spite of the difficulties involved in developing an appropriate vision—it should be built on a rigorous analysis of the data rather than on the egocentric caprice of a chief executive—the available evidence suggests that having one helps a firm improve its performance.[15] A strategic intent can be thought of as a carefully articulated vision augmented by the organizational effort and commitment to bring it about. In fact, a powerful and strategic intent often allows a firm to transcend the limitations of its resource base as conventionally defined, and to tap into the unexploited reserves of employee motivation and imagination. By pursuing 'stretch goals' rather than 'fit goals'—that is, goals that actually expand an organization's capacities rather than merely reflect them—a firm can achieve levels of performance that could not be predicted on the basis of a rational analysis of its resource base alone.[16] In this sense, a strategic intent favours emergent strategies over planned ones.[17]

Emergent strategies cannot be planned in detail and then meticulously executed by following a blueprint. They depend for their success on employees having either shared or complementary mental models of what their firm is trying to achieve. Prahalad and Hamel see top management as providing a driving vision—a 'strategic intent'—with reference to which employees can

---

[15] J. Collins and J. Porras, 'Organizational Vision and Visionary Organizations', *Research paper 1159*, Stanford GSB, 1991.

[16] Hamel and Prahalad, 'Strategic Intent'.

[17] H. Mintzberg, 'Crafting Strategy', *Harvard Business Review*, July–August 1987.

align themselves. The vision might be quite loose and metaphorical, as indeed might employee responses in a fast-moving and dynamic situation. A strategic intent thus provides an integrative framework for the loose coordination of a diversity of mental models. It allows for the emergence of order from the diversity of human action rather than solely from the narrow purposefulness of human design.[18] Hayek saw orderly market processes as the unplanned and unforeseen result of human action; with his concept of emergent strategy, Mintzberg extends Hayek's insights to organizational and strategic processes.

Although not expressly linked in this way by Hamel and Prahalad, in certain cases a core competence can also 'emerge' in response to a strategic intent. The intent, in effect, acts as a selection device, retaining and reinforcing behaviour patterns that appear to serve it. The intent, however, must not be so narrow as to prevent a firm from generating the diversity from which a competence can evolve—a competence, after all, builds upon a repertoire of knowledge assets which it gradually structures into useful patterns. Nor must it be so broad as to deprive the selection process of any useful guidance. To focus a semiconductor manufacturing intent and effort on zero-dimensional quantum confinement technology, for example, may be too narrow; yet to focus it on the emerging field of nanotechnology as a whole, may be too broad.[19]

The link that might bind together a core competence and a strategic intent is far from inevitable. Some firms may develop the intent without ever achieving the competence: in effect, the intent fails to function as a selection device for the competence. Others stumble upon the competence with little in the way of any strategic intent to guide their selection: here, competence is achieved more or less by accident. The relationship between the two terms can be clarified by means of the I-Space, the next section's topic.

8.4 LOCATING CORE COMPETENCES IN THE I-SPACE

In section 3.7 we described a core competence as a set of technology nodes mediated by organizational linkages (see also Figures 5.4(a) and 5.4(b)). In reality, the line that separates a technology node from an organizational link is not always easy to draw, bearing in mind that a technology, as a knowledge asset, can embed its information content in physical objects, documents, or people's heads. Consider, for example, a piece of high-tech production equipment whose control parameters need to be set. The task could be undertaken by a technician using his own judgement, skill, and experience. It could also be carried out by a technician in response to written instructions from a production engineer. Finally, it could also be performed 'telematically' by the production engineer himself working from a distant location. Should such

---

[18] Hayek, 'The Use of Knowledge in Society'.
[19] M. A. Reed, 'Quantum Dots', *Scientific American*, January 1993.

fiddling with control knobs be considered a personal craft skill, an organizational process, or a technical process? Clearly, it could be any of these three, and often a combination of them all.

Drawing boundaries around a core competence, therefore, and deciding what should be included in it will often be a matter of subjective judgement on which reasonable people will disagree. Hamel and Prahalad see it as a time-consuming process.[20] They claim that it could take up to eight months for the managers of a large firm to come to some consensus as to where its core competences actually reside. Competence identification, then, is no trivial exercise, and getting it wrong could lead a firm into a serious misallocation of its strategic resources.[21]

How might the I-Space help to identify a firm's core competences? What would one look like in the I-Space? We know from our earlier discussions that it might not be too difficult to represent technology nodes in the I-Space. They could each be assigned to an appropriate location in the space by asking the kind of questions listed in Table 8.1 (this repeats Table 3.1). But what about the organizational linkages that bind technology nodes together into value-adding configurations? Clearly, it does not follow that because technology nodes are highly codified, concrete, and diffused, the organizational procedures that link them together must also be. Two different nodes, for example, might each stand for a highly automated step in a production process, using readily available technologies. Yet before the output of one step could be accepted as an input for the other, it might require the skilled intervention of a team of experts. These might inspect the output of the first step and subsequently require a number of informal organizational adjustments in order to align the two steps and get them to function in a coordinated manner.

It would appear, then, that organizational linkages that configure technology nodes into competences need to be represented in the I-Space independently of the technology nodes themselves. This can be done by converting the 'key' diagram of Figure 5.4(a) into its dual, as shown in the key of Figure 5.4(b), that is, by treating technologies as links and organizational links as nodes. The keys of Figures 5.4(a) and (b) are reproduced in Figure 8.2. Organizational linkages can now be located in the I-Space in much the same way as technology nodes have been, that is, by answering questions such as those set out in Table 8.1. But what grounds do we have for assuming that either diagram is describing anything that can be called a core competence? Given how rare core competences are supposed to be, we might reasonably hypothesize that only certain I-Space configurations are competence-rich. We shall show that this is indeed the case.

[20] G. Hamel and C. Prahalad, *Competing for the Future*, Boston, Mass: Harvard Business School Press, 1994.
[21] J. Kay, *Foundations of Corporate Success*, Oxford: Oxford University Press, 1993.

TABLE 8.1 Scaling Guide

Position on Scale	Codification	Abstraction	Diffusion
	Is the knowledge:	Is the knowledge:	Is the knowledge:
High	Easily captured in figures and formulae? Does it lend itself to standardization and automation?	Generally applicable to all agents whatever the sector they operate in? Is it heavily science-based?	Readily available to all agents who wish to make use of it?
Medium	Describable in words and diagrams? Can it be readily understood by others from documents and written instructions alone?	Applicable to agents within a few sectors only? Does it need to be adapted to the context in which it is applied?	Available to only a few agents or to only a few sectors?
Low	Hard to articulate? Is it easier to show someone than to tell them about it?	Limited to a single sector and application within that sector? Does it need extensive adaptation to the context in which it is applied?	Available to only one or two agents within a single sector?

Recall that Hamel and Prahalad require a core competence to be unique to a firm—or, at least, available to but a few firms—and largely tacit and hard for competitors to imitate. Only knowledge assets located in the lower region of the I-Space and towards the left effectively meet this requirement. They could do so, however, at different levels of abstraction. That is, a firm's core competences might draw on a very specific set of technologies and find application in a limited number of product-markets, or they might draw on a more generic set of technologies and get used in a wide variety of product-markets. One would expect the pharmaceutical industry, for example, to accommodate the first type of competence and the semiconductor industry to accommodate the second.

To represent a core competence properly, we need to deploy I-Spaces at both the industry and the organizational levels:

1. At the industry level we can locate the technological and organizational know-how that together make up a core competence relative to a firm's competitors, suppliers, and customers (see Figures 8.3(a) and (b)). Here,

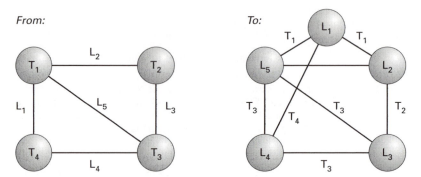

FIG. 8.2 Technologies and Linkages: Two Representations

our diffusion dimension is populated by the firms that make up an industry.

2. At the organizational level, we can see whether the constitutive elements of the competence in question are widely distributed within the organization and hence available for further leveraging—one of its defining characteristics according to Hamel and Prahalad (see Figures 8.4(a) and (b)). Here, our diffusion dimension is populated by the employees of a single firm.

Note that in the industry-level I-Spaces of Figures 8.3(a) and (b) we would expect technologies and linkages to be located towards the left in the diagram if a competence is present, whereas in the firm-level I-Spaces of Figures 8.4(a) and (b) we would expect them to be located towards the right. The knowledge that makes up a core competence, then, is relatively inaccessible to outsiders, but widely accessible within a firm.

Recalling our earlier discussion of technological systems, we can see that a significant part of the knowledge assets that make up a core competence must be located in the region labelled A in the industry-level I-Space of Figure 8.5. It is also likely, given the integrative nature of a core competence, that the centre of gravity of the organizational linkages (circle '0' in the figure) will be located further towards the origin in the diagram than the centre of gravity of the technology nodes (circle 'T' in the figure). The different technologies that make up Canon's core competence in fine optics, for example, are for the most part well documented and available to outsiders. What is less likely to be available to outsiders, however, are the tacit organization skills through which Canon brings these technologies together into a unique, high-performance configuration.

Should the centre of gravity of the organizational linkages turn out to be located further away from the origin than that of the technology nodes—as shown in Figure 8.6—then we are in effect dealing with a *modular* system. Here, it is the organizational linkages that are codified so that they can generate standardized interfaces, while the technologies so linked are treated as

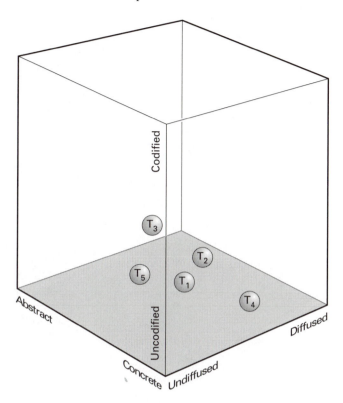

FIG. 8.3(a) Industry-level Representation of Technologies

black boxes. Modularization facilitates decentralization, outsourcing, and hence a controlled diffusion of technological know-how.[22] The way in which system components fit together has to be technically articulated and shared with suppliers if subsequent systems integration is to proceed smoothly. Modularization, however, while effectively leveraging what might be a core competence by facilitating its exploitation on a larger scale, also gradually erodes it. Considerable productivity gains are to be had from the modularization of a production or a business process—when such modularization is radical and holistic, it sometimes goes by the name of business process re-engineering—but its ultimate effect is gradually to dissipate the competence. The organizational integration of technologies ceases to be tacit and firm-specific. By degrees, it becomes explicit and public. For this reason, modularization sooner or later calls for a renewal of a firm's competence base.

[22] R. Sanchez, 'Strategic Flexibility, Firm Organization and Managerial Work in Dynamic Markets: A Strategic Options Perspective', *Advances in Strategic Management*, 9, 1993.

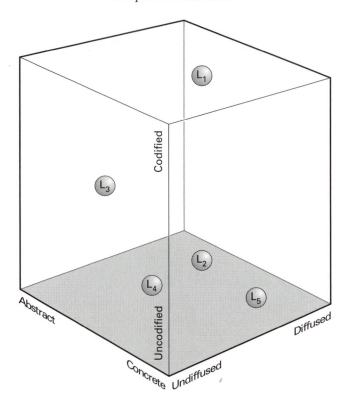

Fig. 8.3(b) Industry-level Representation of Organizational Linkages

A core competence only has strategic relevance to a firm if it can be exploited in value-adding ways.[23] It must allow a firm to move tradeable goods and services into the maximum-value region of the I-Space—region B of Figure 8.5—either in ways that competitors find hard to match, or with a speed and frequency that they cannot keep up with. The first approach extends a good's or a service's residence time in region B; it will thus appeal to N-learners. The second maximizes the throughput of goods and services in region B, and will attract S-learners.

In effect, according to the interpretation that we are giving it, the possession of a core competence facilitates the progress of an SLC through one of the most problematic regions of the I-Space: the fief region. Why is it problematic? Primarily because in this region contributions to the learning cycle are built upon an agent's possession of a unique identity and personal power. Both derive from knowledge which, residing as it does in the heads of individuals, cannot easily be owned by an organization. A core competence

---

[23] Kay, *Foundations of Corporate Success.*

allows a firm to access such knowledge and integrate it across different players. Yet, as the I-Space indicates, to manage and exploit a core competence successfully, a firm must enjoy a measure of cultural and organizational capacity in the lower region of the space. We examine this next.

8.5 THE EVOLUTION OF A CORE COMPETENCE

If a core competence, located as we have hypothesized in the fief region of the I-Space, is the fruit of an organizational learning process, then it must arise, by degrees, from scanning activities conducted in the lower part of the space. Such scanning must take place inside as well as outside the firm: it must draw, first, on the insights of variously situated employees with respect to internal processes, and second, on what outside players—competitors, customers, suppliers—communicate to the firm about the external environment. For this

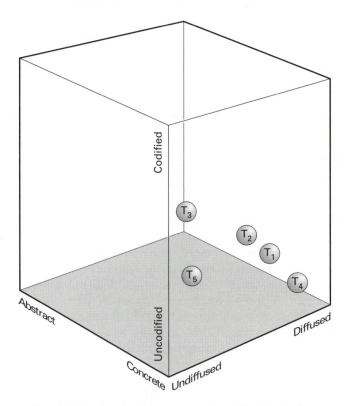

FIG. 8.4(a) Firm-level Representation of Technologies

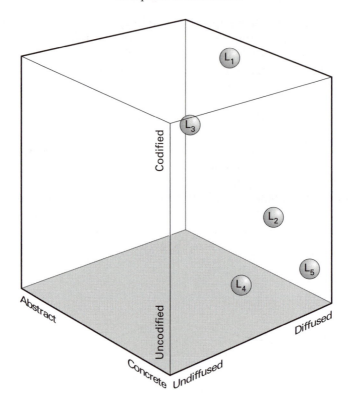

Fɪɢ. 8.4(b) Firm-level Representation of Organizational Linkages

reason, and as already suggested, a core competence can only properly be captured using both a firm-level and an industry-level I-Space.

Scanning, when conducted in the upper reaches of the space, is a well-codified and often quite abstract activity; it is easily imitated and its products are fast to diffuse. It is associated with well-structured incremental changes or product improvements, with statistically based market research activities, and with what consumers say that they want rather than with inferences about their deeper—and often more elusive—needs. It is a relatively safe and unproblematic activity that takes what the data has to say at face value and exploits it as it stands. On its own, however, this kind of scanning cannot lead a firm into region A of the I-Space (see Figure 8.5) where a core competence resides. It is only when, in addition to this kind of scanning, the SLC produces a deepening of the learning effort—and this, recall, should be organization-wide—through processes of absorption and impacting, that region A can be reached. Both processes are associated with learning by doing as well as with a capacity to reflect on experience and to explore alternative patterns. In short, if codified scanning stimulates exploitative learning, uncodified scanning facilitates exploratory learning.

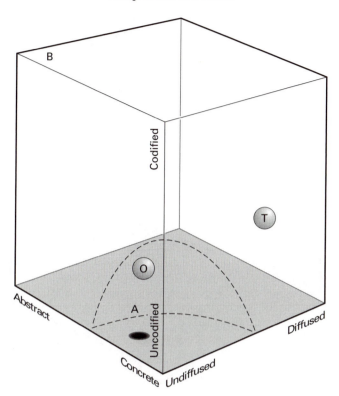

FIG. 8.5 The Centre of Gravity of Technologies T and Organizational Linkages O: The Case of Competence

As discussed in section 3.5, however, pattern-making is a highly personal and sometimes idiosyncratic affair. Where one person sees bricks being laid, another sees a wall being built, and a third will see a future cathedral emerging. We can cast the diversity of pattern-making in evolutionary terms and think of it as the generation of variety. Some of the patterns created will have a greater survival value for a firm than others. Whether any one of them gets 'selected' and subsequently acted upon—as, for example, when articulating a strategic intent or building up a competence—will depend on the procedures followed by the firm in formulating and exercising strategic choices.[24]

Firms usually like to give the impression that such choices are the outcome of careful and rational deliberation. But in reality their decision-making processes are often highly political and uncertain in their outcomes. An irreducibly random element thus pervades a firm's scanning processes, internal or external, inadvertently ensuring that the repertoire of patterns over which

---

[24] Child, 'Organizational Structure'.

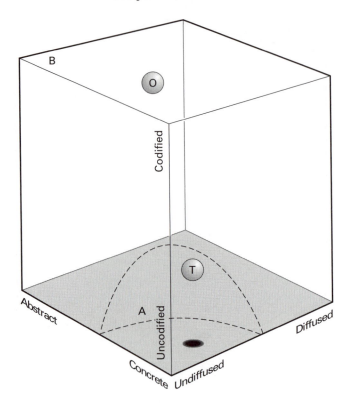

FIG. 8.6 The Centre of Gravity of Technologies T and Organizational Linkages O:
The Case of Modularization

strategic choices are exercised is both expanded and renewed. We might usefully think of patterns generated in this way as possible states of nature with
respect to which a firm's decision-makers take out options. The options last
as long as the states of nature to which they each attach remain live possibilities for decision-makers. Strategic choice then amounts to exercising certain
options while discarding others—in effect, reducing the possible states of
nature that the firm will deal with.

The foregoing leads us to view the pattern-generation and selection
processes out of which core competences are created in region A as emergent.
To repeat the point that we made in the last chapter, they are the outcome of
human action rather than of human design. Hayek drew on the concept of
human action to explain the behaviour of individuals in markets.[25] We use
the term to explain the behaviour of individuals inside firms.

[25] Hayek, 'The Use of Knowledge in Society'; L. von Mises, *Nationalökonomie: Theorie des Handelns und
Wirtschaftens*, Geneva: Editions Union, 1940.

Emergent phenomena are hard to explain or predict and hence cannot be planned for. The reason for this is that the very act of breaking them up into analytically tractable sub-units dissipates the holistic information element that might help to explain them. Emergent phenomena, like quantum ones, are not only indeterminate—they cannot be precisely described or accounted for—they are also discontinuous, so that the causal impact of a well-chosen pattern on a firm's strategic possibilities cannot be fully inferred from the effort that went into creating it. Hamel and Prahalad's treatment of strategic intent brings out the nonlinear potential of such a pattern. Sun Microsystems' cryptic slogan 'The Network is the Computer', for example, might be no more than that—a slogan. But interpreted differently it might also provide the founding vision for a redefinition of the computer industry, turning the Internet itself into a gigantic delocalized computer. Visions and strategic intent are as beguiling as they are risky: who does not remember, for example, the promise of High Definition TV in the early 1990s? The only people who still wax lyrical about HDTV are those who have committed large sums to developing it.[26] The patterns out of which core competences can crystallize have the same alluring quality. Their siren calls challenge the traditional view of the firm as a rational organized entity driven by well-defined market signals.

Treating a core competence as the emergent outcome of political processes highlights a number of problems with managing SLCs in the lower part of the I-Space:

1. The emergent patterns out of which core competences are built cannot be 'managed' in the more traditional 'command and control' sense of the word. They can only be allowed for and responded to.
2. Which emergent patterns get selected and worked on will depend very much on the relative position occupied by those who generate them in the firm's political processes. In many firms, the only patterns on offer will be those that emerge in the heads of the CEO and colleagues. In these firms, variety is likely to be undervalued and underexploited.
3. To the extent that patterns remain in region A of the I-Space, they will stay largely embedded in the heads and behaviours of individuals. These are both mobile and mortal and any firm that employs them will be rightly concerned with the precariousness of knowledge assets stored in such perishable containers. These assets will nevertheless remain hard for a firm to appropriate without codifying them. For this reason it may indeed attempt to codify them.

8.6 MAINTAINING A CORE COMPETENCE

Where a core competence emerges as a response to a scanning process, it reflects the action of an SLC. But SLCs proceed beyond the fief region in

[26] John Rose of McKinsey, quoted in 'Screened out', *The Economist*, 24 October 1994, p. 72.

which, as we have claimed, core competences reside. We argued in the preceding section that the continuation of the SLC beyond the fief region, towards greater codification and abstraction, will tend to show up in product development strategies that move goods and services into the upper region of the I-Space. Yet given the fungibility of knowledge assets and a firm's continuing quest for data-processing and communication economies, it will find it hard to confine its efforts at codification and abstraction solely to the goods and services that it produces. Over time, the tacit knowledge assets that make up its competences also become candidates for codification and abstraction. Many assembly processes that used to be subject to organizational coordination and carried out by human labour—in automobile plants, bottling plants, semiconductor plants, and the like—are now carried out automatically by machines with little or no human intervention.

Firms often have good reasons to attempt to codify and abstract the knowledge that underpins their core competences. This is not to say, however, that they will do so deliberately. The dynamic that drives the process applies to *any* knowledge assets located in fiefs. Sometimes the impulse is provided by new technological or scientific developments that allow a simplification of production activities, a reduction in the number of product parts, or a standardization of products or procedures. In each case, the requirement for tacit coordination and integration skills is reduced, in effect making the competence more visible, more explicit, and hence more replicable—i.e., less firm-specific. The logic of codification and abstraction is driven by a number of considerations:

1. *Property rights*: Firms are often anxious to consolidate their ownership of knowledge assets held implicitly in the heads of key employees. Where such knowledge is simply the sum total of what is held by these people, the returns do not fully accrue to the firm but in large part to the key employees themselves. As John Kay, for example, points out, although in the 1980s Dexel Burnham Lambert was briefly the most profitable firm on Wall Street, the added value it generated was largely due to the know-how locked in the heads of Michael Milken and his associates. They were able to appropriate a large part of this added value for themselves, and when Milken was arrested and put in jail, the firm collapsed.[27] In order to appropriate a greater proportion of the returns on this kind of employee-specific knowledge, the firm has to embed it in visible organizational routines or other articulated processes.[28] That is, it has to shift the knowledge assets from the fief region in the I-Space, where they are a source of personal power for their individual possessors, and

---

[27] Kay, *Foundations of Corporate Success*.

[28] Organizational routines can be either tacit or explicit. Even explicit ones will retain a tacit component. The question then becomes whether the tacit component is the prime determinant of performance. Nelson and Winter fail to distinguish between tacit and explicit routines in their discussion of organizational evolution. They are then led seriously to underestimate the extent to which such routines become replicable outside the firm. See R. Nelson and S. Winter, *An Evolutionary Theory of Economic Change*, Cambridge, Mass: The Belknap Press of Harvard University Press, 1982.

towards the region labelled bureaucracies, where they become a source of power for the organization as a whole. Of course, not all tacit knowledge is in the possession of employees alone. Some of it will be organizationally embedded. Where this is the case, any competence that it underpins will be less threatened with eroding moves up the I-Space.

2. *Uncertainty reduction*: The kind of knowledge located in region A of the I-Space is hard to standardize and has a high degree of uncertainty attached to it. This may or may not be risky. In the case of craft knowledge, variation in outcomes may actually turn out to be a source of value. Applied to surgery or electronic products, however, variation is usually a hazard. For this reason, Motorola in 1987 set itself a target to achieve defect rates of 3.4 defects per million components manufactured by 1992. In that year it achieved 40 defects per million and thus failed to meet its targets. Its performance, however, should be compared with what it was achieving five years earlier: 6,000 defects per million.[29] Typically, firms have an incentive to standardize their knowledge as far as they can in order to reduce the hazards associated with variable outcomes. This moves them out of region A and towards region B in the I-Space.

3. *Economies of scale*: Often the establishment of technical standards spreads out from a firm and into an industry, thus increasing the size of the market for products incorporating the standard. The economies of scale that result sometimes facilitate the further standardization of interfaces between components, and hence the modularization of product and process design.

4. *Co-evolution and dominant design*: Modularization that occurs across firms facilitates the co-evolution of products and the emergence of dominant designs. The design of new aircraft, for example, is highly constrained by the characteristics of the airports out of which they operate—e.g., the length of runways, the dimensions of passenger gates, taxiing patterns, air-traffic control procedures, etc. The degrees of freedom available to aeronautical engineers have thus become severely reduced in comparison with the early pioneering days, with many features of their design tasks being already pre-codified well before they embark on them.

As Kay points out, a core competence remains strategically relevant as long as it is a continuing source of products that are competitive in a firm's chosen markets.[30] The products themselves are in part codifications derivable from the tacit knowledge residing in the competence. A core competence located in region A thus becomes a launch pad for products whose knowledge characteristics will variously be located somewhere on the trajectory between region A and region B (see Figure 8.5). How far a firm attempts either to hoard this product knowledge or to share it with the market turns on whether it is pursuing N- or S-learning strategies or a mix of both. Intel, for example, often exhibits an N-learning orientation, protecting its manufacturing know-how

[29] 'Future Perfect', *The Economist*, 4 January 1992, p. 55.
[30] Kay, *Foundations of Corporate Success*.

through patent battles, entry-forbidding economies of scale, and the rapid introduction of new products.[31] Microsoft, by contrast, while still concerned to protect its critical know-how, is led to share more of it with writers of application software in order to turn it into an emerging industry standard.

To summarize: over time, process knowledge as well as product knowledge migrates towards region B. Links between technologies that were mediated by 'soft' organizational processes gradually get replaced by links that are mediated by 'hard' technological interfaces. Today, for example, the humble household fridge has successfully compressed into a number of compact technological interfaces operations that only two centuries ago required costly and elaborate organization. By way of illustration, consider the following vignette. In 1805, Frederick Tudor (1783–1864), an American entrepreneur who was to become the father of the international ice trade, shipped 120 tons of ice down to Martinique in response to a bad outbreak of yellow fever in the West Indies. He had it cut from a pond on his father's land near Boston and then shipped in a specially bought rig called the *Favourite*. Later, Tudor was granted a monopoly over the ice supply to the British West Indies and to Spanish Havana. He had ice-houses built on the islands to store his cargoes and then extended his network to Georgia and Louisiana.[32]

In the provision of ice, then, products have gradually replaced organizational processes. Where such organizational processes are constitutive of a core competence, they drift up from region A to region B and gradually deplete the core competence of its contents. The firm then confronts the paradox of value with respect to its erstwhile core competence: it moves its knowledge up the I-Space the better to exploit it, only to have it leak out to competitors on account of its greater diffusibility. In the 1990s, the personal computer has fallen victim to the paradox of value. Having successfully done away with the intricate organizational requirements of mainframe manufacturing—many of these now function as highly integrated components, such as microprocessors—computer assembly finds itself relegated to the status of a base technology, one from which all differentiating competences have been squeezed out.

A firm, however, may have little choice but to move its know-how towards region B. The logic of codification and abstraction reflects the competitive pressures that it confronts. If an industry is moving towards automation, the firm may have to follow; if complementary products or powerful clients impose a need for standardization, it will have to adapt. Furthermore, whether or not the firm freely selects the performance dimensions along which it will build its competences, the efficiency gains available in region B may be essential to its competitive posture.

A firm, in effect, pays twice for its move into this region. First, as we now know, the more codified and abstract its knowledge assets, the more diffu-

---

[31] 'Intel', *The Economist*, 3 July 1993, p. 21.
[32] 'The Ice Trade', *The Economist*, 21 December 1991, p. 71.

sion-prone they become. Many banks, for example, fear losing control of the development of their computer systems as well as of proprietary information about their customers to the data-processing firms to which they are outsourcing. Second, moving into region B incurs a loss of flexibility. Codification and abstraction are acts of selection that close off options. Make the right choice and you achieve an increase in utility. Make the wrong choice, however, and it may be hard to backtrack. The problem is that the passage of time often converts what was the right choice at time t_1 into the wrong choice at time t_2. In fast-moving technologies like semiconductors, the problem is becoming acute. At the end of the twentieth century, the cost of the entrance ticket into chip-manufacturing is well over a billion dollars. Yet as the limits to 'Moore's law'—the doubling of the density of transistors on a chip every eighteen months—loom into view, chip manufacturers risk getting stranded with technologies that are no longer competitive but that cannot easily be put to other uses. They then find themselves caught in a 'competence trap': what they are good at, people are no longer willing to pay a premium for. Other dimensions of performance suddenly matter more and these may not be accessible through the firm's current technological base, committed as it has become to ever greater miniaturization as the only game in town.

The only way to renew a core competence, then, as its constituent elements migrate towards the maximum value region B of the I-Space, is gradually to build up new nodes and linkages in region A. Where it is allowed to happen, these will emerge naturally from the firm's scanning and pattern-making activities. In 1969, following Don Frohman's invention of the EPROM (electrically programmable read-only memory), Gordon Moore committed Intel to its production even though no one could tell as yet where the device would find application. Moore's decision built a foundation of know-how and understanding within Intel which, step by step, led to the development of the world's first microprocessor in 1971 and a radically new business for the firm.

Incorporating new linkages and nodes into existing competences, however, is not without problems. The new creations can be either competence-enhancing—thus increasing the performance and potential value of a firm's existing links and nodes—or competence-destroying—undermining the value of such links.[33]

Competence-enchancing additions to the firm's knowledge assets are likely to be the fruit of deep industry-level SLCs located on the left of the I-Space. They will reflect a heavy investment in the absorbing and impacting of a firm's existing technological and organizational know-how. Scanning, to the extent that it occurs at all, will be a tacit and highly personalized business confined to exchanges between a limited number of players—individuals or firms—banding together towards the left in the space. Yet, to the extent that deep SLCs located on the left in the I-Space block out scanning from a larger

---

[33] M. Tushman and P. Anderson, 'Technological Discontinuities and Organizational Environment', *Administrative Science Quarterly*, 31, 1986.

population, there is no guarantee that the competences being reinforced by such cycles are responding to any real need. Indeed, they are often to be found in technology-driven firms where performance gains might be sought for their own sake. Think back to Rockwell producing the 'Cadillac of TV sets' at a price nobody would pay. In these cases, the value of competence-enhancement is more illusory than real.

Competence-destroying additions to the firm's knowledge assets, by contrast, are more likely to reflect scanning from a large number of players and the operation of a broad industry-level SLC. This type of SLC can sometimes be truly Schumpeterian and thus a harbinger of creative destruction. Typically, only a few firms in an industry have the physical or cultural resources required to cope with competence-destroying innovations. Many believe, for example, that IBM surrendered its leadership of the personal computer market because it was unwilling to undermine its prior investments in mainframe computing. It failed to see that the competitive logic of the industry had changed and that what it was trying to hold on to had but a limited future.

8.7 CORE COMPETENCES AS COMPLEX ADAPTIVE SYSTEMS

Core competences that gravitate up the I-Space become, by degrees, technologies and lose the tacit quality that keeps them organizationally tethered to a firm. Yet knowledge assets located too far down the I-Space can also be a source of problems. They lack any clear contours or stability. They cannot much be talked about and for that reason they remain for the most part the unconscious possession of individuals. Unlike an articulate and logical chain of reasoning in which it is possible, with some degree of confidence, to infer one state of a given thought process from what has been established in preceding states, where knowledge is uncodifiable, the links between successive mental states become both less constrained and far more tenuous. The cognitive degrees of freedom available then increase by several orders of magnitude, and the trajectory of a given thought process becomes much more sensitive both to initial conditions and to microscopic disturbances. In effect, uncodified thought processes often exhibit chaotic behaviour in the sense that future mental states cannot be predicted from past ones.

Dreaming and daydreaming, for example, may be instances of chaotic behaviour. In one's waking moments, the need to behave 'heedfully' creates anchoring points in the real world that serve to constrain mental trajectories and render them more predictable.[34] Social interaction can either stimulate or dampen chaotic thought processes. The work of Stewart Kauffman is suggestive in this respect. Kauffman has studied the conditions under which a

---

[34] K. Weick, *The Social Psychology of Organizing*, Reading, Mass: Addison-Wesley, 1979.

system exhibits ordered, complex, and chaotic behaviour as a function of the number of elements it contains and the degree of interaction between them.[35] His approach is schematically shown in Figure 8.7, which describes what Kauffman labels an NK Boolean network in which N stands for the number of nodes and K for the average connectivity of the nodes in the network. The behaviour of the links between the nodes can be tuned by employing a control parameter, P. By manipulating either N, K, or P, Kauffman's network can be made to exhibit order, chaos, or a phase transition between these two states that is known as 'the edge of chaos'. It is in this phase of transition that complex behaviour emerges. Kauffman's results are pertinent to our discussion of core competence. If we take the individual nodes of his systems as data-processing agents and the links between them as communication channels, then Figure 8.7 finds a ready interpretation in the I-Space.

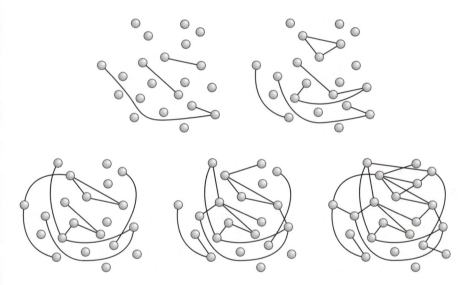

Fig. 8.7 The Foundations of Kauffman's NK Model

The exercise in effect gives us Figure 3.6, here modified as Figure 8.8, with the diffusion scale giving us N, the number of agents acting as nodes in the system, and the codification and abstraction scales giving us P, the control parameter that allows us to 'tune' the communication channels linking them together. The connectivity, K, of the agents in the I-Space becomes an emergent property resulting from the interplay of N and P, giving us, in different circumstances, markets, bureaucracies, clans, and fiefs. Drawing on

[35] S. Kauffman, *The Origins of Order*, Oxford: Oxford University Press, 1993 and 1995.

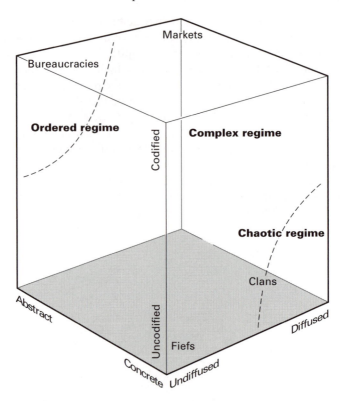

Fig. 8.8 Ordered, Complex, and Chaotic Regimes in the I-Space

Kauffman's analysis, we thus find the same partitioning of the I-Space that we developed in Chapter 3. It yields three distinct phases:

1. The *ordered regime* (phase 1) appears to be the result of highly structured relationships established between a limited number of agents.
2. The *chaotic regime* (phase 3) results from weakly structured relationships between a large number of agents.
3. The *complex regime* (phase 2) emerges either from strongly structured relationships between a large number of agents or weakly structured relationships between a modest number of agents.

Our approach appears to be in line with Kauffman's own. In ours, however, we are left with two distinct levels of complexity. The first operates in the upper reaches of the I-Space, where information is both codified and abstract and reflects a transition from bureaucratic to market processes. The second operates in the lower region of the I-Space, where information is uncodified but concrete; it emerges as one moves from fiefs to clans. In Chapter 3 we distinguished between effective and algorithmic complexity, associating the first with our abstraction scale and the second with our codification scale. Clearly, the move from bureaucracies to markets operates at a lower level of effective and algorithmic complexity than the move from fiefs to clans—i.e., in the first case there are more compressible regularities than in the second. Both moves, however, by increasing N, the size of the population of participating agents, add to the overall increase in complexity.[36]

Drawing on Kauffman's, Gell-Mann's, and other recent work in complexity theory, it makes sense to describe a core competence as a *complex adaptive system*, located in the lower region of the I-Space between an ordered regime in which knowledge assets get frozen into technologies and a chaotic regime in which the stability necessary for effective organizational coordination and integration remains absent. Core competences, then, have their being in a region of the I-Space sandwiched between an excess of usable structure and a total lack of it.

We hypothesize that the possession of a core competence is one measure of a firm's ability to deal with complexity. Firms that find it difficult to cope with complexity are of two types. Some tend to gravitate towards the ordered regime in the I-Space—i.e., towards bureaucracies. Such firms will favour a re-engineering approach to the process of change, focusing their efforts on measurable and stable efficiency gains. Others, by contrast, never manage to get 'organized' at all and simply let entrepreneurial individuals 'do their thing' in the chaotic regime. Such firms rapidly disintegrate under the centrifugal action of opportunistic individuals. In the upper regions of the I-Space these firms might disappear into a network of well-structured market transactions. In the lower regions, however, they simply dissolve as a coherent organizational entity. Only firms that can handle a full SLC, together with the multiple cultures required to drive it, will be able to cope with the many and conflicting demands of a complex regime.

We know from section 1.4 that complex structures operate at a higher level of entropy than more traditional and ordered structures, and that their effective management requires greater data-processing capacities. It follows that firms which operate in the complex regime in the I-Space will need different data-processing strategies than firms that do not. In the next chapter we look at how information and telecommunications technology might affect a firm's choice of data-processing strategies, and, by implication, the management of its knowledge assets.

---

[36] M. Gell-Mann, *The Quark and the Jaguar*, London: Abacus, 1994; G. Chaitin, 'Information-Theoretic Computational Complexity', *IEEE Transactions, Information Theory*, 20 (10), 1974.

9

Information Technology and its Impact

9.1 INTRODUCTION

SOME revolutions creep up upon you by stealth. They do not announce themselves with the fanfare of the French or the Russian Revolutions. In these, even outside onlookers—Burke for the French Revolution, Reed for the Russian—were aware that they were witnessing epoch-making events.

The information revolution has been of the quiet sort. Its early manifestations verged on the banal: in 1953 IBM unveiled its Type 650 Magnetic Drum Calculator, a numerical, stored-program, data-processing machine that had about as much computing power as a modern videocassette recorder. The machine cost $US3,250 a month to rent—equivalent to $US18,000 a month in today's money. The company's expectations were cautious. A few years earlier it had thought the global market for computers to be five machines at best. Type 650, however, could make a profit if fifty were sold.[1]

IBM was similarly cautious when it introduced its PC in 1981. Yet, in 1995, 75 million PCs were sold worldwide. By then, however, IBM had lost the leadership of the industry. One of the initiators of the information revolution was no more able than the onlookers to foresee what direction it would take. Like many other players who rose to prominence in the computer industry during the 1960s, IBM saw data processing requiring ever larger and ever faster machines. The heavy investments in acquiring and operating one of these digital mammoths would favour centralization and ever larger firms.

The opposite turned out to be the case. In the late 1990s a pentium-based PC offers over 10,000 times as much number-crunching power per dollar as an IBM mainframe of the 1970s (see Figure 9.1). And large firms, US ones more than most, have been downsizing and delayering—i.e., decentralizing—their organizations since the mid-1970s. Indeed, with the emergence of the Internet and the virtual corporation some observers are wondering whether, with a further decentralization of data-processing activities, computers or even firms are still necessary. A second, no less fundamental transformation has been going on in the field of telecommunications. The falling cost of a three-minute telephone call is given in Figure 9.2.

These two revolutions in the complementary fields of information structuring and information sharing promise changes in the human condition as fundamental as those that accompanied the advent of settled agriculture or the harnessing of inanimate power to human purposes. The technology that

---

[1] 'A survey of the Computer Industry', *The Economist*, 17 September 1994, p. 3.

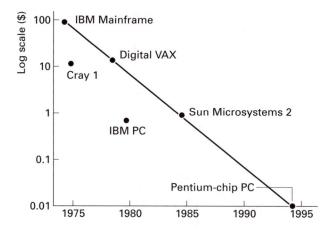

FIG. 9.1 Comparative Costs of Information Processing, 1975–1995

is common to both revolutions, microelectronics, is still undergoing rapid development and is being complemented by advances in materials sciences and in optics. Sometime in the first decade of the twenty-first century, for example, the central processing units of sixteen Cray YNP supercomputers will be manufactured on a single chip, a sliver of silicon containing approximately one billion transistors—in the 1990s, leading-edge devices contain approximately 20 million, and sixteen Crays cost approximately $US320 million. The new chip will cost less than $US100 to make. While this is going on,

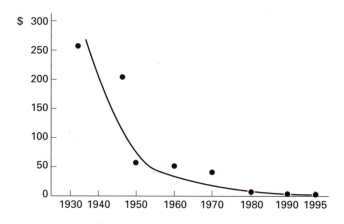

FIG. 9.2 Comparative Cost of a Three-Minute Telephone Call, New York to London, 1930–1995

the 4 kHz telephone lines into America's homes and offices will blossom into some 25 trillion possible hertz of fibre optics.

In this chapter we shall use the term 'microelectronic revolution' to cover those technological developments that affect both information structuring and information sharing, that is, codification and abstraction on the one hand, and diffusion on the other. The term is not a perfect fit since many developments in computing and telecommunications are not electronic in nature. Nevertheless, since microelectronics constitutes the technological paradigm around which the major innovations have clustered, for convenience's sake, we shall stick to the term. The revolution is far from having run its course. It has, however, already transformed the lives of all those living in industrial or post-industrial societies, as well as the lives of a good many who do not. The credit card, the mobile telephone, e-mail, and the laptop computer have today become ubiquitous.

Yet if the depth and pace of the changes that are upon us have become incontrovertible, their direction remains a source of speculation and heated disagreement. Do the information and telecommunications revolutions favour globalization and convergence? Or do they, rather, favour localism? Indeed, could they not in fact foster both at the same time? If so, those living in the global village will want to know whether they should put the emphasis primarily on the world 'global' or on the word 'village'. We are not used to the idea that one can be cosmopolitan and local at the same time.[2] As happened in the scientific revolution three-and-a-half centuries ago, we are, in effect, being called to put on 'a different kind of thinking cap'.[3] What kind of cap might that be?

This book addresses issues of firm-level management and development from an information perspective. The premises on which this perspective has been built up were presented in Chapter 2. We briefly recall two of them here.

First, systems maintain themselves by minimizing the resources they consume per unit of work done as well as by minimizing the amount of work they need to do either in carrying out certain activities, if they are inanimate systems, or in achieving their goals, if they are animate ones. Systems develop and evolve through a gradual—yet sometimes discontinuous—substitution of information for physical resources in securing their own maintenance and survival. Where such substitution is adaptive we can say that the system *learns*. And where its learning is transmissible in space and time to similar systems, we can say that the population of systems *evolves*. As described here, learning is a property of adaptive systems in general and not of biological systems alone—even abstract computer-based simulations of complex adaptive systems display a capacity for learning. What distinguishes the latter from the former is their high degree of complexity.[4]

    [2] A. Gouldner, *Patterns of Industrial Bureaucracy*, Glencoe, Illinois: The Free Press, 1954.
    [3] H. Butterfield, *The Origins of Modern Science*, London: G. Bell and Sons, 1973.
    [4] J. Holland, *Adaptation in Natural and Artificial Systems*, Cambridge, Mass: MIT Press, 1975; S. Kauffman, *The Origins of Order*, Oxford: Oxford University Press, 1993.

Second, in our own day and within human societies, the processes of substituting information for physical resources and of sharing the adaptive benefits that result throughout a population are being accelerated by the microelectronic revolution. Whether the rate of substitution is occurring fast enough to cope with the environmental challenges that human misuse of physical resources has provoked remains an open question.

The I-Space shows how new knowledge is made available for the substitution process that underpins the first of these two premises. Although we have presented the I-Space at a sociological level, that of firms and organization, we believe that as a theory of information production and distribution, it applies to any adaptive system that consumes, processes, and exchanges information in order to survive. Now, if the second premiss is correct, we could expect the microelectronics revolution to have a discernible impact on the dynamics of information flows in the I-Space as well as on how firms and organizations respond to these.

In this chapter we examine what that impact might be. In the next section, 9.2, and in order to set the scene for our subsequent discussion, we briefly interpret the microelectronics revolution in terms of the production function that was presented in Chapter 2. In section 9.3 we assess its impact on information flows in the I-Space. The cultural and institutional implications of the revolution are examined in section 9.4, and the way it might shape knowledge-based competition is discussed in section 9.5. Knowledge-based competition is already provoking a major rethink of what we mean by property rights in knowledge assets, the subject of section 9.6, and how the microelectronics revolution will affect organizational processes in general is addressed in the concluding section, 9.7.

9.2 IT IN THE EVOLUTIONARY PRODUCTION FUNCTION

The evolutionary production function that we developed in Chapter 2 established data and physical factors—space, time, and energy—as the critical inputs for all productive activities that sustain life. In contrast to much inanimate matter that can be treated as a closed system in equilibrium, life is a property of far-from-equilibrium open systems. Such open systems operate at a much higher level of entropy production than do closed systems—Prigogine calls them dissipative systems on account of the energy that they dissipate.[5] Entropy, however, is a measure of disorder, and high entropy production threatens a system's cohesion and integrity. For this reason, therefore, a living system will be concerned to economize on the energy it consumes in order to minimize its production of entropy. What form might such economizing take?

---

[5] I. Prigogine, *From Being to Becoming: Time and Complexity in the Physical Sciences*, New York: W. H. Freeman and Co., 1980.

We hypothesized in Chapter 2 that evolution, over time, would bring about a gradual substitution of data inputs for physical ones, but we also noted that the substitution process itself would be constrained by a system's finite capacity to capture and absorb data. Just as there is a limit to the amount of energy that a system can absorb without disintegrating under the strain, so there is only so much data that it can register and deal with without blowing a fuse. One way of handling such a data-processing constraint is to extract information from data through acts of codification and abstraction, thus reducing the volume of data that needs to be dealt with. This could be done both at the data-capture stage—reducing the amount of data that needs to be taken on board by the system in the first place—and at the data-processing stage—reducing the amount of data that needs to be retained and stored. With the emergence of human cultures and societies, man's capacity efficiently to capture and process data on the one hand, and then to further codify and abstract from it on the other, was greatly enhanced. Critical extensions to this capacity were achieved first with the development of writing in Mesopotamia, some time in the third millennium BC, and then later, in the fifteenth century, with the invention and spread of printing.[6] In our own day, the microelectronics revolution promises similar gains.

Interpreted as a phenomenon on the evolutionary production function, then, the microelectronics revolution promises to accelerate the rate of substitution of information for physical resources in human activity. It increases by several orders of magnitude humankind's capacity to capture, process, transmit, and store data. To illustrate:

1. *Capturing data*: Electronic bar-codes capture data on products and customers on a scale that would have been unthinkable two decades ago. When Kmart, one of the US's leading discount store chains, has its employees zapping bar-coded labels on products, the data is not yet recorded in the store's point-of-sales computer. To keep the finances straight, captured data is transmitted to a second system called Kmart Information Network (KIN). When the store closes at the end of business, the data from KIN is sent to Kmart's head office in Troy by satellite. The head office then logs the information for research purposes and retransmits it to an inventory distribution centre where it is further processed to decide what restocking, if any, is needed at any given store. Fresh stocks then arrive within forty-eight hours. The data so captured and processed is then fed back to Kmart's employees. A display window on the laser gun used for zapping bar-codes provides an instant scorecard. It shows how many items of a given product ought to be on the shelf; how many are still in the stock room; the minimum number that the store is supposed to be carrying; whether fresh ones have been ordered if

---

[6] J. Goody, *The Interface between the Written and the Oral*, Cambridge: Cambridge University Press, 1987; E. Eisenstein, *The Printing Revolution in Early Modern Europe*, Cambridge: Cambridge University Press, 1983. One of the earliest texts bequeathed to us from Mesopotamian times is the epic of Gilgamesh, a legendary Sumerian king.

stocks are too low; what the current price is; and whether that price is the Kmart standard, or has been lowered to beat local competitors.[7]

2. *Processing data*: Since the 1970s, Moore's law—the data-processing power of computing would double every eighteen months—has reigned supreme. The law was revised downwards once, in 1975: performance would henceforth double every two years. During this period, on any given day, therefore, the cost of adding, subtracting, multiplying, and dividing two numbers would be half of what it was twenty-four months earlier. Apart from the obvious computational benefits, one pay-off from these improvements has been the way we use words: at Los Alamos in 1943, for example, a calculator was a woman who carried out calculations for a team organized by the physicist Richard Feynman—a Taylorization of the intellectual function. Today, a calculator is a low-level computing machine, and systems of hundreds of equations are a job for an average PC.

3. *Transmitting data*: Herodotus records that in 490 BC, Philippides, a professional runner, covered the 140 miles between Athens and Sparta in a little under two days in order to appeal for help. The Persians had landed at Marathon just 22 miles from Athens. Although Philippides' exploit passed into legend and gave rise to marathon-running, his message to the Spartans could be compressed into a handful of information bits. In the 1990s, using e-mail, I can transmit the contents of the *Encyclopaedia Britannica* from my house in Sitges to a terminal in Hong Kong in a matter of seconds—without leaving my desk.

4. *Storing data*: The contents of that twenty-volume encyclopaedia can now be stored on a single CD-ROM and carried around in my pocket. Optical storage technology currently under development promises even more compact storage.

The economic effects of the information revolution are a drastic lowering of the costs of data inputs relative to those of physical inputs. This relative change in prices is illustrated in the production function of Figure 9.3. The line drawn tangent to point A on the curve represents the relative prices of data and physical inputs in the energy economy. As can be seen, three units of physical input trade for one unit of data inputs. By substituting data factors for physical factors, we move up the curve towards point B. At this new point the line that lies at a tangent to the curve indicates that the relative scarcity of data and physical resources has been reversed and that one unit of physical inputs will now trade for three units of data inputs. Since one unit of physical inputs used to trade for one third of a unit of data inputs, the latter have now become nine times cheaper in physical terms.

People working in the information economy are intuitively aware of the transformation just described. But, typically, they have not taken on board its implications, namely, *that relative to information goods, physical goods have*

---

[7] 'Remote Control', *The Economist*, 29 May 1993, p. 110.

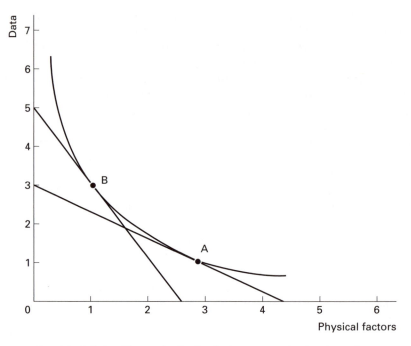

Fig. 9.3 A Price Change in the Evolutionary Production Function

become nine times as costly. In effect, we have retained the mentality of the energy economy, one in which the long-term supply of physical resources is taken to be infinitely elastic. New forms of environmental accounting suggest that we have been systematically underpricing physical inputs by assuming an infinitely elastic supply.[8]

Figure 9.3 highlights two important features of the microelectronics revolution. The first, and the most obvious, is that lowering the relative costs of data inputs, taken together with an increase in the relative costs of physical inputs, imparts a clear direction to social and technological evolution in the production function. The data content of inputs into production will go on increasing in line with falling data costs, and their physical content will go on decreasing in response to evolving price signals.

The second point is much less obvious, even though it is implicit in the shape of the curve in the diagram: the substitution of data for physical resources cannot go on indefinitely. Long before we run off the top of the diagram and up into infinity, we reach the limits of our biological capacity to process and transmit data. To some extent we can increase this capacity through the creation of artefacts—that is precisely what the microelectronic

[8] H. Daly and J. Cobb Jr., *For the Common Good*, London: Merlin Press, 1990.

revolution has allowed us to do. Yet although by doing this we push back the limits, we do not thereby abolish them. Sooner or later we will face the need to economize on data and hence to move back down the vertical scale in Figure 9.3. Should we fail to do so, we risk the fate of Funes the Memorious, a fictional character created by Jorge Luis Borges for one of his short stories. Funes, after falling from a horse, discovered that he had a complete and precise recall of everything he had ever seen: 'He knew by heart the forms of the southern clouds at dawn on 30th April 1882, and could compare them in his memory with the mottled streaks on a book in a Spanish binding he had only seen once.' Unfortunately for Funes, with his phenomenal ability to capture and absorb data he had lost the ability to process and interpret it:

Not only was it difficult for him to comprehend that the generic symbol *dog* embraces so many unlike individuals of diverse size and form; it bothered him that a dog at 3.14 p.m., seen from the side, should have the same name as the dog at 3.15 p.m., seen from the front. His own face in the mirror, his own hands, surprised him every time he saw them.[9]

9.3 THE IMPACT OF IT ON INFORMATION FLOWS IN THE I-SPACE

How should we interpret the microelectronics revolution in the I-Space? It manifests itself in two, somewhat contradictory ways:

1. As we have just seen, it increases an organization's capacity to capture, process, transmit, and store data, thus facilitating moves towards codification, abstraction, and hence towards diffusion.
2. Yet given increased transmission capacities, it also reduces the need to process data just to save on transmission costs. The result is a reduced pressure to codify and abstract. With the advent of the fax, e-mail, the Internet, and, increasingly, video-conferencing facilities, for example, qualitative rather than efficiency considerations come to dictate communication decisions.

Which of these contradictory effects, if any, will come to predominate? To answer this question, we need to consider their impact on the diffusion curve in the I-Space. If the diffusion curve reflects the cost of sharing data within a target population at a given level of codification and abstraction, then any lowering of these costs through technological progress will either increase the size of the population that can be reached or it will reduce the need to codify and abstract data for the purposes of transmitting it. In the I-Space, the first effect shows up as a rightward shift in the diffusion curve from AA' to BB' (see

---

[9] Jorge Luis Borges in his short story 'Funes, the Memorious' introduces us to a poor young Uruguayan, a hapless, friendless prodigy by the name of Ireneo Funes. His blessing, and his curse, is that he could forget nothing. See J. L. Borges, *Labyrinths*, New York: New Directions, 1962.

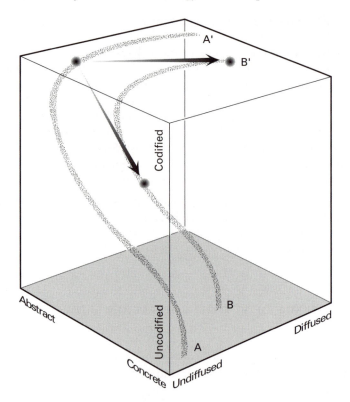

FIG. 9.4 IT Shifts the Diffusion Curve to the Right in the I-Space

Figure 9.4). The size of the population that can be reached at any given level of codification and abstraction thus increases. The horizontal and vertical dotted arrows in the diagram, however, indicate that the rightward shift in the curve in fact opens up two options, the second of which incorporates the second effect. Let us briefly describe each option in turn.

Option 1: The Horizontal Arrow: Obviously, and as is implied by the curve shift itself, for a given level of codification and abstraction, more people will be reachable across a greater distance per unit of time than hitherto. Video-conferencing provides an example of this possibility for messages that are concrete and uncodified, and e-mail illustrates the case for messages that are more codified and abstract. Both of these technological developments increase the potential number of agents that can be involved in the commu-nication nexus.

Option 2: The Vertical Arrow: Less obviously, for a given size of population targeted, information transmitted can be both less codified and more con-crete. An A4 page of text, for example, represents about 100,000 bits of data; a photograph about 10 million bits; a cinema-quality film requires a transmission rate of 20–100 million bits a second. In the 1990s, fibre optic cables have the capacity to handle such transmission rates. As that capacity grows, objects that could only hitherto be represented in a highly codified and abstract manner can increasingly be experienced sensually. The success of scientific visualization since the late 1980s has shown how to harness people's intuitive ability to discern patterns in properly presented data. As virtual reality (VR) evolves, it will become possible to bring into play several senses simultaneously. VR will then be used to visualize all kinds of complex, dynamic systems, ranging from personal investments to global economies, and from micro-organisms to galaxies.[10]

As can be seen from the position of the new curve BB' relative to the original curve AA', the microelectronics revolution affects both the structuring and the sharing of knowledge assets, reducing the need for the first, while increasing the scope for the second. The result is a significant lowering of transaction costs throughout the I-Space, with the savings increasing as one moves downward, forward, and to the right. Information that is concrete, qualitative, and that could once only be reliably transmitted face to face, can now be shared globally and instantaneously by a large number of agents. More significantly, perhaps, much information that once had to be codified and abstracted for the purposes of authentication and transmission can now be widely shared on an informal basis with trusted parties. For example, publication in many scientific journals has become a mere ratification of a result that has already been well disseminated to professional colleagues through e-mail or fax, and, as it were, pre-peer reviewed. For many physicists, the journal *Nature* has become little more than an archive for results that are already common knowledge within certain networks before they are published. Diffusion, then, now takes place at a much lower level of codification and abstraction than hitherto, quickening the pace and intensifying the competition to be first. This is as true of industrial as of scientific competition.

9.4 THE INSTITUTIONAL IMPACT OF IT IN THE I-SPACE

The lowering of transaction costs brought about by the microelectronics revolution is likely to exert a strong influence on the cultural and institutional options available to firms, both for their internal management and for their dealings with each other. If we superimpose the institutional structures discussed in Chapter 6 on the diagram of Figure 9.4, the cultural implications of the microelectronics revolution become immediately apparent (see Figure 9.5). The shift of the diffusion curve from AA' to BB' is likely to stimulate the growth of market and clan institutional forms, both across organizational boundaries as well as inside them.

---

[10] B. Laurel, 'Virtual Reality', *Scientific American*, September 1995, p. 70.

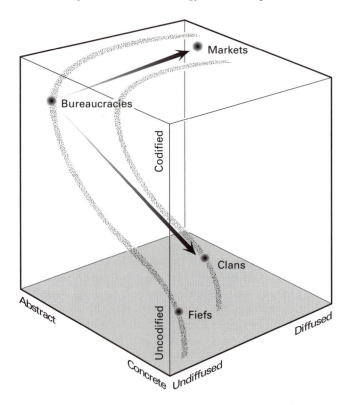

Fɪɢ. 9.5 Institutional Implications of IT in the I-Space

To borrow and loosely adapt a concept from introductory economics, we might think of the curve as defining a 'Transactional Possibility Frontier', that is, a set of transactional options available to data-processing agents as a function of their data-processing and transmission budgets. What the new data-processing and transmission technologies are doing, in effect, is to push outward the transactional possibility frontier, thus extending the options available for a given level of resources. In this way, many transactions that were located either in the fief or bureaucratic region of the I-Space on grounds of cost-effectiveness, can now, if needed, be reassigned to markets or clans.

This does not mean that fief and bureaucratic structures will necessarily disappear. As long as knowledge assets get renewed and SLCs pass through the left-hand region of the I-Space, such transactional forms will remain essential and will therefore persist. Nevertheless, with the shift in the curve, transactional options have expanded and lowered the average cost of transacting per agent involved.

At the end of the nineteenth century, the introduction of the telegraph, along with the advent of the railways, extended the reach of hierarchical coordination and ushered in the era of the giant corporation. Large corporate bureaucracies emerged in response to the new coordination options that were becoming available.[11] Recall, however, that bureaucratic transactions require data to be steered into the most problematic region of the I-Space, one where the value created by codification and abstraction becomes precarious. Bureaucracies are under constant pressure to decentralize authority and to adopt less formal administrative procedures. Moves in the 1990s towards employee empowerment are just one more manifestation of this pressure. For this and other reasons, many transactions handled bureaucratically might be better located elsewhere in the I-Space.

Prior to the advent of the new technologies, reassigning transactions in this way was not possible; a shift to the right or down would have pushed them into the region of the I-Space in which chaos reigned supreme. The outward push of the transaction possibility frontier, however, extends the dominion of the complex regime in the I-Space at the expense of the chaotic one. It also extends the reach of the ordered regime, but, as we saw in the last chapter, we are now more likely to see a substitution of technological for organizational processes in that regime—automation, robotization, etc.—than a further bureaucratization of transactions themselves. Automatic teller machines, for example, do not make banking transactions more bureaucratic; they make them more technological.

In sum, the rightward shift of the diffusion curve is likely to be accompanied by a shift in the centre of gravity of a firm's knowledge assets in the I-Space. Inside the firm, the bulk of these assets is likely to be shared more extensively with employees; outside the firm, they will be more readily available to customers, suppliers, and competitors. Over the long term this is likely to erode the viability of hierarchical forms of organizing. People will operate increasingly within clan structures if they are permanent employees, and within market ones if they are part time.

The critical skills required for organizational effectiveness in clan structures differ from those found in bureaucracies. In the latter, tasks are subdivided in a Tayloristic fashion, and task components find their way on to individual job descriptions. Efficiency considerations require that coordination within and between jobs be carried out by fiat. Managers have to be technically proficient and to show that they know what they are doing. Non-managerial employees, by contrast, have to demonstrate obedience and a willingness to be coordinated, as well as an ability to confine relevant behaviours to what is set out in their job descriptions.

In clan structures, on the other hand, the level of task uncertainty is much higher and no one possesses privileged information on how to carry it out. Coordination is by negotiation and mutual adjustment rather than by fiat,

---

[11] A. Chandler, *The Visible Hand: The Managerial Revolution in American Business*, Cambridge, Mass: The Belknap Press at Harvard University Press, 1977.

and, as a consequence, the quality of interpersonal relationships, trust, and shared values takes on a much greater importance than in bureaucracies.

Markets share with bureaucracies the requirement for a high degree of codification and abstraction of the information they draw on. Tasks can be precisely defined and hence enforceable contracts can be written. Tasks that can be traded in markets, however, do not easily lend themselves to the degree of hierarchical coordination found in bureaucracies, and therefore managerial authority has less purchase. Relationships are much more explicitly competitive in markets, and, being less personalized than in clans, they are less constrained by bonds of reciprocal obligations and mutual regard.

Although, as discussed in Chapter 6, markets can be internal to firms as well as external to them, the decrease in transaction costs associated with external market governance will make this form an attractive option for many tasks that used to be conducted through the internal hierarchy. The growing trend towards outsourcing and part-time or temporary employment, for example, indicates that many tasks in the modern corporation lend themselves to the market form of governance. Where transaction costs remain high, however, clan forms associated with strategic alliances and interorganizational networking will still be preferred.

Whether in a particular case markets or clans are actually preferred may depend in large part on the way that national cultures and institutions shape transactional options. The US business environment, for example, is likely to exert a powerful bias in favour of the market over the clan option. Although inside firms there is a move to promote interpersonal networking and a more informal management style associated with clans, across firms such collaboration continues to be frowned on in many cases, being viewed as collusive and detrimental to the public interest. Yet, to the extent that in the lower region of the I-Space organizational boundaries become fuzzy and ambiguous—i.e., no one quite knows how or where to draw them—cultural constraints on *inter*firm relationships are bound to limit the way that *intra*firm relationships are conducted.

The cultural environment of a country like China, by contrast, with its bias towards uncodified and concrete transactions, is likely to favour the clan option over the market one.[12] In spite of having a Marxist-Leninist regime that aspired to conduct all transactions through bureaucracies, coordinating them centrally by means of a command economy, China never fully succeeded in building up the rational-legal structures of a modern nation-state. As a result, managers and officials have more or less been driven to sort out their relationships in the fief region of the I-Space, where information and power asymmetries predominate. The reforms that were initiated in agricul-

---

[12] M. Boisot and J. Child, 'The Iron Law of Fiefs: Bureaucratic Failure and the Problem of Governance in the Chinese Economic Reforms', in *Administrative Science Quarterly*, 33, 1988, pp. 507–27; M. Boisot and J. Child, 'From Fiefs to Clans and Network Capitalism: Explaining China's Emergent Economic Order', *Administrative Science Quarterly*, 41, 1996, pp. 600–28.

ture in 1978, and extended to industry in 1984, have brought about a gradual decentralization of economic activity. But this decentralization has been taking place predominantly in the lower regions of the I-Space, leaving the upper regions largely untouched. Robust legal infrastructures through which arm's length market and bureaucratic transactions can be conducted are still absent.

As the microelectronic revolution takes hold in China, therefore, it is likely to build on transactional structures already available. With the reforms, these have been extending to the right in the space, shifting the institutional order from fiefs to clans. The idea that China is moving towards a market economy, therefore—that is, decentralizing from bureaucracies to markets in the I-Space—is an illusion that has been fostered by a Chinese leadership with little real understanding of what such an economy entails.

9.5 EVIDENCE AND IMPLICATIONS

Evidence for some of the cultural shifts just hypothesized is already upon us. The advent of information technology has given rise to extensive networking both within and across organizational boundaries. Used generically, a network description can be made to represent any of the transactional forms that were discussed in Chapter 6. As Figure 9.6 indicates, bureaucracies and fiefs, no less than markets and clans, can be described in network terms. Yet it is clear from the examples that people habitually draw on when discussing networking, that what they actually have in mind when using the term is either the market or the clan forms of the activity—i.e., they view networks as an alternative to hierarchical ways of transacting.

One example of the market form of networking is the Internet. In spite of its nifty graphics, it operates largely on the basis of codified information available to everyone—either for free, or for a small price. It also offers anonymity as well as ease of entry and exit. It is largely self-regulating and, until recently, escaped all attempts at control from outside. Indeed, it is ironic to see leaders who claim to be moving their country's culture towards a market economy— the case of China—frantically trying to control their citizens' access to the Internet. It is only because a genuine market economy is in fact so alien to China's culture and institutional structures that the country's leadership fails to see the contradiction.[13]

An example of clan forms of networking is the Italian version of the industrial district. The so-called 'Third Italy', located in the north-central part of Italy and away from the industrial heartland of Milan–Turin–Genoa and the agricultural south, is based on groups of small firms, pursuing strategies of continuous innovation and flexible specialization. Alfred Marshall defined an

---

[13] Boisot and Child, 'From Fiefs to Clans'.

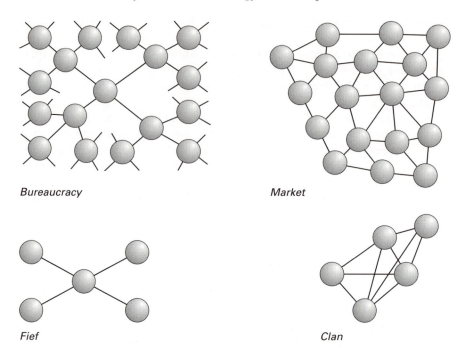

Bureaucracy   Market

Fief   Clan

FIG. 9.6 Institutional Forms Represented as Networks

industrial district as a spatial conglomeration of small firms whose relationships are characterized as much by collaboration as by competition and
whose aggregate output is greater than it would be in the absence of such collaboration.[14] Industrial districts thus benefit from external economies. Silicon
Valley constitutes an American example of an industrial district, and the software firms currently springing up in and around the city of Bangalore, known
locally as the 'Silicon plateau' provide an Indian one.

   In principle, there is nothing to stop a large firm adopting a clan style of
management and operating as if it were a network of smaller firms.
Bureaucratic capacity may have been a prerequisite for the construction of
the large modern corporation in the age of the telegraph and the telephone,
but in the age of the Internet and the video-conference the need for a bureaucratic style of management is much diminished. As a result, firms like
Hewlett-Packard and Asea Brown Bovery (ABB) have adopted a clan-like
approach to running themselves, with considerable success. Indeed, the latter,
by subdividing itself into 1,300 independent companies and 5,000
autonomous profit centres, has become a fluid network that adds value by
coordinating activities across geographical and corporate boundaries. In

[14] A. Marshall, *Principles of Economics*, London: Macmillan, 1947; M. Best, *The New Competition:
Institutions of Industrial Restructuring*, Cambridge: Polity Press, 1990.

such networking, corporate boundaries may well lose their importance. Digital Equipment, for example, uses almost the same performance appraisal system for its suppliers as for its own employees, and Eastman Kodak allows outsiders to run one of its supply rooms.

Mastering the logic and the culture of clans, then, allows a firm to develop an organizational capacity that reaches beyond its corporate boundary, and this even for transactions that are too vague and fuzzy to be conducted through external markets. In Japan such clan networks are known as *Kereitsu*. Like their pre-war brethren the *Zaibatsu*, however, *Kereitsu* sometimes metamorphose into fiefs centred on one or two powerful players, usually banks.

Both market and clan forms of networking are likely to be enhanced by IT. The crucial point to note is that since the 1980s the debate among economists, based largely on the transaction cost perspective, has centred almost exclusively on the diffusion dimension of the I-Space: in seeking to minimize the search, contracting, and monitoring costs associated with transactions, should these be centralized and conducted through bureaucratic hierarchies inside firms, or should they be decentralized and conducted through markets outside firms? This question was posed by Ronald Coase in the 1930s, and we have argued earlier that it needs reformulating.[15] Not only can transactions external to the firm be conducted through bureaucratic hierarchies—as in command economies—but decentralized market transactions can also take place inside the firm—as in internal labour and capital markets. Clans, to be sure, have put in an appearance in recent explorations of Coase's original question, but only as a point along a single (diffusion) dimension.[16] Fiefs do not even get a look in.

The I-Space shows us that the transaction cost perspective offers a very limited view of the options available, one that owes a great deal to orthodox economists' enduring inability to come up with an adequate conceptualization of information. Indeed, in the absence of the codification and the abstraction dimension of the I-Space to counterbalance the emphasis put on the diffusion dimension, fiefs and clans can never even appear as articulate institutional options in their own right: they are therefore cast in the role of hybrids. We believe that it is high time that they were given their proper place in the cultural repertoire of options available to firms and industries.

This certainly seems to be happening at the wider societal level. The growth of communitarianism in the 1980s and 1990s in the USA, for example, points to a cultural revival of institutional forms that have been lost to view.[17] As these forms show up in places like the Internet they clash with the more commercial orientation of market-driven players. At present, the Internet is

---

[15] R. Coase, 'The Nature of the Firm', *Economica*, NS, 4, 1937.

[16] O. Williamson and W. Ouchi, 'The Markets and Hierarchies Program of Research: Origins, Implications, Prospects', in W. Joyce and A. van der Ven (eds), *Organization Design*, New York: Wiley, 1981.

[17] A. Etzioni, *The Spirit of Community*, London: Fontana Press, 1995.

becoming a battleground between those who would like to see its IT potential put at the service of delocalized and possibly global communities governed by a clan ethos, and those who perceive it as extending the global reach of an impersonal market culture. It will probably end up serving both types of aspiration—but through different channels.

9.6 THE IMPLICATIONS OF IT FOR THE CREATION OF KNOW-LEDGE ASSETS

How will a rightward shift of the diffusion curve in the I-Space affect the extraction of value from knowledge assets? It is hard to be very predictive about this, but it is clear that the curve shift can move one either to the right or downward in the I-Space—or both—and hence away from its maximum value region. How are we to interpret this shift?

At a most fundamental level, the issue boils down to one of property rights. To get a feeling for what is at stake, recall that oilfields cannot be photocopied but that the chemical formula for benzene can. Physical goods, by occupying a unique spatio-temporal location, enjoy an irreducible measure of scarcity that is not shared by information goods. In the latter case, if scarcity is required, it has to be artificially contrived. A patent, for example, does not increase the physical scarcity of new knowledge. On the contrary, by requiring its public disclosure, it actually reduces it. And that, of course, is the whole idea. What a patent does, however, is to require would-be recipients and users of newly patented knowledge to treat it *as if* it was scarce. Yet creators of new knowledge have to meet certain stringent conditions before a patent is granted. In particular, they must articulate that knowledge in such a way as to make it readily usable by others. If they fail or refuse to describe new technical knowledge at the right level of codification and abstraction, the patent will not be granted.

By facilitating the diffusion of information that is still uncodified and concrete, IT makes it more difficult to reach the level of codification and abstraction required for legal appropriability before others manage to gain possession of it. Under such circumstances, the problem of deciding who invented what and of enforcing ambiguous property rights in knowledge may reduce the attractiveness of patenting as a way of extracting value from the creation of knowledge assets. With the evolution of IT, then, achieving collaboration in knowledge creation activities may become easier; achieving adequate returns on such collaboration, however, may well become more difficult.

One plausible interpretation of the rightward shift of the diffusion curve in the I-Space, therefore, is that the maximum value region in the space will be more difficult to reach and that it will be more difficult to stay in once reached. The problem has two quite distinct components:

1. Since much information will start to diffuse at lower levels of codification and abstraction, the expected returns on investments in information structuring will drop. It may be that with earlier diffusion, more people will participate in the structuring of information. Yet the increased utility of information so structured will not always compensate for the loss of scarcity entailed by its earlier diffusion.
2. The residential time of structured information that does reach the maximum value region is likely to shorten as a result of increased diffusion pressures brought about by the rightward shift of the curve.

As a consequence of such a dynamic, we would hypothesize that N-learning strategies associated with information hoarding in the maximum value region will be least profitable in those industries most deeply penetrated by IT. In such industries, S-learning strategies based on information sharing and fast learning, are likely to prove more attractive. S-learning, however, is likely to operate through faster, flatter SLCs, in the lower region of the I-Space (see Figure 9.7). We know from our discussion in Chapter 4 that property rights

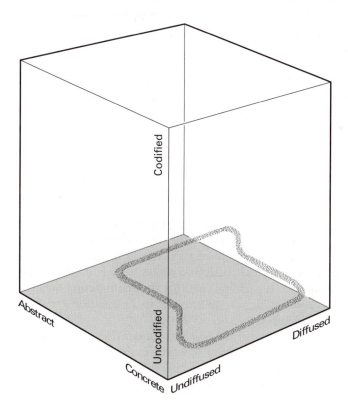

FIG. 9.7 A Flat SLC in the Lower Region of the I-Space

are ambiguous in the lower regions of the I-Space and that there, firms have difficulty making good their ownership claims to knowledge assets. By shifting transactions downward and to the right, IT will, if anything, exacerbate the problem of intellectual property rights.

It has been calculated that in developing countries up to four-fifths of the countryside has no legally recognized owner. The same thing could happen to large stretches of intellectual territory. Much of it will then be up for grabs. If so, we would expect knowledge workers who are located in the lower region of the I-Space, those actively involved in the creation of knowledge assets, to establish a 'new deal' with the organizations they work for, allowing them to appropriate for themselves a much larger share of the value they create. Establishing a deal that will be perceived as fair by all the parties concerned will not be easy. It has been hard enough to shift compensation schemes from an orientation based on effort to one based on contribution. How will these function when that contribution is ambiguous—knowledge does not often come in neatly measurable packages—and its link to performance is subject to divergent interpretations? How will a firm deal with a situation in which five minutes of clear-headed thinking by a middle-level employee may be worth two or three years of muddled effort by a top manager? To make matters worse, in contrast to many physical assets, the real value of knowledge assets can usually only be known *ex post*: the full value of a contribution can only be properly ascertained after—sometimes well after—it has been made. When that contribution is made on the basis of shared knowledge and of informally coordinated team work, the challenge of coming up with a deal that is perceived by all players as being fair becomes formidable indeed.

9.7 IMPLICATION FOR ORGANIZATIONAL PROCESSES

The organizational uncertainty resulting from operating lower down the I-Space will not be resolved through trying to anticipate every contingency and then writing more complete contracts. Firms will have to move away from legal contracting and towards relational contracting, from arrangements enforced by impersonally applied legal sanctions, to those secured through prior familiarity, personal trust, and reputation. Legal ordering, of course, does not disappear. It remains valid for spot-contracting arrangements. But these are less and less likely to be relevant to the creation and development of durable knowledge assets.

The above remarks apply as much to the contracts that bind employees to their firms as to those that bind one firm to another. Yet to the extent that prior familiarity and personal trust take time and effort to develop, employment relationships in a regime of relational contracting are likely to generate higher transaction costs than under a regime of market contracting. 'Hired heads' are more difficult to monitor than 'hired hands'—you can see what the hands are doing but you cannot know what the head is thinking. For this reason, knowledge-based firms are likely to have fewer employees for a given level of sales than more traditional industrial firms. A limited number of high-quality relationships will be preferred to a larger number of average-quality relationships.

With IT, however, prior familiarity, personal trust, and reputation will not be built using traditional forms. Until the microelectronic revolution, trust was built on the basis of shared experiences that required a minimum of co-presence. Co-presence, in turn, required co-location—i.e., parties to a transaction had to coordinate their actions in order to find themselves at the same place at the same time. With the advent of electronic communication—video-conferencing, e-mail, etc.—co-presence can be achieved without co-location. As a result of this, one may well be able to build up a more 'trusting' relationship with a transaction partner located on a neighbouring continent than with one located in a neighbouring room. The deeply held assumption that putting people in the same room or in the same building makes it easier for them to get on the same wavelength may not be invalidated by the microelectronic revolution. But it will have to compete with the insight that people who are already potentially on the same wavelength may be able to get together irrespective of the constraints of time and space, and may thus not have to share a room or a building at all in order to maintain a productive relationship.

The prizes will go to firms that can take advantage of this simple insight. Whatever the benefits to be offered by IT, interpersonal trust itself is a commodity whose supply is inelastic. It is conditioned by an individual's capacity to achieve co-presence, a capacity that is limited by the number of people with whom an individual can meaningfully interact. IT will have but a marginal effect on that capacity, much as it might allow many more people to operate closer to it than do so at present—in itself no mean achievement. Yet, if the capacity for trust is limited, where is the pay-off from IT? It resides mainly in the increasing geographic and cultural diversity that now becomes available within the trust relationship. Until the advent of IT, interpersonal trust was in the nature of things a parochial affair, conditioned primarily by class, ethnic origins, and geographical proximity. In the 1920s, for example, to be labelled a 'cosmopolitan' was to be branded as rootless and shiftless. The delocalization and internationalization of trust will enhance a firm's ability to operate SLCs in the lower regions of the I-Space independently of spatial and—perhaps more importantly—of cultural constraints.

A number of economists, including Paul Krugman and Michael Porter, see competent networking as the ultimate source of competitive advantage for an economy.[18] IT is giving such networking a global reach. As the cost of innovation continues to climb, firms in a growing number of industries—

[18] M. Porter, *Competitive Advantage*, New York: The Free Press, 1985; P. Krugman (ed.), *Strategic Trade Policy and the New International Economics*, Cambridge, Mass: MIT Press, 1986.

pharmaceuticals and telecommunications are the obvious examples of the 1990s—are having to sell globally to recoup their investments. With a careful integration of their knowledge flows, innovative multinationals need only one team of people to design and develop a product platform for the entire world market. In the case of Texas Instruments, for example, design teams in Texas, USA, coordinate their work with design teams in Bangalore, India, in order to be able to work on a problem round the clock.

Some cultures are better placed to profit from the internationalization of trust relationships than others—those, for example, that have a tradition of tolerance and pluralism. But the main message is that whatever their geographical origins, firms will have to build up a culture of trust from the ground up. 'The technology is here', observes Daniel Shubert, director of client/server technical services for Electronic Data Systems Corp. 'The problem is not with the technology, but with the corporate processes. Companies must fundamentally change the way they do business, and that's hard.'[19] As the *Business Week* article in which the above quote went on to observe, 'you can't run a 21st century networked corporation with 1950s rules'. Getting the most out of a network requires substituting trust for control. And if that trust is to extend beyond the parish pump politics that characterizes decision-making at the top of many firms, those that are still saddled with a 1950s 'command and control' culture, then IT must become a constituent part of the trust-building process.

The I-Space offers some pointers to how this might be done. Our basic contention is that the microelectronics revolution has the potential greatly to accelerate movements around an SLC—a development which, as we have already seen, is likely to favour S-learning strategies over N-learning ones. The appropriate use of IT, however, will vary as one moves round an SLC. Consider, for example, Figure 9.8. It depicts the four transactional cultures discussed in Chapter 6 linked together by an SLC. Each of the four phases of the SLC is associated with a distinctive process designed to move social exchanges from one type of transactional culture to another. Networking processes in markets, for instance, may start out as impersonal and arm's length, and rely extensively on the ready availability of codified and abstract data. Over time, however, recurrent transactional patterns will stabilize certain networking relationships, and, as the parties to an exchange get to know and trust each other, a more personalized and 'clannish' transactional style may take over. Knowledge flows inside these subnetworks are likely to be much more informal and qualitative, and where subnetworks interact regularly and share common concerns they will gradually give rise to community processes.

Clearly, markets and clans operate fundamentally different cultures. This is why orthodox economists are often suspicious of the latter. They reek of collusion and exclusion—the other side of the trust coin—and hence com-

[19] Annual Report on Information Technology, *Business Week*, 26 June 1995, p. 47.

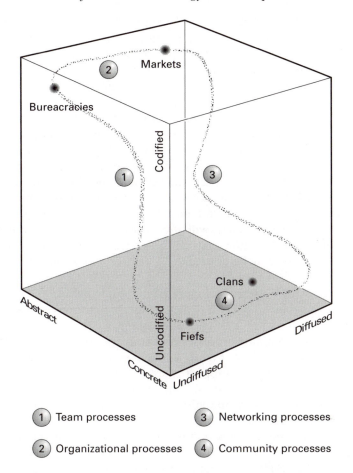

1 Team processes   3 Networking processes

2 Organizational processes   4 Community processes

Fɪɢ. 9.8 Four Different Social Processes in the I-Space

promise the impersonal efficiency of markets. To those who believe that as many transactions as possible should go through markets, the kind of networking that leads from markets to clans is a kind of learning that they could do without. Yet the networking activities that move transactions from markets to clans—and thence on to community processes—are essential to the S-learning perspective. Creative destruction may be the price to be paid by the move away from market equilibrium, but social renewal and development is the prize.

The scanning phase of the SLC, the one that transforms clans into more centralized fief-like structures, is greatly facilitated by community processes because any focusing on shared concerns is neatly counterbalanced by the cognitive and behavioural diversity of community members. The sheer variety of perceptions and interests that a community can accommodate increases the chances that uncodified threats and opportunities will be spotted and acted upon. Communities, however, are not unitary actors. They share concerns rather than goals. Responding in a coherent fashion to opportunities or threats that have been scanned by a community is the work of team processes.

Teams are small groups drawn from the community and operating in a focused problem-solving mode in response to threats and opportunities. They may start as informal 'fief-like' entities with a few powerful individuals making the key decisions. Yet, as teams progress through their life cycles and as both the problems they face and the solution they explore become better structured and understood—a move once more up the I-Space—so team processes become more formalized and bureaucratic. And as the knowledge they create needs to diffuse out to non-team members who do not share the team's tacit knowledge base, so team coordination gradually gives way to organizational processes. These will often diffuse the knowledge created by a team beyond the population that can be subjected to hierarchical bureaucratic control, so that such knowledge, by degrees, moves once more into the market region of the I-Space.

In sum, the picture offered by Figure 9.5 of the microelectronic revolution's impact on firms is incomplete. It depicts a change in the field of forces acting on information flows in the I-Space and strongly suggests that the transformation favours community processes over more traditional ones. As the more dynamic representation of Figure 9.8 makes clear, however, the latter processes do not thereby disappear; they remain a constituent part of the SLC. The skill required will consist in integrating the four different processes just discussed—network, community, team, and organizational—into a single seamless learning cycle.

IT itself is evolving in ways that will facilitate such integration. The distinction that is often made between old-style computing, in which data is processed in a carefully preprogrammed and serial manner, and new-style computing, in which items of data are processed in a parallel and decentralized fashion, corresponds to two different locations in the I-Space (see Figure 9.9). The first expresses a hierarchical approach to data processing that is institutionalized in human organizations as bureaucracies. The second takes data processing to be a horizontal activity requiring mutual adjustment. In human organizations it is institutionalized as clans. Yet while there has been a tendency to present sequential processing and parallel distributed processing—i.e., old and new style computing—as competing computational paradigms, our own analysis suggests that they are best viewed as two moments in a single learning process. Although we cannot address the issue further here, it is important to realize that IT itself offers us today a much expanded repertoire of data-processing options in different parts of the I-Space.[20]

---

[20] Alan Turing argued that sequential- and parallel-processing machines are but two different instantiations of a Universal Turing Machine. See A. Turing, 'On Computable Numbers with an Application to the Entscheidungsproblem', *Proc. Lond. Math. Soc* (Ser. 2) 42, 1937, pp. 230–65; with a correction in 43, 1937, pp. 544–6.

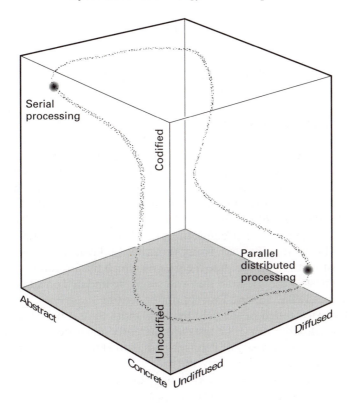

FIG. 9.9 Two Computational Strategies in the I-Space

Using the I-Space as an analytical framework, this chapter has explored the impact of IT on organizational and cultural processes. IT, by dramatically lowering the costs of data processing and transmission, will extend its influence well beyond organizations and culture. By embedding itself in every kind of manufacturing process imaginable, it is already accelerating and changing the terms of the trade-off between information and physical resources that we discussed in Chapter 2. Properly conceptualized, then, the microelectronic revolution provides us with some of the tools that we need to address the environmental challenges that beset us. What this chapter has highlighted, however, is that the type of learning required to meet the challenge calls for an appropriate organizational and cultural orientation. And IT also turns out to be well placed to help develop these as well.

10

Applying the I-Space

IO.I INTRODUCTION

I-SPACE is a conceptual framework built on a theory of information flows. Any theory worth its salt should be tested in encounters with concrete experience. Some of these encounters are explicitly designed to test the theory. Where possible, they take the form of controlled experiments. Others are designed to make use of the theory. Of course, using a theory tests it as well and the wider the range of circumstances in which it can be usefully applied, the more robustly it gets tested. Every time that I take off in a 747, for example, I am testing the aerodynamic theories on which the aircraft is built. They may not be perfect theories and they will surely be updated one day, but they cannot be totally flawed, else I would not be writing these lines. To date, the I-Space has been tested in the field by users more than it has in the laboratory—although laboratory-like tests are currently under development at the Wharton School, University of Pennsylvania, and at the Management School at Imperial College, London University.[1]

The social psychologist Kurt Lewin once quipped that there is nothing so practical as a good theory. Does the I-Space meet the test of practicality? In this chapter we briefly describe two situations, each in a different firm, in which I-Space has been used by practising managers to address practical issues facing their firms. In section 10.2 we describe the procedures managers followed in using the framework. In sections 10.3 and 10.4 we present and interpret the results of their work, and we compare the two firms in section 10.5. We then look in section 10.6 at other situations in which the I-Space has proved useful. We assess applications of the I-Space in the concluding section, 10.7.

IO.2 PROCEDURES

In both cases to be presented—one in the chemical firm Courtaulds, the other in BP's oil exploration business—the framework was used to map and analyse a business's technological posture—the configuration of a particular class of knowledge assets—in a specific area of its operations. Getting the level of analysis right from the outset is crucial if one wants meaningful results.

---

[1] A simulation model is being developed in which the behaviour of agents in the I-Space is tested by means of genetic algorithms. This work is supported both by Courtaulds and BPX.

Mapping at the corporate level, for example, would not look the same as mapping at the business level, or at that of a competence. The populations to be located on the diffusion scale would be different, as would the level of detail at which knowledge assets are to be mapped. The most practical approach is to be guided in one's choice of level by the nature of the problem that one hopes to address.

The analysis we present is that carried out by practising managers themselves. We are thus initially dealing with a collection of individual perspectives and representations that are subjective in nature and that confront each other. Gains in objectivity are achieved gradually through iterated discussions and further investigations. Who gets to participate in this exercise is therefore important. Managers need to be chosen for their thorough familiarity with the issues to be addressed as well as for the relevance of their technical background.

The mapping is typically carried out with a group of up to fifteen managers in a two-day workshop. It proceeds as follows:

1. Participants are asked to identify the area of operations in which knowledge assets are to be mapped. The two businesses under study each chose a technical area, but clearly many other kinds of knowledge assets could be mapped. Usually, an area is selected because it presents a strategic challenge to the firm.
2. Within the cluster of knowledge assets themselves, participants then clearly establish what will be treated, respectively, as elements and as key relationships between elements. In other words, they attempt to describe the knowledge assets selected as a *system* of interrelated parts. This second step takes time and can be full of surprises. A matrix representation of the elements and relationships selected can be helpful and injects some rigour into the analysis. Nevertheless, deciding where exactly to draw boundaries around knowledge assets is often a matter of judgement requiring group consensus. System and matrix representations of knowledge assets are given in Figures 10.1(a) and (b).
3. By means of simple scales, individual participants locate the *elements* e_1 ... e_n of the system in the I-Space along the three dimensions of codification, abstraction, and diffusion.
4. The exercise is then repeated for the linkages l_{ij} between elements where l_{ij} links element i to element j.
5. Participants' individual scores are then compared and discussed. In this phase of the workshop, participants get to appreciate how much or how little shared understanding they have of the area under consideration. The discussion should, if possible, be recorded.
6. Those entries where strong divergences in scores between individual participants suggest ignorance rather than irreconcilable differences should be rescored. However, suggestive outliers should be kept and not discarded.

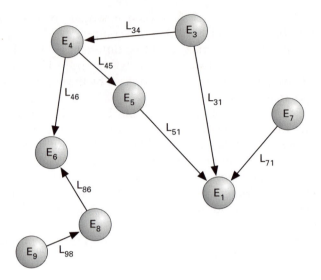

FIG. 10.1(a) A System Representation of Knowledge Assets

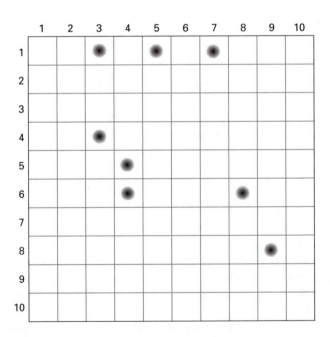

FIG. 10.1(b) Matrix Representation of Knowledge Assets

Notes: The ten key knowledge assets are identified with numbers making up the rows and columns of the matrix. Columns influence rows so that for example a cross placed in columns 3, 5, and 7 of row 1 means that knowledge assets 3, 5, and 7 causally influence knowledge asset 1.

7. The final results are presented in graphic form and participants come up with a coherent interpretation of what they see.

The process described above is greatly facilitated by the use of the groupware. Groupware is computer software designed to foster group interaction and collaboration. In the interventions described, participants used portable Power Macs and a proprietary software package called Council, both to locate key technologies and organizational linkages in the I-Space as well as to record discussions of their individual scores. Using groupware helps to focus on the issues, to exchange ideas, and to track the results of 'electronic discussions'. It creates a novel kind of interaction, since comments entered into the machines are no longer directly attributable to particular individuals and hence, filtered through professional or status differences.

In some circumstances the divergences between the scores of different individuals that show up on the groupware may point to a need for further investigation beyond the workshop. If certain elements or linkages still cannot be located in the space in a way that participants can agree upon, then specialized outsiders may need to be consulted. Elements and linkages might then be redefined and/or relocated. What we are after is a shared understanding based on dialogue, debate, and rigorous analysis. Only when the mapping is one that workshop participants can all live with can the workshop move on to an interpretation of the resulting patterns.

Where there are constraints on the time available for an intervention, a reduced form of the I-Space, that we shall label the I*-Space, can sometimes be used. In this reduced form, the concrete–abstract dimension of the model is initially omitted and only the codification and diffusion dimensions are employed. The third dimension is brought in later, as needed. Both content and process reasons can be given to justify this.

Content reasons: In company work, the issues associated with the dimension of abstraction can often be dealt with independently of those raised by codification and diffusion. They may, for example, involve the generic quality of a firm's knowledge assets, whether the science they draw on resides at the abstract end of the abstraction scale, like, say, physics, in the middle of the scale, like, say, biology, or at the concrete end of the scale, like clinical psychology. Where such issues are not the central focus of an intervention, it is quite feasible to handle them as they arise, bringing in the third dimension in response to the specific needs of the situation.

Process reasons: In consulting interventions, the framework has been used primarily as an elicitation and interpretive conceptual tool. It is typically employed by company managers in one- to three-day workshops that focus on technological or strategic issues related to knowledge management. Given the limited time available, it is often more expedient to focus on two of the three dimensions of the model that workshop participants can master quickly than to grapple with the full complexity of the three-dimensional framework.

The results of such a simplification may be more coarse-grained, but in many situations they will suffice, and cognitive overload will be avoided. Again, if the abstraction dimension is required, it can be introduced once the codification and diffusion dimensions have been fully mastered.

In what follows (sections 10.3 and 10.4), we present interventions based on the I*-Space only. Interventions focusing on the dimensions of codification and abstraction alone—i.e., focusing on the forms taken by knowledge assets rather than their social distribution—are also possible. We first present some background material on the business under study in each firm in order to provide some context for our discussion of the workshops. We then present the mappings that were developed in each of the two workshops and briefly discuss them. The mappings developed in each firm will then be compared in section 10.5, drawing on the concrete–abstract dimension of the full I-Space where appropriate. In section 10.6 we briefly look at a few other corporate applications of the I-Space, and in the concluding section, 10.7, we offer an assessment of the I-Space as an intervention tool.

10.3 COURTAULDS' FIBRE BUSINESS[2]

Background

By the mid-nineteenth century, Courtaulds had become a 'considerable manufacturer of crêpe'. By the 1890s the home market for crêpe was no longer expanding. A slump in the firm's output and profits between 1886 and 1898 made clear the need for diversification. Two new men from outside the family circle, who were to dominate the company for the next twenty-five years, were brought in: Henry Greenwood Tetley and Thomas Paul Latham.

During the second half of the nineteenth century various attempts to get cellulose from cotton or trees into solution had been documented, culminating in de Chardonnet exhibiting 'artificial silk' fibres and textiles in Paris in 1889; these were made via the nitrocellulose route. At this time Samuel Courtauld and Co. were planning stock-market flotation. The firm was looking for opportunities to grow and for new raw materials to target its developed silk markets. In 1904, the year that Samuel Courtauld and Co. became a public company, Tetley persuaded the Board to buy the English rights to the patents for making artificial silk by the viscose process. The new fibre had qualities of its own—one of them being that it possessed the lustrousness of

    [2] The research on which this material is based was funded by the CDP Group of the UK Engineering and Physical Sciences Research Council, grants GR/K24284 and GR/K23591, as part of its Management of Technology initiative. The research was carried out in collaboration with Dorothy Griffiths and Veronica Mole both of Imperial College, and with the help of Dr Hilda Cousley and Dr Terry Lemmon, both of Courtaulds. It also draws heavily on the three-volume history of the firm by D. C. Coleman: *Courtaulds: An Economic and Social History, Vol. 1: The Nineteenth Century, Silk and Crepe*, Oxford: The Clarendon Press, 1969; *Vol. II: Rayon*, Oxford: The Clarendon Press, 1969; *Vol. III: Crisis and Change, 1940–1965*, Oxford: The Clarendon Press, 1980.

silk. It owed much to professional chemists working on the chemistry of cellulose (the essential components of all plant tissue) and it responded to the demands of a quite diverse range of industries: electric-lamp manufacture, paper-making, explosives, etc. The first plant was built in Coventry in 1905.

The development of the viscose process was a mixture of chemistry and engineering in which the company collaborated with the French holders of the viscose patent rights. Partly as a result of this collaboration, between 1905 and 1913 the firm was transformed from a textile firm into a chemical firm with a textile branch: by 1909 profits from the chemical process of turning wood pulp into artificial silk were greater than those that came from making fabrics. The problems of the business were increasingly those of chemical engineering: more and more of the company's main product was yarn to be processed by textile firms, not fabric to be worn by consumers. By 1912 profits had doubled as a result of a rapid growth in the output of viscose yarn and a satisfactory financial position enabled the company to bear years of losses incurred by a process of trial and error at Coventry. Yet once initial success had been achieved in 1908, it was the remarkable productivity wrested from the chemical inputs which enabled profits to be built up and ploughed back at a rate that permitted further expansion.

Viscose—i.e., cellulosic fibres—enjoyed dramatic expansion from 1920 onwards. After 1941, viscose continued to grow, but at a slower rate. This was due to a combination of factors: release from wartime restrictions in Europe, the expiry of most of the basic patents, and a worldwide dissemination of the fundamental technology of 'artificial silk' manufacture. The growth pattern had two main constituents: first, important technical changes which created new yarns and fibres within the generic category of cellulosic fibres, and second, the differing timing of advances in these various types of cellulosic fibres amongst the leading producing countries.

Many of Courtaulds' products were developed by the firm only after the initial invention had been made elsewhere. In Tetley's day the firm had bought the rights to the inventions of others and had then exploited these successfully. In the absence of basic chemical research, technical achievements were brought about by the close alignment of the company's research policy with the demands both of the textile markets and of the firm's production processes; this allowed continuous practical advances which combined quality and product improvements with lower costs; it also allowed repositioning in new but similar markets.

Yet, by 1950 the firm was lagging behind the USA and Europe in its technical development. It had become increasingly apparent that viscose textile yarn, which had made big money for Courtaulds in the past, had had its day. A certain level of 'defensive' research was maintained—in acrylic and nylon it was more than defensive—in order to stay competitive and ensure a continuance of improvements at the margin. Yet the closure in 1962 of the firm's basic research laboratory at Maidenhead was a suitable symbol of the times.

By the 1970s Courtaulds, in response to the oil price rises of the period and to environmental pressures for a cleaner viscose process, was wondering where to go next. Recognizing that the compliance technology patented by Eastman Kodak and being explored by Akzo had potential, Courtaulds bought into it: Akzo had established the feasibility of dissolving cellulose in organic solvent and generating this in fibrous form. But Akzo itself, faced with the difficulties of developing and commercializing the new fibre, had decided not to proceed.

In 1978, Courtaulds began work in its central research and technology (R and T) organization to find a better way to make viscose. The work was kept relatively secret inside the fibres and viscose laboratory and was actually paid for by the viscose business—a certain degree of bootlegging was necessary because the work could be perceived as a threat to the business and its progress therefore hampered. The search was now on for a safer and more environmentally friendly technology and the firm focused on cellulose—not only was it renewable, but Courtaulds had a commercial interest in wood pulp—as a possible source of new fibres. At the same time, cost reduction pressures were making themselves felt.

In the 1970s, R and T at Courtaulds was organized along university lines and characterized by a certain informality. Funding was not as narrowly controlled as it has become since and there was sometimes enough in the budget to indulge in a bit of exploratory research. In the 1980s, on his retirement, the firm recruited Akzo's technical director. With his help, pilot plant work was undertaken, the objectives of which were to develop fibre spinning and solvent recovery operations. It was fibre spinning and cellulose technology expertise that led to the development of the world's first commercial solvent spun fibre. The new cellulosic fibre (NCF) was quickly recognized as a potentially new product in its own right and, in 1983, in order to develop and commercialize it, it was set up as a new and independent business within Courtaulds. In the course of the NCF's development, it became clear that the firm was not only dealing with a compliant process technology, but with a new product technology offering new product properties.

In 1987 an NCF pilot plant was built in Grimsby, Humberside, and introduced to financial analysts in the City of London as an environmental solution to the problem of viscose. In 1992 the first commercial plant became operational in Mobile, Alabama, and in 1994 it was decided to invest in a doubling of the fibre's production capacity in the USA. The strategy was to exploit the fibres in high value end uses to which viscose is unsuited, while continuing to identify potential products for other markets. Courtaulds' investment in the NCF had been initially justified on the grounds that it was an environmentally friendly alternative to viscose. In a paper to the board, however, David Giachardi, the board member responsible for R and T, also mentioned that the fibre had interesting and novel properties of its own, as well as a strong potential for cost savings. There was a clear feeling that the

NCF might turn out to be basically a new fibre for which there would be demand.

Building on its experience of the commercial production of acrylic, poly-ester, nylon, and other fibres, Courtaulds developed a strong competence in the process technologies linked to fibres, bringing together and integrating the diverse technical elements associated with different processes. This led to the development of the cellulose dissolution stage, for example, based on the viscose and acetate experience. And the NCF spinning technology included elements of melt spinning, that is, polyester spinning, of acrylic and of viscose technologies.

In developing a product like the NCF, there is a need to control for the scale of production, and to understand how wide the material's envelope of properties might be. The former aims to increase production volume and bring costs down; the second, by trying out different mixes of raw materials, for example, aims to widen the material's envelope of value-adding proper-ties. The two development endeavours go on in parallel, since product and process improvements are interlinked: some change in the process can trigger a significant improvement in product properties, and vice versa. During this development phase the firm aims to sell more than enough in the market to recover its development costs. There is a delicate balance to be found between extending the range of value-adding properties of the material and keeping its costs competitive.

Some of the senior technical people at Courtaulds believe that the ability to create a NCF was based on an underlying competence in spinning technolo-gies. It was this competence, they argue, that allowed the firm to recognize the new material for what it was. Courtaulds has been involved in three types of spinning: liquid spinning, melt spinning, and air-gap spinning. It was because Courtaulds had mastered a repertoire of spinning processes that it was in a position to devise the kind that was required by the NCF. The two headings under which the claimed competence appears are Spinnable Materials Technology and Spinnable Process Technology. The keys under 'Materials' are Courtaulds' abilities first to produce and handle difficult polymer solu-tions, particularly cellulose, and second to purchase and use low-cost raw materials. The spinning process combines many skills in order to make prod-ucts with properties and at costs that the customer will buy. The firm has a long history of engineering: building kits to its own designs, squeezing costs, and manipulating conditions around the jet and spin bath to produce the properties needed. Moreover, the firm can perform a number of operations on the formed fibre to produce different effects. In spite of all this, Courtaulds only just began to understand the NCF's spinning process in the 1990s, and the material has only recently been given an industry classification in Europe.

Over the course of the twentieth century, Courtaulds demonstrated great skill in the handling and spinning of polymer solutions, particularly cellulose, as well as ingenuity and skill in the building and operating of complex processes to produce the fibre properties needed, improved and optimized to achieve minimum cost. The NCF, for example, being made from natural cellulose, can be produced to have the feel and the fall of silk and the appearance of cotton, even though it is stronger and more versatile than cotton. The NCF, then, has a considerable range of potential applications. Yet it was only when there was enough NCF material already in the market to experiment with that Courtaulds began fully to appreciate its superior properties. Appreciation was facilitated by the fact that the firm had retained its textile business until 1990 and knew its traditional markets well. Such market knowledge gave the firm the confidence—not always justified—to go ahead.

To summarize: for the second time in the twentieth century, Courtaulds, the British chemical firm, stumbled on to a new fibre with considerable commercial potential. It may turn out to be a generic product with a number of different applications in many markets. In this, as in the earlier case, the basic chemistry that led to the discovery of the fibre was performed outside the firm by an organization that did not fully appreciate the fibre's potential. Also, as in the preceding case, the firm has taken a laboratory product and developed it to the point where it could be exploited commercially. This involved, simultaneously, an exploration of the fibre's possible new properties as well as an exploitation of whatever economies of scale might be achieved in its production to increase volume and drive down costs. It was during the development phase itself that Courtaulds came to appreciate and understand many of the new fibre's potential applications. In contrast to what happens in many other industries, the firm's experience points to a development process coexisting with a fair amount of basic research and hence operating at a high level of uncertainty.[3] Courtaulds, then, appears to be good at doing physics and chemistry on a large scale—a form of chemical engineering. Many of the technologies finally developed for the NCF production processes were originally drawn from failed experiments and development projects carried out for other purposes. They were thus present and available in the organization's memory and in its technology repertoire.

The Workshop

Workshop participants were concerned to understand the nature of Courtaulds' success with the NCF and, in particular, what kind of competence, if any, it might be symptomatic of—i.e., what conditions would have to be met for the processes described to be considered a core competence of Courtaulds? Recall from our discussion in Chapter 8 that a core competence can be thought of as an interrelated set of processes or technologies that are operated and integrated in such a way as to yield a higher level of performance than competitors might achieve with the same means. Arguably, and

[3] D. Mowery and N. Rosenberg, *Technology and the Pursuit of Economic Growth*, Cambridge: Cambridge University Press, 1989.

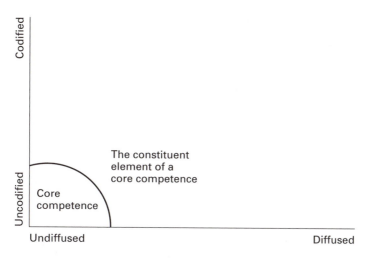

Fig. 10.2 Core Competences in the I*-Space

as has already been hinted at, in so far as tacit knowledge and organizational processes are involved, a core competence would appear in the I*-Space as less codified or diffused than its constituent elements (see Figure 10.2).

The mapping exercises carried out by participants are given in Figures 10.3 and 10.4. The first locates the technologies associated with the production of the NCF, in the I*-Space, and the second locates the critical linkages between these technologies in the space. For purposes of confidentiality, the technologies and linkages are numbered but not named. The mapping exercise carried out by the managers do not support the claim of a core competence in the processes under study. As can be seen in the two diagrams, the lower part of the I*-Space is contentless. Not only do no technologies reside there, but no organization integration is taking place there either. What is apparent, however, is that the firm is strongly positioned in a number of tightly integrated technologies. These are well codified and located on the left in the space.

The exercise provoked some heated discussion among participants. One who had been intimately involved in the development of the NCF objected that it was built on a strong base of uncodified knowledge. Further probing, however, revealed that what the participant was referring to was the kind of tacit knowledge that we all possess—unique, idiosyncratic, and *not necessarily available to the organization*. Other participants, by contrast, found the map both plausible and illuminating. It seemed consistent with their perception of the fibre business at Courtaulds as one that aims to codify everything as quickly as possible. Was this strategy of uncertainty reduction, they wondered, compatible with a continued capacity to innovate? The answer to this question seemed to turn on the innovation dynamics of the industry that Courtaulds found itself in. In a mature business like fibres, characterized by

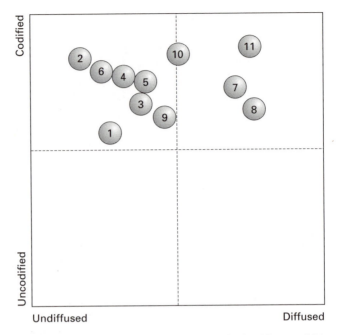

FIG. 10.3 Industry-level C-Space: Technologies (Courtaulds)

economies of scale and comparatively slow SLCs, getting into the maximum value region of the I*-Space and then staying there as long as possible appeared to offer the greatest returns. The issue will be further discussed in section 10.5 below. We now turn to our second intervention.

10.4 BP EXPLORATION (BPX)[4]

Background

Historically, BPX, the exploration arm of BP, was organized into a number of Regional Operating Companies (ROCs) each of which managed a number of exploration and production (E and P) activities. Each ROC had its own staff support—for example, in the form of a human resource and training function—and operating performance was measured at the ROC level. A major change in structure, however, was initiated in July 1994 when BPX removed the ROC management layer and decentralized itself into a federation of assets. An asset was to be a 'project or operation which has the capac-

⁴ The research on which this material is based was funded by the CDP Group of the UK Engineering and Physical Sciences Research Council, grants GR/K24284 and GR/K23591, as part of its Management of Technology initiative. The research was carried out in collaboration with Dorothy Griffiths and Veronica Mole.

ity to produce results in terms of positive cash flow or is close to producing positive cash flow'. Assets could be individual fields or a number of these clustered into a national region. An example of the former is Magnus in the North Sea, and an example of the latter is Vietnam.

Between 1989 and 1996 a drastic downsizing of the organization took place. Like many other performance-focused organizations, BPX had reflected on the nature of its core activities and decided that these should be resourced internally. Non-core activities, on the other hand, might well form the core business of other firms and should therefore be left for them to develop. This line of reasoning has led to a massive growth in outsourcing over the last decade, as large firms got rid of more and more of their non-core activities. BPX has followed the trend and outsourced an increasing number of activities, from IT through to training, with only their strategic components being retained internally. Outsourcing raises many issues for BPX, among the most critical being how to identify core activities, how to remain an informed buyer, and how to avoid becoming overdependent on contractors or suppliers.

The firm's strategic reorientation altered its approach to technology issues. In January 1992, BPX produced a document entitled 'Technology Strategy', in which its new approach to technology provision was outlined. This

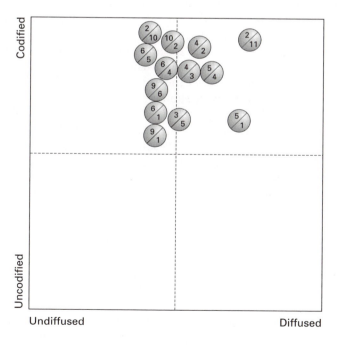

FIG. 10.4 Industry-level C-Space: Organizational Linkages (Courtaulds)

document was the outcome of an extensive series of discussions with a large number of business and research staff. The key element of the strategy was '. . . to focus on the *use* of technology, and not on its creation and ownership' (our emphasis). The discussions that led to the document had concluded that while the possession of technical know-how was a major ingredient of BPX's competitive advantage, the critical success factor was the extent to which such know-how facilitated the adoption and application of new technologies, whether these were generated in-house or externally sourced.

Three arguments were put forward in defence of the new perspective. First, IT is having a major impact on the amount of E and P data which can be produced and the speed with which it can be processed. This is shortening the time-horizon of the exploration process and hence the time available to recoup any investments made in technology development. Second, E and P is a mature business. As befits mature businesses, the major E and P companies now have access to more or less the same technologies. Furthermore, any technological advances diffuse rapidly between service companies, contractors, and the oil majors. Increasingly, therefore, a range of activities which were once resourced in-house are now available and more appropriately resourced from specialized external contractors. Finally, BPX's core business no longer requires direct technology generation. Its core business consists of accessing acreage, making hydrocarbon discoveries, developing fields, getting them into production, and delivering product to the point of sale. Where it might be of benefit to the firm, BPX could assist technology generation indirectly through fostering and participating in an E and P market for technical development. Where the generation of technology does remain important to BPX, then pre-competitive, collaborative activity with other oil majors and service companies has more to offer the firm than in-house development.

The conclusion was clear. BPX should secure competitive advantage for itself through the quality and speed of its decision-making and of its implementation activities. It should be quick to adopt a new technology and quick to apply it. It should not necessarily burden itself with the risks and costs of creating it. The shift from the creation to the use of technology as the central tenet of BPX's technology strategy did not, of course, preclude BPX generating new technology directly where this was deemed appropriate. It did, however, bring about a closer alignment of the firm's R and D with its business needs.

Technology provision for BPX still retains elements of a functional structure. The earlier branch structure has been preserved, but is now crossed in a matrix fashion by activities called Major Technology Levers (MTLs). In January 1996 there were nine MTLs: (1) produced water; (2) production facilities; (3) drilling enhancement; (4) well productivity; (5) gas to market; (6) sub-surface prediction; (7) gas cycling; (8) deepwater facilities; (9) operations support. Central to the MTL concept is the view that research activities must be managed by the businesses themselves. These have the problem of deciding what R and D activities to address or solve. The MTLs consist of networks of people from the assets, from the Exploration Technology Centre (XTC) at Sunbury-on-Thames and, where appropriate, from suppliers and contractors.

In the 1990s, in line with the new orientation, internal XTC staff are focused more on the commissioning and interpretation of R and D and technical service activities than on their direct execution. The change raises a number of strategic issues for the organization. Critical among these is the tricky question of exactly how and where the boundaries will be drawn between BPX and external collaborators. Might BPX one day find itself stranded without technical capacity in some areas because suppliers in, say, an underdeveloped market will not take on the risks of technology development just for BPX? Could BPX then end up as a hostage to such suppliers?

The integration of diverse streams of technical and organizational know-how, both internal and external, is perceived to be one of the most critical requirements for the effective delivery of technology in BPX. The emphasis on integration reflects the move away from a functionally based response to business problems to a more multidisciplinary, business-focused one. It involves 'creating a collective skill set' that is managed by networks. Teams are assembled to address any particular issue or need and are drawn from XTC and the assets, together with participants from contractors, service companies, universities, etc., as appropriate. The approach is designed to bring the right skills to bear on the solution of a problem at the right time.

At the time of our intervention, the produced water MTL was perceived to be one of the most successful—success being defined here in terms of the quality of the relationship with the relevant assets—of the MTLs within BPX. The produced water programme consists of five elements: (1) holistic water management; (2) reservoir; (3) producers; (4) facilities and corrosion; (5) injectors. Each has its own leader and might include a dozen or more pieces of work, ranging from industry joint-ventures to in-house research. The produced water programme was selected as the focus for the workshop mapping exercise that is described next.

The Workshop

Workshop participants were interested to see what light, if any, the I*-Space could shed on the technology management issues that the produced water MTL faced. The mapping carried out by participants is shown in Figures 10.5 and 10.6. As with Courtaulds, the first figure describes technologies and the second linkages between technologies. And as with Courtaulds, technologies and linkages are numbered but not named in order to preserve confidentiality. The results caused a good deal of surprise and discussion.

In line with our own hypotheses concerning the location of core competences in the I*-Space, the technologies mapped are generally more diffused

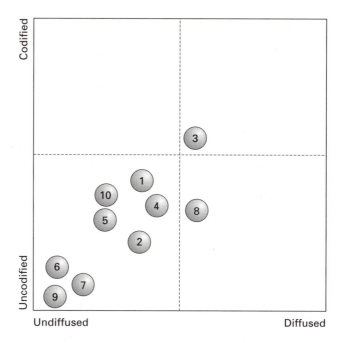

F<small>IG</small>. 10.5 Industry-level C-Space: Technologies (BPX)

than linkages because they are easier to codify and hence tend to move more rapidly to the right across the space. Yet contrary to the expectations of participants, a number of technologies are located in the lower left-hand region of the I*-Space. The discussion provoked by the mapping led to some promising and unexpected insights. It gradually became apparent to participants that, in spite of its strategic reorientation, BPX remains an important generator of technology in its own right, something that challenges the prevailing view of the firm as a technology purchaser only. Discussion of the mappings by workshop participants led to the following tentative re-interpretation of the firm's technology strategy:

1. First, BPX, through the MTLs, generates novel approaches to technical problems and establishes a 'proof of concept'—i.e., that a proposed solution is technically feasible and desirable.

2. The firm then outsources the further development of any novel approach to one or more external contractors or suppliers.

3. Finally, the firm underwrites the external contractors' development risk by acting as a 'lead user'[5] for the proposed solution. It is happy to see this solution diffuse to competitors, as this helps to establish it as an industry standard.

[5] E. von Hippel, *The Sources of Innovation*, Oxford: Oxford University Press, 1988.

Workshop participants concluded that **BPX** had perhaps oversold the idea that it was merely a user rather than a generator of technology. Indeed, to the outside world the message has sometimes been interpreted as 'BP does not have the technology', something that does not go down well with **BPX**'s customers, e.g., host governments with acreage on offer. From analysing the two I*-Spaces, it also emerged that **BPX** is something more than simply an informed buyer. Participants observed that in the 1990s **BPX** has a more innovative R and D portfolio than it had a decade earlier—hardly the sign of a company that no longer generates technology.

The lower left region of the I*-Space—low codification/low diffusion—was recognized by participants as being critical for technology provision at **BPX**. If the firm is indeed a generator of technology, then this is where generation originates. The region is thus perceived as being the 'motor' which drives a technology-based SLC in **BPX**.

The reconceptualization of **BPX**'s technology strategy in the I*-Space raised a number of issues for participants in relation to the maintenance of this motor. First, activity in the lower left-hand region of the space depends on a continuous flow of insights deriving from the scanning activities conducted not only by **BPX** itself, but also by its collaborators in external networks. Although scanning is a boundaryless activity, it needs to be stimulated

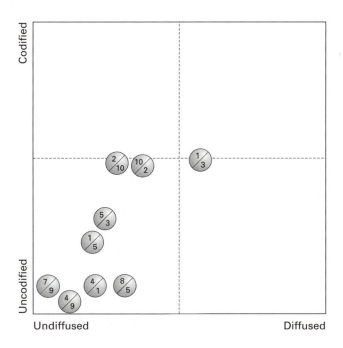

FIG. 10.6 Industry-level C-Space: Organizational Linkages (BPX)

and supported. How is this best done? Second, much of the critical information that is located in this region of the I*-Space resides in people's heads. The literature suggests that such knowledge assets can be more critical than physical assets in turbulent situations. Is this properly recognized in the psychological contract that they are offered and in the career opportunities open to them within BPX? Finally, to sustain a competitive advantage, BPX and its network of collaborators need to respond rapidly to new developments. The process of absorption by which technologies are brought into rapid use and applied thus becomes important. If absorption is a process that moves knowledge down the I*-Space, scanning moves it across to the left once more. Each process is inherently difficult to manage and neither relies on formal mechanisms. Informal networks, face-to-face communication, and personal interactions are required. How well does BPX's culture encourage the social processes that foster effective absorption and scanning activities in the SLC?

The data from Figures 10.5 and 10.6 led to a discussion among participants concerning technology strategies based on the sharing of knowledge versus those based on the hoarding of it. For tactical technologies, the objective seemed to be to absorb new developments as fast and as thoroughly as possible, quickly to improve on them, and then to push them out to the service companies for the next round of development. For strategic technologies, however, some of the workshop participants challenged the appropriateness of this sharing approach. They felt that BPX would not necessarily wish to share these at the earliest opportunity, but might wish to secure for itself a measure of competitive advantage through the more traditional hoarding route prior to doing so.

A workshop discussion on one particular technology threw further interesting light on the hoarding versus sharing issue. Workshop participants and interviewees all agreed that collaborative development was faster than in-house development because it was undertaken by more specialized companies. It was also cheaper because costs were shared. Second, these companies could bring the experience of their work with other clients to bear on any development, hence improving quality. Indeed, in a number of cases, BPX had coaxed its partners into a development partnership by arguing that they would be able to sell the resulting technology to other companies. A third possible advantage which could accrue to BPX, from sharing rather than hoarding, lay in the power this subsequently gave the firm to shape the technological trajectories within which future development would take place. The literature on technological innovation suggests that companies customize the technologies they use. No two companies use a given technology in the same way. Each develops, modifies, and applies it somewhat idiosyncratically in the light of previous technological decisions and the dictates of corporately held tacit knowledge. BPX's development demands of service companies are thus made in the context of its own technological trajectories. When its competitors then seek to adopt and use technologies whose development BPX has initiated, they face adjustment costs which BPX can avoid because the development has taken place along a BPX-inspired trajectory. As a consequence, BPX will find it both easier and quicker to use the technologies it has 'generated' after these have been further developed by the firms with which it collaborated. In this way, the firm secures for itself a first-mover advantage.

Speed of movement around the SLC, however, is critical in allowing BPX to maintain the momentum of its 'generation–development–use' cycle, and speed will partly depend on how extensively BPX is required to share its technical know-how. Hoarding versus sharing, then, turns out not to be a black-and-white issue: selective sharing, in many cases, offers the most effective leverage for fast learning.

BPX's business is characterized by a high degree of operational and technological uncertainty. Moreover, each field developed is, in many respects, unique and requires a tailor-made approach. Nevertheless, best practice and new technologies diffuse quite rapidly within the industry, so that we are dealing with fast-moving industry-level SLCs. In such a regime, it is unlikely that a heavy investment in moving knowledge assets into the maximum value region of the I*-Space will yield durable returns. The trick is therefore to get other potential beneficiaries of a technical innovation to co-invest. If returns have to be shared, why not share the investment risk? Providing that an investment is judiciously carried out and that the new knowledge it creates gets adopted and put to good use throughout the industry—i.e., it becomes an industry standard—BPX stands to gain a first-mover advantage from its adoption. By the time such knowledge becomes generally available, the firm will be further down the industry learning curve than its competitors, and, having initiated and then shaped the technical change to meet its own specific internal requirements, it is likely to face fewer adjustment costs than they will when attempting to master it.

In line with this thinking, during the 1990s BPX's internal organization moved towards a clan-like culture built on networking and outsourcing. It may well be, therefore, that, given the firm's new cultural orientation and the nature of the technical tasks that it confronts, the long-term returns on the sharing of knowledge assets will exceed those on hoarding them. Indeed, BPX, as described by participants, appeared to be almost anxious to share its technical know-how with suppliers and competitors. Participants felt that the firm had little to gain from keeping knowledge assets in the maximum value region of the I*-Space. BPX aimed to act as a customer and 'lead user' for the technologies that it helped to generate, and sought to gain a first-mover advantage from playing out that role. The main challenge facing BPX was how to stake out a position in the lower left-hand region of Figures 10.5 and 10.6 through an effective scanning process. How might it access the tacit know-how of its partners and suppliers in order to derive from it the insights that would drive the SLC through another round?

Although the workshop discussions could not by themselves establish the point, BPX's new posture appeared to be broadly consistent with an S-learning orientation. Whether this was the appropriate posture for the firm to adopt given its competitive environment and its chosen strategy was a subject of vigorous debate among workshop participants.

10.5 COMPARISON

How do Courtaulds and BPX compare in the I*-Space? Do we gain any further insights by bringing the two firms together? Figure 10.7 offers a succinct interpretation of each firm's implicit strategy with respect to its knowledge assets. What the diagram indicates is that Courtaulds is interested in getting its knowledge assets into the maximum value region of the I*-Space, whereas BPX is not. In so far as Courtaulds succeeds, it will face the paradox of value—i.e., strong diffusion forces that will limit the residence time of its assets in the maximum value region. BPX, by contrast, and as we have seen, is no longer interested in getting into that region. It does not believe that it can stay there long enough to recoup whatever costs it incurs in moving up the space.

The mappings carried out within each firm give us, respectively, the I*-Space signatures for a knowledge hoarder (Courtaulds) and a knowledge sharer (BPX). Are these two orientations towards knowledge assets freely chosen by the firms' managers, or do they reflect the logic of each firm's situation in its industry?

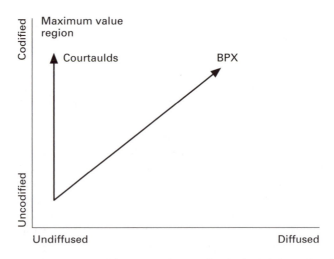

FIG. 10.7 Courtaulds' and BPX's Respective Technological Orientation in the C-Space

Consider Courtaulds. It operates in an industry characterized by continuous process technologies and large volumes. Although the differentiating properties of a new fibre may give the firm a competitive advantage with consumers, the industry essentially competes on costs. This means that ramping up production and rapidly achieving economies of scale is a crucial competitive requirement. It calls for large up-front investments which have to be amortized over a number of years. It is not in the firm's interest to see the technologies that underpin such investments diffuse to competitors or erode too fast. Courtaulds, in contrast to, say, Microsoft, will see no particular advantage in having its technical standards adopted by competitors. The clothes that fibres go into do not have to talk to each other, nor do they necessarily need to be compatible with each other (alas, they often are not!). The scope for creating lock-in is limited.

In such a capital-intensive world, incremental improvements to the technological base located up the I*-Space will extend the life of existing investments, whereas radical improvements located down the space could well undermine it. And since much of the technical knowledge required to produce the NCF eventually gets embedded in plant and machinery, the larger the initial investment in process technology, the greater the barriers to entry that confront potential competitors and, by implication, the greater the barriers to the diffusion of firm-specific know-how out of the maximum value region of the space. Firm-specific process technology typically diffuses much more slowly than product technology.[6]

Contrast Courtaulds' situation with BPX's. The latter operates in an industry which has moved heavily into outsourcing, in which technologies evolve continuously on a project-by-project basis, and in which, given the ever-shorter life cycle of these, the returns to hoarding are correspondingly low. Furthermore, whereas in the continuous process plants operated by Courtaulds, most of the know-how gets embedded in physical equipment, in the oil exploration business much of the critical knowledge resides in the heads of engineers. And those move around—from one oil company to another, or to subcontractors and suppliers, and so on. If returns to hoarding knowledge are correspondingly low in the oil business, the returns to sharing knowledge, by contrast, may be high, but only if one is a fast learner—that is to say, if one can participate in the absorption and impacting phases of the SLC faster than the recipients of one's know-how. What is learnt in this way must then be interpreted—i.e., scanned—digested, and effectively transferred to new projects. In short, any diffusing of knowledge assets to outsiders has to be part of an articulate learning strategy.

Fast learning, however, may still not fully cover the costs of codification and abstraction where this takes place in isolation on the left in the I*-Space. One way of lowering these structuring costs is to make moves up the space a

---

[6] J. Utterback, *Mastering the Dynamics of Innovation*, Cambridge, Mass: Harvard University Press, 1994.

collective enterprise, something carried out with subcontractors, suppliers, and even with competitors. Thus, the returns to learning are achieved not by securing monopoly rents on knowledge assets located in the maximum value region of the I*-Space, but by sharing the costs of moving up the space with outside players.

The mappings on their own merely suggest these hypotheses. They then have to be tested further in conversation with participants. Nevertheless, they yield patterns that are consistent with N-learning and S-learning strategies. How effective each type of strategy proves to be is a function of both technological and industry characteristics. To pursue an N-learning strategy in an industry with rapidly moving SLCs could prove suicidal unless it is executed with a great deal of selectivity and care. Likewise, an S-learner in an N-learning industrial environment may end up giving away the shop with little to show for it unless he or she can be sure that the value of the new learning gained far exceeds that of the learning being discarded.

As we have seen in earlier chapters, an industry's learning environment is not constant. In the early stages of industry growth, S-learning strategies may be preferred over N-learning ones, whereas, as the industry matures, the reverse may be true. Sometimes it works the other way round. In the computer industry, for example, the move from mainframes to PCs signalled a shift from N- to S-learning. Many entrenched N-learners were unable to make the transition. Knowing under what circumstances to adapt a firm's learning strategies to what is warranted by its environment is an important diagnostic skill. The I-Space provides a framework within which such a skill can be developed.

What might the third dimension (concrete–abstract) of the I-Space add to the picture? Although it was not explicitly drawn upon in the interventions described, it could help further to highlight important differences between the two firms discussed. Whereas the produced water network in BPX was focused on very concrete, context-specific applications in their technical concerns, Courtaulds was aiming to broaden the range of applications of the NCF, possibly turning it into a generic product. In other words, the first operated at the concrete end of the third dimension, while the second was concerned to move towards greater abstraction.

Courtaulds' concern to broaden the envelope of properties of the NCF and thus to extend the scope of its applications has a number of interesting consequences of which two can be briefly mentioned here. The first is that the wider the range of applications for the NCF, the larger and the more varied the customer base and hence the more difficult it will prove for the firm to get close to any one group of customers. The second is that with a wide and varied customer base, the firm can only successfully move towards greater abstraction if it is able successfully to identify the critical technological and product attributes around which standardization will be pursued and a core product built. Yet greater abstraction and codification will increase the diffusibility of the firm's know-how—not an attractive prospect for an organization oriented towards N-learning. One way to counter such diffusibility is aggressively to pursue entry-deterring economies of scale and to do so quickly. Yet this is risky: the firm would be entering new markets with new products and hence moving into uncharted waters—and possibly away from its core business. Nevertheless, a successful exploitation of the generic potential of a new technology or product calls for a high level of up-front investment failing which a firm risks creating opportunities that it cannot itself benefit from.

Tentatively summarizing the difference between Courtaulds and BPX with respect to the third I-Space dimension, we could say that BPX's comparative lack of concern with losing proprietary know-how was consistent with having know-how held in a concrete, application-specific, and relatively uncodified form—i.e., one in which it does not readily diffuse. Courtaulds, by contrast, is much more concerned with the protection of its critical know-how. But this know-how is already highly codified and becoming more generic in scope—it is thus more readily diffusible. The attitude of each firm towards its knowledge assets reflects their respective location in the I-Space.

10.6 OTHER APPLICATIONS OF THE I-SPACE

Although space does not allow for further detailed illustrations of the I-Space-in-use, I briefly outline below four quite different situations in which the framework has been used. For reasons of confidentiality none of the firms involved is identified, except in the first example.

1. *Technology transfer*: GEC-Alsthom markets its high-speed train, the TGV, around the world. Would-be clients, however, are often interested not only in acquiring trains, but also in acquiring the technologies that go into them. Which technologies should GEC-Alsthom hold on to and which should it let go of? For a major contract in Asia, a group of GEC-Alsthom engineers used the I-Space to map out and explore the technologies that were candidates for transfer. GEC-Alsthom was unwilling to release one of the critical technologies that the client wanted to see included in the transfer package. An I-Space analysis revealed, however, that by making this technology available, GEC-Alsthom would actually be reinforcing its technological position with the client. It was transferred.

2. *Corporate versus national culture*: A large multinational firm developing its business activities in Central Asia had lost a major piece of business to competitors. Insiders felt that there might be incompatibilities between the firm's corporate culture and the culture of the host country. The two different cultures were mapped by the firm's managers on to the I-Space. It was discovered that the firm's corporate culture was heavily invested in the region of the I-Space labelled 'bureaucracies', whereas the national culture that it

confronted was located in the region labelled 'clans'. In complex negotiations over a multi-billion-dollar project, the firm and the host government had been talking right past each other without even realizing it. A series of workshops inside the firm allowed the cultural issues to be identified and discussed and the I-Space was subsequently drawn upon by the firm in further negotiations in the region.

3.   *Building the virtual organization*: A global firm was concerned to use IT to encourage the sharing of best practice in its operations around the world. In particular, it wanted to develop 'virtual' ways of working across national and time boundaries in order to speed up the firm's learning processes. The I-Space was used as a conceptual framework in a number of internal 'action-learning' projects intended to develop the necessary skills. Using the framework made people aware that IT could only be properly exploited if important cultural changes took place inside the firm and that it would not be sufficient merely to place video-conferencing equipment on people's desk-tops. Collateral investments in organizational development, investments operating over a much longer time-horizon, would also be necessary.

4.   *Technology management in international joint-ventures*: Two major multinational firms, one American and one British, were discussing a joint venture. Each was concerned to strike the right balance between protecting and sharing its knowledge assets. An I-Space mapping of these assets allowed the firms to discuss the issue openly and productively.

Because the I-Space is built on a general theory of information flows, it can be applied wherever knowledge assets are created or eroded by such flows. Nevertheless, the I-Space is not a tool which easily allows outside experts to come in and 'do' something to a firm. It is a framework that facilitates 'strategic conversations' inside a firm between the managers themselves, allowing them to develop and share insights into their operations that would be difficult to arrive at by other means.[7] It is, in effect, a device for handling the scanning phase of an SLC, one that stimulates the emergence of insightful patterns from available fuzzy data. The patterns are usually idiosyncratic, ambiguous, and hard to discern at first. The challenge is to bring them out of the shadows and into the light where all managers can see them and talk about them.

10.7 CONCLUSIONS

We can now offer a brief assessment of what the I-Space contributed to the interventions described in this chapter. It appeared to offer three specific benefits:

---

[7] K. van der Heijden, *Scenarios: The Art of Strategic Conversation*, Chichester: John Wiley, 1996.

1. It allowed a diagnosis—i.e., a mapping of technologies and linkages that organizational players could subscribe to and that would have been difficult to achieve without it. The diagnosis was, for many, counterintuitive. Many workshop participants in the two firms discussed, for example, were surprised by their own configuration of their firm's technologies and processes in the I*-Space.
2. It promoted constructive debate and generated numerous insights. Even competing interpretations were framed in the language of discourse established by the model.
3. It pointed to specific issues that needed dealing with. In the Courtaulds case the challenge was to generate new knowledge assets in the lower region of the I*-Space. For BPX, the challenge was to distinguish between what to share and what not to share—not all firm-specific knowledge should be allowed to travel to the right in the I*-Space along the diffusion curve.

The interventions also indicated how the I-Space, as a conceptual framework, could be further developed and applied. For example, as well as dealing with a firm's technologies and competence, it could be made to yield independent representations of both a firm's products and its culture. Three types of I-Space could then be used in an interlinked fashion to examine: (1) products and the knowledge needed of users; (2) technologies used to manufacture the products; (3) the organizational and cultural processes through which the technologies are managed.

An effective use of the framework requires skilful interpretation of the data. The process is likely to be less rigorous than, say, a radiologist's examination of X-ray pictures. And it is certainly likely to be more political, given the frequently divergent interest of those involved. Yet, the objectivity of the result is in large part a function of the care taken in collecting data and the time allowed for structuring it and working through it. Although much of the data that we collected in workshops was nothing more than subjective estimates, with further work and refinement they could be made more 'intersubjectively objective'. And once they have been given the appropriate tools, the degree of objectivity achievable is very much in the hands of the corporate players themselves.

In sum, in spite of the informality of our data-collection methods, the I-Space provided a framework for an analysis which, judging from the comments offered by workshop participants, generated helpful insights—as one participant put it, it made intuitive understanding explicit. The framework stimulated learning because it enabled participants to see things in a different way. It provided a common 'language' of discourse, and, by allowing them to locate their knowledge assets in the I-Space, it stimulated a fruitful dialogue between different players within the same organization.

11

Recapitulation and Conclusion

11.1 INTRODUCTION

A 1994 survey of sixty-four countries by the International Federation of the Phonographic Industry has estimated that the total retail value of pirate sales of recorded music in 1993 was $US1.9 billion, compared with $US30 billion for legitimate sales. Indeed, pirate sales in some countries, including Poland, Mexico, and China, were larger than legitimate sales of recorded music.[1] Although its utility is aesthetic rather than instrumental, music is information, and to its owner a musical recording must be counted a knowledge asset. The above figures indicate how hard it is becoming in some industries for producers to extract value from knowledge assets. If, as a result of uncontrolled piracy, the supply of recorded music was to dry up, the world would be the poorer for it. Music, to be sure, would go on being produced, but access to it would now be more limited, in many cases becoming the privilege of the minority who attend live concerts rather than a mass phenomenon. A whole class of consumers or would-be consumers would thus be forced out of the market.

Suppose that a failure properly to protect intellectual property rights became pervasive and affected other classes of knowledge assets—for example, in the pharmaceutical industry, the energy industry, or the telecommunication industry. Here, although less immediately perceptible than in the case of music—after all, in certain settings the absence of music can be literally deafening—a fall-off in the supply of intellectual capital could have dramatic long-term consequences for human welfare.

In Chapter 2 we discussed the evolutionary production function and the accelerating rate at which information resources are being substituted for physical ones. As demographic growth and economic development continue to exert their twin pressures upon the finite resources of the biosphere, a continued ability to substitute information for space, time, and energy constitutes the best hope that our species may have to cope with the environmental challenges which lie ahead. The substitution, however, calls for abundant supplies of intellectual capital. Should the supply dry up, substitution would slow down dramatically or possibly even come to a halt. Elementary economic texts teach us that, like any other form of capital, intellectual capital will only be supplied if it is rewarded at a level commensurate with its productivity. Intellectual capital flows into knowledge assets, however, and like these, it is

[1] *The Economist*, 26 November 1994, p. 130.

affected by the paradoxical nature of information flows. The effective management of intellectual capital nevertheless holds the key to securing a continuing supply of knowledge assets.

In this book, we have presented a conceptual framework for the analysis and understanding of knowledge assets. We have proceeded step by step, first by creating a 'space' within which information could flow, and then by examining how new knowledge could emerge from information flows. The paradoxical nature of new knowledge with respect to value has been discussed, and we saw how individual actors might develop specific strategies—N- and S-learning strategies—in response to the paradox of value. When these strategies are pursued in common by a number of actors, whether in firms or other groupings, they often give rise to distinctive cultures and institutional structures.

The technologies and products generated by firms emerged from our analysis as extensions of their cultures and of the institutional structures that they operated. Firms, therefore, in their turn, became amenable to treatment in the I-Space. A firm's distinctive competence could now appear as a unique configuration of knowledge assets embedded in goods, documents, or the minds of agents, located in different regions of the I-Space and organizationally integrated to deliver superior performance. In Chapter 9, we discussed the impact that the electronic revolution would have on the way that we conceive of and manage knowledge assets, and in Chapter 10 we showed how two large firms were using the I-Space as a tool for thinking about their knowledge assets.

In this concluding chapter we shall step back a little and explore the broader implications of our analysis for the strategic management of knowledge assets in the twenty-first century. In industrialized countries, this kind of management probably holds the key to continued prosperity and social stability. In the emerging economies it offers the prospect of by-passing the gruesome and dehumanizing experience of industrialization through which developed countries initially secured their wealth. As things stand, neither industrialized nor industrializing economies have yet developed a managerial orientation appropriate to the needs of the information economy in general, or the phenomenon of knowledge assets in particular. We look at what might be needed in the pages that follow.

In the next three sections (11.2–11.4) we link the relative decline of the energy economy to the rise of the information economy, and discuss the paradoxical nature of the latter. We hypothesize that managers in the information economy will require a degree of intellectual flexibility and a tolerance for ambiguity that would have been positively dysfunctional in the energy economy. In sections 11.5 and 11.6 we develop the point by comparing the management style and philosophy that were required by the energy economy with those that will be called for by the new one. In section 11.7 we argue that the creation and management of knowledge assets entail an approach to learning that challenges some of our most cherished organizational tenets. Finally, we bring the book to a close in section 11.8 with a plea for a political economy appropriate to the information age.

11.2 THE RELATIVE DECLINE OF THE ENERGY ECONOMY

The energy economy deals primarily with physical objects and processes, with things that have a finite extension in space and in time. They have inertia and they have stability. They do not proliferate uncontrollably. The miracle of the loaves and fishes was considered such precisely because it violated deeply held assumptions about the way that the world works. Where proliferation does take place, whether in purely physical entities, in biological organisms, or in the creation of artefacts, it is because information processes are at work. Information gives form to matter—i.e., it in-forms.

In the energy economy, the focus was always more on the matter that was being informed than on the information that did the informing. A country's economic prospects have always seemed to depend far more on resource endowments measured in stocks of raw material and agricultural potential, than on resource endowments measured in, say, the number of designers it possessed. What would Egyptian civilization have achieved, for example, without the fertility of the Nile valley? And without their mines, would Australia and South Africa have ranked among the world's richest countries, on a per capita basis, at the beginning of the twentieth century?

By traditional standards, therefore, it seems puzzling that at the end of the twentieth century so many of the countries with the world's highest income per head are notably poor in natural resources. Think, for example, of Japan, Singapore, and Hong Kong in Asia, or Switzerland and Denmark in Europe. Conversely, several countries with plentiful natural resources have relatively low incomes per head: Nigeria, Argentina, Brazil, and, most notably, Russia.

We have come to realize that far more important than having the physical resources is the ability to do something intelligent with them, to deploy the knowledge required to do the in-forming. Yet the role played by knowledge in adding value to matter is often either misunderstood or ignored by those committed to the paradigms of the energy economy. Nowhere is this more apparent that in the largest of the surviving planned economies: China. A committed Marxist—admittedly, a member of a dying breed, even in China— would have to reject our evolutionary production function out of hand. Information could never be a factor of production having a claim on part of the product for the simple reason that information, to the Marxist, is a public good that is not naturally subject to scarcities. Information scarcities are artificially created by entrepreneurs in order to appropriate for themselves part of the returns that properly belong to the workers. There is only one legitimate factor of production and that is labour power, conceived of purely as an energetic phenomenon. Skilled labour, to be sure, might be paid more than unskilled labour, but only by an amount that reflects the energy expended in acquiring the necessary knowledge and skills.

One feature of an energy economy uncontaminated by knowledge and information stands out. Value-adding is a purely linear phenomenon: 1 + 1 always adds up to 2, never to 3. Such an economy is regulated by Newton's laws of motion and inertia. Small causes produce small effects, and big effects, in turn, require big causes. In socialist economies, the big cause was the state, and many of the big effects that it produced turned out to be quite negative in their impact. An energy economy whose behaviour can be given such a quasi-mechanical interpretation is thus an equilibrium phenomenon regulated by statistical laws. It deals with the average characteristics of large statistical ensembles of actors. Unsurprisingly, its analysis drew on equilibrium concepts from physics. Until the discovery of electromagnetic waves, even information could be thought of as moving according to purely mechanical laws. For with the exception of a few isolated experiments with visual telegraphy during the Napoleonic campaigns, by the middle of the nineteenth century information could still only be moved very slowly across large distances by having it embedded in physical objects.

An important innovation bequeathed to us by the ancient world was the shift from writing on stone or clay tablets to writing on paper. At a stroke, information became more portable and mobile, extending the spatial reach both of state administration and of commercial activity.[2] Communications, however, were still limited by the speed of the carriers available—runners, carrier pigeons, horses, or sails. Furthermore, information itself was rarely treated as an economic good in its own right. It was too immaterial and transient to be thought of as appropriable and hence as tradable. Patents were the exception that proved the rule. Appropriability of new knowledge had to be artificially secured through institutional arrangements that were hard to enforce—it was not a natural attribute of its constituent information as such. Under the circumstances, therefore, it seemed reasonable to think of information as a support to economic transactions rather than as their actual focus. Its function was to describe the object of the transaction as well as the terms on which it would take place. It was rarely itself an object of exchange.

Yet even as the energy economy rose to new heights in the course of the nineteenth and early twentieth centuries, the communicative possibilities that were opened up by the rapid transmission of information using electromagnetic waves wrought profound transformations in the nature of economic organizations. The heavy increases in cost incurred by most firms that sought to operate beyond their immediate localities had conspired to keep most of them small and regional. The advent of the telephone and the telegraph, together with the rapid spread of the railways, suddenly allowed the low-cost

---

[2] J. Goody, *The Interface between the Written and the Oral*, Cambridge: Cambridge University Press, 1987.

coordination and monitoring of transactions across a whole continent.[3] Railway transport itself became one of the main beneficiaries of the new communication technologies. Travel timetables could be aligned and tightened up right across a transport network, and the movement of goods and people became more predictable. For the first time, the effective planning and control of large-scale and widely scattered economic activity became possible, allowing a growing number of firms to operate well beyond their local markets.[4]

Not all firms, of course, chose to do so. The new dispensation appealed primarily to firms which could reap economies of scale by operating in national rather than regional markets. In these firms, a new kind of professional, skilled in the analysis, planning, and coordination of large-scale operations, made an appearance: the industrial manager. In his hands—very few were women—many of the new firms grew to a size that placed them beyond the reach of control by individual families or single owners.[5] Ownership and control of the firm became two different things, the first devolving increasingly to an anonymous mass of passive shareholders, the second accruing to the managers of the enterprise.[6] Given the extent of the changes that cascaded down on economic organizations between 1870 and 1930, it is easy to forget that, as Chandler has stressed, the telegraph and the telephone, no less than the railways, made managerial coordination on a large scale possible, and ushered in the era of the giant corporation.

The large firm, in sum, as we saw in Chapter 6, was the product of new coordination possibilities opened up by the rapid transmission of information on the one hand, and of new codification and abstraction skills embedded in the emerging practices of industrial management, on the other. Both developments, taken together, entailed a massive creation of knowledge assets in the upper reaches of the I-Space, and brought ever larger populations of data-processing agents under either bureaucratic or market control. It is worth pointing out that the emergence of the giant firm might not have happened at all if the creation of corporate bureaucracies had not been accompanied by the parallel development of state bureaucracies. The new communication technologies facilitated the growth of large-scale organizations, whether private or public. And private organizations needed public institutions to provide a stable and predictable framework for their operations. For this reason, the move up the I-Space just referred to should be seen as something more than a development that took place only within firms. It amounted, in effect, to nothing less than the creation of a new institutional order, one which the

---

[3] A. Chandler, *Strategy and Structure: Chapters in the History of the American Industrial Enterprise*, Cambridge, Mass: MIT Press, 1962; *The Visible Hand: The Managerial Revolution in American Business*, Cambridge, Mass: The Belknap Press at Harvard University Press, 1977.

[4] Chandler, *The Visible Hand*.   [5] Ibid.

[6] A. Berle and G. Means, *The Modern Corporation and Private Property*, New York: Harcourt, Brace, and World, Inc., 1932; J. Burnham, *The Managerial Revolution*, Bloomington: Indiana University Press, 1960.

German sociologist Fernand Tönnies described as a movement from *Geimeinschaft* to *Gesellschaft*, i.e., from community to organization.[7]

So powerful an impact on our way of thinking has this move up the I-Space achieved, that we have come to view it as a prerequisite for the process of modernization itself. Indeed, the major ideological battle of the twentieth century was conducted almost exclusively in the upper regions of the I-Space, between those advocating a bureaucratic order (Marxism-Leninism) and those who believe in a market order (liberalism). Rare have been those who suggested that the real contest might in fact turn out to be between the lower and the upper regions of the I-Space, that is, between a personal and an impersonal social order.[8] Yet, since the mid-1970s the average size of firm in the USA, the largest of the advanced industrial economies and a *Gesellschaft* culture if ever there was one, has been going down, as measured by employment, not up. Interestingly, and contrary to predictions that computers would allow firms to grow ever larger and more impersonal, this downward trend has coincided with the rapid spread of information technology. What is going on?

If we discount the possibility that firms are downsizing because they are doing badly—this might be true of a small minority, but hardly of the majority of US firms—then we are left with two quite different explanations for the trend. The first is that firms are either substituting capital for labour, or using labour itself more efficiently. Since firms have effectively been doing both without respite since the industrial revolution, it is bound to be a good part of the story. This explanation is most plausible in the case of manufacturing where the scope for such substitution is greatest. It cannot be the whole story, however, since manufacturing today accounts for an ever smaller proportion of the USA's GDP. In 1970, manufacturing employed 27 per cent of the US labour force; by 1993, the figure had fallen to 16 per cent. Over the same period the share of GDP accounted for by services had climbed from 66 to 78 per cent. The figures must be treated with caution. Up to a point they are statistical artefacts created by the growing popularity of outsourcing, a second explanation for the trend towards downsizing. Many services that used to be provided in-house by manufacturers—such as design—were classified as manufacturing. When these were later outsourced, they were reclassified as services. In such an operation we would then register, first, a reduction in size and activity level of a large firm in the manufacturing sector, and second, the creation of a new firm in the service sector with an increase in the activity level in that sector. The only thing that has changed, however, is that activities that were coordinated hierarchically within one firm, are now coordinated across firms, using either the market mechanism or clan-like forms of collaboration such as joint ventures or strategic alliances.

---

[7] F. Tönnies, *Community and Association*, London: Routledge and Kegan Paul, 1955.

[8] E. Schumacher, *Small is Beautiful: A Study of Economics as if People Mattered*, London: Abacus, 1974; I. Illich, *Tools for Conviviality*, Middlesex: Penguin, 1973; A. Etzioni, *The Spirit of Community*, London: Fontana Press, 1995.

Information technology has made it easier both to substitute capital for labour and to outsource. Yet it was only in the 1980s that the role it could play in outsourcing really came to be recognized. Until then, it had been assumed that it would, if anything, contribute to an increase rather than a decrease in firm size.[9] We need to understand why this did not happen.

11.3 THE EMERGENCE OF THE INFORMATION ECONOMY

By drastically lowering the costs of data processing and transmission, the new electronic revolution is facilitating the creation of knowledge assets throughout the I-Space, not just in its upper regions. And the revolution has not yet run its course. An electronic memory circuit that cost $US10 in the 1950s will have gone down to a hundred-thousandth of a cent fifty years later.[10] Looking at technical performance, the prospects are even more startling: according to Yutaka Kuwahara, head of R and D at Hitachi Europe, by the year 2010 we could have computers that store information as single electrons. Such machines would pack the power of thousands of PCs onto a chip the size of a postage stamp.[11]

The revolution's impact, however, is most likely to be felt in the lower regions of the space, where information is qualitative and highly personalized. Thus, whereas the telex and the telegraph, by favouring the selective transmission of well-codified information, tended to move economic exchange *up* the I-Space, towards bureaucracies and markets, the PC, videoconferencing, e-mail, and the Internet, by allowing transactions to occur less formally and at lower levels of codifications, are moving the centre of gravity of economic exchange once more *down* the I-Space.

To be sure, many transactions will move even further up the I-Space than they are now. The advent of digital money, or e-cash, for example, will do away with the need for human intermediation altogether in, say, routine banking transactions. Yet wherever economic exchange involves risk or uncertainty, the need for an element of interpersonal trust will remain. By lowering the costs of personalizing transactions, the microelectronic revolution will encourage their growth. And because these transactions are becoming free of spatio-temporal constraints, they are ushering in the era of the global village. The greatest beneficiaries of this revolution may well be developing countries. In the late 1990s, half the world's population lives more than two hours away from a telephone—one reason why they find it hard to break out of their poverty. Inexpensive access to participation in the global village offers them new options.

---

[9] T. Whistler, 'The Impact of Information Technology on Organizational Control' in C. Myers (ed.), *The Impact of Computers on Management*, Cambridge, Mass: MIT Press, 1967, pp. 16–60.

[10] G. Styx, 'Toward Point One', *Scientific American*, February 1995, p. 72.

[11] M. Chown, 'Silicon Islands Promise More Power to PCs', *New Scientist*, 15 July 1995, p. 22.

One consequence of being able to transact in the lower region of the I-Space free of space–time constraints will be felt at the level of industrial organization. Outsourcing suddenly becomes an option for many transactions that until now had to remain internal to firms. Outsourcing is viable when one of two conditions obtain:

1. Reasonably complete contracts can be written and their execution monitored at low cost—in which case the transaction can be conducted through markets in the I-Space.
2. Enough interpersonal trust exists between transacting parties to overcome whatever risks or uncertainties might plague the exchange—in this case the transaction can be conducted through clans in the I-Space.

If, as already indicated, firms are getting smaller in advanced industrial economies, one possible explanation is the rightward shift of the diffusion curve in the I-Space that we discussed in Chapter 9 (see Figure 9.4). The curve shift lowers the costs of decentralizing transactions whether such decentralization takes place internally or externally to firms. The net result, however, is likely to favour external transactions and hence outsourcing. The reason for this is that IT, by lowering the spatio-temporal investments required to achieve a given level of trust between transacting agents, also reduces the extent of the commitment that each requires of the other to render the transaction viable. A firm can thus secure for itself most of the benefits of an employment relationship, for example, while avoiding many of its more onerous obligations.

Increasing the density of knowledge assets throughout the I-Space has a second consequence: it also leads to an acceleration of SLCs. Faster learning, in turn, threatens the stability of existing knowledge assets. And where information has become the focus of transacting rather than just a support for it, accelerated flows of it are likely to trigger threatening discontinuities. Nowhere is the problem more apparent than in the globalization of financial markets. In the sixteenth century, imperial Spain's increase in wealth was measured by the rate at which silver could be shipped by sail across the Atlantic from the Potosi mines in Peru. At the close of the twentieth century, wealth is measured by electronic bits flowing at close to the speed of light through fibre optic cables or through the airwaves. Money used to be coin. With the use of banknotes it then became information. And information has now gone electronic. The speed and volume at which electronic money flows across national boundaries makes it increasingly hard to control by sovereign states.

Take, for instance, foreign exchange. In 1973, typical daily foreign exchange trading amounted to $US10–20 billion. In 1983 it was still a modest $US60 billion. Figures compiled by *The Economist* for 1995, however, suggest a daily turnover that was nudging $US1.3 trillion. To put these figures in perspective, the total foreign currency reserves of governments in the rich industrial economies amounted to only $US640 billion at the time that the figures were compiled. Financial deregulation, by shifting foreign exchange transactions to the right in the I-Space, and towards markets, has effectively pushed them beyond the hierarchical reach of domestic bureaucratic controls.[12]

We hypothesize, therefore, that in contrast to the energy economy, the information economy is becoming a far-from-equilibrium phenomenon, characterized by nonlinearities and emergent properties. As indicated by Figure 11.1, the rightward shift of the diffusion curve in the I-Space brought about by the electronic revolution has an important but unforeseen consequence: it renders viable many transactions whose information profile locates them either in or close to the chaotic regime. *The information economy is an edge-of-chaos economy.*

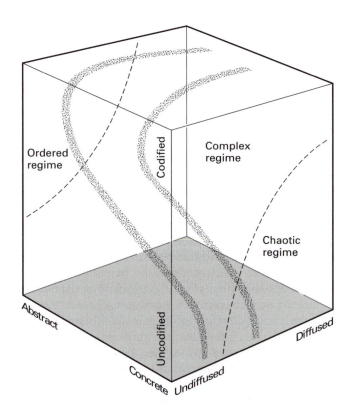

FIG. 11.1 The Shift of the Diffusion Curve into the Chaotic Regime

[12] 'Survey of the World Economy', *The Economist*, 7 October 1995.

11.4 THE PARADOXICAL NATURE OF THE INFORMATION ECONOMY

The discontinuities associated with far-from-equilibrium behaviour impart to the information economy its paradoxical character. In Chapter 5 we argued that learning could be interpreted as a stabilizing or as a destabilizing process. In a stable environment an organization has time to consolidate and exploit the knowledge assets that it creates—i.e., it can pursue an N-learning strategy. In an environment characterized by rapid change, this luxury is no longer available. For there, stabilizing and destabilizing insights work in tandem, and S-learning, as a strategy, then comes to dominate N-learning. S-learning is close to what Argyris and Schön have called 'double-loop' learning and to what Gregory Bateson terms 'Deutero learning' or second-order learning.[13] It requires one to step back and to look at the world, not so much as a given, but more as a set of unexplored possibilities. Such an approach is both creative of new possibilities as well as destructive of existing assumptions. In short, and as the prefix S- reminds us, it is Schumpeterian.

As the expression is used here, creative destruction is a cognitive act: it is knowledge assets that are created and destroyed. The paradox of value that we discussed in Chapter 4, however, is destructive but not creative. When the utility created by codification and abstraction leaks out, value gets eroded by diffusion. Creative destruction, by contrast, is at work when the utility achieved by a given knowledge asset is eroded by competing ones that can offer better performing codifications and abstractions. Here, competing knowledge assets actually dislodge the existing one from the I-Space altogether. Through atrophy, it simply disappears from the available knowledge base. The codified elements of knowledge assets so replaced may survive in a vestigial form in the archives of an organization, but without some access to the context in which the codes must be deployed—i.e., the uncodified knowledge carried in the heads of employees—these elements become increasingly costly to interpret and use.

Sandra Blakeslee offers a poignant example of the role played by tacit knowledge in the interpretation of codes. For thirty years, NASA collected data from space flights. Yet the three thousand images from the Viking mission to Mars in 1975 were never processed. Why? The NASA documents describing data-entry procedures—and hence containing the keys to access—were written in a highly technical jargon. This jargon turned out to be all but incomprehensible to people trying to decipher it two decades later.[14] It had become decontextualized.

---

[13] C. Argyris and D. Shön, *Organizational Learning: A Theory of Action Perspective*, Reading, Mass: Addison-Wesley, 1978; G. Bateson, *Steps to an Ecology of Mind: Collected Essays in Anthropology, Psychiatry, Evolution and Epistemology*, St. Albans: Paladin, 1972.

[14] Sandra Blakeslee, 'Lost on Earth: Wealth of Data found in Space', *New York Times*, 20 March 1990, Sec. C:1; this example is drawn from D. Leonard-Barton, *Wellsprings of Knowledge: Building and Sustaining the Sources of Innovation*, Boston, Mass: Harvard Business School Press, 1995.

Both the paradox of value and the process of creative destruction are most visible in industries characterized by rapid SLCs—those where the residence time of knowledge assets in the maximum value region of the I-Space is cut short, either by rapid diffusion or a high volume of competing codifications or abstractions. Rapid SLCs make the creation of knowledge assets a highly uncertain business and the ability to extract value from them somewhat problematic.

As far back as 1962, Kenneth Arrow was fingering problems of appropriability in explaining the tendency of firms to underinvest in R and D.[15] He did not actually mention the rapid obsolescence of knowledge assets in rapid learning regimes, but such obsolescence can only exacerbate the problem. A tentative solution that we have put forward for rapid learning regimes is to let go, not to hold on, to maximize *throughput* in the maximum value region of the I-Space rather than residential time. This is the strategy being pursued by Microsoft, as it encourages other firms to use and further develop its products. Although it is conscious that it might be creating future competitors for itself, Microsoft freely supplies the technical details that rival programs need in order to write software as good as its own. The result is a vibrant software industry growing at 11 per cent a year.

Managing knowledge assets, then, in a fast-moving information economy, is the cognitive equivalent of white-water rafting, of going with the flow and trying not to capsize. It requires alertness, flexibility, and a light and buoyant craft. It will not do to shoot the rapids in a paddle-steamer.

11.5 TRADITIONAL MANAGEMENT: THE QUEST FOR UNCERTAINTY REDUCTION

Yet, in the typical firm, paddle-steamers are what managers have typically aspired to build. In large corporate bureaucracies the quest for competitive advantage is often little more than a quest for monopoly rents—a move towards bureaucracies in the I-Space. Bureaucracies, however, are built for gentle cruises down the Mississippi, not for white-water rafting. They assume a gentle and placid flow of knowledge through the maximum value region of the I-Space that propels the steamer forward at a speed with which corporate managers feel comfortable. The Nobel laureate Sir John Hicks once quipped that the most attractive returns to monopoly are 'a quiet life'. The search for a 'quiet life' is precisely what pushes so many firms to seek out the ordered regime in the I-Space (see Figure 8.8) and to create a culture built on stability and predictability.

Traditionally, if they wanted to reduce transactional uncertainty and to secure for themselves a measure of stability, organizations moved up the I-

[15] K. Arrow, 'Economic Welfare and the Allocation of Resources for Invention', in *The Rate and Direction of Inventive Activity*, Princeton, New Jersey: Princeton University Press, 1962, pp. 609–25.

Space. Codification and abstraction reduce both the variability of phenomena that have to be processed as well as the number of categories into which they have to be fitted. In this way information overload is avoided and problems can be tackled in a methodical and controllable fashion. In slow-moving industries the residential time of knowledge assets in the bureaucratic region of the I-Space justified the construction of massive administrative structures to trap and systematically structure the relevant knowledge and exploit it. Even in fast-moving industries, such as are found in financial markets, these structures could still function effectively provided that the relevant knowledge base did not evolve too rapidly. Markets may be more dynamic than bureaucracies, but they still operate on the basis of well-codified price-quantity data. There may be uncertainty as to future price movements, but the negative consequences of these can be handled through appropriate hedging strategies. Rational analysis, planning, and control are the key success factors in the upper regions of the I-Space, whether applied to bureaucracies or to markets.

Much of modern management science has been pressed into the service of creating such structures, and many business-school professors earn their stripes by promoting them either through their publications or their teaching. Yet with the acceleration of SLCs in an ever-increasing number of industries, much lighter and more flexible structures are now needed. Exploiting knowledge flows can no longer be achieved by slowing them down; they have to be ridden. The critical requirements are to understand the dynamics of the flows and to steer one's craft accordingly, harnessing the energies available to move one forward.

At the end of the twentieth century, information technology allows us to build these lighter structures, enabling firms to engage more productively with knowledge flows in the lower regions of the I-Space. There, the traditional language of organizations, the language of rational analysis, of planning and control, of order-giving, and of compliance, gives way to a new type of discourse associated with networking, community, and teamwork. The traditional language does not disappear; far from it. Where organizations can effectively reduce uncertainty and economize on data processing, they would be foolish not to do so. Yet uncertainty reduction and data-processing economies are no longer the only recipes on offer for the creation of competitive firms. Through the softer processes just referred to, information technology offers a new option: *uncertainty absorption*.

11.5 THE NEW MANAGEMENT: UNCERTAINTY ABSORPTION

In future, the challenge will be to absorb rather than to reduce uncertainty and complexity. In other words, it will be to manage the trajectory of SLCs in the lower regions of the I-Space. This is not in any way to argue that moves up the I-Space are undesirable. The rising tide of data processing that individuals and firms are having to cope with—the Internet alone is forecast to have more connections than there are people in the world by the early part of the twenty-first century—makes some form of data structuring indispensable. It does, however, suggest that the quest for data-processing economies and a general concern for transactional efficiency need to be counterbalanced by a greater organizational investment in uncodified forms of knowledge, in exploratory as well as exploitative learning, and in the cultural values and beliefs that make these possible.

Some of this uncodified learning will be of a general kind and will benefit organizational members whatever their circumstances. It will enhance their personal effectiveness and their overall capacity to interpret and make sense of experiences. Yet some of this learning will be much more specific to the organizations they work for or with. Properly applied, it stands to benefit the latter at least as much as the members themselves. Yet, given that this second kind of learning is too intangible to be properly defined and legally appropriated, who will it belong to? The employee or the firm? We confront once more the dilemma of ownership versus possession discussed earlier. It will loom ever larger in the emerging information economy.

A second, and equally important point, is that if the information revolution requires organizational members to operate in a decentralized fashion further down the I-Space, it places them closer to the edge of chaos (see Figure 11.1). Popular management texts picked up the increasingly chaotic nature of modern business some time ago.[16] Yet although individuals vary in their capacity to handle uncertainty—and many sociologists view the ability to reduce or absorb uncertainty as a source of personal power and as a prerequisite for leadership—chaos itself is rarely a comfortable experience. For most people it is a source of anxiety and stress. Not everyone can cope. Nevertheless, by asking all employees, and not just senior managers, to operate further down the I-Space, a firm is inviting them to shoulder a greater part of the uncertainty that it confronts than was deemed appropriate by the traditional employment contract. The deal with employees, in fact, used to be quite feudal in its orientation: a firm offered protection and employment security in return for obedience. In the 1990s, the firm has replaced employment security with the less committing and more nebulous promise of 'employability', and in most cases it wants imagination, creativity, and initiative in return.[17]

The lower region of the I-Space is the stamping ground of entrepreneurs, people who thrive on risk-taking and uncertainty. They also thrive on the rewards this brings. Are firms, then, in effect asking their employees to become entrepreneurs? And if so, are they offering entrepreneurial returns to those who make the grade? Employees who are asked to share the pain will undoubtedly expect to share the gain as well. If they do not get the deal they

[16] T. Peters, *Liberation Management*, New York: Alfred A. Knopf, 1992.
[17] N. Tichy and S. Sherman, *Control Your Destiny or Someone Else Will*, New York: Harper Collins, 1994.

want, they may well conclude that they are better off on their own. The paradox is that firms seeking too much of a one-sided entrepreneurial bargain will suffer what economists call 'adverse selection': as genuine entrepreneurs discover their potential they move out in search of greener pastures, leaving their employers with less entrepreneurial talent than if they had left well alone.

A move by firms down the I-Space will be partly a response to the faster and more turbulent knowledge flows that result from a rightward shift in the diffusion curve. It will also be the direct product of such a shift. We saw in Chapter 9 how the electronic revolution, by lowering the costs of transacting externally, was facilitating outsourcing, shrinking the size of firms, and making it economic to flatten internal hierarchies. Smaller firms and flatter hierarchies, in turn, make it ever more difficult to push uncertainty upwards towards the top of the firm. Only in the most stable and traditional lines of business can administrative coordination be centralized and handled by an owner-manager who views his firm as a personal extension of himself, i.e., a fief. In fast-moving, skill-intensive industries decentralization becomes essential, and uncertainty then has to be absorbed at whatever point it originates inside the firm. Of course, the counterpart to uncertainty absorption is empowerment, giving employees the right to deal with uncertainty as they see fit. Empowerment is a generator of tacit knowledge and a mandate for the kind of uncodified exploratory learning that drives an SLC. Yet, as such knowledge accumulates in the heads of empowered employees, the question of who actually owns it will become ever more pressing.

Marx had predicted in the 1860s that the state would wither away when workers owned the means of production. But although knowledge workers in the 1990s increasingly *possess* the means of production—in the shape of tacit knowledge assets—do they in fact *own* them? And making Marx's prediction a little less apocalyptic and somewhat more tractable, are the mini-states that we call firms likely to wither away as the knowledge assets that they own gradually become the possession of their knowledge workers?

Our existing conception of firms draws extensively on the 'command-and-control' models that we associate with the region of the I-Space labelled bureaucracy. It was not always so: in the nineteenth century, the typical firm was more akin to a fief, a small, highly personalized organization under the direct control of an owner. As we saw in Chapter 6, other ways of organizing are available: markets in the upper region of the I-Space, clans in the lower region. Both come across as more 'loosely coupled' and hence less organized than fiefs or bureaucracies. Both are likely to receive a boost from the decentralization made possible by the electronic revolution. What distinguishes markets from clans in an organizational perspective is that, whereas the former require an equilibrating process to function well, the latter can operate as high entropy, far-from-equilibrium phenomena. 'Withering away' may be too strong a word for it, but if withering away there is to be, it is first likely to occur in the lower right-hand region of the I-Space. The organizational response to such withering away is not going to be an alternative location in the space to compete with clans, but a stronger learning cycle that has withering away as a recognizable staging post on its itinerary.

II.7 MANAGING KNOWLEDGE ASSETS AS A SOCIAL LEARNING PROCESS

In the final analysis, whether a firm 'withers away' à la Marx or not will ultimately depend on how it responds to the creative destruction of its knowledge assets. We can guess what it feels about this when such destruction is inflicted on the firm by outsiders. But what about creative destruction brought about by the action of its own employees? The effective management of knowledge assets requires firms to address this issue. Knowledge assets are the fruit of a learning process and, as we have seen at several points throughout this book, learning can be as much competence-destroying as it is competence-enhancing. S-learners appear willing to confront this dilemma more readily than N-learners. But for all types of learner, unlearning, no less than learning, has to be on the corporate agenda.

Unlearning as well as learning is required to drive a firm around the SLC. For the cycle is constantly dislodging existing knowledge assets from the positions they occupy in the I-Space and pushing them hither and thither, or, indeed, causing them to disappear altogether. How easily they are dislodged is both a function of what they are embedded in as well as of the forces of codification, abstraction, and diffusion acting upon them at a given point. They might, for example, be embedded in a piece of long-lived equipment that will be amortized over fifty years—in socialist economies, as we have already seen, the physical life of such equipment artificially prolongs its economic life, significantly reducing the amount of learning that can take place, given that much of it occurs when new equipment is installed. Alternatively, they might be embedded in institutional practices and beliefs whose robustness in the face of opportunities for change will vary considerably from culture to culture.

What is beyond doubt in the closing years of the twentieth century is that, everywhere one looks, learning cycles are accelerating, a situation that favours S-learners and that places N-learners increasingly at a disadvantage. Yet, in many countries, whether it is through their labour laws, their fiscal stance, or their welfare practices, governments pursue policies that tend to favour N-learners. The instinct behind these policies is natural if shortsighted. N-learners are committed to protecting what already exists over what might exist: today's technologies over tomorrow's, current employment over future employment. Governments, however, can only act as custodians for the future to the extent that their electorate asks them to. And within the electorate, constituencies with a stake in the present are usually better entrenched and more clamorous than those with a stake in the future. Furthermore, as it becomes ever more difficult to discern a single, stable future when looking ahead, the natural tendency for governments is to shorten their planning horizons and to concentrate on what is foreseeable. Unfortunately, hard choices do not thereby disappear, and what is called for in making them is not a planning stance—an N-learning solution—but a more flexible entrepreneurial stance characteristic of S-learning.

Firms, like states and other large-scale structures, have been institutionally designed to survive the individuals who create them. They are thus, at base, devices for holding on. Like physical organisms, they maintain their identity by creating boundaries and barriers. Yet, in the emerging information economy boundaries and barriers will be far more permeable than they ever were in the energy economy. Whatever equilibrium is available to firms in the new order is likely to be much more dynamic in nature and will offer little in the way of durable stability. If anything, boundaries and barriers will often act as obstacles to adaptation and innovation. The challenge for firms will therefore be to profit from a culture that requires them to let go of old knowledge assets as they acquire new ones, to unlearn as they learn. Firms will only be able to do this if they can reconceptualize economic processes so as to deal with the information phenomenon on its own terms and not merely as a puzzling variant of the energy processes with which they are already familiar.

11.8 THE NEED FOR A POLITICAL ECONOMY OF INFORMATION

For the time being, we lack an articulate political economy of information. If knowledge is wealth, we lack a coherent account of the production and distribution of wealth-generating information, one that can accommodate its nonlinear, far-from-equilibrium features, as well as the exchange properties that result from these. Such an account is not an academic luxury, a plaything for underemployed theoreticians who have little to say to practical individuals. It is only just dawning on theoreticians and practitioners alike that in physical systems, nonlinearity and far-from-equilibrium states may be the rule rather than the exception—the mathematician Stanislaw Ulam once jokingly described nonlinearity as 'the science of non-elephant life', linearity itself, of course, being elephant life. At least part of the problem that we face in evolving an adapted response to the environmental challenge that confronts us, therefore, is coming up with an appropriate model of what is actually going on.

Until the mid-twentieth century, conventional wisdom had the environment conditioning the possibilities for life on earth. Natural selection created a one-way line of causation from environment to life. Species proposed and the environment disposed. In the 1990s we recognize that the lines of causation run both ways and that life and environment make up a single interdependent system of forbidding complexity.[18] To the extent that life is an information-based phenomenon relying on the existence of myriad feedback loops running both ways between itself and the environment, we cannot even begin to address the environmental challenge without an adequate theory of information flows.

It is a commonplace that it takes a theory to beat a theory. The electronic revolution continues to be viewed by many in the 1990s through the theoretical lens of neoclassical economic theory, a theory deeply rooted in the energy paradigm. Economists themselves are now acknowledging that this paradigm will no longer serve. Indeed, as our discussion of the evolutionary production function in Chapter 2 makes abundantly clear, an exclusive preoccupation with physical factors—and with energy playing a preponderant role—can all too easily blind policy-makers to the crucial trade-offs on offer. As we saw earlier in the chapter, a number of resource-poor countries have successfully exploited the trade-off between energy and information to build for themselves a knowledge-intensive modern economy. Yet many resource-rich countries remain poor because they fail to grasp the nature of the cultural prerequisites that allow the trade-off to be exploited in the first place. A continuing infatuation with the energy paradigm is proving damaging to the health of many industrializing economies.

This book has provided some of the conceptual foundations on which a political economy of information might be built. It is addressed to practising managers and policy-makers, as well as to academics, in the belief that such an economy requires the reflective inputs of practical people addressing practical problems as much as the practical inputs of reflective theoreticians. The ideas presented in these pages reflect my involvement with both practitioners and theoreticians over two decades. The I-Space is thus as much the result of work carried out in companies grappling with concrete problems of knowledge management as it is of musings pursued in the inner recesses of libraries, poring over abstract text. In some phases of its development the theory ran ahead of the practice, producing concepts in need of grounding. In others, the practice took the lead, suggesting new avenues of theoretical development.

Putting a political economy of information on the agenda will require academics, managers, and policy-makers to address issues such as the following:

1. *Institutional issues*: How does the assumption that the world is for the most part nonlinear modify the nature of institution building?
2. *Organizational issues*: How does the 'virtuality' of organizations affect their governance?
3. *Accounting issues*: What impact will the shift from energy-based assets to knowledge assets have on accounting practices?
4. *Educational issues*: What educational practices best equip agents successfully to manage the six steps of an SLC on a lifetime basis?

[18] J. Lovelock, *The Ages of Gaia*, Oxford: Oxford University Press, 1990.

5. *Employment issues*: What kind of employment policies would make creative destruction less threatening and yet productive?
6. *Political issues*: How will nation-states maintain sovereign control over knowledge-based economic activities that have no identifiable spatio-temporal location?

Since theory building and testing is ultimately a collective enterprise, the hope is that those who have found the ideas presented in these pages of interest—practitioners as well as theoreticians—will help to address the above issues and place the evolving theory on a sounder footing. They can do this either by challenging what has been presented, or by building on it. In either case, doubtless, some rebuilding will be called for. Hopefully, however, the concepts presented in these pages will prove to be robust.

BIBLIOGRAPHY

ABBEGLEN, J., *The Japanese Factory* (Glencoe: The Free Press, 1958)

ABELL, D. and S. HAMMOND, *Strategic Market Planning: Problems and Analytical Approaches* (New Jersey: Prentice-Hall, 1979)

ALCHIAN, A. and H. DEMETZ, 'Production, Information, Costs, and Economic Organization', *American Economic Review*, 62 (1972)

ALLEN, T., *Managing the Flow of Technology: Technology Transfer and the Dissemination of Technological Information within the R and D Organization* (Cambridge, Mass: MIT Press, 1977)

ARGYRIS, C. and D. SHÖN, *Organizational Learning: A Theory of Action Perspective* (Reading, Mass: Addison-Wesley, 1978)

ARROW, K., 'Economic Welfare and the Allocation of Resources for Invention', in *The Rate and Direction of Inventive Activity* (Princeton, New Jersey: Princeton University Press, 1962), pp. 609–25

ARTHUR, W. B. 'Competing Technologies, Increasing Returns, and Lock-In by Historical Events', *The Economic Journal*, 99: 394 (1989), pp. 116–31

—— 'Positive Feedbacks in the Economy', *Scientific American* (February 1990)

BARNEY, J., 'Strategic Factor Markets: Expectations, Luck, and Business Strategy', *Management Science*, 32 (1986)

—— 'Firm Resources and Sustained Competitive Advantage', *Journal of Management*, 17: 1 (1991)

BATESON, G., *Steps to an Ecology of Mind: Collected Essays in Anthropology, Psychiatry, Evolution and Epistemology* (St Albans: Paladin, 1972)

BEGG, D., *The Rational Expectations Revolution in Macroeconomics: Theories and Evidence* (Oxford: Philip Allen, 1982)

BERLE, A. and G. MEANS, *The Modern Corporation and Private Property* (New York: Harcourt, Brace, and World, Inc., 1932)

BERNSTEIN, B., *Class, Codes, and Control Vol. I. Theoretical Studies Towards a Sociology of Language* (London: Routledge and Kegan Paul, 1971)

BEST, M., *The New Competition: Institutions of Industrial Restructuring* (Cambridge: Polity Press, 1990)

BIJKER, W., HUGHES, T., and T. PINCH, *The Social Construction of Technological Systems: New Directions in the Sociology and History of Technology* (Cambridge, Mass: MIT Press, 1987)

BIKHCHANDANI, S., HIRSHLEIFER, D., and I. WELCH, 'The Blind Leading the Blind: Social Influence, Fads and Informational Cascades', UCLA Working Paper (October 1993).

BLAUG, M., *Economic Theory in Retrospect* (Cambridge: Cambridge University Press, 1978)

BLOCK, Z. and I. MACMILLAN, *Corporate Venturing: Creating New Businesses within the Firm* (Boston: Harvard Business School Press, 1993)

BOISOT, M., 'The Shaping of Technological Strategy: European Chemical Firms in South-East Asia', *Management International Review*, 2: 3 (1982)

—— 'Convergence Revisited: The Codification and Diffusion of Knowledge in a British and Japanese Firm', *Journal of Management Studies*, 20: 2 (1983)

—— 'Markets and Hierarchies in Cultural Perspective', *Organization Studies*, 7: 2 (1986), pp. 135–58

—— *Information and Organization: The Manager as Anthropologist* (London: Harper and Collins, 1994)

—— *Information Space: A Framework for Learning in Organizations, Institutions and Culture* (London: Routledge, 1995)

—— 'Institutionalizing the Labour Theory of Value: Some Obstacles to the Reform of State-owned Enterprises in China and Vietnam', *Organization Studies*, 17: 6 (1996), pp. 909–28

BOISOT, M. and J. CHILD, 'The Iron Law of Fiefs: Bureaucratic Failure and the Problem of Governance in the Chinese Economic Reforms', *Administrative Science Quarterly*, 33 (1988), pp. 507–27

—— 'From Fiefs to Clans and Network Capitalism: Explaining China's Emergent Economic Order', *Administrative Science Quarterly*, 41 (1996), pp. 600–28

BOISOT, M., LEMMON, T., GRIFFITHS D., and V. MOLE, 'Spinning a Good Yarn: The Identification of Core Competences at Courtaulds', *International Journal of Technology Management*, 2: 3/4 (1996), pp. 425–40

BORGES, J. L., *Labyrinths* (New York: New Directions, 1962)

BOULDING, K., 'The Economics of Knowledge and the Knowledge of Economics', *American Economic Review*, 58 (May 1966), pp. 1–13

BRAUN, E. and S. MACDONALD, *Revolution in Miniature* (Cambridge: Cambridge University Press, 1982)

BROOKS, D. and E. WILEY, *Evolution as Entropy: Towards a Unified Theory of Biology* (Chicago: University of Chicago Press, 1986)

BURGELMAN, R., 'Fading Memories: A Process Theory of Strategic Business Exit in Dynamic Environments', *Administrative Science Quarterly*, 39 (1994), pp. 24–56

BURNHAM, J., *The Managerial Revolution* (Bloomington: Indiana University Press, 1960)

BUTTERFIELD, H., *The Origins of Modern Science* (London: G. Bell and Sons, 1973)

CAIRNS-SMITH, A., *Seven Clues to the Origin of Life* (Cambridge: Cambridge University Press, 1985)

CASTI, J., *Complexification: Explaining a Paradoxical World through the Science of Surprise* (London: Abacus, 1994)

CHAITIN, G., 'Information-Theoretic Computational Complexity', *IEEE Transactions, Information Theory*, 20: 10 (1974)

CHANDLER, A., *Strategy and Structure: Chapters in the History of the American Industrial Enterprise* (Cambridge, Mass: MIT Press, 1962)

—— *The Visible Hand: The Managerial Revolution in American Business* (Cambridge, Mass: The Belknap Press at Harvard University Press, 1977)

CHEUNG, S., 'The Contractual Nature of the Firm', *Journal of Law and Economics*, 3: 1 (April 1983)

CHILD, J., 'Organizational Structure, Environment, and Performance: The Role of Strategic Choice', *Sociology*, 6 (1972), pp. 1–22

CHOWN, M., 'Silicon Islands Promise More Power to PCs', *New Scientist* (15 July 1995), p. 22

CHRISTENSEN, C. and J. BOWER, 'Customer Power, Strategic Investment, and the Failure of Leading Firms', *Strategic Management Journal*, 7: 3 (March 1996), pp. 197–218

COASE, R., 'The Nature of the Firm', *Economica*, NS, 4 (1937)

COLEMAN, D. C., *Courtaulds: An Economic and Social History, Vol. I: The Nineteenth Century, Silk and Crepe* (Oxford: The Clarendon Press, 1969)

—— *Courtaulds: An Economic and Social History, Vol. II: Rayon* (Oxford: The Clarendon Press, 1969)

—— *Courtaulds: An Economic and Social History, Vol. III: Crisis and Change, 1940–1965* (Oxford: The Clarendon Press, 1980)

COLLINS, J. and J. PORRAS, 'Organizational Vision and Visionary Organizations', *Research paper 1159*, Stanford GSB (1991)

DALY, H. and J. COBB JR., *For the Common Good* (London: Merlin Press, 1990)

DAVID, P., 'Clio and the Economics of "Qwerty"', *American Economic Review*, 75 (May 1985), pp. 332–7

DERIAN, J. C., *America's Struggle for Leadership in Technology* (Cambridge, Mass: MIT Press, 1988)

DEUTCH, K., *The Nerves of Government: Models of Political Communication and Control* (New York: The Free Press, 1966)

DIXIT, A. and R. PINDYCK, *Investment Under Uncertainty*, Princeton, New Jersey: Princeton University Press (1994)

DOERINGER, P. and M. PIORE, *Internal Labor Markets and Manpower Analysis* (Lexington, MA: Heath, 1971)

DORE, R., *British Factory—Japanese Factory: The Origins of National Diversity in Industrial Relations* (Berkeley: University of California Press, 1973)

DOUGLAS, M., *Natural Symbols: Explorations in Cosmology* (Middlesex: Penguin Books, 1973)

DREXLER, K., *Engines of Creation* (New York: Anchor Press/Doubleday, 1986)

EISENSTEIN, E., *The Printing Revolution in Early Modern Europe* (Cambridge: Cambridge University Press, 1983)

ETZIONI, A., *The Spirit of Community* (London: Fontana Press, 1995)

FINE, J. A., *The Ancient Greeks: A Critical History* (Cambridge, Mass: Harvard University Press, 1983)

GELL-MANN, M., *The Quark and the Jaguar* (London: Abacus, 1994)

GIDDENS, A., *The Constitution of Society: Outline of the Theory of Structuration* (Cambridge: Polity Press, 1984)

GOODY, J., *The Interface between the Written and the Oral* (Cambridge: Cambridge University Press, 1987)

GOULDNER, A., *Patterns of Industrial Bureaucracy* (Glencoe, Illinois: The Free Press, 1954)

GRANOVETTER, M., 'Economic Action and Social Structure: The Problem of Embeddedness', *American Journal of Sociology*, 91 (1985)

HAGSTROM, W., *The Scientific Community* (New York: Basic Books, 1965)

HALL, E., *The Hidden Dimension* (New York: Doubleday, 1966)

—— *Beyond Culture* (New York: Doubleday, 1976)

HAMEL, G. and A. HEENE (eds), *Competence-Based Competition* (Chichester: John Wiley and Sons, 1994)

HAMEL, G. and C. PRAHALAD, 'Strategic Intent', *Harvard Business Review* (May–June 1989)

—— *Competing for the Future* (Boston, Mass: Harvard Business School Press, 1994)

HAYEK, F., 'The Use of Knowledge in Society', *American Economic Review* (September 1945)

HENDERSON, G., *Gothic* (Middlesex: Penguin Books, 1967)

HILL, C. and G. JONES, *Strategic Management: An Integrated Approach* (Boston: Houghton-Mifflin, 1995)

HIRSCH, F., *The Social Limits to Growth* (London: Routledge and Kegan Paul, 1977)

HOFSTEDE, G., *Culture's Consequences: International Differences in Work-Related Values* (Beverley Hills: Sage Publications, 1980)

HOLLAND, J., *Adaptation in Natural and Artificial Systems* (Cambridge, Mass: MIT Press, 1975)

HOLLAND, J., HOLYOAK, K., NISBETT, R., and P. THAGARD, *Induction: Processes of Inference, Learning and Discovery* (Cambridge, Mass: MIT Press, 1989)

HOLTON, G., *The Scientific Imagination: Case Studies* (Cambridge: Cambridge University Press, 1978)

ILLICH, I., *Tools for Conviviality* (Middlesex: Penguin, 1973)

JARILLO, J. C. and J. MARTINEZ, Benetton Spa (A) Harvard Business School Case 9—389–074 (1988)

JENSEN, M. and W. MECKLING, 'Theory of the Firm: Managerial Behaviour, Agency Costs, and Capital Structure', *Journal of Financial Economics*, 3: 4 (1976)

KAHNEMAN, D., SLOVIC, P., and A. TVERSKY (eds), *Judgement under Uncertainty: Heuristics and Biases* (Cambridge: Cambridge University Press, 1982)

KAUFFMAN, S., *The Origins of Order* (Oxford: Oxford University Press, 1993)

KAY, J., *Foundations of Corporate Success* (Oxford: Oxford University Press, 1993)

KIRZNER, I., *Competition and Entrepreneurship* (Chicago: University of Chicago Press, 1973)

—— *Perception, Opportunity, and Profit: Studies in the Theory of Entrepreneurship* (Chicago: University of Chicago Press, 1979)

KOLGOMOROV, A., 'Three Approaches to the Quantitative Definition of Information', *Problems in Information Transmissions*, 1 (1965), pp. 3–11

KROEBER, A. and C. KLUCKHOHN, *Culture: A Critical Review of Concepts and Definitions*, Papers of the Peabody Museum of American Archeology and Ethnology, Vol. 47 (Cambridge, Mass: Harvard University Press, 1952), p. 181

KRUGMAN, P., (ed.), *Strategic Trade Policy and the New International Economics* (Cambridge, Mass: MIT Press, 1986)

KUHN, T., *The Copernican Revolution: Planetary Astronomy in the Development of Western Thought* (Cambridge, Mass: Harvard University Press, 1957)

—— *The Structure of Scientific Revolutions* (Chicago: University of Chicago Press, 1962)

LAKATOS, I. and A. MUSGRAVE (eds), *Criticism and the Growth of Knowledge* (Cambridge: Cambridge University Press, 1970)

LANGTON, C., *Artificial Life* (Reading, Mass: Addison-Wesley, 1992)

LAUREL, B., 'Virtual Reality', *Scientific American* (September 1995), p. 70

LEONARD-BARTON, D., 'Core Capabilities and Core Rigidities: A Paradox in Managing New Product Development', *Strategic Management Journal*, 13 (1992)

—— *Wellsprings of Knowledge: Building and Sustaining the Sources of Innovation* (Boston, Mass: Harvard Business School Press, 1995)

LEWIN, R., *Complexity: Life at the Edge of Chaos* (Middlesex: Penguin, 1993)

LLOYD, S., 'Mechanical Computers', *Scientific American* (October 1995)

LOVELOCK, J., *The Ages of Gaia* (Oxford: Oxford University Press, 1990)

MAHONEY, J. and R. SANCHEZ, 'Competence Theory as Integrating Product and Process of Thought: Beyond Dissociative Theories of Strategy', unpublished paper (1995)

MARCH, J., 'Exploration and Exploitation in Organizational Learning', *Organization Studies*, 2: 1 (February 1991)

MARSHALL, A., *Principles of Economics* (London: Macmillan, 1947)

MARX, K., *Capital: A Critique of Political Economy* (London: Lawrence and Wishart, 1972)

MAUSS, M., *The Gift: Forms and Functions of Exchange in Archaic Societies* (London: Routledge and Kegan Paul, 1954)

MEADOWS, D. H., MEADOWS, D. L., RANDERS, J., and W. BEHRENS, *The Limits to Growth: A Report on the Club of Rome's Project on the Predicament of Mankind* (London: Earth Island Ltd., 1972)

MINTZBERG, H., 'Crafting Strategy', *Harvard Business Review* (July–August 1987)

MINTZBERG, H., and J. WALTERS, 'Of Strategies, Deliberate and Emergent', *Strategic Management Journal* (July–September 1985)

MIROWSKI P., *More Heat than Light: Economics as Social Physics, Physics as Nature's Economics* (Cambridge: Cambridge University Press, 1989)

MITCHELL WALDROP, M., *Complexity: The Emerging Science at the Edge of Chaos* (London: Penguin Books, 1992)

MOWERY, D. and N. ROSENBERG, *Technology and the Pursuit of Economic Growth* (Cambridge: Cambridge University Press, 1989)

NELSON, R. and S. WINTER, *An Evolutionary Theory of Economic Change* (Cambridge, Mass: The Belknap Press of Harvard University Press, 1982)

NICOLIS, G. and I. PRIGOGINE, *Exploring Complexity: An Introduction* (New York: W. H. Freeman and Co., 1989)

NONAKA, I. and H. TAKEUCHI, *The Knowledge Creating Company: How Japanese Companies Create the Dynamics of Innovation* (New York: Oxford University Press, 1995)

NORTH, D., *Institutions, Institutional Change and Economic Performance* (Cambridge: Cambridge University Press, 1990)

NORTH, D. and R. THOMAS, *The Rise of the Western World* (Cambridge: Cambridge University Press, 1973)

PAIS, A., *Inward Bound: Of Matters and Forces in the Physical World* (New York: Oxford University Press, 1986)

PANOFSKY, E., *Gothic Architecture and Scholasticism* (Cleveland: The World Publishing Company, 1951)

PENROSE, E., *The Theory of the Growth of the Firm* (Oxford: Oxford University Press, 1959)

PETERAF, M., 'The Cornerstones of Competitive Advantage: A Resource-based view', *Strategic Management Journal*, 14 (1993)

PETERS, T., *Thriving on Chaos* (New York: Alfred A. Knopf, 1987)

—— *Liberation Management* (New York: Alfred A. Knopf, 1992)

PIAGET, J., *Play, Dreams and Imitations in Childhood* (New York: W. W. Norton and Company, 1962)

PINCHOT, G., *Intrapreneuring* (New York: Harper and Row, 1985)

POLANYI, M., *Personal Knowledge: Towards a Post-Critical Philosophy* (London: Routledge and Kegan Paul, 1958)

POPPER, K., *Objective Knowledge: An Evolutionary Approach* (Oxford: Clarendon Press, 1972)

PORTER, M., *Competitive Strategy: Techniques for Analyzing Industries and Competitors* (New York: The Free Press, 1980)

—— *Competitive Advantage: Creating and Sustaining Superior Performance* (New York: The Free Press, 1985)

PRAHALAD, C. and R. BETTIS, 'The Dominant Logic: A New Linkage Between Diversity and Performance', *Strategic Management Journal*, 7 (1986), pp. 485–501

PRAHALAD, C. and G. HAMEL, 'The Core Competence of the Corporation', *Harvard Business Review*, 68: 3 (1990)

PRIGOGINE, I., *From Being to Becoming: Time and Complexity in the Physical Sciences* (New York: W. H. Freeman and Co., 1980)

PRIGOGINE, I. and I. STENGERS, *Order out of Chaos: Man's New Dialogue with Nature* (Toronto: Bantam Books, 1984)

PRIGOGINE, I., NICOLIS, G., and A. BABLOYANTZ, 'Thermodynamics of Evolution', *Physics Today*, 25: 11 (1972), pp. 23–8; 25: 12 (1972), pp. 38–44

QUEISSER, H., *The Conquest of the Microchip: Science and Business in the Silicon Age* (Cambridge, Mass: Harvard University Press, 1988)

QUINN, J. B., *Intelligent Enterprise: A New Paradigm for a New Era* (New York: The Free Press, 1992)

REBER, A., *Implicit Learning and Tacit Knowledge: An Essay on the Cognitive Unconscious* (New York: Oxford University Press, 1993)

REED, M. A., 'Quantum Dots', *Scientific American* (January 1993)

REPETTO, R., *Accounts Overdue: Natural Resource Depletion in Costa Rica* (Washington DC: World Resources Institute, 1991)

ROBBINS, L., *An Essay on the Nature and Significance of Economic Science* (London: Macmillan, 1935)

ROMER, P., 'Endogenous Technical Change', *Journal of Political Economy* (1990)

—— 'Are Nonconvexities Important for Understanding Growth?', *American Economic Review* (1990)

RONAN, C. and J. NEEDHAM, *The Shorter Science and Civilisation in China* (Cambridge: Cambridge University Press, 1978)

SANCHEZ, R., 'Strategic Flexibility, Firm Organization and Managerial Work in Dynamic Markets: A Strategic Options Perspective', *Advances in Strategic Management*, 9 (1993), pp. 251–91

—— 'Higher Order Organization and Commitment in Strategic Options Theory: A Reply to Christopher Bartlett', *Advances in Strategic Management*, 106 (1994), pp. 299–307

SANCHEZ, R. and A. HEENE, *Strategic Learning and Knowledge Management* (Chichester: John Wiley and Sons, 1997)

SCHUMACHER, E., *Small is Beautiful: A Study of Economics as if People Mattered* (London: Abacus, 1974)

SCHUMPETER, J., *The Theory of Economic Development: An Inquiry into Profits, Capital, Credit, Interest and the Business Cycle* (London: Oxford University Press, 1961 (1934))

SCOTT, M., *A New View of Economic Growth* (Oxford: Oxford University Press, 1989)

SELZNICK, P., *Leadership in Administration* (New York: Harper and Row, 1957)

SHANNON, C. and W. WEAVER, *The Mathematical Theory of Communication* (Urbana: University of Illinois Press, 1949)

SIMMONS, I., *Changing the Face of the Earth* (Cambridge: Cambridge University Press, 1989)

SIMON, H., 'The Logic of Heuristic Decision Making', in Rescher (ed.), *The Logic of Decision and Action* (Pittsburgh: University of Pittsburgh Press, 1967), pp. 1–20; reprinted in H. Simon, *Models of Discovery* (Dordrecht, Holland: D. Reidel Publishing Co., 1977)

—— *The Sciences of the Artificial* (Cambridge, Mass: MIT Press, 1969)

STALK, G., EVANS, P. and L. SHULMAN, 'Competing on Capabilities', *Harvard Business Review* (March–April 1992)

STYX, G., 'Toward Point One' *Scientific American* (February 1995), p. 72

SWADE, D. D., 'Redeming Charles Babbage's Mechanical Computer', *Scientific American* (February 1993)

TAYLOR, C. and Z. SILBERSTON, *The Economic Impact of the Patent System: A Study of the British Experience* (Cambridge: Cambridge University Press, 1973)

TICHY, N. and S. SHERMAN, *Control Your Destiny or Someone Else Will* (New York: Harper Collins, 1994)

TÖNNIES, F., *Community and Association* (London: Routledge and Kegan Paul, 1955)

TUDGE, C., 'Human Origins: A Family Feud', *New Scientist* (20 May 1995)

TURING, A., 'On Computable Numbers with a Application to the Entscheidungsproblem' *Proc. Lond. Math. Soc* (Ser. 2) 42 (1937), pp. 230–65; a correction 43 (1937), pp. 544–6

TUSHMAN, M. and P. ANDERSON, 'Technological Discontinuities and Organizational Environment', *Administrative Science Quarterly*, 31 (1986)

ULLMAN, A., 'The Swatch', in de Wit and Meyer (eds), *Strategy: Process Content, Context* (Minneapolis, St Paul: West Publishing Company, 1994)

UTTERBACK, J., *Mastering the Dynamics of Innovation* (Cambridge, Mass: Harvard University Press, 1994)

VIDALI, G., *Superconductivity: The Next Revolution?* (Cambridge: Cambridge University Press, 1993)

VAN DER HEIJDEN, K., *Scenarios: The Art of Strategic Conversation* (Chichester: John Wiley, 1996)

VON FOERSTER, H., 'On Self-Organizing Systems and Their Environments', in Youitz and Cameron (eds), *Self-Organizing Systems* (London: Pergamon Press, 1960)

VON HIPPEL, E., *The Sources of Innovation* (Oxford: Oxford University Press, 1988)

VON MISES, L., *Nationalökonomie: Theorie des Handelns und Wirtschaftens* (Geneva: Editions Union, 1940)

WALRAS, L., *Elements of Pure Economics or the Theory of Social Wealth* (Philadelphia: Orion Editions, 1984 (1926))

WEICK, K., *The Social Psychology of Organizing* (Reading, Mass: Addison-Wesley, 1979)

WEICK, K. E. and K. H. ROBERTS, 'Collective Minds in Organizations: Heedful Interrelating on Flight Decks', *Administrative Science Quarterly*, 38 (1993), pp. 357–81

WERNERFELT, B., 'A Resource-based View of the Firm', *Strategic Management Journal*, 5 (1984)

WHISTLER, T., 'The Impact of Information Technology on Organizational Control', in Myers (ed.), *The Impact of Computers on Management* (Cambridge, Mass: MIT Press, 1967), pp. 16–60

WILSON, R. W., 'The Sale of Technology Through Licensing', Ph. D. thesis (Yale University, New Haven Conn., 1975).

WILLIAMSON, O., *Markets and Hierarchies: Analysis and Antitrust Implications* (Glencoe: The Free Press, 1975)

—— *The Economic Institutions of Capitalism: Firms, Markets, Relational Contracting* (New York: The Free Press, 1985).

WILLIAMSON, O. and W. OUCHI, 'The Markets and Hierarchies Program of Research: Origins, Implications, Prospects', in Joyce and van der Ven (eds), *Organization Design* (New York: Wiley, 1981)

WOMACK, J., JONES, D., and D. ROOS, *The Machine that Changed the World: The Story of Lean Production* (New York: Harper Collins, 1991)

WOMACK, J. and D. JONES, *Lean Thinking* (New York: Simon and Schuster, 1996)

YAM, P., 'In the Atomic Corral', *Scientific American* (July 1995), p. 13

INDEX

The letter 'n' following a page number indicates a reference in the notes.

market transactions 126, 127–8, 138, 140,
144, 148, 216, 218, 219, 221, 226–7, 261,
265, 267
Marshall, A. 219–20
Marx, K. 72–3, 150, 164, 267
mass-produced artefacts 13
matrix representation of knowledge assets 232
Matsushiba 180
Maupertius 15
Mauss, M. 140
mercantilists 72
microelectronic revolution 206–29, 255, 260,
267, 270
Microsoft 92, 93, 95, 200, 264
Milken, M. 199
Mintzberg, H. 169, 187
modularization 107, 191, 196
Moore, G. 201
Moore's law 211
motion, Newton's laws of 3
Motorola 183, 199
musical recordings 254

nanotechnology 15, 27
NASA 263
national culture 123, 141–2, 251–2
nature
economy of 15
as source of value 72
NCR 186
NEC 180
Neill, J. 184
neoclassical (N-) learning 96–9, 100, 108,
111–16 *passim*, 166, 168, 199, 223, 250,
255, 263, 268, 269
networking 219–21, 225–7, 265
Newton, I. 3
Nicolis, G. 80
non-linearity 9, 99–100, 269
of knowledge assets 3
Nonaka, I. 56
Noyce, R. 86

order 38, 67, 69, 81–3, 204, 205
chaos as source of 9
excessive 37, 38, 39
organizational processes 153, 154, 166–9,
171–6 *passim*, 200, 224–9
output 23
outsourcing 218, 259, 260, 261, 267

paradigm shifts 93–4, 102
paradigmatic knowledge 93–4, 95, 102
parallel distributed processing 228, 229
Pareto welfare function 34
patents 76 n., 222, 257
Pentium chip 2
Peters, T. 39
physical assets

economic life of 3
locality of 32
substitution of data for 28–30, 41, 67,
208–9, 210, 211, 212–13, 254
physical substrates for knowledge assets 154–60
migration of knowledge across 165–6
physiocrats 72
Polanyi, M. 57
population growth 8, 34
porcelain industry, China 119
Porter, M. 225
positioning view of competitive advantage
152, 181
poverty 8
Prahalad, C. 180, 182–3, 184, 185–6, 188,
189, 197
Prigogine, I. 68, 80, 81, 209
printing technology 122, 210
problem-solving phase of social
learning cycle 59–60, 70, 172
production function
evolutionary 25–33, 36–8, 39–40, 254
information technology in the 209–13
neoclassical 19, 22–5, 31–2
productive factors 21, 22–3, 24–7, 31–2
products 152–4, 165–6, 172, 173, 253, 255
co-evolution of 199
diffusion of 174
dominant design 36–7, 161–4, 199
evolution of 35–6
familiarity with 175
impacting of 176
scanning for 171
standardization of 36, 45, 160–4, 199
property rights 85, 90, 198, 209, 222–4, 254

QWERTY keyboards 103

railway transport 103–4, 257–8
reproduction, biological 81–2
resource-based view of competitive advantage
181, 182
Reuter, E. 186
Ricardo, D. 72
Rockwell 168, 202
Romer, P. 24

Sanchez, R. 148
scale economies 199
scanning phase of social learning cycle 59,
62, 63, 70, 171, 194, 201–2
scarcity 75, 76, 77, 82–3, 90, 96, 222
Schmitt trigger 10
Scholes, C. 103
Schön, D. 263
Schumptererian or S-learning 99–108 *passim*,
111, 112, 114, 115, 116, 166–9, 177, 178,
199, 223, 250, 255, 263, 268, 269
Scott, M. 24